RECULTURING MUSEUMS

Embrace Conflict, Create Change

Doris B. Ash

NEW YORK AND LONDON

Cover image: Pacific Grove, CA. Picture by Doris Ash

First published 2022
by Routledge
605 Third Avenue, New York, NY 10158

and by Routledge
4 Park Square, Milton Park, Abingdon, Oxon, OX14 4RN

Routledge is an imprint of the Taylor & Francis Group, an informa business

© 2022 Doris B. Ash

The right of Doris B. Ash to be identified as author of this work has been asserted in accordance with sections 77 and 78 of the Copyright, Designs and Patents Act 1988.

All rights reserved. No part of this book may be reprinted or reproduced or utilised in any form or by any electronic, mechanical, or other means, now known or hereafter invented, including photocopying and recording, or in any information storage or retrieval system, without permission in writing from the publishers.

Trademark notice: Product or corporate names may be trademarks or registered trademarks, and are used only for identification and explanation without intent to infringe.

Library of Congress Cataloging-in-Publication Data
A catalog record for this title has been requested

ISBN: 978-1-598-74521-4 (hbk)
ISBN: 978-1-598-74522-1 (pbk)
ISBN: 978-1-003-26168-1 (ebk)

DOI: 10.4324/9781003261681

Typeset in Bembo
by SPi Technologies India Pvt Ltd (Straive)

RECULTURING MUSEUMS

Reculturing Museums takes a unified sociocultural theoretical approach to analyze the many conflicts museums experience in the 21st century. Embracing conflict, Ash asks: What can practitioners and researchers do to create the change they want to see when old systems remain stubbornly in place?

Using a unified sociocultural, cultural-historical, activity-theoretical approach to analyzing historically bound conflicts that plague museums, each chapter is organized around a central contradiction, including finances (*"Who will pay for museums?"*), demographic shifts (*"Who will come to museums?"*), the roles of narratives (*"Whose story is it?"*), ownership of objects (*"Who owns the artifact?"*), and learning and teaching (*"What is learning and how can we teach equitably?"*). The *reculturing* stance taken by Ash promotes social justice and equity, 'making change' first, within museums, called *inreach*, rather than outside the museum, called *outreach*; challenges existing norms; is sensitive to neoliberal and deficit ideologies; and pays attention to the structure agency dialectic.

Reculturing Museums will be essential reading for academics, students, museum practitioners, educational researchers, and others who care about museums and want to ensure that *all* people have equal access to the activities, objects, and ideas residing in them.

Doris B. Ash is Professor Emerita in science education in the education department at the University of California Santa Cruz.

Dedication

I dedicate this book to my wife, my children and grandchildren
Liz
Teresa, Deb, Rich, Judy, Becky, Melissa, Kristina and Phoebe
Shelagh, Jan, Noah, Marc and Helene

CONTENTS

List of Figures   ix
List of Tables   x
List of Appendices   xi
Preface   xii
Acknowledgments   xvii

1   Introduction to the Main Theories and Themes of *Reculturing Museums*   1

2   Why Do We Need Theories?   37

3   Who Will Go to Museums?   74

4   Who Will Pay for Museums?   110

5   Whose Story Is It?   143

6   Who Owns the Artifact?   181

7   Where Is the Learning, and Who Gets to Learn?   218

8 What Do We Mean by Equitable Teaching in Museums? 249

9 How Do We Reculture an Institution While Old Systems
   Are Still in Place? 274

Index 304

FIGURES

1.1	First-generation activity system	9
1.2	Equity vs. equality, Interaction Institute for Social Change (2016)	20
2.1	Second-generation activity theory	45
2.2	Two interacting activity systems as a minimal model for the third generation of activity theory	49
2.3	The cycle of expansive transformation	55
4.1	Adapted museum pricing model developed by Rentschler et al. (2004)	125
5.1	Activity system showing secondary contradictions in tension	155
5.2	The Sutter Buttes	159
5.3	Little BigHorn diorama at the Monroe County Historical Museum in Monroe, Michigan, U.S.A.	165
5.4	A display of vintage advertising showing stereotypes of Native Americans at the National Museum of the American Indian in Washington, D.C., U.S.A.	166
8.1	Expansive learning cycle	260
9.1	Multiple-interconnected activity systems	288

TABLES

1.1	Engeström's five core principles for CHAT	6
2.1	CHAT word meanings, the Exxon/Valdez example	40
2.2	Types of contradictions and corresponding epistemic actions	52
2.3	Secondary contradictions in the Valdez spill	53
2.4	The stages of expansive cycle	56
3.1	Theme Index and Museum Index Report	90
4.1	Secondary contradictions exacerbated by finances	117
4.2	Sample of primary, secondary and tertiary contradictions regarding pricing	119
5.1	A representation of some possible secondary contradictions	156
5.2	Commodification vs. conservation	157
5.3	Controversies at three levels	158
5.4	Secondary contradictions in the Californio narrative	162
6.1	Secondary contradictions of uses of artifacts	189
7.1	A taxonomy of learning	227
7.2	Individual vs. social views of learning through a neoliberal lens	237
8.1	Sample deficit discursive traces	257
8.2	Secondary contractions in museum teaching from the *blue/purple* case study	264
9.1	Some aspects of power in museums	289
9.2	Some suggested actions to take	291
9.3	A summary of questions/contradictions/themes used for this book	293

APPENDICES

2.1	Contradictions at Three Levels of Analysis	64
3.1	Museum Social Media That Regularly Address Issues of Race, Equity, Social Justice	97
3.2	The Sciences	99
3.3	Delpit's "Culture of Power"	100
3.4	Levels of Racism	100
4.1	Pricing Details	135
4.2	Museum Executive Pay in New York City	135
5.1	Two Recent Exhibitions About Controversy	169
6.1	Repatriation in the United States: NAGPRA	205
6.2	DNA Testing	205
6.3	Who Owns Nazi Loot?	205
6.4	Alienation	207
6.5	Australia	208
7.1	Learning Research Pragmatics	237
7.2	Some Origins of Social Learning Research in Museums	238
7.3	What's in a Name?	239
8.1	Levels of Interaction	266
8.2	Museum Educator History	267
9.1	Summary of Major Themes	293
9.2	Involving the Community	295
9.3	Critical Reflective Practice	296
9.4	One Example of Museum Reculturing	296

PREFACE

This is the book I have wanted to read. It reflects how I think, conduct research and also one direction I believe the field of museum research needs to go for the future. Like so many other books in the mind of authors, it has been a long time in coming, growing and changing as I've written and rewritten chapters to reflect both history and modern times but always pitched for the future. Researching and writing this analysis has been thoroughly challenging, requiring years of effort. In the early days, it was one book; in the middle days, it was another; and now in the final days, it is a third. This third version includes more theory to guide us through the hard times and addresses societal concerns as they impact museums. In these years of COVID and Black Lives Matter, I cannot remain neutral in my research position. I believe it is too important to be clear, self-reflective and self-critical in the work we do together. This book is the culmination of many years of reflection, doing and thinking. Use it as you think best.

Museums are not neutral, and I am not neutral. Neutrality is often claimed, but as Jean Lave said many years ago, to paraphrase, we all wear glasses; it's important to know what color they are. I am telling you the color of my glasses. Societal change has to some degree helped us to be more reflective, and now that I am an emerita professor, I can afford to be more critically reflective of myself, my field and its practices. I am first and foremost a socioculturalist theorist, focusing on activity theory, with equity as a core value of my world and all my work. I have long believed that museums need to change from the inside out, what I have called *inreach* instead of *outreach*, focusing on others. I embrace conflict and contradiction as tools for change, and I ask others to embrace conflict throughout this book. I believe that we are indebted to and must pay attention to history. I believe that resistance is not futile and hopefully, with the help of many, we may engage in new ways to challenge what we call the *norm* or 'business as usual'. I argue that we need to change ourselves inside museums before we have any hope of working collaboratively and flexibly with and for the minoritized populations we hope will become part of our museums. Not because we want them to assimilate to white Western European ways of visiting museums, but because we want to expand our own horizons to what other ways we might meet there. As the title suggests, we embrace conflict, and we seek change. I believe that theory is the essential foundation for what we see and do; ignore it at your peril. This book reflects all of this.

From our current stance, we may look back decades from now and recognize that this moment in time is the tipping point for truly understanding that museums *must* do things differently in order to be the kind of institutions they can and should be for future generations. As I delved into the literature of each chapter, some far from my home discipline of science education, I came to see the world writ large in exciting new ways. What a pleasure to learn about finances (really), narrative and objects. These subjects have been important to me in my personal life, but happily, in this book, I have been able to hybridize the personal and professional in a new way. I could indulge my lifelong passion for alternative ideologies, new ways of framing the world. As an immigrant to the United States, I am, as many others are, in a constant state of 'outsiderness', even though I have been here many years. That outsiderness stays with me when I conduct research with and for nondominant populations in places like museums. I believe it gives me a different set of eyes and especially makes me suspicious of any claimed 'norms'.

Writing this book has allowed me to step into several alternative realities for each of the major topics we discuss. Thus, the book has been a gift to me and a major opportunity to expand my horizons. What a luxury! I have recently retired from academia and have found the unbounded life of fewer rules and being open to new thinking much to my liking. With this book, I have done what I am recommending for others in the chapters that follow: break away from the 'norm'. I have broken away from my old norms.

I apologize for any errors, misunderstandings or misinterpretation on my part. I recognize I am a white woman speaking of tender subjects, such as Native American rights, in a racialized world. Please understand I am searching but do call me out if I have misstepped. That is how I learn and grow. Speaking of errors and conflict, it has been comforting to know, as I repeatedly argue in this book, that deviations and conflict are normal, expected and to be valued for what they can teach us. Tensions lead to creating new opportunities. One of those new opportunities for me is to reframe how we view museums and informal research and to share these insights with others who might have perceived conflict as failure. Conflict is part of our future. And, as the title suggests, this book is about embracing conflict and working for change.

I want to say a little about how I came to be at this moment in time with this book. I taught in elementary, community college and high school almost 20 years before receiving my Ph.D. from the University of California, Berkeley. My dissertation was set in East Oakland, part of Ann Brown and Joe Campione's *fostering community of learners* classroom research project. There, I learned about Vygotsky, the zone of proximal development (ZPD) and sociocultural theory. I learned early on the value of providing challenging disciplinary content, using sociocultural theoretical foundations of learning and teaching, always trying to understand equity and social justice in new ways. I worked next at the Exploratorium; there I learned about hands-on learning, inquiry and interpretations of constructivist learning. After five years, I went to the University of California Santa Cruz, conducting research at the Seymour Center, the Monterey Bay Aquarium, the California Academy of Sciences, consulting at the Bishop Museum in Honolulu on their Voyaging project, then to a larger grant and Tampa's Museum of Science and Industry. All those experiences inform who I am now, a firm believer in the value of museums but not blind to their conflicts.

Many others have paved my road. In the museum field, during the early days, the work of Elaine Gurian, Minda Borun, Zahava Doering, George Hein, Paulette McManus, John Falk and Lynn Dierking and others got me started. Along the way, I encountered the work of Kevin Crowley, Maureen Callanan, Nina Simon, and Kirsten Ellenbogen, among others. Later, the advice of Angela Calabrese Barton, Jrene Rahm, Laura Martin, Sarah Ward, Gordon Wells and Jim Wertsch, among others, provided invaluable insights into how equity and activity theory could inform all I do and, most importantly, gave me the strength to embrace a theory that does not sweep conflict under the rug. Lori Fogarty of the Oakland Museum; Julie Barrett Heffington at the Seymour Center, Sam Taylor, then at the Cal Academy of Sciences; Judith Lombana at the Museum of Science and Industry, Tampa; and Rita Bell at the Monterey Bay Aquarium all provided me homes for my research. Anne Marie Palincsar helped me stay in the game when I was not sure academia was what I wanted. None of this would have been possible without the mentoring of Ann Brown and Joe Campione.

I have been catholic in my use of resources. I am an academic and use academic sources; I also use blogs, newspapers and social media because they are more current and often more relevant to our immediate sociopolitical, cultural world. I have paid special attention to sources that some academics might find marginal. I do not share their view of marginal. It has been my experience that marginalized people, often those 'emboldened disruptors' we discuss later, must revert to so-called marginalized forms of communicating, because academic routes are not open to them. A recent study by Stanford psychologist Steven Roberts confirms this, noting that "race is almost absent from top psychological publications" (de Witte, 2020). Thus, I have used alternative sources such as the *Incluseum*, *Museums and Race*, *Transformation and Justice*, *MASS Action*, *Museums Are Not Neutral* and *Decolonize This Place*, which are contemporary, forward-thinking, sometimes unfiltered but also quite revealing of the 'here and now' of museums. Museum critiques by reputable journalists such as in the *New York Times* offer warning signs through their urgency, resistance and contemporariness. Just as I ask you to embrace conflict, I have asked myself to do so.

Similarly, I have relied on recent dissertations, finding this work forward-thinking and refreshingly complex. Some of these are by Cortell, Dartt-Newton, Dailey and Ward. You will see them referenced. Such young scholars help imagine the way to the future, without being overly blinded by past norms. Similarly, I have made ample and intentional use of endnotes and appendices. When I read a scholarly text, I always want to know a bit more; if there is an endnote or appendix to go to, I often will do so. You can feel free to ignore them. I was much influenced in this matter after reading the book *Zealot* by Reza Aslan, which had wonderful endnotes.

This book has some sensitive material. I make constant reference in the following chapters to how we position the *other*. We consider Native American artifacts and narratives. I am neither Native nor a person of color, so I have tried to be very careful in what I write, always going to scholars who know more than I. I focus on Native sources that are authentic and consistent with sensitive handling of spiritual matters. I don't know Amy Lonetree, Meghan Bang, Gregory Rodriguez or John Kuo Wei Tchen personally but have appreciated their fearless speaking truth to power, offering me and others a path to step outside the Western world. I also believe that it is imperative for white scholars to challenge deficit, racist ideologies, not expecting POC to constantly carry that burden.

Why We Need Reculturing

Elaine Gurian (1995) suggested that changing the course of a museum is like changing the course of a large ocean liner. Simon, using the same metaphor said, "[I]t takes an engine room full of people straining as hard as they can to make even the slightest ripple" (Simon, 2013; p. xvii). *Reculturing Museums i*s meant for a broad audience of museum practitioners, researchers, teachers, administrators, funders, and others who wish to dissect how educational settings like museums can help ensure that *all* people have equal access to the activities, objects, and ideas residing in them. We look toward the future, by which we mean the next 20–80 years or the rest of the 21st century. To *reculture* is to *reimagine* how museum workplaces can advance a collective ethos of equity and social justice for visitors and staff at multiple levels, both in and outside the museum.

This book differs from other museum-based books in several main features. I have purposely and continuously expected conflict and called for dynamic, flexible change at all levels. I argue for the comprehensive and tested, flexible theoretical framework of cultural-historical activity theory (CHAT) to analyze museum systems. I have tried to reimagine equity and social justice as thoroughly integrated in all aspects of policy and practice of museums and their staff. I insist on an examination of power in all of its many manifestations, as well as confront ideological differences, whether recognized or not, as they work in museums. I recognize that we will need to replace the old with the new while the old is still in place. Some of these topics have been discussed singly before, but very few books that I am aware of have incorporated most or all these aspects into one overview of how we might understand and change museums. Using examples from the everyday world of museums, one goal of *Reculturing Museums* is to make CHAT more accessible for museum professionals as a practical tool for understanding the seemingly intractable contradictions that plague so many modern museums. I touch on many examples of dialectical relationships, such as the individual vs. social orientation, resources vs. deficit ideologies, monetary vs. social good goals and the relationship between agency and structure.

Resistance Is Not Futile

In the following nine chapters, I touch on a number of conflicts that *resist* change and support 'business as usual', some intentional and overt, some unintentional and covert, some surprising, others not so much. Structural tensions of the past, present and future concerning money, demographics, narrative, objects, learning and teaching reveal themselves in these chapters as they will as we move into the 21st century, and hopefully past the COVID crisis, the defining feature of 2020. Personal and collective resistance to structural constraints can be difficult to notice as they often quietly manifest on different levels. Dawson (2017) recounted when a Sierra Leonean participant "recognized a bird among a display of several animals, which triggered members of the group to dance and sing next to the exhibit for several minutes". Dawson said later,

> [T]he Sierra Leonean participants had tried to find a role for themselves in the museum, working to be more like the "ideal" visitor; they later felt they behaved in ways that marked them as "other."… Such actions can also be understood as a form of transgression and resistance to the museum, with its objects imprisoned in glass, inaccessible texts, unknown codes of conduct, and incomprehensible language.

I explore other forms of resistance in this book, including an alternative curriculum created by one family using humor as an alternative path through exhibits, museum educators working in the ZPD rather than 'telling and yelling', and board members and directors being asked to resign. Who knows where all resistance will lead? Embrace conflict, create change!

Reference

de Witte, M. (2020). Psychological research has a racism problem. https://news.standard.edu/press-releases/2020/06/24/Psychological record-scholar-says/

ACKNOWLEDGMENTS

There are many people who provided support, emotional, psychological and physical in terms of editing, reading and providing valuable feedback. I'd like to first thank Dr. Elizabeth Krainer, my artful and dedicated editor; she has been my steadfast support all these years. I'd like to thank Dr. Sarah Ward, an activity theory specialist who read for content and continuity and who was available to talk over many gnarly ideas. I'd like to thank Kristina Ortiz who organized the references over the last year. Those references were quite complex, and she did a magnificent job. I'd like to thank my two current graduate students Caroline Spurgin and Alexandra Race for the work they did in reading and editing in the early days. For my friends and family, thank you so much for your help and for 'being there' with advice, cookies, and just to listen. Sincere gratitude to Heidi Lowther, my patient and supportive editor and her team at Museum & Heritage Studies at Routledge.

1
INTRODUCTION TO THE MAIN THEORIES AND THEMES OF *RECULTURING MUSEUMS*

Overview

This book is called *Reculturing Museums*. The *reculturing* stance relies on promoting change within museum culture, *inreach*, rather than relying on and promoting cultural and linguistic changes outside the museum, *outreach*. Underlying all my arguments is the need for social justice and equity. Unlike many other books concerning museum transformation, I use a unified sociocultural, historical theory to analyze historically bound contradictions that plague museums in all areas, for example, finances, narratives and ownership of objects.

I especially focus on the minoritized, nondominant visitors of color museums wish to attract. Whereas *outreach* is focused on assimilation (Dawson, 2014b) of diverse voices into museum practice, reculturing is a shift that begins internally and is dependent on changing the *norms* that impact all we see and do in and around museums (B. Moore, 2013).

This desire for equity and social justice recognizes that *reculturing* and major internal structural shifts along several axes of museum organization are essential. Such reculturing reverberates in how museums structure events, build and cut budgets, hire and fire, design exhibits, conduct public relations, speak to the press and conduct educator training, among other policies and practices.

I argue that institutions need to *change* themselves, including the frontline and administrative staff, educators, directors, board members, CFOs, etc., *in order to* collaborate with 'museum outsiders' in equitable, socially just ways (Dawson, 2014b). Current expectations for 'museum outsiders' to assimilate have not worked in creating equity or socially just practices (Dawson, 2014b).

I rely on a four-part theoretical foundation that is based on cultural-historical activity theory (CHAT) as the central analytic tool. The other analytic tools provide additional lenses. The structure agency dialectic (SAD; Giddens, 1984; Varelas et al., 2015) gives us a way to study power in more detail. I provide a critique of sociopolitical economic philosophy of neoliberal (late capitalist) consumerism and individualism as it applies to educational systems with the help of Apple (2010) and Au and Ferrare (2015).

Finally, I critique *othering*, a form of *deficit ideology* (powell & Menendian, 2017) throughout each chapter. These four core perspectives dovetail reciprocally in our analysis of museum structure, and they help guide our suggestions for structural transformation—that is, reculturing in the 21st century. This discussion is meaningless without touching on power and how it is interwoven into all aspects of museums.

VIGNETTE

It is rare that a public figure such as the past first lady comments on the equity aspirations and social conscience of museums. Yet, here was Michelle Obama, who had been invited to speak to a crowd of museum elite and reporters at the dedication of the new Whitney Museum of American Art[1] in New York City in 2015, commenting on what it might mean for a girl from South Chicago to *belong* to a museum like this one (Cochran, 2015).

The inaugural exhibit "'America Is Hard to See', used the challenge of truly seeing America in all of its glory and complexity" (The White House, 2015). This new exhibit was an important one for the Whitney, an expansion and invitation to attract new visitors. Moments like this are important to highlight precisely because it is quite rare to witness an African American in a place of prominence in such a prestigious museum and because Michelle Obama ever so gently chided museums to do better, "to give disadvantaged children access to another world" (Durkin, 2015).

> You see, there are so many kids in this country who look at places like museums and concert halls and other cultural centers and they think to themselves, well, that's not a place for me, for someone who looks like me, for someone who comes from my neighborhood. In fact, I guarantee you that right now, there are kids living less than a mile from here who would never in a million years dream that they would be welcome in this museum. … And growing up on the South Side of Chicago, I was one of those kids myself. So, I know that feeling of not belonging in a place like this. And today, as First Lady, I know how that feeling limits the horizons of far too many of our young people.
>
> … If you run a museum, make sure that you're reaching out to kids in struggling communities. Invite them in to see those exhibits. Maybe you could inspire a young person to rise above the circumstances of their life and reach for something better. …
>
> One visit, one performance, one touch, and who knows how you could spark a child's imagination (The White House, 2015).

(Adapted from Cochran, 2015; Durkin, 2015; White House, 2015)

Introduction: Changing 'the Way We Do Things Around Here'

Change is necessary. But what needs to change? A central question throughout this book is, "What does it take to replace old systems with new when old systems stubbornly stay in place?" If institutions are, by definition, firmly rooted in taken-for-granted rules, norms, and routines, and if those institutions are so powerful that other organizations and individuals are apt to automatically conform to them, "then how are new institutions created or existing ones changed over time?" (DiMaggio & Powell, 1991, in Seo & Creed, 2002, p. 222).

Simon suggested, "Change is hard. Change is a kind of sausage that we rarely feel comfortable making or showing off. …Change is cruel" (Simon, 2013, p. xvii). In the vignette highlighting Michelle Obama, change is being sought by the Whitney Museum, as it recognizes that people of color don't often feel that they *belong* in museums; research confirms this view (Dawson, 2014a; Garibay, 2009, 2011). The Whitney Museum deliberately invited an African American icon to help challenge that view.

We know from research literature, however, that institutions are remarkably resistant to change. Change demands understanding complex social, cultural and historical theoretical underpinnings, and change needs to be structural, rather than piecemeal or offering temporary shifts (Foot, 2014) in programming or financing. Those who have written about institutional change in museums (Bennett, 2018; Griffin, 1987; James, 2013), Gurian (2017) and the Pew Charitable Trust, among others, have concluded that transformation takes a long time; it is hard to recognize its barriers; it requires significant commitment and a strong driving force—for example, funding, new leadership or some necessity (Hein, 2014). What these experts leave out is that change requires powerful, holistic and flexible theory to guide the process.

Change here is focused on museums. I have adopted a broad definition of what museums have been, are now and may be. The definition of the word 'museum' has recently been contested; the arguments at the International Council of Museums (ICOM) meetings closely reflect those made in this book. As a socioculturalist, I believe museums are more than a collection of pretty artifacts. They are or can be "democratizing, inclusive and polyphonic spaces for critical dialogue about the pasts and futures" (Marshall, 2020, para. 5); they can be safe places of community dialogue, disagreement and unity. I include in 'museums' those that show art, natural history, culture, history, maritime, military and war history, as well as histories of migrations, old and new. Museums are often established entities and edifices whose purpose and goals are on their websites and whose values are reflected in their exhibitions, staff and public relations. Yet, age, geography, endowment, and boards of directors are not defining features in my analysis. Also, I have expanded some chapters to include data from zoos, aquariums and other informal learning spaces because the conflicts we analyze in museums are common to these other learning spaces, as well.

I have focused primarily on American museums because they show evidence of being on the leading edge of visible and contemporary conflict. Their funding is insecure, the demographics are changing rapidly and larger societal cultural movements, such as decolonizing, are ongoing. I believe we can learn valuable lessons from the many experiments in progress in U.S. museums that can carry over to other countries and continents.

As a general organizing principle, we will focus on one central sociohistorical contradiction currently challenging modern museums in each chapter. I will use the word 'contradictions' instead of 'problems' or 'conflicts' because they occur "within and between activity systems" (Engeström, 2009, p. 57). When we learn to discern them, historically accumulating structural contradictions are everywhere. For example, is the purpose of museums to be educational or moneymaking or both? (Cortell, 2011; Gurian, 2020). Should exhibits be didactic or visitor-centered? Who determines the content and interpretation; does the curator or educator most influence the teaching (Ash, 2014a; Barab et al., 2004)? As Seo and Creed (2002) and Ward (2016) suggested, the transformative role of dialectically related contradictions and the relationships that accompany them can reciprocally change both institutions and staff. But how does that work?

Precisely because long-standing contradictions are active and being re-generated in museums, I consider them holistically, as well as locally and personally, asking how they might transform people and their systems and how they are transformed in turn, always assuming reciprocity. We may focus, for example, on balancing the budget, a fraught activity in most museums, and requiring directors, boards and administrative staff to weigh and balance the needs of the whole. One typical pre-pandemic example in 2016 concerned the Metropolitan Museum of Art in New York as it was

> planning to tighten its belt in the face of a projected deficit of $9 million to $10 million, a figure that museum officials said could swell to $40 million over the next 18 months if no action is taken.
>
> (Smith, 2016, para. 3)

The squeeze in the budget in this case included laying off or furloughing personnel and curtailing new digital efforts. These areas are essential to the long-term well-being of the museum, but the money was not there.

In this case, it is easy to recognize the larger contradiction between overall finances and ongoing and future service to the public; this is a long-standing, historically and culturally bound contradiction.[2] The framework I use does not sweep this contradiction under the rug or look for a 'quick fix'; rather, I highlight these issues as 'opportunities for change' (Engeström, 2001, p. 137).

This fits squarely into some education researchers' views of institutional change (Barab et al., 2004; Foot, 2014; Rahm, 2010, 2018; Yamagata Lynch, 2010). Contradictions help explicate how social actors (curators, museum professionals, administrators, etc.) can work to keep the status quo by resisting new policies and practices in institutions within which they work. On the other hand, the framework of contradictions also allows us to discern how people working in museums can dynamically negotiate objects and share ideas and agency with each other, become more self-determined in their professional careers and collaborate in expansive ways within an organization to create change.

Michelle Obama highlighted the contradiction between the desire for the museum to attract new visitors and the museum's lack of knowledge of how to genuinely include minoritized visitors once they are inside the museum. Like the contradiction created by money and service, wishing to be inclusive and socially conscious across the entire museum is not yet within the skill set or policies of many museums. This is another historically situated, accumulated tension for museums (see Chapter 3). As I locate contradictions and show how they impact museums, we can hopefully gain insights for lasting fruitful change. In each chapter, I explore how the contradictions play out in localized, superficially different but deeply related ways.

Some Basics

We can thank Lev Vygotsky for the basic tenets of sociocultural theory, including dialectic relationships and reciprocity between inner and outer worlds, the zone of proximal development (ZPD) and the primacy of mediation. Kaptelinin (2005) argued, "The main conceptual thrust of the sociocultural perspective was to overcome the divide between...human mind, and...culture and society" (p. 5); this dialectic is central to all our discussions.

Mahn and John-Steiner (2012) suggested that Vygotsky's dialectical approach has four central tenets: "a historical, developmental approach; seeing change as a constant; transformation...[is] through the unification of contradictory, distinct processes; and unifications... embody the essence of the whole". I include constant change, transformation, contradictory process and unification as basics in the analyses in this book.[3]

These are some foundations for CHAT, which provides a richness to research and practice by allowing us to study dynamics of transformation on a larger structural scale (Ward, 2016; Yamagata Lynch, 2010).[4] Foot (2014) argues that CHAT incorporates these three essential points:

> Humans act collectively, learn by doing and communicate in and via their actions;
> *We incorporate collective actions in all aspects of this book; including communicative actions (discursive manifestations);*
> Humans make, employ and adapt tools of all kinds [mediational means][5] to learn and communicate;
> *We analyze tool use (mediational means) as it appears in each chapter, e.g., exhibits, stories, entrance fees, language, teaching strategies, signs and so on;*
> Community is central to the process of making and interpreting meaning—and thus to all forms of communicating and acting;
> *Communities of like practitioners, for example, curators, educators, visitors and administrators are key aspects of each chapter.*
>
> (Adapted from Foot, 2014, p. 3)

TABLE 1.1 Engeström's five core principles for CHAT

1. The prime unit of analysis is a collective, artifact-mediated and object-oriented activity system, which is seen in its network relation to other activity systems.
2. Activity systems are multivoiced and are a nexus of many points of view, traditions and interests…a source of both tension and innovation.
3. Activity systems take shape and are developed over long periods…analyzed in terms of history, objectives and outcomes…as well as the conceptual tools that have shaped it over time.
4. Contradictions between and within activity systems are potential sources of change and development.
5. Activity systems have the potential for expansive transformations…when the object and motive of an activity have been reconceptualized to embrace a much wider horizon of possibilities than originally imagined.

(Adapted from Engeström, 2001, pp. 136–137, in Ward, 2016, p. 63).

CHAT builds on the original tenets of sociocultural theory in multiple ways. I use CHAT to analyze multiple interacting systems, to observe transformations in action and to explore the effects of power and hierarchy within systems. To understand how this might work, we first need to consider Engeström's five core principles for CHAT in Table 1.1.

These five points are essential to understanding how CHAT views learning systems like museums and each is crucial. Point 3 highlights how contradictions between and within activity systems can become *potential* sources of change and development, though we also see institutions fail to grow and change dynamically in the face of contradictions. CHAT helps us understand, though, that contradictions are the real drivers of transformation, rather than things to be avoided. As Roth and Tobin note, "In dialectical logic, contradictions are not evils but the engine of development… [so that] development arises from the resolution of contradictions and conflict" (Roth & Tobin, 2002, p.165).

Throughout this book, we will come to understand that contradictions are deeply embedded in all museum activity, that they are complex and that they cannot be handled just by adjusting hiring numbers, increasing entrance fees, providing free evenings on Thursday or hiring a new outreach coordinator who happens to be a person of color. As Foot (2014), Foot and Groleau (2011), Gurian (2017), Kaptelinin (2011) and others have noted, simple fixes are not adequate for transforming complex systems of activity.

Contradictions manifest from core historical, ideological commitments, such as blaming the victim in deficit logic, suggesting that visitors must pay for what they see or that learners need to be led to the content. I will therefore seek to identify the ideologies behind historical and current policies that determine what is done or said within museums, as well as the relationships (*outreach*) with those *others* outside the museum. Notice the different ideological commitment behind questions and statements such as, "How do we see and collaborate with those who we perceive to be different?", and, "How does this exhibit *position* the 'norm'?", rather than "They will just break things on free days", or, "Why don't they come to our museums?" Identifying underlying beliefs requires confronting some secondary contradictions that currently plague modern museums, such as to pay entrance fees or not to pay, to claim ownership of a sacred object or not, to rely on a Western master narrative or not? I will argue that such seemingly opposite views actually presuppose each other and cannot be considered except in a dialectical relationship.[6]

Reculturing Museums[7] intends to promote critically reflective, tension-filled dialogue designed to change museums from within while recognizing the need to collaborate with *others*. Critical reflection encourages us to look for the tensions and contradictions, especially as they manifest from conflict, for example, between dollars and demographics, or between my story or another's story. The *other* refers to those outside the 'business as usual' museum circles—namely, communities of color, the poor, minorities and those 'new to museums'.[8] Such groups have often been lumped together under the umbrella concept of *outreach*, which generally refers to the *other* (Othering and Belonging Institute, 2019). We discuss *othering* as one aspect of deficit ideology throughout this book.

My main goal here is to closely examine the many tentacles of what is now seen as 'business as usual' or 'the way we always do things around here' (Thompson, 2005), often referred to as the 'norm' (B. Moore, 2013) or as 'settled expectations' (Bang & Marin, 2015), to free museums up for transformation. I have chosen everyday examples for each chapter that best suit a particular contradiction, different types of museums and the broader themes of social justice and equity. In some cases, I have chosen a natural history or science museum, in others, an art museum, and a cultural museum, in order to offer relevant material across a range of museums.

In this book, I confront deficit ideologies, such as racism, genderism, ableism and other 'isms' noting that social justice and equity are increasingly important topics within museums and society. As everywhere in society, though, it has been challenging to *reculture* institutional core structures and beliefs in fundamental ways (Center for the Future of Museums (CFM), 2009; Dubin, 1999, 2014; Gurian, 1999; Jennings & Jones-Rizzi, 2017). Throughout this book, I will argue that it is important for museums to undertake change internally—*inreach*—before they can ask their visitors to change—*outreach*. I also argue that outreach invokes deficit/othering ideologies while clinging to the increasingly outdated view that that minoritized visitors must change or assimilate to a supposed 'norm'.

Challenging and Transforming 'Norms'

Changing norms is never as easy as it may sound. At the macrolevel, changing norms could involve pressure on a board to diversify. At the intermediate level, it might focus on reducing the power inequality between the curator and educator departments. At the microlevel, it might consist of changing individual orientations toward microaggressions. I will operate on macro-, intermediate and microlevels throughout (Ash, 2019).

8 Introduction to the Main Theories and Themes

The focus on supposed *norms* and *settled expectations* (Bang & Marin, 2015) interweaves throughout the book because they govern how we interpret learning, teaching, finances, narratives and the objects that make up museums, in short, the entire institution. Once we recognize what we mean by *norms, settled expectations* or *'the way we do things around here'*, and come to understand better how they determine how visitors are greeted, treated and taught, we then are able to conceive how museums can be transformed, or *recultured*, to reflect a more equitable stance.

Norms (B. Moore, 2013) and *settled expectations* (Bang & Marin, 2015; Bang et al., 2012) both in the past and still today reflect the status and power of in-groups in museums and all institutions. Hobsbawm and Ranger (2012) argued that norms are

> a set of practices…or tacitly accepted rules…which seek to inculcate certain values and norms of behaviour by repetition, [and] which automatically implies continuity with the past.
>
> (Hobsbawm & Ranger, 2012, p. 2)

Speaking more pointedly and less neutrally,[9] Coffee has argued,

> Museums are not neutral organizations…fundamentally they define…social narratives…[are] collections of ideological symbols…[and have a] legitimizing role. The narratives conveyed by museums are…definitive and authoritative, and the objects displayed are understood as emblematic of *normative culture*.
>
> (Coffee, 2007, p. 435)

Bang and Marin (2015) suggest that *settled expectations* are

> the set of assumptions, privileges, and benefits that accompany the status… that whites have come to expect and rely on (Harris, 1995, p. 277) across the many contexts of daily life.
>
> (Bang & Marin, 2015, p. 532)

I have included these three quotes because they shed light on the definitive power of supposed neutrality of *normed* behaviors, accepted as societal standards, promoted in social, cultural contexts, as well as reflected and reified by cultural institutions like museums and schools. Related to *norming*, I position *othering* as deficit thinking and as a jumping-off point for studying ideological positions and how they may shift relative to power (Leonardo, 2003). In terms of ideological shifts, museums are currently actively reflecting on the origins and perpetuation of such normative culture and settled expectations. In the United States, the National Museum of American Indians has been under pressure to revisit their interpretations (Hatzipanagos, 2018; Lonetree, 2009). In Europe, Migration Museums have examined sociopolitical realities related to migration (Network Migration in Europe, n.d.).[10] We discuss such 'normed' and 'settled expectations' and their alternatives in greater detail in the following chapters.

Theoretical Foundations

I have just enumerated many of the core aspects of museums that need to be understood and transformed. To do so, we need a powerful, yet flexible theoretical frame, large enough to contain entire museum systems and small enough to see shifts at intermediate and microlevels. Our core theoretical foundation is CHAT, informed by the lenses of the structure agency dialectic (SAD), a critique of deficit/othering ideologies and neoliberal (late capitalism) policies and practices. Taken together, these four lenses allow us to deeply examine the many conflicting ideologies and subsequent contradictions endemic to modern museums. I briefly introduce these four strands next and then describe them in more detail in Chapter 2.

CHAT

CHAT, a sociocultural theory, thrives on the dialectic inherent in relationships, is dynamic and is designed to explore the interrelationships among all aspects of a system. In Table 1.1, Engeström's five core principles, we see that CHAT's unit of analysis is collective, artifact-mediated, object-oriented, multivoiced and held in relationship to other systems; change is understood to be dynamic and takes time; contradictions are inherent; and systems have the potential to expand. A system may be a museum, or a subsection of the museum, like the education, public relations or curatorial departments.

One way to unpack a system is to, first, note and then explain the interacting aspects, called nodes, which, at a minimum, include (1) people, (2) tools (artifacts) or mediational means and (3) object of activity (desired outcome; see Figure 1.1). All figures shown here are analytic tools, i.e., tools for thinking, which function as guides rather than gospel.

To better understand CHAT, we must refer first to its sociocultural roots in Vygotsky, Ilyenkov, Leon'tev and others who recognized the fundamental social nature of learning. The original treatment that Vygotsky (1978) suggested is sometimes called first-generation activity theory, represented by the triangle in Figure 1.1. Smagorinsky (2010) suggests that Vygotsky was primarily speaking from

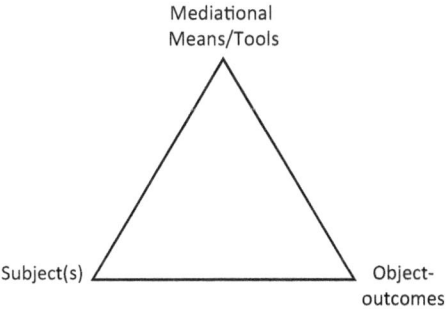

FIGURE 1.1 First-generation activity system (Adapted from Engeström's, 1999)

the point of view of the individual, even as he acknowledged the social advancement from collective to individual. It was Leont'ev's work that expanded activity to "the mediated activity collective, to social and cultural patterns of actions…routine actions that contribute to collective conceptions…of whole societies. Leon'tev foregrounded the social group rather than the individual" (Smagorinsky, 2010, p. 13).[11]

Vygotsky emphasized the role of mediational means (tools)—all actions are mediated; the zone of proximal development (ZPD) mediates between the individual and the social and is the fundamental dialectical relationship that undergirds it within object-oriented activity. Speaking more practically though, we can say that within CHAT,

> people create systems and systems create people and all of this is tethered to a cultural, social, historical unfolding. That relationship is dialectic, you can't separate yourself as a museum practitioner from the practice of museums. So if you want to change the system, you have to understand the system, that is CHAT.
>
> (Ward, 2018, p. 72)

The notion of being 'mutually and inseparably constituted' is essential to dialectical thinking; we must understand that as the institution changes the worker, the worker also changes the institution, and together they 'develop/transform'. 'Mutually constituted/inseparable' reflects the dialectical nature of sociocultural theory. CHAT is sociocultural and thus contains all the aspects we noted earlier and more.

Kaptelinin reminds us that dialectical relationships "encourage us to forgo hard and fast dualities in favor of more complex and dynamic interactions" (Sannino et al., 2016, p. 246), where complexity is sought rather than opposed. Generally speaking, contradictions allow the activity system to expand and transform.

Seo and Creed begin to address the fundamental conundrum of how we move from 'business as usual' to a *reculturing* stance in this way:

> [D]rawing upon [a] dialectical perspective, we [can] identify concrete mechanisms that delineate how institutional arrangements create various inconsistencies and tensions within and between social systems (contradictions), how those contradictions transform the embedded social actors into the change agents of the very institutional arrangements, and how those contradictions further enable and foster the subsequent change processes.
>
> (p. 223)

Discursive Manifestations: Making Contradictions Visible

CHAT is designed to analyze and trace change as it occurs. So how do we track change within this framework? Tsoukas (2003) suggested that a suitable motto for the study of organizational change might be: "Don't search for the logic of organizing; look for the discursive practices involved in organizing" (Sannino et al., 2009, p. 619). By this they mean to follow the discursive traces that people use to reveal underlying ideologies typically seen in the form of conflict/contradictions. Discursive traces can tell us much about the ethos and inner workings of an organization. We can see discursive traces of a deficit orientation, for example, in comments such as "those people are doing the exhibit wrong".

Similarly, Engeström and Sannino (2010) argued that "contradictions cannot be observed directly", suggesting "they can only be identified through their manifestations" (p. 369), by which they mean closely following the things that people actually do and say. They argue that discursive manifestations "track change as institutional contradictions, experienced by the affected people, both in the moment and over time" (p. 369). Discursive manifestations can help in the sometimes-challenging task of seeing transformation in action.

A few common discursive manifestations of internal resistance to change, for example, were provided in the *Design Thinking for Museums* blog (2013) and include, "This will never work here", when institutional change is suggested. This statement and those listed next 'give away' the sentiments of the staff. These traces may sound familiar to anyone who has worked to transform 'how things are done around here'.

> We don't work this way in XYZ Museum/Institution.
> Now is not the time to change our process [or] try something new.
> (Silvers, 2015)

Making contradictions visible by tracking discursive manifestations allows us to trace how and where they originate, are appropriated (or not) and how they transform over time. As anyone familiar with audio and video discourse analysis can tell you, it is very time-consuming to track these manifestations. Luckily, we have a beginning tool to help us 'see' such discursive patterns. Engeström and Sannino (2010) discussed four types of discursive manifestations. We will come to see over time that contradictions we encounter over the next eight chapters generally fall into one or more of these discursive manifestation categories. We list the categories next and foreshadow the future chapters that most closely match each category.

1. Dilemmas are expressions or exchanges of incompatibility evaluations, either between people or within the discourse of a single person.
   Example: Chapter 8. How do we teach in museums?

   Museum educator: *"These people are doing it all wrong. I don't know how to teach them?"*

   At a science museum, a newly trained museum educator expressed this judgment to their peers after watching families new to museums. It was a dilemma for her, as there was no obvious solution. This dilemma led to new forms of professional development in this and similar cases.

2. Conflicts take the form of resistance or disagreement
   Example: Chapter 6. Who owns the object?

   > Scientist...[repatriation is] *the equivalent of the historian burning documents after he has studied them.... It* [is] *impossible for scientists to carry out a genuinely scientific study of American Indian prehistory...an entire field of academic study may be put out of business.*
   >
   > Some scientists believe Native American bones must be kept in museums and storehouses for future use, for science. They resist efforts to repatriate (that is, return bones to native tribes for whom they are sacred). The anti-repatriation stance had been dominant before NAGPRA (Native American Graves Protection and Repatriation Act) and is still present today. There are still many ongoing court battles over the ownership of Native Hawaiian and other Indigenous people's bones.[12]

3. Critical conflicts are situations in which people face inner doubts that paralyze them when faced with contradictory motives unsolvable by the subject alone.
   Example: Chapter 5. Who owns the story?

   > *About a dozen families own the majority of land in the Sutter Buttes, much of which is still used as ranchland...[creating] a family relationship with the land that spans more than 100 years. They are proud of their ranching heritage and their private stewardship of the land and want to see it remain undeveloped. They felt a threat...to their private control of this area with the state of California's recent acquisition of a parcel of land.*
   >
   > (Sacred Land Project, 2020)

   The long-time California ranchers felt they were being good custodians of the land; they argued that the state of California, by coming in, was taking away their historical task of caretaking this land for themselves and Native tribes, accustomed to being allowed to use it for ceremony. If the state took over the land, they were powerless to fight (the state). The state has not yet opened this land to the public.

4. Double binds are processes in which actors repeatedly face pressing and equally unacceptable alternatives in their activity system, with seemingly no way out.
   Example in Chapter 8: How do we teach in museums? Educators were told they must use a script (new tool) and be forceful on the museum floor:

   > *One day I came [to work] to be a "purple educator" and I was told that [the mid-level manager] said to ignore everything I've learned as a [blue educator] and go back to [purple] training because that's what they want to see...They [purple manager] said we should be the "dragons" of the floor.*

This museum educator felt 'as if' he had little choice. If he was true to his beliefs, he could not work as a *purple*. He stood to lose money and prestige. If he gave in and acted like a 'dragon on the floor', he would betray his *blue* training.

Another example of discursive manifestation seen in different guises is the question: "*Why don't they come here?*" (Feinstein & Meshoulam, 2014) referring to a *dual deficit model*: They (outsiders) lack science, and museums lack them (outsiders). This question, "Why don't they come here?, carries several intended or unintended, deficit-laced messages, including whether there is a *they* to be identified and whether *they* should want to come to museums (see Dawson, 2014a & 2014b). Variants of this question exist throughout museums as they try to attract minoritized visitors.

SAD (Structure Agency Dialectic)

My second theoretical lens is the structure agency dialectic (SAD; Giddens, 1984;[13] Sewell, 1992), which focuses on the dialectical relationship between the agency of engaged workers and the structures that constrains their activities (Dowding, 2008; Gutiérrez & Calabrese Barton, 2015; Varelas et al., 2015). From both sociocultural and cultural-historical standpoints, agency and structure "presuppose each other in a dialectical relationship; that is, structures shape people's agency and, conversely, people's agency reproduces and/or transforms structures" (Emirbayer & Mische, 1998, p. 963). Gutiérrez and Calabrese Barton (2015) noted, "The dialectic between structure and agency helps us to see how individual actions, occurring in particular times and places, are both constrained and enabled by the social structures therein" (Gutiérrez & Calabrese Barton, 2015, p. 581). We can recognize the SAD at various interfaces of museum structure—for example, the degrees of freedom of curatorial staff versus educator staff, or of administrators versus restaurant staff, etc.

Although SAD has a different theoretical grounding than CHAT, arising primarily from sociologists Giddens (1984) and Sewell (1992), I suggest that it is compatible with CHAT and, taken together, they allow our analysis to include museum workers, and the mediational means available to them or under design, as well as hierarchies and rules, to see the more detailed individual agentic action in dialectical relationship with structural constraints (Gutiérrez & Calabrese Barton, 2015).

When SAD is used in conjunction with CHAT, we have a specific dialectically oriented tool to analyze power relationships among museum staff, especially museum educators' shifting agency and the sometimes-invisible structural constraints, that either competitively or collaboratively affect their agency within the larger museum institution's activity system, especially in terms of hierarchies of power. We discuss this in more detail in Chapter 8.

Neoliberal Policies and Practices

The third lens is my critique of neoliberalism, or as it is also called, late capitalism, as it applies to educational organizations and systems. Neoliberalism has many interpretations, a long history and is a contentious topic across the globe. Harvey (2007) explains, "[N]eoliberalism is a theory…proposing that human well-being can be best advanced by the maximization of entrepreneurial freedoms…characterized by private property rights, individual liberty, unencumbered markets, and free trade" (p. 22). Neoliberalism also allows us to locate contradictions in cases where individual liberty typically comes at the cost of collective action. In such cases, a second and important corollary contradiction concerns the lack of social justice and the presence of inequity that are embedded within neoliberalism. These appear in arguments that "the voices and collective power of marginalized communities, the poor, and people of color must also be limited" (Lipman, 2011).

The neoliberal adjectives, 'marketized' 'consumerist' and 'competitive' are not typically used for educational settings, especially given socioculturally based learning and teaching theories. Now, though, they are becoming more frequently used in museums and schools in conjunction with ascendant neoliberal policies at all levels of interaction.

I critique neoliberalism throughout the next chapters, especially interpretations of neoliberalism used to analyze educational systems. To be more specific about the roots of power inequality, Apple (1993) laid out these four main aspects of neoliberal goals in education aimed at increasing international competitiveness: emphasize profit and discipline, to make them an idealized free-market economy; raise standards [for] both teacher and student; attacks on the aspects of the curriculum; and pressure to make the perceived needs of business and industry into the primary goals of schools (Apple, 1993, p. 228). These school-based aspects transfer directly to museums, which have received such critiques over the past decades[14] (Dailey, 2006; Ekström, 2020). Karp et al. (1992) argued that museums are a part of neoliberalist policies that result in limiting the "selection and presentation of ideas, images and information" (Karp et al., 1992, p. 1).

Dailey's research suggests that the role of museum staff may be dominated by concerns of acquiring money for the museum. After Dailey asked the question, "Please tell me about your job", she was startled by the number of responses that mentioned money or funding, especially staff member's feelings of responsibility "for finding funding or for contributing to funding efforts" (p. 8)

She noted,

> They talked about the challenges of working under pressures of budget cuts…struggling with increasing pressures to "market" their exhibits to specific "audiences"…meeting demands from sponsors requiring them to quantify effectiveness…much of their time was spent worrying about issues that are technically outside their traditional role and responsibility.
>
> (Dailey, 2006, p. 9)

Clearly, it is not most staff members' job to find funding, yet it appears they now feel that it is. This reflects the contradiction of being a nonprofit organization in a neoliberal system that turns to profit-making organizations for money and where profit-making organizations and their workers receive tax breaks for donating to nonprofits. Simultaneously our most vulnerable communities are diminished as nonprofits find themselves subverted toward a for-profit model.

These ideologically informed and cyclic practices—e.g., staff are expected to understand and manage accountability for time and money (Groninger, 2016; Weil, 2007) and then turn to for-profit models in times of stress—may seem inherently counterproductive. Yet, as Apple and others argue, that is exactly the point. Neoliberalism and the emphasis on commodification counteract and negate any and all collective equity and social justice goals.

Deficit/Othering

I focus on contradictions and dialectical relationships in this book, positioning reculturing as part of deep internal structural change. So, how do we get to that larger vision of reculturing? My fourth theoretical frame is a critique of what we call *othering/deficit* ideologies. I intentionally combine the two terms *deficit* and *othering* in order to braid together several different theoretical strands that inform this interpretation. The experts powell and Menendian (2017) have defined *othering* as

> a set of dynamics, processes, and structures that engender marginality and persistent inequality across any of the full range of human differences based on group identities.
>
> (p. 17)

They noted that 'othering' captures expressions of prejudice and behaviors, but it is also a term that "points toward deeper processes that dominate ideological positions about race and class, especially poverty and the myth of meritocracy" (McNamee & Miller, 2004). Gorski (2010) has noted that *deficit* thinking is characterized "by pointing to the supposed deficiencies within disenfranchised individuals and communities" (p. 4), essentially blaming those who have been disenfranchised and have little power. This view is aligned with the myth of meritocracy (McNamee & Miller, 2004), a position strongly aligned with neoliberalism. Davis and Museus (2019) have suggested deficit thinking can have several interpretations, but "all of them incorporate 'blame the victim' thinking that attribute students' failures to their individual, family, or community traits" (p. 117). For the word 'student', substitute the word 'visitors' in museums.

This is increasingly important in museums because *deficit* thinking and *othering* are often combined with expectations of 'assimilation' by visitors from minoritized groups to the museum's *norms*. By assimilation here I mean behaving and speaking closer to the socioculturally, historically established white, middle-class *norm* (Dawson, 2014a). Yet, expecting *assimilation to the norm* is often not recognized as such, precisely because even that expectation conforms to 'how we do things around here'.¹⁵

Ideologies and Critical Reflection

Reculturing requires recognition of, critical reflection on, and subsequent action toward, outcomes based on fundamental ideologies (Mezirow, 1990). If norms are to change, we need to recognize them. Examining ideologies helps us do that.

Coffee (2007) has been clear about the role of ideologies, arguing that museums determine/reflect culture as it is represented:

> [V]isitors are to be entertained and beguiled by the show up front, to "view… Chelsea Clinton's ballet slippers…Harrison Ford's costume from 'Air Force One'" (NMAH, 2006). This is only effective if they already accept the larger belief system, the overarching ideology from which this culture projects.
>
> (p. 436)

Coffee's examples of ideologies at work include 'westward expansion', so-called 'victory in WW2', the role of slavery in the early Americas and others. Dubin (1999) and others have explored the role of ideologies using conflict-raising exhibits (e.g., Enola Gay) as a focus. These macro ideological contradictions are very much part of museum culture.

Moreover, all the contradictions I discuss are driven by historically informed ideological commitments. For example, expecting assimilation is classist, racist and/or gender insensitive (Ash, 2018; Dawson, 2014b; B. Moore, 2013) and defies any concept of belonging.

I suggest museums are the sites of numerous ideological (dialectical) skirmishes. Ideologies are not just ideas; they eventuate in both even and uneven real-world distribution of goods and services (i.e., resources) and are the foundation for contradictions and dialectical relationships.

By ideology I mean the

> taken for granted assumptions that are often "fragmentary and disjointed and episodic" (S. Hall, 1986, p. 432), specifically sensemaking that stabilizes, challenges and or transforms the distribution of material and symbolic resources in society.
>
> (Philip et al., 2018, p. 2)

The previous definition conveys a less-hegemonic interpretation of ideology, i.e. the recognition that ideologies can be fragmentary and episodic. This interpretation appears to more accurately describe the fragmented ways that people and communities go about their daily lives, which are, of course, colored by structural constraints, such as class, gender, race and so on. Throughout this book, I will ask the fundamental question, "*How can change happen when unquestioned ideologies dominate activity systems?*"

Critical reflection helps to uncover and explore ideologically based assumptions and change them when they no longer match the evidence. Using a critical perspective means making power relations explicit, especially as they intersect with race and class (Dawson, 2014a). Critical reflection is essential to reculturing because it examines beliefs about what is not working, as well as actions to be taken as a consequence.[16] When ideologies are considered "worldviews" that individuals use to mediate and explain their experiences, then ideology as a concept becomes dynamic and capable of change, but ideology must be visible before change can occur (B. Moore, 2013).

Thus, the essential feature is being aware of how ideological constraints inform outcomes such as the choice of master narrative (e.g., Western vs. Indigenous), which are the product of such beliefs. Without this, we are blind to culture, history and societal change. In short, we are at the whim of ideologies[17] we may not know, understand or agree with.

The sources of ideological contention are both internal and external. Coffee (2007) argues that the culture of museums is to "present a visual ideology of the dominant social narrative[s]…[which] tend to be rather closely held and tightly monitored" (p. 436). Ideologies fomenting contention may erupt, for example, when curators or directors present alternative narratives, such as

> when the director of the Cincinnati Contemporary Arts Center sponsored a Robert Mapplethorpe retrospective and was criminally prosecuted for 'pandering obscenity'.
>
> (Coffee, 2008, p. 264)

When ideologies are so tightly held and monitored, it becomes our challenge to critically identify and examine them; each chapter that follows does this. Coffee instructs us on how ideological commitments create important confrontations, concerning, for example, the historical role of Alexander Hamilton or the representation of American Indians at the Smithsonian. In the parlance of CHAT, I consider Coffee's examples to be incipient contradictions that force us to uncover and explore the ideological commitments informing our sense of fundamental 'norms' in museums.

Even as ideologies are always at work, there is strong evidence from several sources that ideologies can change. Leonardo, for example, has argued that

> ideologies are not static…ideology is understood, perpetuated, or challenged through discourse. …Ideology never stands on its own…[and] is involved in relations with other ideologies. It is never complete but instead is evolving and modifying itself.
>
> (Leonardo, 2009, p. 207)

One example of such change is noticing how views of the *other* have shifted over the past two decades, "most specifically in terms of racism, validating our point that individual biases are changeable…long-term change in six social group attitudes: sexual orientation, race, skin tone, age, disability, and body weight" (Cikara and van Beval, 2015, p. 246).

Leonardo suggested that not only do beliefs change, but rather the language of beliefs also changes, so that "the words and ideas we use as terminologies are also changing rapidly; this is but one *indicator* of both the shift we are experiencing and the tensions underlying such shifts" (Leonardo, 2009, p. 430). Shifts in the language are thus strong indicators of societal change. World views, ideologies and the language about them are shifting under our feet (Leonardo, 2003).

Competing Ideologies

In this section, I want to present several ongoing dialectically related, ideological mismatches that particularly impact museum activity systems.

Individualism Versus Collectivism

I address individualism vs. collectivism in several dialectically related ways, relying on both CHAT and SAD. One of the classic conundrums in learning and teaching was choosing how we positioned learners, individually or collectively. In chapter seven I deliberately return to the robust debate of the late 1990s concerning where 'learning is located', posing the question of primacy between social vs. individual views.

A second concern is the way individualism and collectivism are positioned in neoliberal theory. Neoliberalism is, first and foremost, individualist and actively resists collective agency aimed at changing existing power structures. This active diminishment of collectivism helps to create considerable collateral damage (Steger & Roy, 2013), such as destroying equitable access to education (and other resources) for those least able to experience it in the first place, while blaming them as well (Andersen, 2020; Apple, 2017).

An overemphasis on individualism is also detrimental for educator professional development (Ash & Race, 2021; Tolbert et al., 2021). As collective power is deliberately diminished, educators are blamed for problems arising in classroom situations. Children may be too hungry to learn, there may not be adequate resources, but the teacher is made to feel responsible. Similarly, minoritized students are blamed for their individual lack of ability, despite enormous systemic constraints.

Equity/Social Justice vs. Equality

Naming (equality/equity) is but one aspect of a critically reflective agenda. I examine equity versus equality, to get clear on what we actually mean. I assume that the majority in our world seeks social justice. Language shifts as ideologies shift. Language and meaning are recurring refrains in each chapter. Tolbert (2015) has suggested, for example, using the term *minoritized* to reflect the way *other* populations have been treated in public educational spaces. The term minoritized is useful as it connotes the action of active 'othering' involved in making some members into a power-minority group. Marginalized serves a similar function (Gibbons, 2015).

Rodriguez uses the phrase *new mainstream* (Rodriguez, 2009) to reflect changing demographics. The *new mainstream* includes Latino, black, Asian, and other non-Caucasian groups; the largest group is Hispanic/Latino. The term *Latinx* is also recent, less used among Latino populations generally but more often used by young Latinix women (Meraji, 2020).[18] I have in the past used the phrase 'culturally and linguistically diverse' populations to indicate focal areas of difference. The word *diversity* has become overused and under-precise (P. Moore, 2014). In this book, I use the terms *nondominant* or *minoritized*, as these terms more accurately reflect the power dynamics at the heart of most discriminatory practices. Yet, there are worries that changes in language are not accompanied by changes in beliefs. For example, Gorski notes, "I worry that our evolution from "diversity" and "multiculturalism" to "social justice" is more a shift in language than a shift in consciousness or shifts in institutional cultures" (p. 4).

Naming is just the tip of the iceberg. We must ask, "*What would it take for museums to become more socially just?*" Social justice theorists have long been concerned with how resources might be distributed most equally (redistributive social justice) and now, more recently, most equitably (relational social justice; Dawson, 2017, p. 540).

In the first model, justice is about equality of access and distribution between social groups; everybody being able to do, enjoy or use the same amounts of the same things (Rawls, 1971). The second model, in contrast, emphasizes the value of recognizing difference. This means recognizing, respecting, and valuing that people differ and taking their differences into account, rather than treating everyone's needs as the same (Young, 1990). According to Parker, equity is "not about everybody getting the same thing, it's about everybody getting what they need in order to improve the quality of their situation" (Parker, 2016). I adopt the equity/social justice view throughout this book, while I also recognize that equity and social justice are not the same (Figure 1.2).

Outreach vs. Inreach

What's wrong with 'outreach'? After all, outreach is an accepted, well-known term in museums and other circles. Bell et al. (2009) identified some troubling aspects ten years ago:

> [M]useum staffs conceptualize efforts to broaden participation as "outreach," they implicitly endorse this [staff-centric] view of ownership. The term "outreach" implies that some communities are external to the institution.
> (p. 232)

Bell identifies the dichotomizing nature of outreach, but *inreach* and *outreach* exist in a dialectical relationship. *Inreach*, a newer term, requires that museums view

FIGURE 1.2 Equity vs. equality, Interaction Institute for Social Change (2016). Artist Angus Maguire, open source

linguistically, economically, culturally or ethnically different populations as resource-full, rather than deficient.

The very word *outreach* carries the implication that some people are outside and, thus, less powerful than those inside. By *outreach* we typically mean going *out* into the community, sometimes conducting workshops in targeted neighborhoods, summer camps, afterschool programs and other specifically tasked programs. The idea is to *reach* those who are not currently patrons of museums. These populations are often linguistically, economically, culturally or ethnically different.

Dawson similarly noted that "implications of identifying and representing people or groups as 'other' – whether as 'non-participants', 'non-visitors', 'new audiences' or 'excluded'—are problematic and risk the implication that their differences from some *norm* are problematic or at fault" (Levitas, 2004 in Dawson, 2014b, p. 211). Externalizing or *othering* is troubling as it infers an 'us vs. them' ideology. As we already noted, reculturing requires critical reflection on dominant norms at all levels, to understand how deficit, assimilationist or neoliberal consumerist views have shaped modern museum policy and practice.

Many researchers have found middle-level professional development work in the museum workplace to be a valid entry point for tracing how change does and does not occur (Anderson et al., n.d.; Martin et al., 2019; Ward, 2016). Working in or collaborating with different institutions, including aquariums, science centers, museums, zoos and other settings, I have found similar dynamics to apply throughout all these settings. Museum, zoo and aquarium efforts can and sometimes do incorporate critically reflective practice, which asks educators, curators and administrators to examine their own theories and practices, both as subjects for action research and active promoters of the goals of greater equity and inclusivity (Anderson et al., n.d.; Ash & deGregoria, 2013; deGregoria Kelly, 2009).

A growing group of museum scholars and practitioners are conducting related research across many institutions in the hope that the results of our combined efforts will effect long-lasting change in museum educators and institutional culture (Bevan & Ramos, 2021; Martin et al., 2019; Tran & Halverson, 2021). The institutions studied cut across a wide swath of scientific interests. As a group, we are using reflective practice as a central organizing theme, although each of us has a different view of what it means for institutions to change, and each of our efforts has taken a slightly different approach. Consistent with activity theory, our experiments indicate a healthy outgrowth of the current tensions and contradictions noted in the coming chapters.

The concept of *inreach* does not carry assimilation as a prerequisite; rather, it allows us to keep the visitors' agendas in the forefront, to develop a sense of shared purpose, practices, values and beliefs; to make a deep commitment to collaborate with all visitors; to use reflective practices; to develop a resource view of the minoritized visitors and, most crucially, to share power at all levels. It also requires enhanced listening, communication and paying attention to the needs of the outside community in new and different ways by museum staff. Many of the ideas are not *new*, yet when taken in conjunction with the expectation of large-scale institutional change, in the company of theory to explain change at all levels, past concerns perhaps may be repurposed. These expectations are fulsome and will not be achieved easily, yet they are part of creating a future ethos of museums unstuck on past *norms* or *settled expectations*. For all these reasons, we must move beyond *outreach*.

Deficit vs. Resource Orientation

Feinstein and Meshoulam (2014) noted that museum staff ask, "Why don't *they* come to our museum?" This phrasing refers to the audience whose needs are not yet met, typically the poor, the underrepresented and the invisible and/or specific ethnic groups, i.e., the *other*. Paired with the general tendency of museums to conduct *outreach* to change 'nonparticipants', 'nonvisitors' or 'new audiences', museum staff typically focus on how to inculcate *others* into the museum's normative culture, ideas and ways of speaking and doing. Such *othering or* treating a person or group of people as basically different from oneself, or "not one of us", widens any perceived gap between insider and outsider. Deficit orientation can be more broadly defined as

> a worldview that explains and justifies outcome inequalities—standardized test scores or levels of educational attainment, for example—by pointing to supposed deficiencies within disenfranchised individuals and communities.
>
> (Gorski, 2010, p. 6)

Gorski argues that when one uses the deficit view, difference is mistaken for deficit, and this misunderstanding is then "woven into the fabric of society and its socializing institutions" (p. 7).

We can see the impact of such *othering* beliefs at all levels of museum activity systems. For example, if a ticket taker is rude to visitors of color, these visitors will probably not come back. If people feel unwelcome or uncomfortable, why should they come back? If administrators decide it is too expensive to support free passes, then people may not come. If people of color are made to feel like tokens for their community, they also may not want to come.

One corollary of difference as deficit is trying 'to fix' the individuals rather than fixing the structural conditions that inform how we interpret such differences. As Dawson and others have argued, "[T]he 'rules of the game' that non-dominant visitors are expected to be able to notice, understand and operate successfully are… norms and expectations that may not be their own" (Dawson, 2014b, p. 226).

Taking the opposite tack, the resource view, requires us to recognize that all people have ways of knowing, funds of knowledge (González et al., 2005; Moll et al., 1992), as well as everyday ways of thinking and reasoning that can fit well with and use what museums have to offer if we take the time to recognize them (Ash, 2014b; Dawson, 2014a). Taking time means looking closely at what is said, rather than expecting specialized language (Ash et al., 2008; Lemke, 1990).

In the sciences, for example, words such as *species, predation, trophic levels* are looked for; in art, *abstract, representational, the blue period* are anticipated and expected. Museum exhibit designers, curators, educators and other insiders all learned science and art using those words and may believe that these words are the actual knowledge. Scientific or artistic sensemaking does not rely on specialized language (Bruna, 2010; Lemke, 1990; Warren & Rosebery, 2008). I revisit this topic in chapter seven devoted to learning.

Viewed from the confines of deficit ideology, it is not only possible to see the words people use about art and science as *wrong*, but it also even leads insiders to believe that people are 'doing the exhibit' wrong (Mai & Ash, 2012). Numerous conflicts exist, seen and unseen, with respect to the museum's intention and "what are we supposed to do here?" Any exhibit curriculum, that is, what the visitor is intended to learn, either explicitly or implicitly drives how the museum exhibit's designers, administrators and educators interpret the activity of the people who subsequently interact, read signs and interpret what they see as they try to engage with the exhibit. When we take an equitable stance, we discover that it is not essential that the visitor grasp the designers' intent in order to make sense of the exhibit (Ash, 2018; Mai & Ash, 2012).

Among the implicit and unexamined ideas in museum culture, there is a belief that right ways *to do* an exhibit actually do exist. Any deviation is judged to be the fault of the visitor, or 'doing it wrong'. An educator's expectation of a 'normal' visit can create an authoritative tone that can be particularly discouraging for those new to museums. This can create a negative feedback loop that eventuates in reluctant offerings of resources by new visitors, met by a lack of receptivity on the part of the museum educator, as well as resistance to significant change on the part of the institution. This toxic combination virtually ensures diminishing returns.

Assimilate or Resist

Dawson (2014a) questioned the core assumption of "science museums, that exposing more people to science is *de facto* a good thing, whether they want it or not" (p. 214). Lee & Buxton, 2010) describe this assumption as assimilationist (Lee & Buxton, 2010). Dawson and others have pointed out that assimilationist views assume minoritized people will only be successful if they adapt to Western European-American, white, middle-class norms, especially ways of communicating, that most museums currently reflect. Dawson noted,

> Assimilation refers to attempting to increase inclusion in a practice [such as museum visiting]…without considering the cultural, social, linguistic or other changes that may be required for that practice to be appealing, accessible and equitable.
> (Bell et al., 2009; Fenichel & Schweingruber, 2010, in Dawson, 2014b, p. 215)

Regarding the question of which norm we aim to assimilate toward, B. A. Moore (2013) has been eloquent on this subject in schools (we may substitute the word museums for schools):

> The conceptualization of *normal* in schools is problematic. It mediates perceptions about ability, achievement and behavior. *Normal* implies a hierarchy, naturalizing the idea that some students can achieve better than others. This practice places the *blame* on the student by locating the problem within the child while failing to consider ways to make educational contexts more responsive. Those seen as deviating from normal are often characterized by race, language use, socioeconomic status, or perceived ability. Historically, this has led to educational inequities.
> (B. A. Moore, 2013. p. *iii*)

Looking at museums from these perspectives, we may ask, "Who is trying to change whom?" I suggest that a noncollaborative *outreach* stance, explicitly or implicitly focused on changing museum outsiders so that they can *learn to assimilate* and learn to imitate the 'museum norm' (Dawson, 2017), is counterproductive to long-term transformation, especially if the goal is to increase minoritized visitor attendance.

Power, Stratification, Hierarchy

Dubin (1999) has argued that museums always engage in *displays of power* that can be identified in the museum's message, mission, exhibition choices, interpretations and internal dynamics. If we are concerned with what is socioculturally and historically perceived as the *norm* (B. Moore, 2013) or 'settled expectations' (Bang et al., 2012), then we need to understand and tackle the analysis of power relationships. As Davis argues, "[N]ormalizing conceptual binaries", such as straight/gay, rich/poor, black/white, male/female that act in similar ways, "are embedded in ideologies of power, fear and marginalization" (Davis, 2010, p. 54). Apple (2017), Au and Ferrare (2015), B. A. Moore (2013) and powell and Menendian (2017) all refer to the lack of power of those considered 'other', those on the 'wrong side' of the neoliberal divide.[19]

One aspect of power at a personal level is self-reflection and self-knowledge as a form of agency. Self-knowledge of hierarchical position is inevitable as part of any work environment; Lucy Suchman said this of self-knowledge as empowerment:

> [S]pecial authority in relation to our own fields of knowledge and experience [suggests that we] should have the ability to shape not only how we work [but also] with how our work appears to others. Self-representation on this view is a form of empowerment.
>
> (Suchman, 1995, p. 56)

What does *self-representation and the ability to share our work* look like for museum curators, educators or administrators? The research community is still pondering this particular question, as we are actively reshaping it. Seeing museum staff empowerment in new ways has been influenced by the 'social turn' of the 1990s that I discuss in Chapter 7 and the sociopolitical turn we discuss throughout (R. Gutiérrez, 2013).

In museums, power traditionally peaks at the administrative and then curatorial levels, a system reflected in almost every museum organization chart.[20] Power hierarchies implicitly or explicitly stem from historically situated ideologies and the resultant policies and practices (Bourdieu & Wacquant, 1992). Using a critical perspective means making power relations explicit, especially as they intersect with race and class (Dawson, 2014a). Many museums are conducting experiments in community collaboration (Science Museum of Minnesota, Oakland Museum of California, Dallas Museum of Fine Arts, to name but a few). This will require that evaluators, researchers, administrators and educators need to know where, when and under what conditions *different* groups of learners can become more comfortable in museum settings and begin to develop a sense of 'belongingness' there. Understanding these dimensions requires a different kind of research and practice using the analysis tools I discuss.

The Structure of the Book

In the chapters that follow, I describe several structural tensions common to museums. The tensions have historical roots that reflect the broader society. Specifically, I explore demographics and finances, narrative and objects and learning and teaching.

I have organized these chapters in pairs that operate dialectically, informing and changing each other. Chapters 3 and 4 examine demographics and dollars, Chapters 5 and 6 stories and objects and Chapters 7 and 8 examine learning and teaching. Each pair operates in dynamic tension with one another. Highlighting these dialectical relationships here, I hope to familiarize the reader with the pleasure of 'working the dialectic'. The questions I ask throughout this book include, "Are museums social, cultural and societal forums for *all* the public, or are they forums for only *some* of the public?" "Are visitors *clients or collaborators?*" (Feinstein & Meshoulam, 2014). "Must visitors pay for the right to see/appreciate cultural artifacts, or is this a free right for all?" "How can we break through an *us vs. them* divide that pervades society and is reflected in museums?" (powell & Menendian, 2017). And, "How can we adopt a truly equitable view?" as Dawson (2014a), Gurian (2020) and many others have demanded.

The Chapters

Each chapter begins with a brief overview designed to let the reader know quickly what material is to be discussed. I then provide a real-world vignette that typifies the particular contradiction/dialectic museums face. The vignette helps us to situate the ideas explored in the chapter. Each chapter ends with a brief discussion of power dynamics, vis-à-vis the topics discussed.

Although the order of the book has been carefully planned, we know that the reader often has other ideas; the overviews are designed to allow the reader to pick and choose the order of chapters they wish to engage with. Each chapter is meant to be self-contained but also to be braided with the aforementioned themes so that the interlinking and reciprocity of issues and analyses will become increasingly apparent.

Chapter 1: Introduction to the Main Theories and Themes of *Reculturing Museums*
A review of the structural tensions concerning social justice and equity in informal institutions, including deficit ideology, assimilation, decolonization, power, outreach vs. *inreach* and the need for a reexamination of the norm, the status quo or 'how we do things around here'.

Chapter 2: Why Do We Need Theories?
We discuss the core elements of CHAT in the context of a real-world example involving the Exxon oil spill in Valdez, Canada. We relate CHAT analyses to actual museum day-to-day decision-making and, also, to the topics addressed in the ensuing chapters. We also discuss the SAD basic principles, as well as the basics of neoliberal and othering/deficit ideologies, which we critique. I argue we are at a major historical *tipping point* within museums.

Chapter 3: Who Will Go to Museums?
Museums are being asked to reexamine their traditional norms, to think differently about *equity and social justice*, and to seriously question their strategies for the future.

This chapter discusses some of these challenges. I argue that 'demographics' are but a proxy, disguising underlying ideologies. The central contradiction of this chapter concerns the difference between the desire of informal learning institutions for increasing diversity, compared with current data concerning actual and projected future attendance. These two factors—the desired and the actual—are far out of alignment—a discrepancy that creates new tensions.

Chapter 4: Who Will Pay for Museums?
Museums face continuing financial hardships, which often are 'quick fixed' by layoffs, deaccession and other temporary cost-cutting efforts. Using admission as a proxy and as a focus contradiction for discussion, I pose the question, "Should museums offer free admission to all?" "Do visitors really need to pay for what they see to appreciate art", as one museum director has suggested? We review but do not suggest a particular solution, using a spectrum of pricing proposals and focus on the underlying contradictions, which are tied to competing ideologies that reflect the heightened tension at the nexus of money and power.

Chapter 5: Whose Story Is It?
How do contradictory views of history and culture affect what is said on the museum floor and in the surrounding community? We explore narratives as multi-sided, dynamic and often contradictory, rather than linear, chronological or fossilized positioning. Master narratives reflect the philosophical cultural stance underlying the stories that are told; counter-narratives offer resistance to master narratives. We focus here on another proxy in history and cultural museums, specifically those portraying Native Americans in the United States and Canada because they provide a clear case study of contradictions. We explore the basis of framing master narratives, including contested land in Central California, the American Museum of Natural History, and the National Museum of the American Indian. I invoke the dialectic between narratives of westward expansion vs. cultural genocide.

Chapter 6: Who Owns the Artifact?
"What does it mean to own something?" I explore the ways museums and politics have treated sacred, stolen and 'found' objects, referencing the Native American Graves Protection and Repatriation Act of 1990, the repatriation of the 'ancient one' Kennewick Man in Washington, and of Hawaiian bones (Iwi kūpuna) from London to Hawaii. We discuss the meaning of sacred; I suggest that any cultural object, whether sacred or practical or both, is given meaning by the context of how and when it was used, and for what purpose. The repatriation of Hawaiian and Native American bones in the United Sates acts as a proxy for similar international cases.

Chapter 7: Where Is the Learning, and Who Gets To Learn?
Examining learning in informal settings such as museums is challenging. Chief among the reasons for this is agreeing on what we mean by learning and then

locating instances to prove our point. I describe multiple theoretical perspectives concerning learning and explore these in the context of a real-life family visit at a science museum. I offer a taxonomy of learning theories developed in the 1990s to guide our thinking and explore the critical role of mediational means in sociocultural theory. We explore two contradictions: whether we view learning as individual or social and whether we view learners from a deficit or a resource stance. I relate the main themes from other chapters as they relate to learning.

Chapter 8: What Do We Mean by Equitable Teaching in Museums?
In this chapter, I pose the essential question: "What do we mean by equitable teaching in museums?" I use a case study approach to examine a case of an incomplete expansive learning cycle and the SAD in a museum context. This research and practice project addressed the dialectic between didactic and scaffolded teaching theory and practice as central features of a large museum. I examine here the power relations that cut across all levels of museums and especially impact how we can best conduct professional development that leads to transformative agency (Sannino, 2020) and equitable teaching.

Chapter 9: How do we reculture museums while old systems are still in place?
By working through the issues museums face with learning, teaching, finances, demographics, storytelling and objects, we can truly appreciate just how challenging it is to actually transform institutions in fundamental ways. It can be particularly difficult to think about change with respect to issues of equity, diversity and social inclusion or exclusion. I summarize why and how CHAT, SAD and ideological critiques allow researchers to uncover the dialectical forces at work and follow how these dynamics actually play out and ways to begin to effect change. I highlight how power is reflected in museums and make suggestions for how change can happen for museums wishing to do so. This is not prescriptive but a starting point. Finally, I describe recent work that reflects reculturing in process.

Summary

I have introduced the central features of my analytic tools: CHAT, SAD, and a critique of deficit ideologies as well as neoliberal policies and practices. These four theoretical frames inform how we situate change in museums. CHAT allows us to simultaneously capture multiple layers of how people, objects and meaning are interrelated and mutually constructed across time. Contradictions, based on historically produced tensions, are broad ranging, both past and future oriented and dialectical. This is important for museums, as each contradiction implicitly or explicitly informs decision-making and, thus, transforms or reifies 'the way we do things around here'. I consider change at all levels of museum functions.

SAD allows us to look more closely at power dynamics in new ways, as well as to explore the limits of individual agency in the neoliberal world of work, eventually seeking out transformative agency (Sannino, 2020). I note the rise of individualism over the past half-century at the expense of human rights and collectivism, where the individual does not gain systemic power in isolation but feels as if they might (Harvey, 2007).

Successful reculturing also requires critical reflection of what has passed as the *norm* and then finding pathways to challenge and transform 'the way we do things around here' by critiquing the way museums engage in *displays of power* (Dubin, 1999). I argue that reculturing requires change from within the museum (*inreach*), rather than expecting others to change (*outreach*) and that neoliberal ideology and resultant policies have significantly diminished equitable access to education in museums and schools (Apple, 2017; Au & Ferrare, 2015). Each chapter discusses power. I examine four dialectic relationships: Individualism vs. Collectivism, Equity/Social Justice vs. Equality, Outreach vs. Inreach, and Deficit vs. Resource Orientation and Assimilate or Resist and initiate a dialogue concerning Power, Stratification, and Hierarchy continued throughout this book.

In the chapters that follow, I explicate my analytic methodology and address historically accumulating structural tensions of the past, present and yet to emerge concerning money, demographics, narrative, objects, learning and teaching using the tools and concepts introduced here.

Notes

1 "The 220,000-square-foot, Renzo Piano–designed stunner now turning heads at the base of Manhattan's High Line Park" (Cochran, 2015).
2 See Bennett (1995, 2013).
3 Stensenko (2013) argued, "Conceptualizing the subtle dialectics of individual and collective planes of human praxis whereby *each* individual…is revealed as constituted by, embodying, participating, and most importantly, *contributing* to the dynamic materiality of collective history and collaborative practices" (p. 9).
4 We have now seen several powerful examples of how useful CHAT is for analyzing museum systems (Ash, 2019; deGregoria Kelly, 2009; Ward, 2016).
5 Mediational means/tools are signs and symbols such as, words (do this), visual tools (picture), physical tools (hammer), digital (email, video), symbolic (semaphore). They act as agents for, and served as intervening links to consciousness (Wertsch, 1985). Tools are created and transformed during the development of the activity itself.
6 Activity theory argues that contradictions are designed to explore these dialectical relationships.
7 Reculturing desires change of…"shared beliefs, history, assumptions, norms, and values that manifest themselves in patterns of behavior, or, in other words, the way we do things around here" (Strategies, the Panasonic Foundation, 2005, p. 1).
8 There are many ways to describe the *other* (see Othering and Belonging Institute).
9 See also the museums are not neutral website (https://www.museumsarenotneutral.com/).

10 "To provide information about migration, integration, immigration politics and population development worldwide, mainly focusing on Germany, Europe and North America". http://www.network.(migration.org/pr_migration_museum_eng.php
11 As discussed in Chapter 2, we note that Vygotsky's original model, subject (S), object (O), and mediating artifact triad, emphasizes both mediated action and dialectical relationships, where each node affects the other, as well as the activity as a whole (Engeström, 2001).
12 One of the most recent cases is the Kennewick man, the skeleton of an 8,500-year-old man discussed in Chapter 6.
13 Giddens (1984) argued agency determines structure, which determines the possibilities for the expression of agency and so on, ad infinitum.
14 As Ekström (2020) noted, "Culture and business have become increasingly intertwined, and cultural institutions need to be aware of their place in the market".
15 Such a basic schism of views is diagnostic of the overall tensions in the museum world. The notion of *double deficit* is especially alarming, as it points to a common perception that minoritized visitors don't know enough and that the museums themselves cannot attract enough minoritized visitors. Most certainly, if belief in the first deficit is deeply ingrained, any action based on this inaccurate worldview becomes doomed to failure.
16 We highlight the importance of individual and institutional critical reflection (Ash, 2019; Bequette, 2018; Mezirow, 1990) to accommodate conflicting issues of power as they relate to equity and social justice.
17 We also know that ideologies (sometimes called frames (Lakoff & Ferguson, 2006) or worldviews) *matter* in any institution and that often "the relationship between ideology and learning remains insufficiently theorized and investigated" (Philip et al., 2018, p. 185).
18 Pew's latest survey of Latinx adults living in the United States, found that only 3% self-identify as Latinx (Meraji, 2020).
19 Lisa Delpit calls this the culture of power (Delpit, 1988), suggesting that it operates as if these (nondominant) children (read visitors) were incapable of critical and higher-order thinking and reasoning.
20 One quick example, educators in museums do not enjoy commensurate salaries with other job categories, such as curators.

References

Anderson, D., Cosson, A, & McIntosh, L. (n.d.). *Diverse audiences, challenging topics, and reflective praxis*. Sense Publishers. https://doi.org/10.1007
Andersen, K. (2020). *Evil geniuses: The unmaking of America: A recent history*. Random House.
Apple, M. W. (1993). *Cultural Politics and education* (2nd ed., Vol. 95). Teachers College Press.
Apple, M. W. (2010). Theory, research, and the critical scholar/activist. *Educational Researcher*, 39(2), 152–155. https://doi.org/10.3102/0013189x10362591
Apple, M. W. (Eds.). (2017). *Cultural and economic reproduction in education: Essays on class, ideology and the state* (Vol. 53). Routledge.
Ash, D. (2014a). Positioning informal learning research in museums within activity theory: From theory to practice and back again. *Curator: The Museum Journal, 57*, 107–118. http://dx.doi.org/10.1111/cura.1205
Ash, D. (2014b). Creating hybrid spaces for talk: Humor as a resource learners bring to informal learning context. *National Society for the Study of Education, 113*(2), 535–55.

Ash, D. (2018). Cultural conflict: The stories Dioramas tell and don't tell. In A. Scheersoi & S. D. Tunnicliffe (Eds.), *Natural history dioramas – Traditional exhibits for current educational themes: socio-cultural aspects* (pp. 113–130). Springer International Publishing.

Ash, D. (2019). Reflective practice in action research: Moving beyond the "standard model". In L. Martin, L. Tran, & D. Ash (Eds.), *The reflective museum practitioner: Expanding practice in science museums* (pp. 23–38). Routledge. https://doi.org/10.4324/9780429025242-3

Ash, D., Crain, R., Brandt, C., Loomis, M., Wheaton, M., & Bennett, C. (2008). Talk, tools, and tensions: Observing biological talk over time. *International Journal of Science Education, 29*(12), 1581–1602.

Ash, D., & deGregoria Kelly, L. A. (2013). Thoughts on improvable objects, contradiction and object/tool reciprocity in a study of zoo educator professional development. *Cultural Studies in Science Education, 3,* 587–594.

Ash, D., & Race, A. (2021). Hybridizing equity-focused, field-based theory and practice for pre-service science teachers. *Journal of Informal Science and Environmental Learning.*

Au, W., & Ferrare, J. A. (Eds.). (2015). *Mapping corporate education reform: Power and policy networks in the neoliberal state.* Routledge.

Bang, M., & Marin, A. (2015). Nature-culture constructs in science learning: Human/non-human agency and intentionality. *Journal of Research in Science Teaching, 52*(4), 530–544. doi:10.1002/tea.21204

Bang, M., Warren, B., & Rosebery, A. S., & Medin, D. (2012). Desettling expectations in science education. *Human Development, 55*(5–6), 302–318. doi:10.1159/000345322

Barab, S., Schatz, S., & Scheckler, R. (2004). Using activity theory to conceptualize online community and using online community to conceptualize activity theory. *Mind, Culture, and Activity, 11*(1), 25–47. http://dx.doi.org/10.1207/s15327884mca1101_3

Bell, P., Lewenstein, B., Shouse, A. W., & Feder, M. A. (Eds.). (2009). *Learning science in informal environments: People, places, and pursuits.* National Academies Press.

Bennett, T. (1995). *The birth of the museum: History, theory, politics.* Routledge.

Bennett, T. (2013). *Making culture, changing society.* Routledge.

Bennett, T. (2018). *Museums, Power and knowledge: Selected essays*: Routledge

Bequette, M. (2018). *Minnesota museum of science: Making connections.* Museum Internal Report.

Bevan, B., & Ramos, B. (Eds.). (2021). *Theorizing equity in the museum integrating perspectives from research and practice.* Routledge.

Bourdieu, P., & Wacquant, L. J. D. (1992). *An invitation to reflexive sociology.* University of Chicago Press.

Bruna, K. R. (2010). *Ways with words: Language play and the science learning of Mexican newcomer adolescents.* Education Publications. https://lib.dr.iastate.edu/edu_pubs/32

Center for the Future of Museums. (2009). *Demographic transformation and the future of museums.* American Association of Museums. http://www.aam-us.org/resources/center-for-the-future-of-museums/demographic-

Charlesworth, T. E. S., & Banaji, M. R. (2019). Patterns of implicit and explicit attitudes: I. Long-term change and stability from 2007 to 2016. *Psychological Science, 30*(2), 174–192. https://doi.org/10.1177/0956797618813087

Cikara, M., & Van Beval, J. (2015, June 2). The flexibility of racial bias. *Scientific American.* https://www.scientificamerican.com/article/the-flexibility-of-racial-bias/

Cochran, S. (2015, March 31). First Lady Michelle Obama speaks at the dedication of the new Whitney Museum of American Art. *Architectural Digest.* https://www.architectural-digest.com/story/michelle-obama-whitney-dedication.

Coffee, K. (2007). Audience research and the museum experience as social practice. *Museum Management and Curatorship, 22*(4), 377–389.

Coffee, K. (2008). Cultural inclusion, exclusion and the formative roles of museums. *Museum Management and Curatorship*, *23*(3), 261–279. https://doi.org/10.1080/09647770802234078

Cortell, S. (2011). *The cost of free admission: A comparative study examining the feasibility of eliminating museum admission charges*. [Master's thesis, Ohio State University]. OhioLINK. https://etd.ohiolink.edu/

Dailey, T. L. (2006). *Museums in the age of neoliberalism: A multi-sited analysis of science and health museums*. [Master's thesis, Georgia State University]. ScholarWorks. https://scholarworks.gsu.edu/anthro_theses/20

Davis, N. (2010). The Exxon Valdez oil spill, Alaska. In J. K. Mitchell (Eds.), *The long road to recovery: Community responses to industrial disaster* (pp. 231–272). United Nations University Press.

Davis, P., & Museus, S. (2019). What is deficit thinking? An analysis of conceptualizations of deficit thinking and implications for scholarly research. *Currents*, *1*(1), 117–130. http://dx.doi.org/10.3998/currents.17387731.0001.110

Dawson, E. (2014a). "Not designed for us": How Science museums and science centers socially exclude low-income, minority ethnic groups. *Science Education*, *98*(6), 981–1008.

Dawson, E. (2014b). Equity in formal science education: Developing an access and equity framework for science museums and science centres. *Studies in Science Education*, *50*(2), 209–247.

Dawson, E. (2017). Social justice and out-of-school science learning: Exploring equity in science television, science clubs and maker spaces. *Science Education*, *101*(4), 539–547. https://doi.org/10.1002/sce.21288

deGregoria Kelly, L. A. (2009). Action research as professional development for zoo educators. *Visitor Studies*, *12*(1), 30–46.

Delpit, L. (1988). The silenced dialogue: Power and pedagogy in educating other people's children. *Harvard Educational Review*, *58*(3), 280–299.

DiMaggio, P. J., Powell, W. W. (Eds.). (1991). *The new institutionalism in organizational analysis*. University of Chicago Press.

Dowding, K. (2008). Agency and structure: Interpreting power relationships. *Journal of Power*, *1*(1), 21–36. doi:10.1080/17540290801943380

Dubin, S. (1999). *Displays of power: Memory and amnesia in the American Museum*. New York University Press.

Dubin, S. (2014). *Displays of power: Memory and amnesia in the American Museum*. New York University Press.

Durkin, E. (2015). Michelle Obama urges cultural institutions to provide free access to children in struggling communities. *NY Daily News*. http://www.nydailynews.com/news/politics/michelle-obama-urges-museums-kids-free-article-1.2205987

Ekström, K. M. (2020). *Museum marketization: Cultural institutions in the Neoliberal Era*. Routledge.

Emirbayer, M., & Mische, A. (1998). What is agency? *American Journal of Sociology*, *103*(4), 962–1023. doi:10.1086/231294

Engeström, J. (2001). Expansive learning at work: Toward an activity theoretical reconceptualization. *Journal of Education and Work*, *14*(1), 133–156.

Engeström, Y. (1999). Activity theory and individual and social transformation. In Y. Engeström, R. Miettinen, & R. Punamäki (Eds.), *Perspectives on activity theory (learning in doing): Social, cognitive and computational perspectives* (pp. 19–38). Cambridge University Press. doi:10.1017/CBO9780511812774.003

Engeström, Y. (2009). The future of activity theory: A rough draft. *Learning and Expanding with Activity Theory*, 303–328. https://doi.org/10.1017/cbo9780511809989.020

Engeström, Y., & Sannino, A. (2010). Studies of expansive learning: Foundations, findings and future challenges. *Educational Research Review, 5*(1), 1–24. doi:10.1016/j.edurev.2009.12.002

Feinstein, N. W., & Meshoulam, D. (2014). Science for what public? Addressing equity in American Science Museums and Science Centers. *Journal of Research in Science Teaching, 51*(3), 368–394.

Fenichel, M., & Schweingruber, H. A. (Eds.). (2010). *Surrounded by science: Learning science in informal environments*. National Academies Press.

Foot, K., & Groleau, C. (2011). Contradictions, transitions, and materiality in organizing processes: An activity theory perspective. *First Monday, 16*(6), 1–21. doi:10.5210/fm.v16i6.3479

Foot, K. A. (2014). Cultural-historical activity theory: Exploring a theory to inform practice and research. *Journal of Human Behavior in the Social Environment, 24*(3), 329–347. doi:10.1080/10911359.2013.831011

Garibay, C. (2009). Latinos, leisure values, and decisions: Implications for informal science learning and engagement. *The Informal Learning Review, 94*, 10–13.

Garibay, C. (2011). *Responsive and accessible: How museums are using research to better engage diverse cultural communities*. ASTC Dimensions. http://www.astc.org/blog/2011/02/28/responsive-and-accessible-how-museums-are-using-research-to-better-engage-diverse-cultural-communities/

Giddens, A. (1984). *The theory of structuration*. Berkeley and Los Angeles: University of California Press.

Gibbons, E. (2015). Museums and marginalized historical narratives. In D. Anderson, A. Cosson, & L. McIntosh (Eds.), *Research informing the practice of museum educators*. Sense Publishers. https://doi.org/10.1007

González, N., Moll, L., & Amanti, C. (Eds.) (2005). *Funds of knowledge: Theorizing practices in households, communities, and classrooms*. Lawrence Erlbaum Associates.

Gorski, P. (2010). *Unlearning deficit ideology and the scornful gaze: Thoughts on authenticating the class discourse in education*. EdChange. http://www.edchange.org/publications/deficit-ideology-scornful-gaze.pdf

Griffin, D. J. (1987). Managing in the MUSEUM organization: I. Leadership and communication. *International Journal of Museum Management and Curatorship, 6*(4), 387–398. https://doi.org/10.1080/09647778709515091

Groninger, K. R. (2016). An introduction to museum accountability. *The Museum Scholar, 1*(1). http://articles.themuseumscholar.org/vol1no1groninger

Gurian, E. (2017). *Transforming practice*. Routledge.

Gurian, E. H. (1999). What is the object of this exercise? A meandering exploration of the many meanings of objects in museums. *Daedalus, 128*, 163–183.

Gurian, E. H. (2020). Curator: From soloist to impresario. In C. Fiona & L. Kelly (Eds.), *Hot topics, public culture, museums* (pp. 95–111). Cambridge Scholars Publishing.

Gutiérrez, K. D., & Calabrese Barton, A. (2015). The possibilities and limits of the structure—agency dialectic in advancing science for all. *Journal of Research in Science Teaching, 52*(4), 574–583.

Gutiérrez, R. (2013). The sociopolitical turn in mathematics education. *Journal of Research in Mathematics Education, 44*(1), 37–68. https://doi.org/10.5951/jresematheduc.44.1.0037

Hall, S. (1986). Gramsci's relevance for the study of race and ethnicity. *Journal of Communication Inquiry, 10*(2), 5–27. https://doi.org/10.1177/019685998601000202

Harris, C. I. (1995). Whiteness as property. In K. Crenshaw, N. Gotanda, G. Peller, & K. Thomas (Eds.), *Critical race theory* (pp. 276–291). The New Press.

Harvey, D. (2007). Neoliberalism as creative destruction. *The ANNALS of the American Academy of Political and Social Science, 610*(1), 21–44. https://doi.org/10.1177/0002716206296780

Hatzipanagos, R. (2018, October 11). The 'decolonization' of the American Museum, *The Washington Post*. https://www.washingtonpost.com/nation/2018/10/12/decolonization-american-museum/

Hein, G. (2014). Museum: Knowledge, democracy and transformation conference on organizational change within participating institutions related to the citizenship project, Helsingor, Denmark (May 26–127). https://silo.tips/download/kronburg-castle-and-danish-maritime-museum-helsingr-denmark-may-2014-museums-kno

Hobsbawm, E., & Ranger, T. (2012). *The invention of tradition (Canto classics)*. Cambridge University Press.

James, R. (2013). *Museums and the paradox of change*. Routledge.

Jennings, G., & Jones-Rizzi, J. (2017). Museums, white privilege, and diversity: A systemic perspective. *Dimensions*, *18*(5), 66–67.

Kaptelinin, V. (2005). The object of activity: Making sense of the sense-maker. *Mind, Culture, and Activity*, *12*(1), 4–18. https://doi.org/10.1207/s15327884mca1201_2

Kaptelinin, V. (2011). *Activity theory*. The Interaction Design Foundation. https://www.interaction-design.org/literature/book/the-encyclopedia-of-human-computer-interaction-2nd-ed/activity-theory.

Karp, I., Kreamer, C. M., & Lavine, S. D. (Eds.) (1992). *Museums and communities: The politics of public culture*. Smithsonian Institution Press.

Lakoff, G., & Ferguson, S. (2006). The framing of immigration. *Huffington Post*. http://www.huffingtonpost.com/george-lakoff-and-sam-ferguson/the-framing-ofimmigration

Lee, O., & Buxton, C. (2010). *Diversity and equity in science education: Research, policy, and practice (multicultural education series)*. Teachers College Press.

Lemke, J. L. (1990). *Talking science: Language, learning and values*. Ablex Publishing.

Leonardo, Z. (2003). Discourse and critique: Outlines of a post-structural theory of ideology. *Journal of Education Policy*, *18*(2), 203–214. doi:10.1080/0268093022000043038

Leonardo, Z. (2009). *Race, whiteness, and education*. Routledge

Levitas, R. (2004). Let's hear it for Humpty: Social exclusion, the third way and cultural capital. *Cultural Trends*, *13*(2), 41–56. doi:10.1080/0954896042000267414

Lipman, P. (2011). *The new political economy of urban education: Neoliberalism, race and the right to the city*. Routledge.

Lonetree, A. (2009). Museums as sites of decolonization: Truth telling in national and tribal museums. In Smith, S. S. (Ed.), *Contesting knowledge: Museums and indigenous perspectives* (pp. 322–337). University of Nebraska Press.

Mahn, H., & John-Steiner, V. (2012). Vygotsky and sociocultural approaches to teaching and learning. In I. Weiner, W. M. Reynolds, & G. E. Miller (Eds.), *Handbook of psychology* (2nd ed., vol. 7). https://doi.org/10.1002/9781118133880.hop207006

Mai, T., & Ash, D. (2012). Tracing our methodological steps: Making meaning of families' hybrid "figuring out" practices at science museum exhibits. In D. Ash, J. Rahm, & L. Melber (Eds.), *Putting theory into practice: Methodologies for informal learning research* (pp. 97–117). Sense Publishers.

Marshall, A. (2020, August 6). What is a museum? A dispute erupts over a new definition. *New York Times*. https://www.nytimes.com/2020/08/06/arts/what-is-a-museum.html

Martin, L. Tran, L. U., & Ash, D. (2019). *The reflective museum practitioner: Expanding practice in science museums*. Routledge.

McLaughlin, M. W., & Talbert, J. E. (2007). Building professional communities in high schools: Challenges and promises practices. In L. Stoll & K. Seashore Louis (Eds.), *Professional learning communities: Divergence, depth and dilemmas* (pp. 151–165). Open University Press.

McNamee, S., & Miller, S. (2004). *The meritocracy myth*. Rowman & Littlefield.

Meraji, S. M. (2020, August 11). 'Hispanic,' 'Latino,' Or 'Latinx'? survey says ... NPR. https://www.npr.org/sections/codeswitch/2020/08/11/901398248/hispanic-latino-or-latinx-survey-says.

Mezirow, J. (1990). *How critical reflection triggers transformative learning*. Academia. https://pdfs.semanticscholar.org/0e6c/5327e7e0c395d35ff57676f2ef666a9644bd.pdf

Moll, L. C., Amanti, C., Neff, D., & Gonzalez, N. (1992). Funds of knowledge for teaching: Using a qualitative approach to connect homes and classrooms. *Theory into Practice*, *31*(2), 132–141. doi:10.1080/00405849209543534

Moore, B. (2013). Understanding the ideology of normal: Making visible the ways in which educators think about students who seem different. [Unpublished doctoral dissertation]. University of Colorado.

Moore, P. (2014, January 20). *The danger of the "D" word: Museums and diversity*. The Incluseum. https://incluseum.com/2014/01/20/the-danger-of-the-d-word-museums-and-diversity/

Network Migration in Europe. (n.d.). Migration in museums: Narratives of diversity in Europe. http://www.network-migration.org/pr_migration_museum_eng.php

NMAH. (2006). National Museum of American History. https://americanhistory.si.edu/.

Othering and Belonging Institute. (2019). *Vision*. https://belonging.berkeley.edu/vision

Parker, C. S. (2016, January 13). *Illustrating equality vs equity*. Interaction Institute for Social Change. https://interactioninstitute.org/illustrating-equality-vs-equity/.

Philip, T. M., Gupta, A., Elby, A., & Turpen, C. (2018). Why ideology matters for learning: A case of ideological convergence in an engineering ethics classroom discussion on drone warfare. *Journal of the Learning Sciences*, *27*(2), 183–223. doi:10.1080/10508406.2017.1381964

Powell, J., & Menendian, S. (2017, June 29). The problem of othering: Towards inclusiveness and belonging. *Othering and Belonging: Expanding the Circle of Human Concern*, *1*, 14–39. https://otheringandbelonging.org/wp-content/uploads/2016/07/OtheringAndBelonging_Issue1.pdf

Rahm, J. (2010). *Science in the making at the margin: A Multisited ethnography of learning and becoming in an afterschool program, a garden and a math and science upward bound program*. Brill.

Rahm, J. (2018). Youths' navigations of botanical gardens: Bids for recognition, ways to desettle practice. *Environmental Education Research*, *24*(8), 1115–1127. https://doi.org/10.1080/13504622.2018.1469731

Rawls, J. (1971). *A theory of justice*. Harvard University Press.

Rodriguez, G. (2009). *Towards a new mainstream?* Center for the Future of Museums. https://www.aam-us.org/2009/11/23/towards-a-new-mainstream/

Roth, W.-M., & Tobin, K. (2002). *At the elbow of another. Learning to teach by co-teaching*. Peter Lang.

Sacred Land Project. (2020). *Our story lives forever*. https://sacredland.org/

Sannino, A. (2020). Transformative agency as warping: How collectives accomplish change amidst uncertainty. *Pedagogy, Culture, & Society*. https://doi.org/10.1080/14681366.2020.1805493

Sannino, A., Daniels, H., & Gutiérrez, K. D. (Eds.) (2009). *Learning and expanding with activity theory*. Cambridge University Press.

Sannino, A., Engeström, Y., & Lahikainen, J. (2016). The dialectics of AUTHORING expansive learning: Tracing the long tail of a change laboratory. *Journal of Workplace Learning*, *28*(4), 245–262. https://doi.org/10.1108/jwl-01-2016-0003

Seo, M. G., & Creed, D. (2002). Institutional contradictions, praxis, and institutional change: A dialectical perspective. *The Academy of Management Review*, *27*(2), 222–247. doi:10.2307/4134353

Sewell, W. (1992). A theory of structure: Duality, agency, and transformation. *American Journal of Sociology, 98*(1), 1–29. doi:10.2307/2781191

Silvers, D. M. (2015, February 8). *"This will never work here": Six strategies for facing internal resistance to design thinking.* Design Thinking for Museums. https://designthinkingformuseums.net/2013/08/06/six-strategies/.

Simon, N. (2013). *On white privilege and museums.* Museum 2.0. http://museumtwo.blogspot.com/2013/03/on-white-privilege-and-museums.html.

Smagorinsky, P. (2010). The culture of learning to teach: The self-perpetuating cycle of conservative schooling. *Teacher Education Quarterly, 37*, 19–31. doi:10.2307/23479587.

Smith, J. (2016, April 22). Met Museum to cut spending as deficit looms. *Wall Street Journal.* https://www.wsj.com/articles/met-museum-to-cut-spending-as-deficit-looms-1461287217.

Steger, M. B., & Roy, R. K. (2013). *Neoliberalism: A very short introduction.* Oxford University Press.

Stensenko, A, (2013). The challenge of individuality in cultural- historical activity theory: "Collectividual" dialectics from a transformative activist stance. *Outlines – Critical Practice Studies 14*(2). 7–28. http://www.outlines.dk

Strategies, the Panasonic Foundation. (2005). *Equity vs equality.* Interaction Institute for Social Change. http://interactioninstitute.org/illustrating-equality-vs-equity/

Suchman, L. (1995). Making work visible. *Communications of the ACM, 38*(9), 56–64. https://doi.org/10.1145/223248.223263

The White House. (2015, April 30). *Remarks by the First Lady at opening of the Whitney Museum.* National Archives and Records Administration. https://obamawhitehouse.archives.gov/the-press-office/2015/04/30/remarks-first-lady-opening-whitney-museum.

Thompson, S. (2005). Reculturing for all means all. *Strategies, 1*(1), 1–16. http://www.aasa.org/uploadedFiles/Publications/Strategies/Fall%202005%20Final.pdf.

Tolbert, S. (2015). "Because they want to teach you about their culture": Analyzing effective mentoring conversations between culturally responsible mentors and secondary science teachers of indigenous students in mainstream schools. *Journal of Research in Science Teaching, 52*(10), 1325–1361. doi:10.1002/tea.21240

Tolbert, S., Spurgin, C., & Ash, D. (2021, April 7). *'Staying with the trouble': Praxis crisis in science teacher education for emergent bilingual learners.* Annual meeting of NARST online. https://ir.canterbury.ac.nz/bitstream/handle/10092/102211/NARST%202021%20SAD%20final.pdf?sequence=2&isAllowed=y

Tran, L. U., & Halverson, C. (2021). *Reflecting on practice for STEM educators: A guide for museums, out-of-school, and other informal settings.* Routledge.

Tsoukas, H. (2003). Do we really understand tacit knowledge? In M. Easterby-Smith & M. A. Lyles (Eds.), *Handbook of orgnizational learning and knowledge* (pp. 410–427). Blackwell.

Varelas, M., Settlage, J., & Mensah, F. M. (2015). Explorations of the structure-agency dialectic as a tool for framing equity in science education. *Journal of Research in Science Teaching, 52*(4), 439–447. https://doi.org/10.1002/tea.21230

Vygotsky, L. S. (1978). *Mind in society: The development of higher psychological processes.* Harvard University Press.

Ward, S. J. (2016). *Understanding contradictions in times of change: A CHAT analysis in an art museum.* [Doctoral dissertation, University of Washington]. ResearchWorks Archive. http://hdl.handle.net/1773/37091

Ward, S. J. (2018). Interconnected impact: Using CHAT to understand art museums as systems. *Museum Management and Curatorship, 33*(2), 178–194. https://doi.org/10.1080/09647775.2018.1440359

Warren, B., & Rosebery, A. (2008). Using everyday experience to teach science. In A. Rosebery and B. Warren (Eds.), *Teaching Science to English language learners*, (pp. 39–50). NSTA Press.

Weil, S. (2007). From being about something to being for somebody: The ongoing transformation of the American Museum. In R. Sanell & R. R. Janes (Eds.), *Museum management and marketing*. Routledge.

Wertsch, J.V. (1985). *Vygotsky and the social formation of mind*. Harvard University Press.

Yamagata Lynch, L. C. (2010). *Activity systems analysis methods: Understanding complex learning environments*. Springer Science & Business Media.

Young, I. M. (1990). *Justice and the politics of difference*. Princeton University Press.

2
WHY DO WE NEED THEORIES?

Overview

In this chapter, we delve deeper into the four theoretical foundations introduced in Chapter 1. Sociocultural theories emphasize collaborative communication and mediation with tools of all kinds,[1] created first by Vygotsky (1978). These theories, expanded to include the collective by Leon'tev and modified by Engeström as modern CHAT, taken together are a theoretical foundation for systems thinking.[2] CHAT is the ideal tool to use in an analysis of complex cases that contain 'historically accumulating structural tensions' for intersecting institutional, environmental, governmental and personal rights, sometimes erupting dramatically in the world as oil spills (Taylor, 2014). We augment CHAT with structure agency dialectic (SAD) and critiques of neoliberal and deficit/*othering* ideologies.

When examining specific contradictions in systems, I rely on dialectical logic, which as Kaptelinin notes "starts from the assumption that development is driven by contradictions" (Kaptelinin, 2011) in museum systems[3] (p. 33). I also refer to the SAD that provides new "analytic tools for re-reading and re-naming some of the enduring equity dilemmas" (Gutiérrez & Calabrese Barton, 2015) I argue that museums have been operating on inherited vestiges of colonialist, neoliberal and ideological "othering". Until recently, such views have helped museums maintain legitimacy, now they are under attack. Using all four theoretical tools allows us to challenge these underlying assumptions, to better understand how museums can critically reflect and move toward reculturing and establish a new 'business as usual'. These tools help us recognize dilemmas, conflicts and double binds as everyday events within any museum system so that they can change.

I first demonstrate the usefulness of this analytic framework by analyzing aspects of the Exxon/Valdez spill in 1989, emphasizing dialectically based contradictions. This foundation sets the stage for looking at contradictions and the potential for

38 Why Do We Need Theories?

expansive learning in the chapters that follow. I also use the Exxon/Valdez case to explain how these analytic tools can help in finding potential for change in other specific aspects of museum structure and activities.

VIGNETTE: THE EXXON VALDEZ OIL SPILL

The Valdez Museum preserves and presents the heritage and culture of Valdez, Alaska, the Copper River Basin and the Prince William Sound. One of its exhibits focuses on the Exxon oil spill. Valdez is a culturally rich, historic area and home to the Valdez Native Tribe (VNT). Valdez is also a port city at the end of the Trans-Alaska Pipeline System. Its economy relies heavily on oil.

On March 24, 1989, the oil tanker Exxon/Valdez ran aground on Bligh Reef, spilling 11.2 million U.S. gallons of oil into Prince William Sound. This event naturally holds historic significance for Valdez, as a center for oil spill cleanup activity in the aftermath of the spill. The long-term effects of the oil spill are still being felt today in terms of environmental impact and negative economic effects on industries such as fishing and tourism. The 30-plus years since the oil spill have been marked by heated litigation and legislation, and scrutiny of the oil industry by environmental groups. The same time span has also seen many changes and improvements to the technology and procedures surrounding oil spill prevention and response, resulting in an unprecedented level of service important for protecting the environment of Prince William Sound.

One visitor to the Valdez Museum and Heritage Center commented on the exhibit:

> Just so much to see, lots of memorabilia, lots of vignettes, a lot of history to digest. We thought the display related to Valdez [oil spill] was particularly memorable. They have the audio tape of the captain that just seemed to underline his [the captain's] apparent indifference to what was unfolding. Also a great tool to help "scale" the spill on various locations of a large world map. Definitely needed more than an hour to see this one!

The woman visitor also commented on the lack of accountability for the captain as he received no jail time, only a fine and community service.

Adapted from the Valdez Museum (2021), Taylor (2014) and Tripadvisor (2012) websites (see https://ateec.org/exxon-valdez-oil-spill-google-earth-virtual-field-trip-activity/for a virtual tour of the spill).

Introduction

The Exxon/Valdez vignette sheds light on how major standing historical tensions can eventuate in environmental disasters. These historical events shape our world but also serve as proxies for underlying ideologies, thus allowing us to unpack the dialectical forces at work. CHAT helps us understand such events in terms of activity systems, contradictions, dialectical/reciprocal relationships, multiple voices and power relationships at the macro-, intermediate and microlevels. At the macrolevel, we are critically reflective of the Exxon/Valdez oil spill as one example of the long-existing historical tension between 'big oil' and human rights, in this case Native (Indigenous) peoples for water and land use.

Using CHAT at the intermediate level to analyze the museum exhibit design, we can describe the museum designer's attempts to achieve the particular object/outcome of how one disaster unfolded, using selected tools of the areas, maps of global spills and the tape recording of the captain as mediational means. In this chapter, I use this example to demonstrate some of the language and core concepts of the activity system, the unit of analysis of activity for CHAT. An activity system typically consists of Subjects(s), Mediational means (tools), Object (what the system is working toward), Rules, Community and Division of labor. We learned in Chapter 1 that CHAT has five main principles: Activity is the unit of analysis, time matters, contradictions arise, relationships are multivoiced and expansion may occur. I view activity systems to be the foundational unit of analysis in CHAT, as "systems of collaborative human practice [and]…the generator[s] of a constantly and continuously emerging context" (Foot & Groleau, 2011, p. 2; see also Engeström, 1987; Foot, 2014; Yamagata-Lynch, 2014).

Analyzing the commentary of the woman visitor, we can note, on the microlevel, how upset she was by the indifference of the captain and by his lenient sentence, just a fine and community service rather than jail. At the macro international level, this same visitor was pleased that the exhibit allowed visitors to relate this particular oil spill to other spills by using global maps "to help 'scale' the spill in various locations".

The museum curators and educators achieved several outcomes with this exhibit. The thoughtfulness expressed in the multifaceted exhibit suggests that dialogue was invited with the recognition that both the personal and the political are valid concerns and exist simultaneously in such cases. It is a museum's job to present these multiple facets of the conflict (mediational means), to help visitors (subjects) make meaning (object) for themselves. In this case, much of that seems to have been achieved. Yet the exhibit was not neutral, as museums are not neutral (Murakowski, 2017; Steward, 2018).

In this exhibit did the museum wish to inform visitors of the emerging or existent contradictions inherent in this larger activity system? Historically museums have had problematic funding ties with big oil; this fact makes it difficult for some museums to be 'impartial'. Events of the last decade have uncovered these connections. A large protest at the British Museum in 2020, against British Petroleum (BP) funding and ties to the board of trustees, broke open a long-standing tension between funding and personnel under the control of oil companies (Walawalkar, 2020). Using activity systems analysis in each case, we can uncover where "contradictions reveal the growing edges of the activity system" (Foot, 2001, p. 63) (see Table 2.1).

TABLE 2.1 CHAT word meanings, the Exxon/Valdez example

1. Cultural points to the premise that everything people do is shaped by and draws upon their cultural values and resources (sociocultural theory).
   In this context, our visitor brought one specific resource to the Valdez Museum—namely, her ethical concerns regarding responsibility.
2. The term historical is used together with culture to indicate that since cultures are grounded in histories, and evolve over time, analyses of what people do at any point in time must therefore be viewed in light of the historical trajectories in which their actions take place.
   The Exxon/Valdez spill presents a complex historical context, including Native American interests and oil interests, as well as the history of the visitors, which together color the entire exhibit, the text and pictures offered in signs.
3. The term activity refers to what people do together and is modified by both the cultural and historical to convey its 'situatedness'.
   The activity is by proxy making sense of the exhibit, and the spill itself, including the captain's insouciance and the global context of environmental damage.
4. Theory is used in this acronym to denote a conceptual framework for understanding and explaining human activity.
   In this case a theory to tie together all of the above aspects into a congruent whole.

Adapted from Foot (2014, p. 3)

Contradictions

The meaning of contradiction has sometimes been simplified to be 'competing priorities'. Engeström and Sannino (2010) suggested that "contradictions are often mentioned as a significant factor behind organizational change" but "tend to be watered down" (p. 368). They argued strongly against this:

> Contradiction is a foundational philosophical concept that should not be equated with paradox, tension, inconsistency, conflict, dilemma or double bind. Many of the terms misused as equivalents of contradiction may better be understood as manifestations of contradictions.
>
> (p. 369)

Kuutti (1996) explained, "Activity theory uses the term contradiction to indicate a misfit within elements [of an activity system], between them, between different activities, or between different developmental phases of a single activity" (p. 18).

People and institutions may try to alter the activity system in order to alleviate or attempt to resolve contradictions/historical tensions as they surface in disturbances, conflicts and various forms of problems that originate in contradictions. For example, particular individual board members affiliated with the oil industry can be asked to leave. Often, such temporary fixes only exacerbate the system further (Foot, 2002).

Engeström, Foot and others have reminded us that contradictions do not signal failure, nor are they 'problems to be fixed', or 'obstacles to be overridden' or are they amenable to 'quick fixes' (Foot, 2014). Contradictions are dialectical and reciprocal relationships that already exist and are continuously at work. They become noticeable because of increased tensions, and they should not be 'swept under the rug'. I situate them as opportunities for transformation and expansion. They are not simple problems, but instead "are historically accumulating structural tensions within and between activity systems" (Engeström, 2009, p. 57).

CHAT suggested that contradictions in messy systems like the Valdez are mutually constituted, or as Kaptelinin suggests, "Activities and their subjects mutually determine one another" (Kaptelinin, 2011, p. 31), making it unproductive to isolate any single entity in a system. In this chapter, I remind us to focus on the many intertwining relationships that create contradictions, rather than any individual event by itself. As in Chapter 1, and throughout this book, following Engeström, Foot and Groleau, Kaptelinin, Roth, Kuuti, and others, I use contradiction as a technical term that encompasses the following key features:

- Contradictions are historically occurring and accumulating structural tensions within and between activity systems (Engeström, 2009, p. 57);
- The primary contradiction between use value and exchange value informs all other contradictions…"the dual construction of everything and everyone as both having inherent worth and being a commodity within market–based socioeconomic relations" (Foot & Groleau, 2011, p. 6);
- Activity systems are also continually evolving; through the dialectical contradictions between the different levels and elements of the system.… Such dialectical relations again emphasize that elements pre-suppose each other and cannot be considered except in relation to others (Timmis, 2014, p. 13);
- Dialectically organized: (a) "both sides of these pairs are mutually contradictory, (b) they are 'mutually constitutive', and (c) their relationship guarantees development automatically" (Roth, 2002, p. 165)[4];
- Any solution intended to resolve such contradictions is temporary, for it gives rise to new contradictions (Kaptelinin, 2011, p. 30); and
- "contradiction…indicate[s] a misfit within elements [of an activity system], between them, between different activities, or between different developmental phases of a single activity" Kuuti (1996, p.18).

Kuuti focused on the misfit aspect of contradictions.[5] The Valdez exhibit represents an excellent example of a 'misfit within elements of an activity system', as it includes people (the woman visitor, captain, educators), mediational means (exhibits, dialogue), object(ive) (making meaning), expected roles (museum as storyteller), hierarchy/power relationship (museum as expert) and the larger community (Valdez community, museum community). The Exxon/Valdez disaster exhibit involved all these nodes at multiple levels of analysis, from exhibit design to global politics. I consider these 'misfits' or tensions to be cause for increased watchfulness at the micro, intermediate and macro levels. Museums must work with' and negotiate these concrete manifestations of real-world contradictions. The places where misfits show up allow us to uncover the underlying ideological forces at work. Another way of describing the *misfits* is as secondary contradictions. Secondary contradictions arise when two nodes of an activity system are in tension. They are useful markers of disruption. In this and following chapters, I note such nodes in tension as secondary constrictions for the reader.

At the macrolevel, the Exxon spill is tailor-made to invoke neoliberal politics, as it perfectly mirrors the contradiction between exchange and use value. Commoditization, consumerism, monetary gain, individualism and less concern for so-called *collateral* damage or what Whyte calls 'calculated indifference' (Whyte, 2019), often to nondominant populations, are traits that those critiquing neoliberalism cite as hallmarks of this ideology and its consequences (Harvey, 2005). If we adopt the neoliberal ideological stance, on the other hand, we might argue that such actions have trade-offs, thus it is worth the collateral environmental damage to the community to make sure oil arrives where it is needed. In short, we can afford to be indifferent. These basic tenets of neoliberal ideology are seldom said out loud.

At the intermediate level, CHAT requires that social actors, subjects, museum professionals, administrators (Blackler, 1993) work to change themselves and the institutions within which they work (Engeström & Sannino, 2011). This concept provides hope that people working in institutions can negotiate and share ideas with each other and, as people's consciousness and understanding evolve, so can the organization. CHAT theory suggests that each institution is a collective of rules, community and hierarchies, people and mediational means, as well as expected outcomes, a contextualization that fits well with multidepartmental, multilayered museum power.

The Exxon/Valdez is an example of how the primary contradiction of use vs. exchange value, drives all such systems (Bonneau, 2013; Engeström, 1987; Foot, 2014). Here the use value is the aesthetics and usefulness to the community, and exchange[6] value is the monetary value we attach to oil. This fundamental contradiction is ready-made for analysis by CHAT. The spill occurred on Prince Edward Sound, an area ideal for nature and human interaction and the center of a bucolic vacation area and home to the Valdez Native Tribe[7]; the spill had catastrophic effects for the VNT who fished these waters.

Multivoicedness[8]

CHAT's principle of multivoicedness is meant to include the voice of many, including *others*. The critique, for example, of the diminishing collective rights for Indigenous peoples is echoed in all settler-colonialism contexts (Bang & Marin, 2015), especially with regard to land, rights and other property conflicts. I return to Indigenous and Native land rights in more depth in Chapter 5. For now, though, I want to emphasize that we should leave nothing out when exploring activity systems; in fact, such complexity of human/natural resources interaction is to be expected and needs to be represented.

Time

Foot argues that this feature of activity theory "makes possible the analysis of a multitude of relations...both at a particular point in time, and evolving over time" (Foot, 2014, p. 3). Time[9] assumes and expects that systems are always emergent and in transition, thus we expect change, surprising or not. Design theorists already know this, especially in complex classroom or museum interventions (Ash, 2014; A. Brown, 1992). Taken together these lenses provide a foundation for examining shifting relationships (Martin et al., 2019). As Engeström and Sannino (2020) suggest, "[an] activity system is more than a mechanical sum of its components...an activity system weaves together its own dynamic context" (p. 46).

Because the activity is the unit of analysis, this systemic view frees researchers from isolating single factors and validates what we already know is true—in any classroom, museum or other workplace setting, there are always multiple competing, socially and historically informed pressures on any one individual, staff, funder, exhibit or board of directors.

Levels of Analysis

The Exxon/Valdez episode helps us to unpack levels of analysis (see Appendix 2.1) with causes and conditions that are local, nationwide and global. Environmental disasters can be positioned from the larger global perspective—e.g., oil vs. aesthetics—but they can also be presented at the human personal level. CHAT recognizes both levels of analysis as intersecting aspects of systems. This analytic complexity does not oversimplify systems or reduce them to the lowest common denominator.

The macrolevel allows us to examine the dynamic contradictions that include the historical tensions between Native rights and large corporations, as well as between environmental and aesthetic 'value' and valuing the maintenance of the energy supply at all costs. The macrolevel includes many disasters humans now experience.[10] The intermediate level includes all the ways the museum may have presented this catastrophe. The micro includes the personal dismay of the women visitor and lack of dismay of the captain.

Museums need not oversimplify these levels of analysis, expanding time, contradictions, multivoicedness and holistic units of analysis, but rather, following Foot, examine them for signs of "emergent opportunities for...development" (Foot, 2014, p. 16). The idea of emergent opportunities is important because we cannot assume that we know the particular outcome in advance of any activity involving individuals and groups (subjects), tools/mediational means (tools) and desired outcomes (object), the three critical nodes of Vygotsky's mediated action and first-generation activity theory (Figure 1.1).

CHAT keeps entire systems in mind, instead of limiting our analysis to the people of Valdez, the economy, leisure, museum visitors, the exhibit, value of oil or any single sociopolitical concern. CHAT can handle the messy, complex systems that the Exxon/Valdez spill or other natural or man-made disasters present, focusing on specific aspects of contradiction without losing sight of the whole. In the vignette, we saw glimpses of all these levels, first as the woman visitor was concerned at the microlevel that the captain didn't seem to care and at the macrolevel when she noted that this particular Exxon/Valdez example represents the global issues at work. She considered both levels simultaneously. I will argue not only that this is not unusual but also that our theoretical frame needs to seamlessly consider and simultaneously capture the personal, as well as the global. Real people are involved. Focusing on contradictions allows us to do just that.

The Exxon/Valdez incident presents several ideologically and dialectically intertwined contradictions, which are typical of other global incidents—namely, Native vs. white rights, tourist vs. local interest, ecosystem vs. energy needs and more. Ideology matters in how we *see* value, how we position people and money, objects and story and much more. Leonardo (2009a) has also argued for the mutuality of actions and beliefs, suggesting that ideology is both "determining of people and is determined by people…[and] both structures are structured by social practices" (Leonardo, 2009, p. 5). This describes the reciprocal relationship of mutually constituting mutable entities, i.e., these competing ideologies are the underpinning of all dialectically situated contradictions.

Even with just these two levels of activity operating, the global and the personal, we can appreciate the need for a rich theoretical framework to encompass the multiple layers of a framework that uses a *unit of analysis* expansive enough to be capable of exploring global, sociopolitical forces while small enough to understand human feelings in action. At all levels, the irreducible minimum is the activity system itself (Foot, 2014).

When we examine the intermediate level, the exhibit design here, we can assume it was intended to introduce visitors to this controversial spill, to present the facts and perhaps even include underlying historical tensions, as represented by pipelines and oil carriers. At first glance, this may appear simple, but CHAT reveals the complex and often competing underlying ideologies at work; the oil spill is ready-made for probing neoliberal values of advancing commoditization for the economic bottom line while ignoring collateral damage to fishing livelihoods for *others*. Ideology is at the core of these contradictions. We must remember that these same ideologies are never far from how museums function and represent themselves.

Basics of CHAT Theory

I want to clarify here the meaning of CHAT, a "cultural–historical theory of human activity…originally developed in the early 1900s by Lev Vygotsky and his student A.N. Leont'ev…[and now including]…the revised version of this framework proposed by Yrjö Engeström (1987)" (Foot & Groleau, 2011, p. 2). The acronym CHAT is informative. Taken one at a time, these four terms, cultural, historical activity theory are reasonable and intelligible, yet it can be challenging to apply them semantically into a single holistic concept.

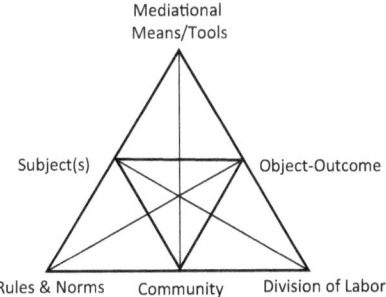

FIGURE 2.1 Second-generation activity theory (adapted from Engeström, 1999)

Breaking Down the Exxon/Valdez Using CHAT

Because activity systems are complex, it is helpful to present events such as the Exxon/Valdez spill by using diagrams. This allows us to see the interacting pieces without losing sight of the whole. As with any serious learning and teaching theory, there is disagreement in the field regarding how best to represent ideas via diagrams; still, researchers have found diagrams useful in clarifying complex phenomena, especially for systemic contradictions. We saw the generic version of first-generation activity system (Figure 1.1) in Chapter 1. Next, I show one possible representation of the Exxon/Valdez activity system in Figure 2.1, using second-generation activity theory.

Figure 2.1 places the woman visitor as subject, using the words, signs, tape and pictures in the exhibit as mediational means to achieve an object(ive)—that is, to make sense of the event using the exhibit. This triad of nodes can apply to any activity. We can assume that people, object(ive)s and mediational means (tools) are always changing, depending on the activity, and that we do not necessarily know the outcome in advance (Foot, 2014). To clarify, mediational means[11] are the interface between individual and social. I emphasize this because activity theory places the individual subject(s) within an organized social system, where movement between the outer and inner world can and does occur in the zone of proximal development (ZPD) using tools/artifacts/mediational means.[12] This point is essential to remember; it is crucial to recognize this tool as a mechanism for studying reciprocal movement between the individual and social in the ZPD, which has been defined by Vygotsky as "the region of activity that learners can navigate with aid from a supporting context, including but not limited to people" (Vygotsky, 1978, in Brown et al., 1993).

The subject(s), and the cultural, historical conceptions they each bring with them may seem a relatively straightforward conception of a person or persons doing the action. Object/outcome, and tool or mediational means may require clarification. Activity theory always centers on object-driven activity—that is, 'what the system is working toward' (Foot, 2014). There is always some motivation, focus of attention or desire behind action. Also, actions require tools or mediational means.

In our Exxon/Valdez example, the woman visitor was trying to make sense of the oil spill, and the museum exhibit was acting as one mediational means for her to do so.

A further clarification of the object[13] of activity is that it encompasses both "the thing that is transformed through their participation" and, following Foot, the motivation, even if "we don't understand what people are doing, we understand why they are doing it" (Foot, 2014, in Ward, 2016, p. 60). The object(ive) of the activity is always *what the system is working toward*. In the object category, we then include both the object (desired outcomes, goal) and the motivation behind it. The woman visitor, for example, uses the exhibit to grapple with both the captain's indifference and the global harm done.

Mediational means/tools always carry their own historical-cultural reminders from their own development, which includes their history. In the Exxon/Valdez exhibit, the tools, or mediational means, include diagrams, maps, the audiotape of the captain and similar resources. The audio of the captain reveals some of his 'history.' In short, all players and mediational means leave historical/cultural remainders and reminders.

Moreover, tools/mediational means are both a result of, as well as a transmission of social, cultural, historical knowledge, even as they are also changed by use. Another visitor (subject), might have had a different object(ive) in mind and, perhaps have used the same mediational means to achieve different ends. A recently designed object (outcome) such as a group-designed laboratory experiment, for example, can subsequently be made into a mediational means and then be used for a different experiment. The new lab exercise would then help mediate students to understand a new object of activity. Similarly, visitors can learn information/practices at one exhibit and then transfer them to another or within the same activity.

There are always communities outside the museum that share an "interest in and an involvement with the same object(ive)". In our example, the Native American population (VNT) has a fishing-based economy that "depends on the Sound for their livelihoods and subsistence food needs…[but] there is little discussion…of the effects of environmental disasters and toxins on Native American communities and their responses to those problems" (Lynch, 2014, para. 4–5). The Valdez Native population relies on clean waters and has serious concerns with both the spill and the way it has been interpreted, cleaned up and paid for, and the effects have lasted decades (WBUR, 2014). As Chief Walter Meganack from Port Graham said in 1989,

> The excitement of the season had just begun, and then, we heard the news, oil in the water, lots of oil killing lots of water. It is too shocking to understand. Never in the millennium of our tradition have we thought it possible for the water to die, but it's true.
>
> (Gill & Picou, 1997, p. 167)

These comments make the spill real, giving voice to those affected, tracing feelings from years later, but remembered. We are also invited into an alternative narrative of water, when the Chief said, "lots of oil killing lots of water". Our Western epistemology does not consider water alive.

This contrast underscores the differences in worldview.

Alternatively, a family or a school field trip might eventuate in a debate regarding environmental responsibilities despite the need for obtaining sufficient oil. These are some potential scenarios of objects and mediational means we can envision using in an object-oriented activity systems approach. The main point here is that all aspects of the activity are included, the people, the mediational means and the potential outcomes. Moreover, any activity involving visitors and exhibits will include other components, such as prior knowledge, exhibit content, the presence or absence of a docent or interpreter, multivoicedness, historicity and contradictions.

To allow analytic space for these further components, second-generation activity theory (Engeström, 1987; Leont'ev, 1978) has incorporated *rules, community of significant others* and *division of labor* as further essential features of activity system analysis. This ensures the inclusion of the larger context within which any activity occurs, and without which an analysis would be incomplete. These three aspects (*rules, community, division of labor*) are apparent within any museum workplace structure and need to be included in the analysis of 'business as usual' or 'how we do things around here'.

We consider these three additional aspects in Figure 2.1, each in turn. Most museums have explicit and implicit *rules* to regulate staff and administration interacting with visitors and with each other. Rules for visitor behavior may be posted at the entrance. For museum educators, rules may be conveyed at hiring, during informal interactions, during professional development sessions and/or formal documents. If a specific sub-group such as educators is situated as a community of practice, we assume common practices, language and content would be promoted and appropriated by staff across different levels of experience. Additionally, many workers may be given a dress code, ways to address the public, hours to work, what work to do and what not to do. The institutional ethos that such rules and roles embody is thus reified by most museum activities.

The community, as we have already noted, may include a larger group of those in policy making, that is, vice presidents, educators, board members, parents and others. These communities may be tightly bound or not. The Valdez Museum staff community at that time was small, an executive director, curator, education specialist and a few others. A full-time curator and a part-time museum educator were hired in 1998. Larger museums have more detailed divisions of labor, often represented in organization charts. Most museum websites display these.

The hierarchies or divisions of labor in Figure 2.1 are typical of any business; such hierarchies are organized both vertically and horizontally. Horizontally, division of labor refers to collaboration between workers at the same level, such as peer counseling and other lateral efforts. For example, educators might share ideas and strategies laterally. Vertically, bosses at various levels provide structures, schedules, and other aspects of the hierarchy, which may be either rigidly or flexibly interpreted in the workplace. Power is embedded in any hierarchical structure and is seen at all levels of analysis, in any organization. I discuss in each chapter how secondary contradictions arise from tension between any of these nodes, flagging them as areas for ongoing negotiation.

It may be difficult, however, to pinpoint power relationships using organization charts.[14] I address issues of power later in this chapter, as well as at the end of each remaining chapter. Many specialized communities such as educators or curators are subsets of the larger museum community. They thereby offer an entry point for an analysis of existing or potential power struggles within and across institutions (Gurian, 2020). We often use third-generation activity theory for this type of analysis (Engeström, 1999; Engeström, 1987).

Third-Generation Activity Theory[15]

Blackler and McDonald (2000) claimed that CHAT is a weak tool for power analysis (Daniels & Warmington, 2007). Engeström argued that: "It is indeed not easy to depict and analyze hierarchical power relations within a single activity system" (Engeström, 1999, 2012, p. 8). He proposed combining two or more activity systems to more directly address competing object-oriented activities, using differing interpretations of the object(ive) and the power differential such negotiation can generate. Vossoughi and Gutiérrez (2014) further suggested that

> a phenomenon should be examined across a minimum of two activity systems (Engeström, 2005)…[a] methodological imperative of understanding learning as "movement" within and across activity systems—a sensibility central to equity-oriented and humanist research.
>
> (p. 604)

In other words, viewing different activity systems as they interact is valuable for equity-oriented, humanist research—that is, a potential tool for analyzing power dynamics involving different levels. Imagine, for example, the vice president of research has asked the curatorial and educator departments to collaborate on exhibit and curriculum[16] development on a controversial topic, such as the Exxon/Valdez, and then to devise teaching strategies to interpret these ideas.[17] The VP asks both departments to be sensitive to the environmental issues that impact the Native population. Suppose the VP asks the curators and educators to fully collaborate with the local Native tribe in their design, which group might suggest incorporating core spiritual (for example, the horror of allowing 'the water to die') or alternative ideological commitments such as the collective ownership of land and water, respect for all living things and how the water is used for livelihood (Gill & Picou, 1997).

Such a situation as this can be analyzed by third-generation CHAT, which is specifically designed to explore what happens when two or more activity systems interact and negotiate a shared object, such as exhibit design or curriculum.

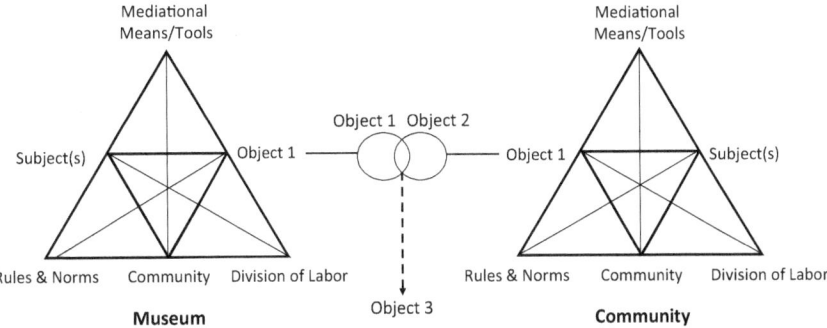

FIGURE 2.2 Two interacting activity systems as a minimal model for the third generation of activity theory (adapted from Engeström, 1999)

During this process, power can become more apparent and observable (see Figure 2.2), when two systems (with objects 1 and 2) work to negotiate a 'shared object' (Object 3). Each community contains all the nodes (subject, rules, and so on) described earlier.

The "*community of significant others*" in Figure 2.2 contains 'museum educator and curator community object',[18] (Object 1), and 'Native tribe' object (Object 2), working toward a 'common object' (Object 3), the 'design and curriculum' for a particular exhibit. This is but one scenario for using third-generation activity theory. We can imagine others.

Within the existing Exxon/Valdez oil spill exhibit, the choice of object was determined by designers, in this case perhaps curators and educators who may had negotiated internally regarding the object. They seem to have settled on offering plentiful data, perhaps intended to allow visitors to make sense for themselves, without being told which point of view to adopt. In such a case, educators, if present, would likely ask leading questions of visitors, encouraging them to think for themselves about the different aspects of the issues without forcing a particular perspective. The relevant and differing perspectives would already have been built into the exhibit by its designers.

In yet another alternative scenario, the oil industry might fund an exhibit with the underlying prime directive of convincing visitors of the importance of providing enough oil to a hungry country. In this case, the exhibit might strongly reflect neoliberal policies of trade-offs, 'calculated indifference' (Whyte, 2019) and minimization of collateral damage. In yet another scenario, the museum might be firmly rooted in environmentalism. In this case, the exhibit would promote the view that the commercial at the expense of the environment and people are not to be tolerated. In each case we can imagine a negotiation of a newly created and shared Object 3.

In our real world, differing perspectives exist in a dialectical relationship typically informed by ideological beliefs, with different intended outcomes (pro/anti-oil, pro/anti-environment, pro/anti-Native American systems and values). In exploring these hypothetical scenarios, take note of the opportunities for conflict to arise at multiple workplace levels. As we noted, one way to study the contradictions that do arise is to follow the "discursive manifestations" (Engeström & Sannino, 2011) that are triggered in such negotiations. Discursive manifestations serve the function of reifying the exhibit/museum message, sometimes as "resistance, disagreement, argument and criticism". Such 'resistance' can come from educators, visitors, staff or the public press. In the Exxon/Valdez exhibit, the visitor criticized the captain; perhaps that was the exhibit designers' intent, as well.

Each activity system, be it the educator, the politicians or the Native American, would come into any set of interacting systems with its own goals, language, mediational means and motivations. The newly negotiated Object 3 then becomes the site around which two or more communities interact and perhaps conflict, which shows up in 'misfits'/tensions between hierarchy, rules, mediational means or other nodes.

Such interactions between two or more activity systems are relatively common occurrences (Ash, 2014; deGregoria Kelly, 2009; C. Lee, 2007; Seig & Bubp, 2008). Reality is this complex. The expectation *is* that activity systems interact and generate *new* objects and outcomes.

Contradictions Expanded

Contradictions exist whether we pay attention to them or not, and they will likely eventuate in more contradictions. Engeström and Sannino (2011) noted, "Our own concept of contradiction stems from Marxist dialectics":

> First, contradiction is a foundational philosophical concept that should not be equated with paradox, tension, inconsistency, conflict, dilemma or double bind. Second, contradictions are historical and must be traced in their real historical development. The primary contradiction of capitalism resides in every commodity, between its use value and (exchange) value.
>
> (pp. 370–371)

I have tried not to conflate terms like tension, inconsistency, conflict, dilemma or double bind, but it is challenging

A typical contradiction most museums face is identifying how they wish to educate or teach the public; for example, shall they 'teach as telling' or rather 'scaffold' learning after first listening to the visitors,[19] admittedly an overly simplistic dyad. These two views are reflections of competing ideological stances regarding the nature of learning and teaching; are learners to be trusted to make sense for themselves, or do they need to be 'shown'? Lisa Roberts in her work on narrative alluded to this basic contradiction in her seminal book in 1997.

This essential tension shows up in many places, especially in how educators are trained to help the public understand exhibits (Anderson et al., 2015; Martin et al.,

2019; Patrick, 2017). Imagine for the moment that 'our' museum leans toward the didactic end of the teaching spectrum. Perhaps educators are asked to use a scripted text for teaching and are not allowed to stray. In this case, neither educator nor visitor is allowed to be agentive when processing information. This may make it difficult for educators who wish to listen to and converse with visitors before telling them information.

This is reminiscent of the doctor's dilemma: Do I treat the patient more fully, or do I save time and money? In each case, the visitor or the patient is treated either as a cog in a wheel or as an individual to be listened to and responded to. Both refer back to the primary contradiction where some museums or health care systems decide to control employees in order to maximize the bottom line. Engeström's (1987) classic example of contradictions is taken from the medical system, where for example, the object of a typical U.S. health clinic's activity system is inextricably dual and a contradiction between fostering health and producing revenue. This dual nature is intrinsic to primary contradictions in all activity systems. Even though museums are nonprofits, they track the bottom line, and it may determine their very existence.

Efficient 'handling' of visitors is a neoliberal value, which can lead to profitability, especially when the museum staff feel responsible for funding as Dailey (2006) suggests. When we put efficiency in medicine to the test, we create the following question: "Should the doctor spend only ten minutes per patient, prescribing only cost-effective solutions, or should she spend as much time as necessary with each patient and prescribe whatever is necessary?"

The comparison of museum staff and doctors in the United States is not an ideal match, yet it provides insights into the monetization of all things, including health, learning and leisure. We note that all contradictions and their manifestations rest on the primary contradiction from which, according to Engeström and others, all the other contradictions arise (Engeström, 1987; Foot, 2014; Foot & Groleau, 2011).

Primary Contradictions

As already noted, the primary contradiction reflects the "opposition between use value and exchange value", where use value reflects the "direct benefits of an activity's outcomes for the activity's participants, [and] exchange value denotes the worth of something when it is exchanged for something else" (Foot, p. 20). Primary contradictions play out as secondary, tertiary and quaternary contradictions, just as Kuutti (1996) has suggested, between phases, activities and element/nodes.

It is relatively easy in our example for this chapter to identify a contradiction between public use and financial gain, essentially use vs. exchange value.[20] Where do our loyalties lie? We note that the international need for oil and the need to protect the environment from oil spills creates a global contradiction, operating in a dialectical relationship.

Foot (following Engeström) notes that primary contradictions serve to keep the activity system in a constant state of tension (Foot, 2014), which tension helps to generate secondary, tertiary and quaternary contradictions). See Table 2.2 for a definition and the associated epistemic action appropriate to each type of contradiction (Foot & Groleau, 2011). As Ward (2016) noted,

> [B]y identifying the levels of the contradictions and not treating the contradictions as all the same, we can begin to understand how aggravating one level leads to another aggravated level while uncovering some of the interconnectedness of the system in question. To do this kind of work requires two different focuses: one that takes into account the historicity of a system, and another that allows the system a chance to imagine what it can become.
>
> (Ward, 2016, p. 61)

Dailey has already verified the pervasive quality of 'the bottom line' in everyday museum life, permeating staff at all levels, saying, "It became clear that my informants were acutely aware of their museum's economic position" (Dailey, 2006, p. 10). One secondary contradiction then (Ash, 2014; Yamagata-Lynch, 2014; Ward, 2016), which grows out of the primary one, concerns how museum staff must sometimes choose between serving visitors well vs. remaining mindful of overall financial constraints of the museum system (Kundu & Kalin, 2015). Is the educator meant to spend as much time as possible with every visitor, especially minoritized and/or those new to museums, or is the educator supposed to make sure she helps treats everyone the same, which is not equitable (see Chapter 8)? In the neoliberal version of the museum (Dailey, 2006; Kundu & Kalin, 2015), cutting costs (as measured by time) has become the answer.[21] Neoliberal policies tilt toward efficiency and commodification, and ignore collateral damage. Museum staff are caught in these contradictions that affect livelihood, well-being and agency.

Such routine but difficult decisions are made at every level of any system. Museum educators are torn between seeing visitors as clients (monetary value) or

TABLE 2.2 Types of contradictions and corresponding epistemic actions

Type of contradiction	Characteristics	Corresponding epistemic action(s)
Primary	Occurs between the use value and exchange value of any corner of an activity system.	Questioning
Secondary	Develops between two corners of an activity system.	Analyzing Modeling
Tertiary	Arises when the object of a more developed activity is introduced into the central activity system.	Examining model Implementing model Evaluating process
Quaternary	Occurs between central activity and neighboring activities.	Consolidating new practice Questioning

(Adapted from Foot & Groleau, 2011)

as collaborators (use value) Feinstein & Meshoulam, 2014). Incipient contradictions occur within every museum system, any time and at any level of interaction, encompassing conflict in designing exhibits, teaching the public or setting up organizational charts.[22] Some may concern budget wars, hiring practices, establishing appropriate rules for worker conduct, keeping pace with new demographics, recruiting volunteers and many other critical aspects of everyday business. I examine those that do rise to the level of secondary contradiction in each chapter. Each of these issues includes multiple, and, typically, varying perspectives, which are often accompanied by further unresolved contradictions.

Secondary, Tertiary, Quaternary Contradictions

Secondary contradictions occur when two nodes are in conflict with one another. This type of contradiction prompts the latent primary contradiction in the activity system to surface and take the form of a specific and visible problem as tension builds between different nodes. According to Foot and Groleau,

> The secondary, tertiary and quaternary contradictions form a sequence that explains the process of cyclical development characterized in CHAT. Secondary contradictions take place when two nodes of the activity system conflict with one another.
>
> (p. 3)

Secondary contradictions often take the form of a specific problem as tension builds between different nodes of an activity system (Table 2.3), for example between rules and tools.

> Tertiary contradictions within an activity system arise when the object of a more "culturally advanced" activity (Engeström, 1987) is introduced into that system…typically to find relief from one or more secondary contradictions

TABLE 2.3 Secondary contradictions in the Valdez spill

Activity systems	Secondary contradiction	Nodes	Possibly more "culturally advanced" forms
Personal/micro	Lack of concern/ danger to others/ lack of punishment	Subject/rules or tools	Investigate ethical dilemmas more generally (see Chapter 7)
Exhibit design/ intermediate	Oil vs. environment vs. neutral Didactic vs. open-ended	Object/tools	Borrow another exhibit design (see Chapter 6)
Global/macro	Local vs. larger effects of oils spills	Community/ rules	Import information from other examples (see Chapter 4)

54 Why Do We Need Theories?

> and the tensions stemming from them…quaternary contradictions arise between the central activity and its neighboring activity systems when a new form of practice is employed based on a reformed and/or expanded object.
>
> (Foot & Groleau, 2011, p. 5)

In the case of the Exxon/Valdez disaster, the primary contradiction between use vs. exchange value promotes tension between nodes of an activity system creating several secondary contradictions for example, the tension between the exhibit content and the woman visitor's discomfort and inability to reconcile the captain's seeming disregard, his negligent behavior with the degree of danger the disaster posed for others. We might position the tension in this case between subject and rules (proper seafaring conduct) as the affected nodes or perhaps between subject and mediational means depending on how we interpret the interaction. This tension was personally motivated.

We also do not know what charge the exhibit designers were given for the exhibit. Were they advised, for example, to minizine or emphasize the detrimental effects on the VNT community? In this case, community and division of labor might be in tension. We might include the aspect of hierarchy between the captain and any rules he was subject to, which in this case is the tension between the division of labor and rules. Another secondary contradiction might have included the exhibit designers being charged with telling a neutral story. We need to know much more information about this episode to parse this any further. These are but a few obvious examples of possible secondary contradictions arising from competing needs, alternative ideologies/epistemologies and/or personal views. Secondary contradictions arise at different levels of analysis, personal (visitor), departmental level of the museum hierarchy (how to design the exhibit) and the global (global impact of oil spills). To be clear, the secondary contradictions noted here occur in different but related activity systems (Table 2.3).

In each of these next six chapters, I explore how the primary contradiction between exchange and use value manifests in the form of secondary, tertiary and quaternary contradictions at multiple levels and across various nodes of other systems (Bonneau, 2013). I delve into how the secondary contradictions that emerge concern finance, demographics, the use of objects, the stories museums tell and how we view learning and teaching in activity systems.

Expansive Learning in CHAT

In expansive learning, learners learn something that is not yet there; they learn something that is emerging.[23] Further, the emergent is driven by contradictions. Through the various stages of analysis: the questioning, analysis, modeling, applying and reflection, outcomes are not predictable, and the dynamic cycle can and will repeat. Various levels of the work hierarchy within museums can have competing and alternative objectives. For example, exhibit designers may have different objectives than the educators, or the community outreach director may lobby for free admittance one day a month to increase museum attendance with diverse audiences, thereby forgoing some revenue. When we study institutional systems as they attempt to change, and as they deal with large and small contradictions, we find they generally go through the same processes researchers do, such as questioning, analyzing, and developing and testing new models before change can be institutionalized. This is called the cycle of expansive learning in activity systems. Figure 2.3 represents the stages of the *expansive learning cycle*.[24]

This cycle walks us through the expected stages of change as activity systems encounter contradictions, new goals, mediational means, practices, epistemological views, etc. Using both Figures 2.2 and 2.3, we note that contradictions in any activity system may be aggravated when participants question the established norm (stage 1), especially if new practices radically deviate from previous activity. By aggravated we mean one of the ways in which tensions occur; for example, different modalities for teaching or designing an exhibit, how much money to charge, which story to tell and so on. The expansive cycle works with these aggravated areas. Figure 2.3 reflects Engeström's view of how contradictions may 'drive' an activity system (see also Ash, 2014).

There are several examples of expansive learning for transformation in the field of museology (Ash, 2014; Ash & deGregoria Kelly, 2013; Ward, 2016) known. A typical sequence of actions is as follows (Table 2.4).

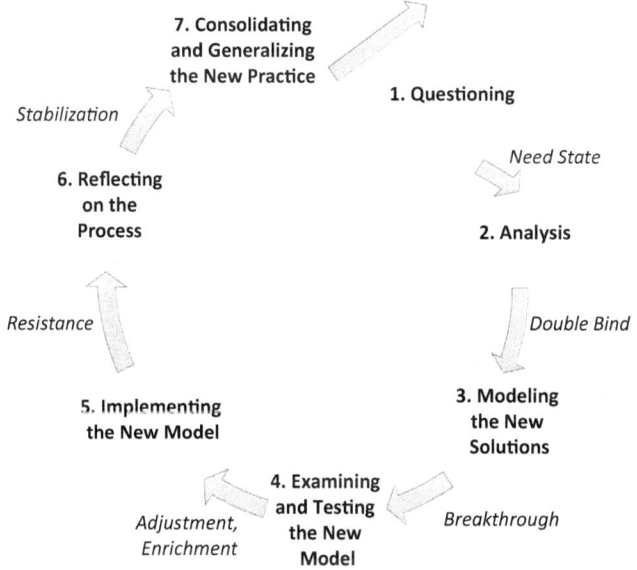

FIGURE 2.3 The cycle of expansive transformation (Adapted from Engeström, 1987, p. 189; Miettinen, 2009, p. 163)

TABLE 2.4 The stages of expansive cycle

1. *Questioning, criticizing* or *rejecting* aspects of the current accepted practice and wisdom;
2. *Analyzing* the situation through mental, discursive or practical transformation in order to understand what is happening;
3. *Modeling* the discovered relationship through some publicly observable and transmittable medium;
4. *Examining* and *experimenting* on the model to understand its dynamics, potentials and limitations;
5. *Implementing* the model in practice, enrichments, and conceptual extensions;
6. *Reflecting* and *evaluating* on the process; and
7. *Consolidating* the outcomes into a new and stable form of practice.

(Adapted from Engeström, 2014)

Moving through these five stages or even just some of the stages depends at least partially on the structural constraints within the system. It is important to remember that there is no predetermined single path in activity systems because, by definition, they include multiple voices, cultural and historical backgrounds and contexts. Thus,

> it is only natural that different understandings and goals will emerge during an expansive cycle and may contradict one another.
> (Engeström, 1991, in Ward, 2016, p. 59)

Designing Exhibits: 'Working the Dialectic'

What I have called 'working the dialectic' relies on uncovering tensions between activity systems or parts of them. Consistent with other sociocultural perspectives, CHAT allows one to see the world differently from most other learning/teaching theories, because it specifically invites us to see the dialectical contradictions within systems, and to "grasp the systemic whole of an activity, not just its separate components" (Foot, 2014, p. 3). Dialectical logic is different from traditional logic which "considers contradictions as indicators of problems that need to be addressed… eliminated"; there is no development in traditional logic (Kaptelinin, 2011. p. 32). Dialectical logic and developmental processes are dynamic; change is "temporary, for it gives rise to new contradictions" (p. 32); [and]…activity systems are constantly developing…[where] development is understood in a dialectical sense as a process driven by contradictions" (Kaptelinin, 2011, p. 34). Perhaps this helps us recognize that contradictions are useful analytical tools to study change. Outcomes are not predictable, and change is constant.

Imagine that the oil spill was not recognized as an ongoing serious dynamic problem. The contradictions of oil supply vs. any perspective centered on environmental/human rights would not be recognized, just as other environmental disasters, such as glacial melting, have been minimized. Then, there would be no development beyond the status quo.

Recognizing the importance of seeing contradictions, we can wonder how a museum might choose to represent them. Different personnel (e.g., educators, curators, administration) or competing notions of harm vs. good for the environment or for profit will pull the design process in different directions. Each view is embedded in an ideological perspective while also focusing on practical or more esoteric goals, such as public relations, legacy endowments, working with limited resources and being situated within historically-fraught sociopolitical contexts. The set of beliefs that a museum adopts for an exhibit informs, by default, all subsequent activity at other levels, such as teaching, advertising and so on (Coffee, 2008; Dubin, 1999). Do the developers deliberately engage with the dialectic in their process of design? If they do, what would the exhibit look like? Would they, could they, engage with dialectical logic? [25]

Timmis (2014) has argued that even though CHAT is used for research in educational contexts "it is often employed only descriptively or as a set of guiding principles; the dialectical method, which focuses on emergent contradictions and tensions, is not always fully explored" (p. 8). In short, dialectics can be abandoned even when CHAT is used. Langemeyer and Roth (2006) have similarly warned that we must pay serious attention to dialectics to avoid falling into reductionist or functionalist thinking…[noting that] CHAT's non-reductionist approach to human development…is due to its affinity to dialectic"[26] (p. 21). We must constantly argue for complexity and against simplicity.

Using CHAT and dialectic logic for exhibit design, then, would emphasize contradictions as dynamic forces for transformation. Exhibit teams can deliberately seek out potent contradictions, expose their ideological underpinnings and position them in dialectical relationships with one another, and within the museum structure overall (Ash & deGregoria Kelly, 2013; Ward, 2016; Yamagata-Lynch, 2010, 2014).

Like the Valdez Museum, every museum decides which overall ideology(ies) to adopt, for example, the overriding necessity for oil, or protecting the environment or neither or both. The carefully worded script in the vignette, perhaps, suggests seeking the dialectic.

Transformative Agency at Work

Change scholars such Gutiérrez and Barton, Dubin, Engeström, Gurian, Sannino, and Ward, among others, collectively argue that changing work organizations can be transformative but also highly problematic. To disrupt traditional power structures, we must examine the often-implicit messaging of 'business as usual', relative to museum professionals' work, and then reposition these within both contradictory and dialectical frames. The SAD calls attention to" how human activity is embedded in structured historicity. Individual and collective action is enabled and constrained by the social structures-in-motion, both in the moment and over time" (Gutiérrez & Calabrese Barton, 2015, p. 575).

In line with CHAT thinking, we position 'museum staff work' in terms of working with both structural and agentic forces, not necessarily set in opposition to each other but rather in a dialectical relationship when negotiating power relationships at all levels. Taken together, they allow us to address power, agency and contradictions.

Discussing 'business as usual,' Suchman argued that "how people work is one of the best kept secrets in America" (Suchman, 1995, pp. 3–4). By this she implied that the subtleties of work (both exhibit creation/curation and museum teaching are work) are often invisible or taken for granted. Examining work in almost any context is a tricky business, as "too often assumptions are made as to how tasks are performed" (Suchman, 1995, p. 56). Suchman wrote this in 1995; the fact that this still seems to hold true is remarkable, as work has been studied for decades.

With a focus on museum educator agency, as an example, what can we say about museums as workplaces for those who teach and have "the ability to shape not only how we work but how our work appears to others" (Suchman, 1995, p. 5). We already know that museums are typically organized hierarchically, yet often expect collaborative, team-based, peer-to-peer work among staff, sometimes organized as communities of practice. Obviously, these dual (vertical and horizontal) arrangements are often at odds with each other. In practical terms, the work of museum educators can best be analyzed using both the theoretical frames of activity theory and the SAD.

Implementing sustainable transformations requires staff to have a substantive role in such change (Ash, in preparation; Gurian, 2020; Karim-Jaffer, 2013), and requires valuing museum employees as "important resources, which should not be wasted" (Haapasaari et al., 2014, p. 233). However, increasing individual agency in the face of structural constraints can be fraught (Varelas et al., 2015). Here we refer to agency in the sense that individuals or groups of individuals have the wherewithal to affect personal and structural transformation within institutional hierarchies.

CHAT's notion of *transformative agency* fits for studying transformation by tracking encounters within the system and for examining disturbances, conflicts and contradictions in the activity system as well (Haapasaari et al., 2014). Transformative agency challenges "individual oriented theories of agency" (Engeström, 2006) because it "develops the participants' joint activity by explicating and envisioning new possibilities" for collective activity (Haapasaari et al., 2014, in Ward, 2016, p. 67). Note the phrase *joint activity*—that is, collective activity—which is explicitly not part of any neoliberal agenda. Transformative agency in the CHAT view promotes collective power. Regarding collective power, Gutiérrez and Calabrese Barton (2015) argued that the SAD provides a window into the issue of equity, such as "the challenge of preparing white middle class people to teach effectively and justly in classrooms, schools, and communities different from their own" (p. 575).

The same applies for museum educators, most of whom are also white and middle class but are expected to help museums move toward visibly equitable practices. However, if the administration requires neutrality on controversial subjects, or educators and curators are limited in how they 'interpret' exhibits or, more simply, are restricted to implementing even a partially scripted curriculum, then individual and collective educator agency is diminished. SAD is designed to examine these reciprocal relationships between individual and administrative power.

Yet, this too has been critiqued as overly individualist and accepting the 'status quo' Stetsenko (2019) has suggested that transformative agency is needed

> in order to expose and overcome ideologies of passive adaptation to, and acquiescence with, the existing order of things and the world as is". Stetsenko argued further that "overcoming the notions of passivity…[is an] indispensable ingredient for combating inequality, racism and quietism in our schools.
>
> (p. 1)

We extend this to museums. Transformative agency occurs when participants are able to actually take action to change the activity, its outcomes and mediational means (Haapasaari et al., 2014).

Such transformative agency requires a good deal of effort as well as more research.[27] Often the full contours of the structure of the system are not fully realized until participants push against its boundaries so that hidden pockets of resistance become visible (see Chapter 8). One gentle form of resistance is using evidence from other experiments in the field, saying, for example, that another museum tried this strategy/exhibit/director, and it worked for them. This adds power to resistance because staff/boards/press can refer to positive experiences as motivation to change (also known as tertiary contradictions). Another form of resistance is the act of envisioning new patterns or models of the activity, which include using imagination to explore what the system could be. Such concrete actions of resistance actually can change the overall activity (Haapasaari et al., 2014). Stensenko (2019) rightfully contests individualistic notions of agency; she argues "work remains to be done in order to conceptualize agency more…deeply dialectical—and importantly, critical-dialectical, or radical-transformative, that is, politically and ideologically non-neutral—premises…[accepting] the existing order of things and the world as it 'is'".

Neoliberalism, Education and Museums

The monetization/consumerism/commodification or exchange value view has been ascendant since the 1970s in the past century but has its roots much earlier.[28] Apple argued in 2017 that neoliberalism is

> one of the roots of power inequality in the education system…[which]… supplants collectivism with individual choice and a marketized educational system, where social, cultural and financial norms emphasize consumerism and competition.
>
> (p. 149)

Robertson (2007) argued similarly that neoliberalism demands:

(i) redistribution of wealth upward to the ruling elites through new structures of governance;

(ii) transformation of education systems so that the production of workers for the economy is the primary mandate; and
(iii) [the] breaking down of education as a public sector monopoly, opening it up to strategic investment by for-profit firms.

(p. 8)

Here we consider how neoliberal policies and practices have exacerbated preexisting problems and weakened most educational systems, including museums. Some have argued that educational systems have been transformed radically "in the last 10 years to reflect a corporate model of market competition…at the intersection of economy, power, and access, both locally and globally" (Rahm & Brandt, 2016, pp. 183–184).

Among other characteristics, the neoliberal model of 'knowledge economy' (McDermott, 2015) and commodification makes it essential to constantly evaluate the performance of students, faculty, schools, districts and states through quantitative assessments designed to sort and place people, often based on biased tests.[29] For example, it is well documented that there are "hidden injuries of the neoliberal university" that advances the notion of individual agency, often in name only, or, as Gill and Donaghue (2016)[30] argued, faculty members become 'reluctant individualists' because of unreal and unreasonable expectations (p. 93).[31] These authors argue that faculty, workers and, of course, students in colleges and universities suffer from an emphasis on competition and commodification while the system claims increased individualism. Yet, this individualism is still strongly restricted by structural constraints (Gill, 2017, Gill & Donaghue, 2016; Gjorgjioska & Tomicic, 2019).

Similarly, in critiquing the neoliberal educational system, McDermott (2015) linked neoliberalism ideologies in education with overvaluing "isolated cognitive skills, stockpiling knowledge' and competition…correlating [lack of isolated skills] with diminished power for those considered inferior in race or class" (McDermott, 2015, para 12). The latter correlation with so-called inferior race or class is mentioned in other such critiques (Apple, 2017; Au & Ferrare, 2015). This argument would suggest that those unable to take part in 'stockpiling knowledge', as it is currently taught, will not be able/allowed to compete and thus lose any competition— in short, more collateral damage or 'calculated indifference' (Whyte, 2019). We who are uniformed can remain indifferent. Moreover, the notion of isolated cognitive skills and stockpiling knowledge typically reflect the individualistic (often behaviorist/cognitivist) views of learning we mentioned earlier.

Neoliberalism is similarly active in museums,[32] promoting increased emphasis on individualism, competition and commodification. As Coffee (2007) noted,

> While many museum specialists recognize visitation as a social activity…[t]his recognition of a social museum experience is often overlaid onto a perception of communication or learning as the independent effort of individuals… [much as] mainstream learning theory and pedagogy, especially in the United States, remain centered on concepts of individual "intelligence".
>
> (pp. 377–378)[33]

Coffee argued that while museums may pay lip service to social learning, they still prize individual learning. I explore this further in Chapter 7. Research and views on learning have shifted since this 2007 article, but the point is still well taken in the 2020s. It is possible to pay lip service to social learning even as different ideologies aim exhibits, educators and public relations squarely toward the individual.

Power and the Theories That Inform the Analysis of Power

I briefly discuss the theories we have already introduced in an abbreviated power analysis, which we introduced at the end of Chapter 1. In the chapters to come, I will consider how we might 'trace' power in action using discursive manifestations with real-world examples.

CHAT provides a flexibility and predisposition for the dialectics of power (Dubin, 2014; Roth et al., 2012). By this I mean that power is involved in the inner workings of any activity system, where rules, hierarchies and competing ideologies are invoked and result in dynamic and unpredictable outcomes.

CHAT has been critiqued for not providing a more nuanced analysis of power (Spurgin, 2021). That is one reason we use four theoretical lenses. Power is recognizable in the SAD, which also has been critiqued. Our critiques of neoliberal and *deficit/ othering* ideologies (Apple, 2017; Au & Ferrare, 2015; P. Moore, 2014; Powell and Menendian, 2017) center on power inequalities. All of these authors refer to the lack of power of those on the 'wrong' side of the neoliberal divide and those considered different. Combining CHAT with SAD and a critique of neoliberal and deficit ideologies, by acknowledging race and class, *othering and belonging* allows us to become at least a bit more nuanced in recognizing just how these underlying ideologies actually do function and how they eventuate as contradictions.

On a global level, contradictions involving oil spills, tar sands or property rights exacerbate existing power conflicts but are being brought to the forefront because an historical tension has been disturbed. CHAT's emphasis on the history of primary contradictions is essential to any power analysis. This is true especially in older museums, many of which have questionable origins, policies and practices, often reflecting colonialist past or current neoliberal tendencies.

This sets the stage for dialogue concerning power differentials as they manifest at all levels of museum function from board to ticket taker. Manifestations of power are intertwined with all everyday aspects of "doing museums", including institutionally approved purchases, salary structure, use of endowment, board membership, administrative structures, expected teaching practices for museum educators, whether volunteer or paid, curatorial practices, exhibit design, cafeteria, fundraising and public relations. I have already introduced contradictions of power between departments in museums in such issues as what to display, how to interpret it and so on. We return to these areas in the chapters to come, as we delve into several aspects of hierarchy: power of display (Dubin, 1999), power of demographics, money, story, objects and more.

Power[34] can be overtly and covertly expressed, for example, in the selective use of an authoritative voice. Deficit-laden discursive traces reveal power, for example, when an educator argues that the visitors are *doing the exhibit wrong*, or an exhibit designer suggests that an object *speaks for itself* or a high-level administrator argues that if *visitors don't pay, they don't appreciate their experience* (de Montebello, 2017). As we noted previously, when everyday discursive events such as these occur, it is important to 'tag' them and to link them to hierarchical issues related to community and rules, to power and hegemony, as well as any theories (production and consumption, neoliberalism, structure/agency dialectic, CHAT, etc.) that inform these topics either directly or indirectly in workplace settings (Engeström, 2014; Gutiérrez & Calabrese Barton, 2015; Sannino, 2020).

I do this because it is important to link hierarchical issues with issues of power and hegemony, as well as with theory. A rather ordinary example is recognizing the increasing role of modern collaborative team-based efforts in designing/displaying/advertising/interpreting museums, which requires we consider both vertical and horizontal hierarchies, levels that may not agree. Teams have been interesting to follow, especially when contradictions inevitably occur. Researchers disagree about the root cause for differing orientations, or disagreement, within teams asked to co-design exhibits. Charlotte Lee argued,

> Disputes are very much seen as tied to the professional identities of team members, with particularly deep divisions running between the museum staff (e.g., educators and design personnel) on one side, and curators and museum directorship on the other.
> (Roberts, 1997; Macdonald, 2001, in C. Lee, 2004, p. 183)[35]

Curators, educators and other staff may disagree as to what exhibits should look like, their degree of difficulty and the nature of any curriculum contained in teaching style, meaning of objects, story, etc., in practical terms (C. Lee, 2004, 2007; Roberts, 1997). Lee noted that in such teams, "disputes in the collaborative development of exhibitions are typically discussed in terms of tensions between scholarship and popularization" (C. Lee, 2007, p. 184). For example, curators critique the 'dumbing down' of exhibitions by other staff members. Of 'dumbing down',[36] Lee said,

> It's an odd idea when you think about it. The whole reason to reach people who don't know what you know, as an expert, is so that they might know about it. Giving them reason to care, process, and understand is precisely the point.
> (C. Lee, 2007, p 158)

Such popularization has been interpreted as giving visitors an opportunity to care. Bogost (2018) argued that giving people reason to care is exactly what exhibits can do, and the idea of 'dumbing down' is antithetical to that.

I underscore that the disturbing use of the discursive trace of 'dumbing down' carries an explicit deficit orientation. As Bogost (2018) claimed and I discuss in Chapter 7, "After all, people have areas in their own lives in which *they* are the experts. Everyone is capable of deep understanding" (para 4–5). MacDonald (2001) described the process of developing an exhibition as one where the team must constantly manage relations with others and maintain control over authorship in the face of others trying to "muscle in" (in C. Lee, 2007) and claim power. In this case, from the outside, 'dumbing down' appears to rely on an ideological stance justified by 'deeper' content, while underneath it actually involves pejorative interpretations of people's capacities to learn (Bogost, 2018). This struggle fits well within CHAT's framing of power differences. Curators historically have had more power than educators in museums; Gurian famously suggested,

> If the curator's pleasure in the job derives from the power that control of information gives him or her, then sharing the role of expert with others will feel like a diminishment of stature.
>
> (Gurian, 2020, paras. 5–6)

Whether the struggle is over curriculum design, professional identity or, as Charlotte Lee also suggests, merging communities of practice, we note that there are at least two communities centered on some potential shared object of importance—that is, the 'curriculum or content' of what should be conveyed to the public and how.

Throughout this book, I will discuss how different levels of personnel, job titles and interest areas within museums can be affected by the anticipated tensions, for example, within the museum between exhibit designers, educators, publicists and administrators, and outside the museum among news sources, investors and local political entities. These historical hierarchical levels, which exist around any museum, have competing or collaborative goals.

Summary

CHAT[37] allows us to examine multilayered, contradictory events like the Exxon/Valdez spill but also recognizes the hidden ideologies and power dynamics beneath such events. CHAT allows us much freedom to explore how museums actually work as systems, replete with neoliberal, colonist history and othering/deficit baggage. These theories, taken together, liberate us from exploring only single aspects, such as the composition of signs or determining whether people are learning certain new concepts in the presence of an educator, instead offering a multidimensional, systemic approach that includes both psychological motives and all kinds of tools, as well as the always-present dynamics of power, money, culture and history. We recognize that everything to do with museums is socially, culturally, historically and hierarchically situated—for example, name, salary, objects, exhibit design, staff clothing, job title and so on.

I have argued that activity theory allows us to analyze difficult situations like the Exxon Valdez Spill as complex historically, culturally situated systems, replete with competing beliefs, underlying philosophies, people involved, rules invoked and communities activated, as well as hierarchies and goals. It is useful to frame contradictions in more theoretical terms, to make it easier to deal with such gnarly issues by allowing us to consider multiple concerns and multiple theories in tandem.

I have argued that such analyses, while complex, are worth the time we take to understand them because they are so very useful in understanding a vast assortment of contradictions that plague modern institutions like museums. CHAT and SAD together are useful when considering the nitty-gritty, day-to-day difficulties of museums, as practical tools that museums can use to unpack complexity. These theories enable researchers to analyze complex and evolving professional practices, without oversimplification. They can therefore engage in reflective research (c.f. Foot, 2014; Yliruka & Karvinen-Niinikoski, 2013, in Foot, 2014, p. 2).

I promote using discursive traces (discussed in Chapter 1) to better understand deficit and neoliberal ideologies and manage the many seemingly disparate elements of what is otherwise an unwieldy and multifaceted museum system so that the basic notion of mediated activity within a community bound by cultural, historical and social norms and the dialectic between agency and structure can be retained without losing the many important details.

Appendix 2.1: Contradictions at Three Levels of Analysis

Engeström claimed that contradictions reverberate at different levels of any institution. Competing motives (money/social good) affect each aspect of an activity system, which typically includes people (visitors, designers, politicians), goals (education, money, social good), mediational means (exhibit, public relations, newspapers), community (museum, city of Valdez, schools) rules (who is allowed to speak) and division of labor (hierarchies of personnel).

An Individual or Small Group With an Educator

One of the goals of the exhibit designers and educators can be that museum visitors bring their own learning objectives and perspectives into interactions. The object(ive) of a visitor may be to learn or, alternatively, to simply enjoy a fun activity with the family. Educators, too, bring their own motives; whether paid or volunteer, their beliefs (ideologies about learning and teaching might be very different from each other or the museum; see Chapters 7 and 8).

A typical contradiction includes how we educate/teach the public—that is, how educators are trained to help the public understand exhibits. Imagine for the moment that 'our' museum leans toward the didactic end of the teaching spectrum. Then, educators are asked to spend less time with each visitor or to use a particular scripted text for teaching. Educators would need to 'teach' in a certain way. This is difficult for those who have been trained to 'listen to visitors' before telling them information. This is reminiscent of Engeström's doctor's dilemma—that is, whether to treat the patient fully or save money. It takes time and money to listen to visitors.

Mid-Level Management

There can be disagreement between curators and educators as to how to interpret an exhibit at middle management levels. We will note in Chapter 8, for example, that two different teaching communities in the same museum can view learning and teaching very differently (desired outcomes, different object(ive)), differing views of power, from the top down or lateral and/or content or process driven, and so on. We note in Chapters 6 and 7 how narratives very much reflect epistemologies. And in Chapters 5 and 6, we see that, often, competing narratives regarding the interpretation of 'history' or an object inform personal and institutional thinking and actions.

We recognize that these design perspectives exist in a dialectical relationship. Both stances are underpinned by differing ideological beliefs. And each dialogue (didactic or scaffolding) would likely have different desired outcomes.

Top-Level Management

There have been numerous examples over the past years where the top administration and the board of directors have not agreed. Typically, that has meant the director is fired or asked to resign.[38] Clearly then, there are serious contradictions at the top level that impact all the other levels. The Met vignette in the next chapter is a well-known example. We can foresee many others. On other hierarchical levels, the community outreach director may lobby for free admittance one day a month to increase museum attendance with diverse audiences, thereby forgoing some revenue, while the CFO may wish to increase visitor entrance fees to support the museum's educational and/or exhibit design activities.

Notes

1 They can be physical tools, such as books, conceptual tools or language.
2 My own research over the years has relied on several different interpretations of socio-culturally based theory, such as mediation in the ZPD (Vygotsky, 1978) and communities of practice (Lave & Wenger, 1991) and, over the past decade, cultural historical activity theory or CHAT (Engeström, 1999, 2017; Engeström, 1987).
3 Dialectical logic is a fundamental aspect of all imaginable objects of study. While some "superficial" contradictions can be eliminated in a relatively straightforward way, there are also other, deeper contradictions that cannot be simply resolved once and for all.
4 Mahn (2003) suggested that Vygotsky's dialectical approach has four central tenets:

   (1) A historical, developmental process from their origins to their terminus.
   (2) Change, a constant, is most clearly seen at times of qualitative transformation in phenomena.
   (3) Transformations take place through the unification of contradictory, distinct processes.
   (4) These unifications or unities are irreducible and embody the essence of the whole.

5 Some have used terms such as 'tensions' or 'dilemmas', 'double binds' (Barab et al., 2004; Ward, 2016) to indicate contradictions. I follow Engeström and Sannino (2011) and acknowledge the conundrum of determining what rises to the level of genuine contradiction.
6 Marx's concepts about use value, that which gives work its inherent worth, vs. exchange value, that which makes work a commodity, underline the primary contradiction. For example, a doctor provides a service of helping the ill (use value) but to do so, they get paid for that work (exchange value). This contradiction is always present within each node of the activity system, and it reveals itself when tensions arise "from the dual construction of everything and everyone as both having inherent worth and being a commodity within market–based socioeconomic relations" (Foot & Groleau, 2011, p. 6).
7 The Valdez Native Tribe (VNT) is located in Valdez, Alaska, in Prince William Sound and approximately 300 miles from Anchorage. For the Alaskan Native people of this region, Valdez was historically a favorite place to hunt, fish, gather, and trade.
8 Approximately 20 Native Alaskan communities were directly impacted by the spill (Davis, 2010).
9 Bang and Marin (2015) also comment on the issue of time in precolonial and colonial settings, noting that the latter typically subsumes the former, which is different in quality.
10 Such as gas leaks nuclear meltdown and industrial or man-made fires.
11 In *mediated* action the Subject, Object and *Artifact* stand in *a dialectical* relationship whereby each affects the other and the activity as a whole.
12 Artifacts/mediational means change and are changed in their intermediate positioning.
13 By object we mean a thing to be acted upon, (e.g., an illness, questions). Second, it is an objectified motive (the search for a cure; Christiansen, 1996). Third, it is a desired outcome (e.g., restored health). In CHAT, each object has all three of these facets, and any of these facets may be constructed or perceived differently by various members of the community.
14 The search for 'flatter' organizational charts has been ongoing over the last decade (Merritt, 2013).
15 The possibility of a fourth generation of CHAT was put forward in 2009 (Engeström, 2009; Sannino et al., 2009). It was most poignantly proposed by Sannino (2020) in a keynote address discussing the challenge of eradicating homelessness (Engeström & Sannino, 2020).
16 By curriculum I mean the standard signage and/or narrative explanations that docents and educators are expected to interpret at exhibits.
17 Lee and others have discussed just such disagreement in the context of ever more frequent team-based efforts used to accomplish museum goals. Such tensions have been an active area of scholarship (Macdonald, 2001; Roberts, 1997).
18 There can be several smaller communities, exhibit designers, education department, technology experts, administrators, maintenance and so on.
19 This distinction has been called 'sage on the stage' or 'guide on the side' in classrooms.
20 On one hand, we want a bucolic area for recreation and living (use value), and on the other hand, we need fuel (exchange value).
21 As Feinstein and Meshoulam (2014) have argued, educators may view visitors either as clients (exchange) or collaborators (use), another instantiation of the same dialectic.
22 Mwanza has argued that tasks are usually divided horizontally [but] power and status vertically (Mwanza, 2001).

23 In other words, the "learners construct a new object and concept for their collective activity, and implement this new object and concept in practice" (Foot & Groleau, 2011, p. 17).
24 The idea behind expansive learning as Ward (2016) noted is the "capacity to reinterpret and expand the definition of the object of the activity…is epistemologically grounded in dialectics that move from the abstract to the concrete" (Sannino & Ellis, 2014, in Ward, 2016, p. 59).
25 Chapter 5 provides an example of an exhibit that 'works the dialectic"— Sutter Buttes at the Oakland Museum of California.
26 To explore CHAT dialectical relationships, consult Langemeyer and Roth (2006) for an in-depth treatment of this subject.
27 Perhaps the beginning of such transformative agency lies with work in museum systems where staff already have more agency; for example, all hands-on-deck meetings where staff are listened to and suggestions are taken seriously.
28 See Andersen, 2020; Apple, 2017; Steger & Roy, 2013)
29 Hall and Pulsford (2019) discussed "neoliberal discourse in U.K. primary schools focusing on metrics that damage self-actualisation…[emphasize] efficiency, excellence and value-for-money…competitive individualism and individuation [and] pit members or factions of communities against each other…because those individuals look different or behave differently, carry different characteristics, have different characters or mobilise weak forms of human capital" (pp. 241–242).
30 "Hidden injuries of the neoliberal university" (Gill & Donaghue, 2016). See also Gill (2017).
31 Gjorgjioska and Tomicic (2019) echo these views "considering the hegemony of neoliberalism and individualism in academic work…[with] emphasis on production of knowledge…and corresponding hegemony of conceptual and methodological individualism in the social sciences" (p. 34).
32 Harrison's (1997) more critical assessment of neocolonialist and neoliberal forces in museums.
33 Dailey (2006) has studied this phenomenon in museums more broadly suggesting, "both [museum] evaluation…and also tracking learning outcomes are reflective of neoliberal ideals" (p. 8).
34 Karp, et al. noted that power derives from ideological views, suggesting "the selection and presentation of ideas, images and information can only take place within a context that imparts its own messages about power (Karp et al., 1992, p. 1)
35 In the case of educators and curators, Lee suggested that there are differences of opinion as to the root of their tension; one noted by (Macdonald, 2001) and (Roberts, 1997): "resulting from a struggle amongst different professional roles", whereas others (Lindauer, 2004) characterize them as differences over curriculum theories rather than as a professional divide (Lee, 2007, p. 183).
36 The phrase *dumbing down* got its start in entertainment. During the golden age of Hollywood, in the 1930s, dumbing down became a screenwriter's shorthand for making an idea simple enough that people with limited education or experience could understand it (Bogost, 2018).
37 For greater clarity, we rely on Foot's (2014) paper "Cultural-Historical Activity Theory: Exploring a Theory to Inform Practice and Research" as a main resource in this chapter, as it explains CHAT in a user-friendly way.
38 Presidents of two Czech museums were fired reportedly for financial (but actually for political) reasons in May 2019.

References

Anderson, D., Cosson, A., & McIntosh, L. (n.d.). *Informing the practice of museum educators: Diverse audiences, challenging topics, and reflective praxis.* Sense Publishers. https//doi.org/10.1007

Andersen, K. (2020). *Evil geniuses: The unmaking of America: A recent history.* Random House.

Apple, M.W. (Ed.). (2017). *Cultural and economic reproduction in education: Essays on class, ideology and the state* (Vol. 53). Routledge.

Ash, D. (2014). Positioning informal learning research in museums within activity theory: From theory to practice and back again. *Curator, 57*(1), 107–119.

Ash, D. (in preparation). Expansive learning in a large urban museum: Contradictions in teaching and learning, power, resistance, and transformation. To be submitted to *Cultural Studies in Science Education*.

Ash, D., & deGregoria Kelly, L.Â. (2013). Thoughts on improvable objects, contradiction and object/tool reciprocity in a study of zoo educator professional development. *Cultural Studies in Science Education, 3*, 587–594.

Au, W., & Ferrare, J.A. (Eds.). (2015). *Mapping corporate education reform: Power and policy networks in the neoliberal state (critical social thought).* Routledge.

Bang, M., & Marin, A. (2015). Nature-culture constructs in science learning: Human/non-human agency and intentionality. *Journal of Research in Science Teaching, 52*(4), 530–544. doi:10.1002/tea.21204

Barab, S., Schatz, S., & Scheckler, R. (2004). Using activity theory to conceptualize online community and using online community to conceptualize activity theory. *Mind, Culture, and Activity, 11*(1), 25–47. http://dx.doi.org/10.1207/s15327884mca1101_3

Blackler, F. (1993). Knowledge and the theory of organizations: Organizations as activity systems and the reframing of management. *Journal of Management Studies, 30*(6), 863–884. https://doi.org/10.1111/j.1467-6486.1993.tb00470.x

Blackler, F., & McDonald, S. (2000). Power, mastery and organizational learning. *Journal of Management Studies, 37*(6), 833–852.

Bogost, I. (2018, October 26). The myth of 'dumbing down'. *TheAtlantic.* https://www.theatlantic.com/science/archive/2018/10/scholars-shouldnt-fear-dumbing-down-public/573979/.

Bonneau, C. (2013). *Contradictions and their concrete manifestations: An activity theoretical analysis of the intra-organizational co-configuration of open-source software.* Paper presented at the 29th EGOS Colloquium. https://www.egosnet.org/jart/prj3/egos/resources/dbcon_def/uploads/a4Uzt_EGOS2013_full-paper_ST-50_CBonneau-final2.pdf

Brown, A. (1992). Design experiments: Theoretical and methodological challenges in creating complex interventions in classroom settings. *Journal of the Learning Sciences, 2*, 141–178.

Brown, A. L., Ash, D., Rutherford, M., Nakagawa, K., Gordon, A., & Campione, J. C. (1993). Distributed expertise in the classroom. In G. Salomon (Ed.), *Distributed cognitions: Psychological and educational considerations* (pp. 188–288). Cambridge University Press.

Christiansen, E. (1996). Tamed by a rose: Computers as tools in human activity. In B.A. Nardi (Ed.), *Context and consciousness: Activity theory and human-computer interaction* (pp. 175–198). MIT Press.

Coffee, K. (2007). Audience research and the museum experience as social practice. *Museum Management and Curatorship, 22*(4), 377–389.

Coffee, K. (2008). Cultural inclusion, exclusion and the formative roles of museums. *Museum Management and Curatorship, 23*(3), 261–279. https://doi.org/10.1080/09647770802234078

Dailey, T. L. (2006). *Museums in the age of neoliberalism: A multi-sited analysis of science and health museums.* [Master's thesis, Georgia State University]. ScholarWorks. https://scholarworks.gsu.edu/anthro_theses/20

Daniels, H., & Warmington, P. (2007). Analysing third generation activity systems: Labour-power, subject position and personal transformation. *Journal of Workplace Learning, 19*(6), 377–391. https://doi.org/10.1108/13665620710777110

Davis, N. (2010). The Exxon Valdez oil spill, Alaska. In J.K. Mitchell (Ed.), *The long road to recovery: Community responses to industrial disaster* (pp. 231–272). United Nations University Press.

de Montebello, P. (2017). Art in conversation. The New Criterion. https://newcriterion.com/issues/2017/6/art-in-conversation.

deGregoria Kelly, L.A. (2009). Action research as professional development for zoo educators. *Visitor Studies 12*(1), 30–46.

Dubin, S. (1999). *Displays of power: Memory and amnesia in the American museum*. New York University Press.

Dubin, S. (2014). *Displays of power: Memory and amnesia in the American museum*. New York University Press.

Engeström, Y. (1987). *Learning by expanding. An activity-theoretical approach to developmental research*. Orienta-Konsultit. http://lchc.ucsd.edu/mca/Paper/Engestrom/Learning-by-Expanding.pdf

Engeström, Y. (1991). *Learning by expanding: Ten years after*. http://lchc.ucsd.edu/mca/Paper/Engestrom/expanding/intro.htm

Engeström, Y. (1999). Innovative learning in work teams: Analysing cycles of knowledge creation in practice. In Y. Engeström et al. (Eds.), *Perspectives on activity theory* (pp. 377–406). Cambridge University Press.

Engeström, Y. (2005). *The future of activity theory: A rough draft*. http://lchc.ucsd.edu/mca/Paper/ISCARkeyEngestrom.pdf

Engeström, Y. (2006). Activity theory and expansive design. In S. Bagnara & G. Crampton Smith (Eds.), *Theories and practice in interaction design: Interaction design* (pp. 3–25). Lawrence Erlbaum.

Engeström, Y. (2009). The future of activity theory: A rough draft. *Learning and Expanding with Activity Theory*, 303–328. https://doi.org/10.1017/cbo9780511809989.020

Engeström, Y. (2014). Activity theory and learning at work. *Tätigkeit – Aneignung – Bildung*, 67–96. https://doi.org/10.1007/978-3-658-02120-7_3

Engeström, Y. (2017). Expanding the scope of science education: An activity-theoretical perspective. *Cognitive and Affective Aspects in Science Education Research*, 357–370. https://doi.org/10.1007/978-3-319-58685-4_26

Engeström, Y., & Sannino, A. (2010). Studies of expansive learning: Foundations, findings and future challenges. *Educational Research Review, 5*(1), 1–24. doi:10.1016/j.edurev.2009.12.002

Engeström, Y., & Sannino, A. (2011). Discursive manifestations of contradictions in organizational change efforts: A methodological framework. *Journal of Organizational Change Management, 24*(3), 368–387. doi:10.1108/ 09534811111132758

Engeström, Y., & Sannino, A. (2020). From mediated actions to heterogenous coalitions: Four generations of activity-theoretical studies of work and learning. *Mind, Culture, and Activity, 28*(1), 4–23. https://doi.org/10.1080/10749039.2020.1806328

Feinstein, N., & Meshoulam, D. (2014). Science for what public? Equity-oriented work in American science museums and science centers. *Journal of Research in Science Teaching, 51*(3), 368–394

Foot, K., & Groleau, C. (2011). Contradictions, transitions, and materiality in organizing processes: An activity theory perspective. *First Monday, 16*(6), 1–21. doi:10.5210/fm.v16i6.3479

Foot, K. A. (2001). Cultural-historical activity theory as practice theory: Illuminating the development of conflict-monitoring network. *Communication Theory, 11*(1), 56– 83.

Foot, K. A. (2002). Pursuing an evolving object: Object formation and identification in a conflict monitoring network. *Mind, Culture and Activity, Summer, 9*(2), 132–149.

Foot, K. A. (2014). Cultural-historical activity theory: Exploring a theory to inform practice and research. *Journal of Human Behavior in the Social Environment, 24*(3), 329–347. https://doi.org/10.1080/10911359.2013.831011

Gill, D. A., & Picou. S. (1997). The day the water died: Cultural impacts of the Exxon Valdez oil spill. In J. Steven Picou, D. A. Gill, & M. J. Cohen (Eds.), *The Exxon Valdez disaster: Readings on a modern social problem* (pp. 167–192). Kendall-Hunt.

Gill, R., & Donaghue, N. (2016). Resilience, apps and reluctant individualism: Technologies of self in the neoliberal academy. *Women's Studies International Forum, 54*, 91–99. https://doi.org/10.1016/j.wsif.2015.06.016

Gill, R. (2017). Beyond individualism: The psychosocial life of the neoliberal university. In M. Spooner (Ed.), *A critical guide to higher education & the politics of evidence: Resisting colonialism, neoliberalism, & audit culture*. University of Regina Press.

Gjorgjioska, M. A., & Tomicic, A. (2019). The crisis in social psychology under neoliberalism: Reflections from social representations theory. *Journal of Social Issues, 75*(1), 169–188. https://doi.org/10.1111/josi.12315

Gurian, E. H. (2020). Curator: From soloist to impresario. In C. Fiona & L. Kelly (Eds.), *Hot topics, public culture, museums* (pp. 95–111). Cambridge Scholars Publishing.

Gutiérrez, K. D., & Calabrese Barton, A. (2015). The possibilities and limits of the structure-agency dialectic in advancing science for all. *Journal of Research in Science Teaching, 52*(4), 574–583. https://doi.org/10.1002/tea.21229

Haapasaari, A., Engeström, Y., & Kerosuo, H. (2014). The emergence of learners' transformative agency in a Change Laboratory intervention. *Journal of Education and Work, 29*(2), 232–262. https://doi.org/10.1080/13639080.2014.900168

Hall, R., & Pulsford, M. (2019). Neoliberalism and primary education: Impacts of neoliberal policy on the lived experiences of primary school communities. *Power and Education, 11*(3), 241–251. https://doi.org/10.1177/1757743819877344

Harrison, J. (1997). Museums as agencies of neocolonialism in a postmodern world. *Studies in Cultures, Organizations and Societies, 3*(1), 41–65. doi:10.1080/10245289708523487

Harvey, D. (2005). *A brief history of neoliberalism*. Oxford University Press.

Kaptelinin, V. (2011). *Activity theory*. The Interaction Design Foundation. https://www.interaction-design.org/literature/book/the-encyclopedia-of-human-computer-interaction-2nd-ed/activity-theory.

Karim-Jaffer, S. (2013). *Making power visible for museum educators: A theoretical framework for multicultural museum education*. Bank Street College of Education. http://educate.bankstreet.edu/independent-studies/129

Karp, I., Kreamer, C. M., & Lavine, S. D. (1992). *Museums and communities: The politics of public culture*. Smithsonian Institution Press.

Kundu, R., & Kalin, N. M. (2015). Participating in the neoliberal art museum. *Studies in Art Education, 57*(1), 39–52. https://doi.org/10.1080/00393541.2015.11666281.

Kuutti, K. (1996). Activity theory as a potential framework for human–computer interaction research. In B. Nardi (Ed.), *Context and consciousness: Activity theory and human–computer interaction* (pp. 17–44). MIT.

Langemeyer, I., & Roth, W-M. (2006). Is cultural-historical activity theory threatened to fall short of its own principles and possibilities as a dialectical social science? *Outlines*, (2), 20– 42. http://lchc.ucsd.edu/MCA/Mail/xmcamail.2013_05.dir/pdfbRMMR2RsmR.pdf

Lave, J., & Wenger, E. (1991). *Situated learning: Legitimate peripheral participation*. Cambridge University Press.
Lee, C. (2004). *The role of boundary negotiating artifacts in the collaborative design of a museum exhibition*. [Doctoral. dissertation, University of California, Los Angeles]. ProQuest. https://search.proquest.com/openview/a90d6863e398cf58b5f2ab0596d9e27f/1?pq-origsite=gscholar&cbl=18750&diss=y
Lee, C. P. (2007). Reconsidering conflict in exhibition development teams. *Museum Management and Curatorship*, *22*(2), 183–199. https://doi.org/10.1080/09647770701470427
Leonardo, Z. (2009). *Race, whiteness, and education*. Routledge.
Leont'ev, A. N. (1978). *Activity, consciousness, and personality*. Prentice-Hall.
Lindauer, M. A. (2004). From salad bars to vivid stories: Four game plans for developing 'educationally successful' exhibitions. *Museum Management and Curatorship*, *20*(1), 41–55. https://doi.org/10.1080/09647770500502001
Lynch, M. (2014, September 6). *Native Americans and the Exxon Valdez oil spill*. Green Criminology. http://greencriminology.org/glossary/native-americans-and-the-exxon-valdez-oil-spill/
Macdonald, S. (2001). Behind the scenes at the Science Museum; London: Knowing, making and using. In M. Bouquet (Ed.), *Academic anthropology and the museum: Back to the future* (pp. 117–140). Berghahn Books.
Mahn, H. (2003). Periods in child development: Vygotsky's perspective. In L. S. Vygotsky (Ed.), *Vygotsky's educational theory in cultural context*. Cambridge University Press.
Martin, L. W., Tran, L. U., & Ash, D. (Eds.) (2019). *The reflective museum practitioner: Expanding practice in science museums*. Routledge.
McDermott, R. (2015). Does "learning" exist? *Word*, *61*(4), 335–349. https://doi.org/10.1080/00437956.2015.1112956
Merritt, E. (2013). *Flower power: A story of organizational re-blossoming*. American Alliance of Museums. https://www.aam-us.org/2013/08/13/flower-power-a-story-of-organizational-re-blossoming/
Miettinen, R. (2009). *Dialogue and creativity: Activity theory in the study of science, technology and innovations*. Lehmanns International.
Moore, P. (2014, January 20). *The danger of the "D" word: Museums and diversity*. The Incluseum. https://incluseum.com/2014/01/20/the-danger-of-the-d-word-museums-and-diversity/
Murakowski, M. (2017, October). *We are stronger together. Museums are not neutral*. https://www.museumsarenotneutral.com/learn-more/we-are-stronger-together
Mwanza, D. (2001, July 9–13). Where theory meets practice: A case for an activity theory based methodology to guide computer system design. *Proceedings of INTERACT' 2001: Eighth IFIP TC 13 Conference on Human-Computer Interaction*, Tokyo, Japan.
Patrick, P. (2017). *Preparing informal science educators: Perspectives from science communication and education*. Springer Nature.
Powell, J., & Menendian, S. (2017, June 29). The problem of othering: Towards inclusiveness and belonging. *Othering and Belonging: Expanding the Circle of Human Concern*, *1*, 14–39. https://otheringandbelonging.org/wp-content/uploads/2016/07/OtheringAndBelonging_Issue1.pdf
Preston, J. (2013). Neoliberal settler colonialism, Canada and the tar sands. *Race & Class*, *55*(2), 42–59. https://doi.org/10.1177/0306396813497877
Rahm, J., & Brandt, C. B. (2016). Reimagining science education in neoliberal global contexts: Sociocultural accounts of science learning in underserved communities. *Mind, Culture, and Activity*, *23*(3), 183–187. https://doi.org/10.1080/10749039.2016.1201514
Roberts, L. (1997). *From knowledge to narrative: Educators and the changing museum*. Smithsonian Institution Press.

Robertson, S. (2007). *'Remaking the world': Neo-liberalism and the transformation of education and teachers' labour*. Centre for Globalisation, Education and Societies. https://susanleerobertson.files.wordpress.com/2009/10/2007-weis-teachers.pdf

Roth, W.-M. (2002). From action to discourse: The bridging function of gestures. *Cognitive Systems Research, 3*(3), 535–554. https://doi.org/10.1016/s1389-0417(02)00056-6

Roth, W. M., Radford, L., & LaCroix, L. (2012). Working with cultural-historical activity theory *Forum Qualitative Sozialforschung/Forum: Qualitative Social Research, 13*(2), Art. 23, http://www.qualitative-research.net/index.php/fqs/article/view/1814/3379

Sannino, A. (2020). Enacting the utopia of eradicating homelessness: Toward a new generation of activity-theoretical studies of learning. *Studies in Continuing Education, 42*(2), 163–179. https://doi.org/10.1080/0158037X.2020.1725459

Sannino, A., Daniels, H., & Gutiérrez, K. D. (Eds.) (2009). *Learning and expanding with activity theory*. Cambridge University Press.

Sannino, A., & Ellis, V. (2014). *Learning and collective creativity: Activity-theoretical and sociocultural studies*. Routledge.

Seig, M. T., & Bubp, K. (2008). The culture of empowerment: Driving and sustaining change at conner prairie. *Curator: The Museum Journal, 51*(2), 203–220. https://doi.org/10.1111/j.2151-6952.2008.tb00306.x

Spurgin, C. (2021). *Discourses of power in science teacher becoming: Science and equity in conflict* [PhD dissertation]. Univeristy of California Santa Cruz.

Steger, M. B., & Roy, R. K. (2013). *Neoliberalism: A very short introduction*. Oxford University Press.

Stetsenko, A. (2019). Radical-transformative agency: Continuities and contrasts with Relational agency and implications for education. *Frontiers in Education, 4*. https://doi.org/10.3389/feduc.2019.00148

Steward, L. (2018, July 12). *Museums are not neutral: A discussion on why there is no museum neutrality in museum education*. Medium. https://medium.com/@steward.lindsey/museums-are-not-neutral-a-discussion-on-why-there-is-no-museum-neutrality-in-museum-education-526e8de21f77

Suchman, L. (1995). Making work visible. *Communications of the ACM, 38*(9), 56–64. https://doi.org/10.1145/223248.223263

Taylor, A. (2014, March 24). Remembering the Exxon Valdez oil spill. *The Atlantic*. https://www.theatlantic.com/photo/2014/03/remembering-the-exxon-valdez-oil-spill/100703/.

Timmis, S. (2014). The dialectical potential of CULTURAL historical Activity theory for researching SUSTAINABLE CSCL practices. *International Journal of Computer-Supported Collaborative Learning, 9*(1), 7–32. https://doi.org/10.1007/s11412-013-9178-z

Tripadvisor. (2012, August 19). *The Valdez Museum and historical archive: "Thoroughly enjoyed this museum…"* [Review]. "https://www.tripadvisor.com/LocationPhotoDirectLink-g31156-d319358-i46374231-The_Valdez_Museum_and_Historical_Archive-Valdez_Alaska.html

Valdez Museum & Historical Archive. (2021, April 14). *Oil spill lab at the Valdez Museum*. https://www.valdezmuseum.org/oil-spill-lab-at-the-valdez-museum/?highlight=oil+spill%3Fref

Valdez Native Tribe (n.d.). *Many tribes, one people*. https://valdeznativetribe.org

Varelas, M., Settlage, J., & Mensah, F. M. (2015). Explorations of the structure-agency dialectic as a tool for framing equity in science education. *Journal of Research in Science Teaching, 52*(4), 439–447. https://doi.org/10.1002/tea.21230

Vossoughi, S., & Gutiérrez, K. D. (2014). Studying movement, hybridity, and change: Toward a multi-sited sensibility for research on learning across contexts and borders. *Teachers College Record, 116*(14), 603–632.

Vygotsky, L. S. (1978). *Mind in society: The development of higher psychological processes*. Harvard University Press.
Walawalkar, A. (2020, February 8). Activists try to occupy British Museum in protest against BP ties. *The Guardian*. https://www.theguardian.com/culture/2020/feb/08/activists-try-to-occupy-british-museum-in-protest-against-bp-ties.
Ward, S. J. (2016). *Understanding contradictions in times of change: A CHAT analysis in an art museum*. [Doctoral dissertation, University of Washington]. ResearchWorks Archive. http://hdl.handle.net/1773/37091
WBUR. (2014, March 24). Native Alaskans still reeling 25 years after Exxon-Valdez oil spill. *Here & Now*. https://www.wbur.org/hereandnow/2014/03/24/exxon-spill-anniversary.
Whyte, J. (2019). Calculated indifference: The politics of collateral damage. *Journal of Genocide Research, 21*(2), 263–268. https://doi.org/10.1080/14623528.2019.1589928
Yamagata-Lynch, L. C. (2010). *Activity systems analysis methods: Understanding complex learning environments*. Springer.
Yamagata-Lynch, L. C. (2014). Understanding and examining design activities with cultural-historical activity theory. In A. Gibbons & B. Hokanson (Eds.), *Design in educational technology* (pp. 89–106). Springer. doi:10.1007/978-3-319-00927-8_6.
Yliruka, L., & Karvinen-Niinikoski, S. (2013). How can we enhance productivity in social work? Dynamically reflective structures, dialogic leadership and the development of transformative expertise. *Journal of Social Work Practice: Psychotherapeutic Approaches in Health, Welfare and the Community, 27*(2), 191–206.

3
WHO WILL GO TO MUSEUMS

Overview

It has been claimed that by 2042 people currently considered to be part of the minority population in the United States will have become the majority, forming what Rodriguez calls the "*new mainstream*" (Rodriguez, 2009) of the majority/minority. The *new mainstream* in the United States will include Latino, Black, Asian and other non-Caucasian groups, the largest group being Latinx.

Given the rapidly changing demographics across the globe, museums need to ask who's going to be walking through the doors in the coming decades (Rodriguez, 2009). Questions concerning how to achieve equity and social justice in museums have recently become a focus for local, national and international press, blogs and other media (Bell et al., 2009; Dawson, 2014a, 2014b; Gurian, 2014; Ng et al., 2017). Some even argue that if things do not change quickly, museums may be out of a job (Rodriguez, 2009). Callihan and Feldman (2018) have argued that

> without direct intervention, museums will continue to replicate societal patterns of oppression such as sexism, racism, and ableism. It will take an intentional and comprehensive strategy to transform museum practices.
>
> (p. 182)

The contradictions we consider in this chapter directly address these concerns. These contradictions, as always, stem from the primary contradiction of use vs. exchange value. Among them are the difference between desire and reality, that is, the stated desire of museums for increasing cultural, socioeconomic, linguistic and social visitor diversity and the *actual* demographic data that do not now reflect that rich diversity; the seeming preference of museums for short-term or quick-fix solutions rather than fundamental internal restructuring; and, lastly, the external influence of decolonizing efforts, seeking to change 'the way things are done around here'.

Ng et al. (2017) noted, "When examined closely, the quick fixes often reveal hidden problematic power dynamics that actually maintain the status quo" (p. 132), thus widening the gap of the central contradiction, and creating other contradictions as well. By widening the gap we mean supporting the status quo by continuing to receive funds from (and have directors from) a small, largely white, cultural elite and maintaining the context of neoliberal policies focused on the bottom line, while trying to connect to a more diverse audience.

What museums hope that they are doing vs. what they are doing when they engage in these quick fixes do not align. Neoliberal policies both drive and exacerbate these contradictions, as the disposable income of the middle and lower classes has and will continue to diminish with the commodification of everything (F. Patrick, 2013). Thus, a widening gap will grow between haves and have nots who can't even visit many traditional museums. Demographic projections are only the leading edge of these contradictions; the ideological conflicts underlying these questions of the demographics, therefore, demand our investigation.

VIGNETTE

An African American family of five walked into a museum of science they had not visited before. They had been invited to the museum as part of the Head Start program from the school across the street. After looking at the exhibit, the teenage daughter, Tanisha, looked around and said in a firm voice, "What are we supposed to do here?" The signage at the museum was minimal; the space was designed for interactive hands-on science exhibits and was without the usual 'to do and notice' signs; there was no clear path to 'doing the exhibit' (Mai & Ash, 2012).

The museum of science was big, but the space they were in was sectioned off from the rest of the museum so that it felt somewhat protected. Still, the kids and parents looked nervously at each other, trying to get their bearings, seeming to wonder what it was 'you're supposed to do'. As part of a research project the museum was conducting, they had been asked to visit four particular exhibits. They received free entry and a voucher for the book store in exchange for their participation.

A paid museum educator[1] stood about three feet away but near enough to watch the family. When Tanisha, the oldest daughter, asked, "What are we supposed to do here?", the educator responded, "Hi. My name is Marci. Maybe I can help". Stepping a foot closer and talking quietly and directly to Tanisha and the other children, Marci continued, "Maybe you want to do this and see what happens?" She demonstrated pulling gently on part of the exhibit and then stepped back. Two children did that a few times, talking together about what might be happening and eventually asking Marci questions. It eventuated that one of the boys actually had a good deal of experience with levers and gears and offered examples of what to do next to the rest of his family.

Introduction

As the world is rapidly becoming a more colorful, less white-dominated global society, demographic projections have the international, education-related world pondering what they will need to do to serve these new populations, including how to transform internally (*inreach*) within their own institutions. At the same time, "museums are being asked to better compute and quantify the benefits they bring to their audiences and to do so in obeisance to market forces"[2] (Rodney, 2018). While the stated goal of many museums and museum organizations[3] is for museums to both survive *and* welcome new visitors, it is far from clear how best to reach these ends (Dawson, 2014a, 2014b; Gurian, 2014; Jennings & Jones-Rizzi, 2017). This question is the focus of the discussion in this chapter.

I take a dialectical approach to addressing the central question, *Who will visit the museums of the future?*, which again is a proxy for competing underlying ideological positioning. The dialectic in this case refers to the issue of desire vs. reality; museums want more minoritized visitors to attend but seem unwilling or unable to make the fundamental internal changes to make this happen. Museums often opt for easier cosmetic changes instead, which bring no lasting results. To truly succeed at their desired outcome, museums will need to change from the inside out (Ash & Lombana, 2019; Bevan & Ramos, 2021).[4]

Controversy, dialogue and debate concerning how to achieve genuine racial, linguistic and ethnic inclusion, as well as serve an increasingly diverse public, are not new in the museum world. Scholars such as Anderson (2004), Dawson (2014a, 2019), Hooper-Greenhill (2000), Garibay (2009), Gurian (1990, 2005, 2006), Lonetree (2012), Macdonald (2006), P. Moore (2014) and many new blog sites such as the *Incluseum, Museums Are Not Neutral*, and *Decolonize This Place* have written eloquently about these concerns (see Appendix 3.1).

Ford Bell, then president of the American Alliance of Museums (AAM), hinted back in 2007 at the disconnect between museums and their intended new public, citing a core lack of understanding of "cultural, linguistic, economic and other forms of diversity". That was 13 years ago; the situation Bell spoke of then has not changed significantly. In 2014, the Center for the Future of Museums (CFM) noted that only 9% of the core support group of visitors in U.S. museums were minorities. Their phrasing is deliberately dire, in an attempt to awaken museums to the challenges they face. Precisely because demographic projections are overwhelming, both society in general and museums tend to focus on statistics, i.e., the numbers, instead of on the cultural, sociopolitical and ideological forces at work. It is easier to cite the soon-to-be majority/minority statistics in the United States, for example, or the immigration tensions in Europe (Jones, 2017) than to engage in uncovering and mitigating underlying contradictions. There are increasingly insistent calls for museums to *do something* before the majority/minority shift occurs. However, it is dangerous to believe the problem is only about the numbers. Such oversimplification hides any real sources of effective change and merely feeds fear.

Demographics have been situated as something to fear, which is a not-so-subtle manifestation of deficit ideology. Furthermore, when we talk about demographics, museums are quick to point out the number of People of Color (POC) who work for them or visit the museum, but when and if more minoritized visitors actually do come to museums in greater numbers, they will need to find more than cosmetic change there. Understanding that we are 'working in the dialectic' of competing ideologies, we can also recognize that asking museums to fundamentally shift their structures and beliefs will engender fear from those who have long held power in the museum, as it threatens their positions. As Li (2020) has suggested, "Cultural institutions have faced hard questions about racial inclusivity for decades, and now American museums are going through an identity crisis" (paras 13–14). The specific event she was discussing concerns an open letter of 100 respected artists pointing to the "longstanding failure [of museums] to have educated, integrated, and prepared themselves to meet the challenge of the renewed pressure for racial justice that has developed over the past five years" (Li, 2020, paras. 13–15). The needs of our changing society and the lack of meaningful structural response by museums is a well-recognized phenomenon.

Psychologist Jennifer Richeson did an experiment to determine if the "minority/majority threat" was a powerful enough concept to change people's thoughts and behavior. It was. After hearing the minority/majority projection, "White participants feel less warm toward members of other races" (Resnick, 2017). They were worried, among other things, about the 'social order' after the majority/minority flip. Nikole Hannah-Jones said this more bluntly, "Whites feel like they are losing their personal stake" (2021, MSNBC). Kalshed, a noted psychologist, said that "this [past] year's events have often reflected past trauma and conflict" (Kalshed, 2020). Kalshed was referring to the past trauma of our country, exemplified by the work that Jones did on *The 1619 Project*.

Numbers and Change

I highlight here two issues concerning museum numbers. First, we have struggled with the difficulty of collecting and analyzing museum attendance over the past decades. Counting is uneven across museums, countries and continents, and quite often subject to *cherry-picking* the best data to highlight successes (Chung & Wilkening, 2008; Simon, 2010). Also, museums everywhere have been relatively undisciplined in reporting how minoritized visitor attendance numbers coordinate with general attendance patterns. The same lack of rigor and critical thinking applies in both cases. In addition, the interactions between these two aspects are also confusing. Numbers are counted, yet analysis and collection theory can be quite idiosyncratic (Chung & Wilkening, 2008). Time spans, type of activity and funding vary, and, most important, what gets counted varies significantly.

Here is a quick summary of past attendance patterns and future museum attendance projections. In the United States, we see projections (adapted from the Reach

Study, in AAM/CFM, 2010) showing future decline in Caucasian attendance, and as whites decrease overall, there will be more older and younger (and more Latinx) visitors (CFM, 2014). Every data source suggests that minority populations are increasing but that these families do not visit museums proportionally (CFM, 2014).[5]

In 2020, during the COVID pandemic, the top 100 art museums recorded that attendance dropped by 77% worldwide (Sharpe & Da Silva, 2021). Taking the long view, though, U.S. art museums recorded declining attendance even before the 2008 financial challenges. Attendance of minoritized populations (in arts and humanities museums) decreased between 1984 and 2005 (The Ralph and Goldy, 2006). Researchers at the Smithsonian in the past had already observed a linkage between income, education and attendance. Households with incomes under $40,000 (at that time) that lacked a college education were less likely to attend museums (Doering, 1995).

Americans with more formal education were more likely to engage in informal science activities; adults in other education categories were less likely to do so (Horrigan, 2006). One interesting phenomenon in Europe is a recent wave by Western museums and curators to grapple with migration and the people who undergo it. The 'museumization of migration' as one academic has put it, is a significant shift in the history of museums[6]. According to Jenkins (2016) migration museums, which are becoming more popular across Western nations, are more about sociopolitics than migration.

Overall American white museum attendance is diminishing because that portion of the population is diminishing in proportion to other populations. *This is old news.* The changing face of America and Europe are agreed upon, yet with variations in future projections, the picture is not as clear when we try to anticipate minority attendance data across countries, across museum types and across demographic groups.

It is difficult to know how minoritized audience attendance in museums in the United States has generally fared. This is because counting and categories often don't match across settings. In a recent report (NEA, 2018), using data from 2002–2017, art museum attendance[7] overall showed "greater numbers of art-goers among African Americans, 18–24-year-olds and 35–44 year-olds, and adults who received only 'some college' education". This contributed to the overall rise in art museum/gallery attendance rates between 2012 and 2017 (NEA, 2018). This is good news. The report continued, "the number of older—predominantly white…and the number of younger (predominantly Hispanic and non-Hispanic non-white) patrons will increase as well" (p. 10). This bifurcated prediction presents a challenge.

To get a more accurate picture, we must rely on umbrella organizations such as the American Alliance of Museums, American Association of Museum Directors (AAMD), Association of Science and Technology Centers (ASTC), the Network of European Museum Organisations NEMO), the Asian National Museums Association, the Chinese Association of Museums (CAM), among others. Yet, counting varies across umbrella organizations as well (see Appendix 3.2 for additional information).

To add to the confusion, a smaller study of 196 American mixed museums conducted by Museum Audience Insight in 2012 gave opposing rationales for changes in attendance. Those reporting increased attendance argued that growth was caused by the specific things the museum had done to attract visitors, while those reporting decreases claimed that the causes were external to the museums.

The AAM was also daunted by the pace of change. "The world is morphing so quickly that the traditional time frame for serious, scholarly research studies may simply be too long to keep up" (Chung & Wilkening, 2008, p. 6). The AAM is verifying fear and trepidation. Why should museums be different from the rest of society regarding concerns about the so-called social order? They have much to lose if they don't meet the demographic challenges, yet they have a heavy investment in the status quo.

They recognize that the numbers are morphing so quickly that it is hard to catch up. As Li (2020) suggested, "The threat of demographic change—and the loss of status that comes with it — provokes a broad sense of wanting to hunker down" (para 4). Hunkering down doesn't support major change.

Asking museums to respond internally to these societal changes by shifting their structures and beliefs also engenders fear. It seems easier to change small things like increasing or decreasing entrance fees, an act that signals 'doing something'. We are asking museums to work more inclusively within the framework of social justice, which challenges every aspect of our society. As a preliminary step then, let us study what is and what is projected to be, as best we can. To simplify our analysis, we isolate some of the prevailing trends, their characteristics and the accompanying rhetoric.

All this need not daunt the researchers and practitioners trying to understand internal, as well as external, transitions, both of which have been studied in the past (Bennett, 2018). We take heart from the fact that "the museum is a contact zone,[8] a place for dialogue, inclusion and participation" (Ünsal, 2019, p. 595). While the term 'contact zone' has been alive in museums for more than 20 years, Ünsal's argument is quite relevant now to our focus on museums as dynamic places of change (Boast, 2011). As Ünsal has argued,

> If museums are going to act as agents of social change, they must first recognize the knowledge systems that have historically shaped their museological practices and then intervene to incorporate the diversity of knowledges that have been excluded.
>
> (p. 595)

We explore in a reconfigured *contact zone* what these specific social change/recognition/ knowledges look like. I explore these ideas across several existing fault lines of controversy surrounding 'diversity, equity and inclusion' (or diversity, equity, accessibility and inclusion (DEAI) in museums; CCLI, 2020). The Cultural Competence Learning Institute (CCLI) argues that while museums do pay attention to DEAI, they

1. have not taken strategic, consistent action at an organizational level foundational for enduring equity and inclusion;
2. have not integrated DEAI into the core work;

3. focus less on the internal organizational dimensions of DEAI compared with public-facing aspects;
4. do not collect or use data; and
5. do use some DEAI-related practices.

(Adapted from CCLI, 2020)

Looking more globally, much has been written in larger sociopolitical arenas and especially in formal schooling about how our societies deal or do not deal with changing demographics (Sleeter, 1996), yet little has been written about *how museums* as a group can and do deal with changing demographics (Merritt, 2016, 2017). By relying both on current demographic data and on an increasing body of research scholarship focused on issues on equity and inclusion in museums (Ash, 2019; Dawson, 2014a, 2014b; Feinstein & Meshoulam, 2014; Garibay, 2009; Gurian, 1990,[9] 2014), as well as by examining ideological strongholds in museums, we may begin to answer the question, *Who will go to museums?*

Who Will Go to Museums?

Museums want visitor attendance numbers to mirror the racial composition of their communities (AAM, 2019), often framing such change in terms of seeking *diversity*. The term *diversity* has become overused and less meaningful, however (P. Moore, 2014; Merritt, 2019). Further, many argue that, even though diversity is important and measurable, without equity, justice and, ideally, decolonizing practices, diversity is mostly cosmetic. Diversity is not inclusion or equity, nor was it designed to be. Museums are actively shifting to other terms such as equity and social justice, inclusion and decolonizing (Lonetree, 2009; Merritt, 2017*)*. Museums include DEI (diversity, equity and inclusion) as part of their focus on this question (AAM, 2019), yet there are inconsistencies. Moving to DEI or DEAI organizationally only adds so much to the conversation. Merritt points out that "debate on definitions must not hinder progress" (Merritt, 2017, p. 8). However, this issue goes far beyond and much deeper than definitions.

Museums have not been clear about what true inclusion might mean (Jennings & Jones-Rizzi, 2017) in terms of internal restructuring/reculturing, power relationships (Dubin, 1999) or outreach relationships, even as they express the desire to do better in this regard (Dawson, 2014b; Gurian, 2020; Ng et al., 2017). Some efforts toward inclusion and equity have been met with criticisms concerning internal policies, such as half-measures, tokenism, poor hiring choices, insensitive staff, intransigent monied-class board members (Pogrebin, 2017), high entrance fees (see Chapter 4) and more in both academic research and popular press and blogs (Fota, 2019: Dawson, 2014a; *Decolonize This Place*; *Incluseum; Museums Are Not Neutral*).[10] Speaking sociopolitically, museums have also been critiqued for a reluctance to address equity and social justice, not just diversity (Dawson, 2014a; Moore, 2014); maintaining an underlying deficit bias in how nondominant visitors are viewed (Dawson, 2014a); avoiding core issues of belonging (Garibay, 2009; powell &

Menendian, 2017); and the reification of white European-American middle-class values. I examine some of these contradictions here, as well as in future chapters.

Certainly, many museums *are* beginning to reexamine traditional *norms*, especially notions of *deficit/othering* and *belonging* (Gorski, 2010; powell & Menendian, 2017)[11] and to work toward understanding equitable access, even as an ever-greater proportion of the population opts out of museum-going. Any unwillingness of museums to reexamine exclusionary ideologies, however, will make equity and inclusion almost impossible to achieve (Ash, 2018; Dawson, 2014a). Even without such restructuring, museums run the risk of seeing their 'normal' (white, middle-class, educated) patronage dwindle, and concurrently having fewer members of nondominant populations attending (Rodriguez, 2009).[12]

An increased understanding of the new mainstream is but a first step toward such reculturing (Black, 2015). I argue here, as elsewhere, that museums must reculture while still being enmeshed within the old systems. Such misalignments give rise to contradictions, such as the clash between status quo vs. structural change, and the deeper underlying differences informing them. CHAT is useful for analyzing contradictions between maintaining the status quo and becoming something new, which cannot be fully anticipated and is itself the product of dialectical logic and negotiation.

Who Is Expected to Change?

Most museums (and schools) expect visitors/learners to change, a process we have called assimilation to dominant forms of behavior, a normative *principle* (P. Moore, 2014, 2016; Dawson, 2014a; Jennings & Jones-Rizzi, 2017). Those in power define what *normative behavior* is or can be (and this changes with geographic, linguistic or other sociocultural factors), but, as Tchen (2005) argues, such normative *correctness* gets in the way of human needs and problems. The vignette at the beginning of this chapter is an example of the unwritten, but generally known, expectations of *normative* correctness for nontraditional visitors designed to inform *others* how to do things to match the behavior 'we' expect in a museum (Dawson, 2014b; P. Moore, 2014). As I noted in Chapter 1 this dominant expectation is ideologically deficient-laden as well as assimilationist[13] (Dawson, 2014a; Noorani, 2019). powell and Menendian (2017) argue that this kind of "assimilation seeks to erase the differences upon which othering is structured" (p. 16). By this we mean we expect *them* to become more like *us* and less like *themselves* (Noorani, 2019).

An interesting example of normative and assimilationist expectations in the museum world is provided by Dilenschneider's (2017) 'standard view' of the demographic challenge:

> If cultural organizations do not get better at *cultivating and converting* "nontraditional audiences" into regular attendees, these organizations…risk experiencing declining attendance and revenues.
>
> (para. 5; italics added)

The above comment is deeply deficit-laden. Feeling the need to *convert* visitors implies having the power to do so and that *they* require conversion in the first place. This particular aspect of deficit thinking is not uncommon in formal educational contexts (Apple, 2017; Gorski, 2010; Sleeter, 2004).

Such views have their roots in racism (Kendi, 2017), neoliberalism (Apple, 2017; Giroux, 2002), genderism, ableism, cultural and other power inequities. The so-called *melting pot analogy* is well known and accepted, as are so-called color-blind beliefs, both of which wash out differences from the temporally, geographically and socioculturally determined *norm*. Kendi (2019) has pointed out that 'anti-racist choices' can be made anywhere; we apply this maxim to museums, many of which were originally founded on racist principles and products:

> The museum's beginnings are inseparable from the story of Western colonialism and its racist ideologies.... As museums became public...they disowned this explicitly racist history, but continued to reinforce national identities and global racial hierarchies.
>
> (Leung, 2020, para. 5)

Moving beyond racial/cultural hierarchies toward anti-racism requires restructuring rather than 'quick fixes'. As Ng et al. (2017) noted, many so-called quick fixes address surface features but do not address core institutional issues of power, privilege, hierarchy or deficit orientation, despite mission statements with aspirations to diversity in many areas such as staff, visitors and administration.

The Giraffe and the Elephant

Jennings and Jones-Rizzi (2017) argued, "Whites are taught to think of their lives as morally neutral, normative, and average, and also ideal, so that when we work to benefit others, this is seen as work that will allow them to be more like us" (McIntosh, 1989, in Jennings & Jones-Rizzi, p. 4). Dilenschneider (2017) suggested that *they* (minoritized) *convert*. Any assimilationist view arises from the perspective of those in power, those who manage and maintain museums, not from the perspective of those who are **not yet** visiting museums and perhaps never will. The expectation is that minoritized visitors adapt themselves completely, rather than having the museum staff and materials (educators, curators administrators, boards, exhibit production and other written products) need to *reculture* their own frames of reference.

Below is a short parable of such assimilationist/deficit ideology in action, which helps us think about expectations of change in practical terms. The elephant and the giraffe parable was told in by Julie O'Mara (2014), coauthor of *Global Diversity & Inclusion Benchmarks*, in a professional development session on diversity:

> [A] giraffe...builds his home/business with his own needs in mind.... But when the giraffe hires an elephant...it gets stuck trying to get through the

skinny doors and can't climb the stairs without crushing them. The giraffe's solution is to suggest the elephant lose weight or go to ballet class to become more nimble in the skinny house.

(paraphrased in part) O'Mara, 2014)

The moral of the story, of course, is that

> we can't expect those who are different to adapt to our norms, ie "it is impossible for people to change, necessarily, to fit into an institution that is built for one type of people. [Instead…] we need to change our systems, our policies and literally our structures so that somebody for whom the house is not designed can come to work and fit [there]".
>
> (Sarubbi, 2014, para. 2–3)

In our opening vignette, the family was expected to know the rules of 'how to do exhibits' (Mai & Ash, 2012), as well as to first stand quietly and listen to the lecture, not interrupting or asking questions. We must therefore question who and what needs to change? This is especially true when inviting *them* to be part of the museum community. Moss (2013) argued critically about museum motivation:

> I sometimes wonder if some of the motivation behind the drive to diversify audiences for traditionally European art forms comes from a place of wanting to assimilate people of color so that we can all be one, big, happy family—on white people's terms.
>
> (p. 7)

Speaking more globally Ng et al. (2017) argued we must be more critical in examining "changes [that] appear to have resulted, for a variety of complex reasons, in surface rather than deep transformation" (p. 133). Deeper change looks different, as P. Moore argued:

> [M]inority visitors are [not] merely niche or annual visitors…[they are] long-term invested stakeholders with a unique set of values whose narratives are celebrated as [being] equally as important and complementary to the system of values which permeate the traditional white mainstream museum.
>
> (Moore, 2016)

Othering and Belonging

As we noted in the introductory vignette, one notable signal of exclusion—that is, of not belonging—is a visitor having to ask, "What are we supposed to do here?" For outsiders, it may seem that some unknown or secret code words are necessary before *being recognized* or *seen* as familiar (enough) with museums. Of course, from a larger sociocultural and political perspective, membership in the white middle class typically provides that signal. As Jennings and Jones-Rizzi (2017) noted, this issue of lack of signals may partially be a result of being part of a group

> who are not white, male, English-speaking, educated, heterosexual, or who have a disability or do not have class privilege or gender normative identities; it is often hard to find our voice within the majority of U.S. museums.
>
> (p. 4)

Other signals include asking the right kind of questions; touching exhibits in the right way; and talking with docents as expected (see Chapters 7 and 8 on learning and teaching). Powell and Menendian (2017) suggested viewing

> othering…[as] a broadly inclusive term…suggesting something fundamental or essential about the nature of group-based exclusion…
> "[B]elonging" connotes something fundamental about how groups are positioned within society…perceived and regarded. It reflects an objective position of power and resources as well as the intersubjective nature of group-based identities.
>
> (powell & Menendian, 2017, p. 17)

They suggested that "belongingness must be more than expressive; it must be institutionalized as well". In other words, changing surface language is not enough; day-to-day, institutionalized practices must echo *belonging* as the new norm. For example, Marci, the educator in the initial vignette, was putting into practice a belonging ideology by her soft entry and responsive scaffolding-oriented approach.

However, precisely because *belonging* seems like a simple term, we fail to imbue it with the sophistication it deserves. It could be oversimplified to merely mean greeting visitors or smiling. Another vignette capturing the sense of *not* belonging, offered by Bonnici (2019),[14] can help us experience the profound difference:

> While the exhibits at the children's museum were thoughtful and playful, somehow the experience left me feeling isolated and alone, like I didn't really belong. There weren't any signs…helping me figure out my role in this unfamiliar play environment, or pointing me to reflect on what the exhibits might teach. Looking around at the other groups of parents, I felt different from them; they seemed to have an understanding or secret code that I didn't have. As a relatively new parent and a first-time visitor to this kind of museum, I felt the familiar twinge of "otherness" from my own childhood in an immigrant family. I felt it especially after my daughter had a hard time taking turns and sharing with another child, leading to an awkward encounter with a parent. Ultimately, our visit ended with us sitting on a bench as I read her a book, an activity I knew well and felt comfortable doing, and then we left.
>
> (paras. 6–7)

The road from *othering* to *belonging* can be a rocky one, because belonging should not mean morphing from an elephant into a giraffe. As Bonnici noted, belonging is signaled subtly. Michelle Obama said it most simply in the Chapter 1 vignette:

> So I know that feeling of not *belonging* in a place like this. And today, as First Lady, I know how that feeling limits the horizons of far too many of our young people.
>
> (Durkin, 2015; italics added)

The giraffe parable, the Michelle Obama quote, the vignette and the Bonnici quote are all powerful examples of how the unwritten but generally known expectations of those in power reinforce the common expectations that nontraditional (*other, they*) visitors are expected to change in order to *belong* (AAM, 2019; Dawson, 2014b; P. Moore, 2014).

A different kind of narrative on belonging comes from the United Kingdom, a study of the Cornish people, who long for a sense of *belonging* to their own subculture:

> There is a network of small museums dotted around the Cornish landscape… helping to generate that much sought-after sense of *belonging* that locals and those that return are seeking.
>
> (Heal, 2015, para 4–5)

In this case, belonging involves 'what was' and might be disappearing. This kind of belonging is triggered by the loss of old cultural ways. We can compare this with the widespread movements in Europe for new migration/ethic museums to analyze "how to define Europe, Europeans, and European heritage, especially mindful of the region's colonial and migratory pasts". Modest et al. (2019) have discussed ethnographic museums that are "at the centre of ongoing debates about Europe's shifting polity and questions around heritage, citizenship and belonging". Core to their thinking is the notion that it "may exactly be in their entanglement with the colonial past that these museums can become important sites for thinking about colonial entailments in the present" Modest et al., 2019, p. 13).

Moreover, competing underlying ideologies make expansive transformation challenging to achieve without a deeper understanding of system dynamics. I will discuss this next.

Contradictions: Competing Ideologies

As always, I start with the primary contradiction, the dialectic between use and exchange value, which translates into terms of production and consumption within activity systems. This is not difficult to determine in museums, whose work includes maintaining and viewing (use) expensive collections, recruiting customers and charging for entry (exchange). One secondary contradiction concerns the conflict between the desire of museums (as noted in many mission statements) for increasing cultural, socioeconomic, linguistic and social visitor *diversity*, and the reluctance to perform the long-lasting reculturing/restructuring essential for accomplishing this goal.[15]

This, then, is one starting point for using CHAT. Here are two constituencies, the status quo and an outside community seeking to *decolonize this place* or seeking structural change in museums. I do not position them as a dualism; rather, I envision a dialectical relationship. I can use third-generation CHAT to position the two different ideological stances, the status quo vs.[16] substantive change, and to include that they have different desired outcomes (Object 1 and Object 2) and different mediational means to achieve them (as we saw in Figure 2.2). We represent this as two activity systems (triangle on left and right) attempting to negotiate a new common object (Object 3; see also Ash, 2014; Engeström, 1999; Foot, 2014; Foot & Groleau, 2011; Ward, 2016).

Here, the triangle on the left represents 'business as usual', understanding that business as usual means quick fixes, or partial reculturing efforts, typically assumes gradualism and more or less steady/continuous identity as an institution; its object/goal of activity is Object 1. The triangle on the right represents racial/gender and intersectional structural transformation, promoted perhaps by the many decolonizing efforts outside the museum, with the goal of more radical/structural change, Object 2, and perhaps even rebranding the institution entirely. Object 3 is the attempted new negotiated object. In our hypothetical scenario, there could be some overlap between constituencies but also considerable differences among community, rules, hierarchy and other aspects. One can imagine the level of negotiation needed to start the process.[17]

On the left we can place a community composed of upper-level administrators, vice presidents, board members and some outside funders (Gopnick, 2020), on the right perhaps some on-the-floor museum staff, community organizations and outside museum-related nonprofit and/or small government organizations proposing decolonizing (Lonetree, 2009, 2012), seeking board membership change (McCambridge, 2017) or at minimum, increased transparency. We cannot predict in advance how and where within the museum any radical transformation—that is, expansive learning might originate.

To accomplish praxis, by which we mean a common understanding of and actions toward a fully negotiated joint Object 3, we would need to examine how the core contradictions have informed other aspects of museum practice. We do this by critically examining tensions arising, for example, in boardroom negotiations, proposed financial cuts, mission statements, policies and strategies for teaching, as well as public relations.[18] These markers of day-to-day practices cut across levels of analysis, for example how money is allocated in department budgets and what normative actually means in a particular museum, as well as mission and public relations statements and more. I expand on these in Chapter 4, as I focus on finances.

Any negotiations concerning the mission and purpose of museums must include the impacts of neoliberalism, especially in issues related to production and consumption (Harrison et al., 2013; Roth et al., 2009) because museums are in the business of producing exhibitions, ideas and interpreting selected curated objects, histories and narratives for visitors to consume. In the classic representation, the second-generation activity triangle (Figure 2.2.) shows production in the uppermost triangles and consumption in the bottom triangle. We use this representation to examine these paired entities both in the CHAT (dialectical) sense and within the neoliberal philosophy, which supports the belief that 'everything is for sale'. Neoliberalism puts a heavy emphasis on exchange value, emphasizing the 'commodification of everything'. The two triangles in Figure 2.2 represent very different ideologies concerning value. Harvey argued that neoliberalism "presumes the existence of property rights over processes, things and social relations" (Harvey, 2005, p. 1)[19] and more generally a "consumption of goods and leisure…rather than materials and services" (McDonald et al., 2017, p. 3). Where do the two triangles locate themselves in this aspect of commodity?

If one adopts the consumer culture perspective, then the purpose of museum production is only for the consumption of goods and leisure; this is one neoliberal core belief represented on the left in Figure 2.2. The underlying epistemological sequelae of the neoliberal stance are quite apparent.

Equity and social justice aspects of decolonizing, then, are major aspects represented by the right triangle. These become diminished by consumer-take-all beliefs, as well as detrimental to the middle and lower classes, as the money 'flows up and not down' in a neoliberal economy (Harvey, 2005). Similarly, Ng et al. (2017) suggested,

> Within the museum field's recent emphasis on diversity and inclusion to create meaningful experiences for visitors, there remain problematic power dynamics that maintain white supremacy and re-inscribe disparities in privilege among museum workers and visitors.
>
> (p. 136)

This is exactly why we need the larger analysis such as in Figure 2.2, where we can represent deeper epistemological/ideological differences at work.

Placing this analysis in the larger context, Fernando argued, "What museums call 'neutral' is all part of a status quo system.… And that system perpetuates oppression, racism, injustice and colonialism" (Fernando, 2020, p. 1).

It's Not Only About the Numbers

Third-generation CHAT analysis makes it clear that the challenge is not simply a matter of changing visitor numbers, even though numbers are important.[20] Focusing on numbers, as I have already argued, encourages us to miss the long-term, deeply embedded, ideologically-bound, normative beliefs informing day-to-day policies and practices. Once we focus on the ideologies, it becomes clear that numbers are actually a reflection of deeper, larger conflicts, not the root cause. Demographics, then, are yet another *proxy* for dueling ideologies typically involving power, *othering* and *belonging* and *commodification*.

What we mean by *genuine racial/cultural/economic/educational inclusion* is an open question. John Kuo Wei Tchen has done a great deal to educate museum researchers and practitioners toward understanding and partnership with nondominant populations.

> I…bridle against forms of normative correctness—especially from the mainstream—that get in the way of addressing human needs and problems. Learning from the expertise of lived experience necessitates our engaging, especially with minoritized and marginalized knowledges.
>
> (Tchen, 2005, paras. 12–13)

Tchen and others insist there is much work to be done in changing the museum's climate from *othering* to *belonging*.

Critical Perspectives: Museums and Diversity

Jennings and Jones-Rizzi argued, "Changing the structure around language would require museums…to fundamentally change structures of power, authority, and value in words and in actions" (Jennings & Jones-Rizzi, 2017, p. 72). Just as the two activity triangles in Figure 2.2 differed markedly, we gain a sense of what all is involved in transformation, rules, hierarchy, larger community, tools and more. Speaking structurally, Ng et al have argued that only anti-oppressive museum education can enact social good and social change. They argued that

> without an anti-oppressive framework, museum education is at best upholding a vacant notion of diversity and at worst actively re-inscribing and perpetuating privilege by excluding or disempowering visitors with marginalized identities.
>
> (p. 136)

"Achieving a collective, community-based, power sharing, equity and inclusion as the standard" (B. Moore, 2013; Dawson, 2014a; Ash, 2019; Ng et al., 2017) requires *critical theory* perspectives that seek to uncover the underlying belief systems embedded in *othering*. This requires calling into question current language labels such as *multicultural, underrepresented, minority, culturally and linguistically diverse (CLD), marginalized, minoritized* or *nondominant*.[21]

Critical analysis allows us to examine discursive manifestations in a field in flux. For example, the words *diversity, equity* and *inclusion* often appear in tandem (Henderson, 2018), alongside the word *belonging* (Merritt, 2014), as part of museum mission statements. But what museums mean when they use the term *diversity* may be quite different than what is meant by those who write about social justice. Diversity means different things to different people. Does diversity imply we should make museums into assimilationist melting pots (AAM, 2018; ICOM, 2019)?

Museum scholar Porchia Moore discussed the term diversity with respect to museum inclusion:

> The truth is that I do not like the term "*diversity*" because I find it to be a racially coded term which exacts all sorts of confusing sentimentalities and hidden agendas.
>
> (Moore, 2014, paras. 8–9)

Reflecting ideological shifts more generally (Hajnal & Baldassare, 2001; Leonardo, 2003), the last few decades have seen terminology shift toward terms such as *minoritized*, *marginalized* or *nondominant* to reflect on the growing awareness of the lack of *power* experienced by 'diverse' populations. Phrases such as *CLD* assign specific criteria to 'diversity'. This struggle for precision may reflect that the internal renegotiation of structure has not occurred or, referring to Figure 2.2, Object 3, the jointly negotiated object is still under negotiation.

AAM's current president Elizabeth Merritt emphasized the word *inclusion* rather than *diversity*, suggesting that *inclusion* means change from the inside out:

> The inclusion gauntlet has been thrown before the museum field, but we are not building the necessary skills in our staff to meet the challenge. To sum up, the work related to *inclusion is more internal than it is external*.
>
> (Merritt, 2016, paras 2–3; italics added)

At the Cleveland Museum of Art[22] which has attempted internal change, inclusion has been defined as

> the confrontation of historical exclusion based on race, gender, sexual orientation, and economic status by bringing those affected into institutional activities and decision-making to address disparities, increase awareness, and foster understanding.
>
> (Henderson, 2018, paras. 9–10)

In contrast, past efforts to develop strategies for *diversity*, which have included developing new programs, hiring *outreach* coordinators, offering special exhibits, procuring special grants, diversifying boards, were predictably only partially successful (Ng et al., 2017). These seemingly loosely coupled *diversity* approaches often eventuated in isolated program efforts, such as Cinco de Mayo celebrations. These partial efforts avoided the essential and harder, but necessary, reculturing efforts across museum staff and boards and most importantly have often not included the external community in joint decision-making (Gurian, 2020; Jung, 2015; Lonetree, 2009).

Larger changes require sharing power. Ng et al. (2017) argued that more criticality and more rigor are needed "to reveal hidden problematic power dynamics that actually maintain the status quo" (p. 132). I will discuss power explicitly at the end of this chapter.

The Numbers: What Counts?

After a careful review of many different sites and situations, I can confidently argue that numbers alone, usually presented devoid of a larger context, are relatively uninformative. According to an international study published recently concerning theme parks, museums and other entertainment venues, Theme Index and Museum Index Report (TEA/AECOM, 2019), attendance, averaged over the top 20 museums in North America, was down 3% during 2017–2018, while in Europe, attendance, also averaged over the top 20 museums, was up 9%.[23] A modest 0.6% increase was noted in Asia's top 20. Many of Europe's largest and most popular museums, such as the Louvre, had visitor overflow. While the Louvre had a +25%+ increase between 2017 and 2018, the Van Gogh Museum decreased by almost 10%. The unevenness of these data is startling but quite typical of different museum types, geographies, age and surrounding population (see Table 3.1). We actually understand very little from these figures, which are pre-COVID.

To give but one small sample of how data can be used for different ends, we see that Jones (2017) reported that

> Britain's leading museums and galleries…have dramatically lost visitors. Museums including the Tate Gallery, National Gallery, V&A, and British Museum collectively clocked up 47.6 million people from April 2015 to March 2016—a significant fall from the previous year.

Jones' data (2015–2016) differs from the TEA/AECOM data (17–18), reporting −1.3% for the Tate, +9.7% National Gallery London and −4.8% British Museum.

TABLE 3.1 Theme Index and Museum Index Report (TEA/AECOM Report, 2019)

Continent	Average change 2017–2018	Sample change
North America	−3%	−15% Field Museum Chicago −20% Natural History Museum Washington +5.1% Metropolitan Museum of Art +19% California Science Center 0% American Museum of Natural History
Europe	+6.1 %	+25.9% Louvre −9% Van Gogh Museum −1.3% Tate +17% Natural History Museum London + 4.8% British Museum +9.7% National Gallery London
Asia-Pacific	+0.06 %	+17% Suzhou Museum −13% National Palace Museum Taiwan +11.5% National Gallery of Victoria −11.5% Tokyo National Museum +10.5 China Science Technology Museum

The gloom noted by Jones for 2015–2016 contrasts with the cautious optimism of 2017–2018 TEA/AECOM data. The Victoria and Albert Museum wasn't included in the TEA/AECOM Report data, and these two studies counted different years. So, if you read Jones, you are worried that Britain's art museums are in trouble, and if you read the TEA/AECOM Report, you are not. If you were to follow the data for several years, you might conclude there was an uptick between 2015 and 2018. Maybe and maybe not. The differences we see in tone and interpretation of numbers reflect the literature in the field; thus differences recorded over years and even decades are confusing.

It is no better in the United States. For example, the median art museum attendance from 2000 to 2010 went from 76,500 to 85,000 per thousand with a peak of 97,509 in 2005 (Statistica, 2020). While some have chosen to interpret this as an uptick, a careful analysis over the decade showed significant loss after 2005. Which aspect do we focus on? It turns out we typically use data that support the argument we are proposing. The Statistica model counts #/thousand, while the TEA/AECOM Report is in %, and Jones uses neither.

Rodney (2018) argued,[5]

> [T]he percentage of Americans visiting art museums and galleries has dropped by 21% since its peak.... In terms of audience size, art museums have lost 5 million visitors, while history has lost over 8 million visitors, since their respective peaks.
>
> (paras 6–7)

So, which is it, small loss, small gain, stay the same or yet another choice? Museum data collection and presentation are idiosyncratic at best, with little uniformity (Reach, 2013). When we ask if overall museum attendance is increasing, decreasing or static, the answer depends completely on who is counting, what and how, and where the counts are taken. The answer to that seemingly simple question depends on multiple factors such as geographical location (urban/rural), disciplinary topic (art, history, science), size, age, target audience or degree of endowment, among several other parameters we discuss in the following section.

Tensions and Emerging Contradictions

Next, I review several emerging secondary contradictions created by tensions between the various nodes of an activity system attempting to 'deal with' demographics in contemporary museums. I will delve deeper into secondary contradictions in subsequent chapters. Here I mention them as an introduction to the way they may present themselves. The emerging secondary contradictions possibly include:

1. Which data count?— Cherry-picking data vs. impartial
   To support specific, typically positive arguments (Reach Advisors, 2013) vs. a more uniform collection and analytic frame

a. tension between mediational means and object;
2. Creative attendance counting (or sausage making) vs. impartial
To enhance impact—(Simon, 2013) vs. a more uniform collection and analytic frame
   a. tension between mediational means and object;
3. Who does the counting? —Tokenism vs. transformation.
Role of museum boards (Diaz, 2019; Jennings & Jones-Rizzi, 2017; McCambridge, 2017)
   a. tension between division of labor and subjects;
4. Positioning the other—Diversity vs. intersectionality
(Callihan & Feldman, 2018; Gan et al., 2014).
   a. tension between rules and subjects.

Which Data Count?—Cherry-Picking Data vs. Impartial

Museum Audience Insights (2012) suggested that

> [m]useums have been willing to allow the field to pick the data trends they like, and push aside the harder facts that may not support proposed actions or that reflect poorly on them. It is difficult to obtain comprehensive museum attendance patterns; different museums and museum organizations *count* their visitors differently, and they routinely *cherry pick* what they report.
> (Museum Insights, 2012)

Cherry-picking data is an old strategy designed to help public relations efforts or allow particular programs to put their best foot forward. These are strategies most businesses might use, but if everything is 'positive', these numbers will dull possibilities of structural change.

Such numbers often leave out discussions of exactly who visits museums, or more to the point here, who does not visit museums. Also, cherry-picking reflects deficit thinking by not counting some visitors. Most troubling, cherry-picking is consistent with a neoliberal philosophy of consumerism and competition for museums as businesses. The field needs reliable statistics, however, not consumerist advertising. We position statistics as mediational means used to achieve a specific outcome.

Creative Attendance Counting (or Sausage Making) vs. Impartial

Nina Simon called juggling the numbers *Creative Counting* (Simon, 2013). She asked the question: *Who counts?: Grappling with attendance as a proxy for impact* and used the City of St. Louis museums to illustrate the ways *creative attendance counting* can work.

> St. Louis Post-Dispatch published the kind of "how sausage is made" story that rarely gets written about the arts. *It's about museum attendance and how the*

> *five big, free museums in St. Louis count it....* Summertime concerts at the history museum? Those count. Outdoor movies at the art museum? Nope. At the St. Louis Science Center...there was a particularly creative perspective...including numbers for offsite board meetings, parades where staff made a showing, and attendance at a school next door. The only form of engagement lacking in the article is online participation.... Small wonder the attendance picture is so muddled.
>
> (para. 7–8)

Just as there is no one way of counting, there is no way of generalizing what we mean by *attendance*. It is difficult to put forth a reculturing agenda if everything counts. What then eventuates is a maintenance of the status quo, the left activity triangle that we saw in Figure 2.2. Again, 'creative counting' is consistent with a neoliberal business philosophy of competition among museums. We position statistics as mediational means used to achieve a specific outcome.

Who Does the Counting?—Tokenism vs. Transformation.

We cannot just critique policies regarding counting. We must also critique, "Who does the counting?" Jennings and Jones-Rizzi (2017) claimed that in the ASTC-ACM 2011 Workforce Survey "with the exception of Directors of Human Resources, between 80% and 95% of directors and senior staff in U.S. children's museums and science centers are white....CEOs responding to the ASTC-ACM 2016 Workforce Survey self-identify as white and 96.8% self-identify as non-Hispanic" (Workforce Survey, p. 244, in Jennings & Jones-Rizzi, p. 6).

The inside of the museum is also skewed white. [24]

And Leading with Intent (2017) reported,

> The demographic profile of museum board members reveals considerable ethnic and racial homogeneity along with minimal age diversity. Board composition is tipped to white, older males—more so than at other nonprofit organizations. Forty-six percent...of museum boards are all white, compared to 30 percent of nonprofit boards.
>
> (paras 3–14)

Quite recently, we have seen pushback as black trustees join forces to make art museums more diverse (Pogrebin, 2020). Warren Kanders, President of the Ford Foundation, argued "everything that moves an institution forward, or holds it back, can be traced to its board... boards need to stop seeing diversity as subtracting from their annual revenue, but rather as adding strength...[and] museum boards must move from tokenism to transformation" (Diaz, 2019, paras 2–4). The numbers have increased but so too has the criticism (McCambridge, 2017; Pogrebin, 2017). The secondary contradiction reflects the tension between the division of labor and subjects.

Positioning the Other—*From Diversity to Intersectionality*

While intersectionality has also become increasingly recognized as important in educational systems such as museums, museums seem stuck in paying lip service to diversity (Diaz, 2019; Merritt, 2016; P. Moore, 2014). "Museum professionals have long grappled with the problems of identity-based exclusion within museum exhibits, programs, and collections" Robert (2014, p, 23). Robert (2014) noted that the approach museums have taken has been additive and fractional—focusing on a single identity, such as black, female or disabled; she argued this is inadequate, that we need *intersectional thinking, a person can be all three*:

> The very idea that identities do not operate alone but intersect with each other in dynamic and complex ways—that identities are intersectional—presents new possibilities for solving the challenges of identity-based inclusion.
> (Robert, 2014, p. 25)

Arguing that intersectionality can't wait, Crenshaw (2015) said,

> Racial and gender discrimination overlapped not only in the workplace... equally significant, these burdens were almost completely absent from feminist and anti-racist advocacy.
> (para. 2)[25]

Thinking intersectionally is important at all levels of museum function, administration, staff and visitors. Bringing this closer to museums, Callihan and Feldman (2018) have suggested,

> Gender inequity has affected museums for as long as these institutions have existed. While it seems true that museums now have many women on staff, they are often in less powerful positions, and if they are Directors they make a smaller comparable salary. Thus, increased representation of women in the workplace over the past 50 years has not brought about large scale change in upper echelons.
> (p. 6)

In art museums, for example,

> women hold less than 50% of directorships, and the average female director's salary lags behind that of the average male director. The overall disparities... are mostly driven by the largest museums.
> (Gan et al., 2014, p. 3)

Callihan and Feldman (2018), Jennings and Jones-Rizzi (2017) and Turner (2002) have all argued that it is not only women but women of color and other gender minorities that lack power. Despite the fact that white women now dominate many areas of the museum, like education departments, women of color are not equally represented, and there are continued gaps in compensation and access to power for women and gender minorities across race and ability (Callihan & Feldman, 2018, p. 180).

Robert concluded that we must reflect "critically and intersectionally on the… systems museum professionals employ…[and] develop conscious understanding of the organizing structures that create marginalization and exclusion" (2014, p. 32). This lack of vision or expansion maintains museums' hierarchical systems. I have preliminarily positioned this tension between rules and subjects.

Power

The issues we have discussed in this chapter reflect power relationships that manifest in museums in different ways, sometimes visibly and often invisibly. Many museum specialists have addressed the issue of power in museums (Bennett, 2018; Anderson, 2004; Dubin, 2014; Golding, 2013; Macdonald, 2006). There is no consensus among them. Power is strongly enmeshed with neoliberalism and *othering/deficit* views and the Structure Agency Dialectic. Power and inequality may be hard to 'spot and reconcile' because they lurk beneath the *norms*, those nuanced, less visible and 'taken-for-granted' aspects of modern museum functioning.

Examples from the past of so-called power in action include "a nineteenth-century cleric [who] could believe that paintings had the power to civilise his community of London's poorest", (Bennett, 2018, p. 169) or Dilenschneider's (2017) call 'to convert' *them*.

These expressions of the power of assimilation are pervasive. Chapter 2 discussed the Native American population in Valdez (VNT), whose fishing-based economy had been rendered powerless in the face of environmental disaster. Those Native American communities had very serious concerns yet lacked collective agency and power over the spill and the way it has been interpreted. Dailey (2006) pointed out that "museum professionals also no longer feel a sense of personal agency, but instead demonstrate feelings of being 'controlled by the market'" (p. 3).

Using structure/agency dynamics, researchers could differentiate whether individuals or groups of individuals do or do not have the power to affect personal and collective structural transformation in specific circumstances. Using CHAT's concept of 'transformative agency', one can identify disturbances, conflicts and contradictions in the activity system (Haapasaari et al., 2014).

Most of these examples of diminished power promote and protect neoliberal values of competition and individualism (Apple, 2017), with concomitant *deficit/other* orientations of winner and losers (Danilova, 2014). Third-generation activity theory (Figure 2.2) can facilitate the dissection of power relationships more directly, particularly involving challenges to hierarchical standing as we noted earlier, for example, between boards and staff, and also between more than one activity system.[26] Karp et al. (1992) noted that "the selection and presentation of ideas, images and information can only take place within a context that imparts its own messages about power" (p. 1). For example, what "selection and presentation of ideas, images and information" are we presenting if we act "as if" certain people don't' "belong", if they don't assimilate, or if we cherry-pick the numbers to look good?

Beyond ideologies or theoretical orientations, manifestations of power are intertwined with all everyday aspects of 'doing museums'. One place to observe them is in the institutionally approved teaching practices for museum educators (volunteer or paid), curator design and interpretation practices, exhibit design, fundraising and public relations.

Power is overtly and covertly expressed, for example, in the selective use of an authoritative voice. Deficit discursive traces reveal bias, for example, when an educator argues that the visitors are *doing the exhibit wrong*, or an exhibit designer suggests that an object *speaks for itself*, when designers are reluctant to 'dumb down' or a high-level administrator argues that if *visitors don't pay, they don't appreciate their experience* (Giuliano, 2008).

Lastly, power for decisions at the top has gone awry. Whenever top administration and the board of directors have not agreed, typically, the director is fired or asked to resign. The most glaring example, in New York, involved the director of the Metropolitan Museum of Art, the largest museum in the United States.

> Thomas P. Campbell resigned under pressure on Tuesday as the director and chief executive of the Metropolitan Museum of Art, after months of growing concerns among staff members and some trustees about its financial health and his capacity to lead the largest museum in the country.
>
> (Pogrebin, 2017)

In this case, the Met Board, especially CFO and the director disagreed. It was argued in the popular press and by groups wishing structural change that the board bore responsibility as well.[27]

I discuss financial issues in more detail in Chapter 4. It is important to remember that people outside the museum share an interest in museum policy, practice, culture and history, and very actively promote the cause of change, often framed as decolonizing. These deserve a place at the board table. I consider both external and internal communities in each of the following chapters.

Summary

Demographic projections should not distract us from delving deeper into clashes of normed ideologies/epistemologies. Numbers can be a distraction; therefore, we need to understand how they are generated and what they actually mean in order to confidently use them or challenge them. I use the elephant and the giraffe parable to illustrate assimilationist/deficit ideology in action, which helps us think about expectations of change in practical terms.

I argue for using "CHAT to identify power dynamics 'as CHAT challenges individual oriented theories of agency' (Engeström, 2006), [and] develops a picture of participants' joint activity and explicates and envisions new possibilities for collective activity" (Haapasaari et al., 2014)

Museums have become more cognizant of some of the most intractable problems, yet often use quick fixes or tweaks at staff levels rather than creating structural change. Structural change is mirrored in CHAT methodology. Using CHAT helps researchers make the case that real expansive learning must involve all levels of the staff at a museum, from ticket takers and parking lot attendants to executive director, CFO and board members.

Appendix 3.1: Museum Social Media That Regularly Address Issues of Race, Equity, Social Justice

Artsblog

The blog of Americans for the Arts, features posts on a variety of arts topics written by leading field experts…a curated space for our staff, members, stakeholders and constituents to share and learn from each other …from Arts Education to Public Art to Community Engagement through the arts and more.

https://blog.americansforthearts.org/2019/05/15/expanding-equity-diversity-and-inclusion-in-museums-through-teen-programming

Beautiful Trouble

A book, web toolbox and international network of artist-activist trainers. An international network of artist-activist-trainers helping grassroots movements become more creative and effective.

https://www.beautifultrouble.org/

Decolonize This Place

A movement based in New York City that organizes around Indigenous rights, black liberation, Palestinian nationalism, de-gentrification and encourages a sharp resurgence of social movements, within which artists and cultural workers are playing leading roles. Land, air, and water are central to decolonization.

https://decolonizethisplace.org/

Empathetic Museum

Maturity Model and diagnostic tools for organizational change across five dimensions: civic vision, institutional body language, community resonance, timeliness and sustainability and performance measures. Visitor-centered, Civic-minded, Diverse. Inclusive, Welcoming, Responsive, Participatory.

http://empatheticmuseum.weebly.com/

GEMM Gender Equity in Museums Movement

The Gender Equity in Museums Movement (GEMM) is a coalition of individuals and organizations committed to raising awareness, affecting change, and championing transparency about intersectional gender equity in the museum workplace

https://www.genderequitymuseums.com/blog-1/archive/2020/04

Gurian website—Elaine Hermann

Elaine is a consultant/adviser to museums that are beginning, building or reinventing themselves, writer and lecturer to many museum studies programs worldwide. She has written *Civilizing the Museum* and many other works.

http://www.egurian.com/

Incluseum

The Incluseum advances new ways of being a museum through critical dialogue, community building and collaborative practice related to inclusion in museums.

https://incluseum.com/

Sample resource—(Re)Frame: The Case for New Language in the 21st Century Museum (2016).

Museums strive to be welcoming places, but the ways museums communicate can inadvertently exclude and alienate visitors. Words have the power to reinforce or negate the social value of museums.

MASS Action: Museum as Site for Social Action

MASS Action, in collaboration with stakeholders across the field, is creating a platform for public dialogues on a variety of topics and issues affecting our communities locally and globally, leading to actionable practices for greater equity and inclusion in our institutions.

https://www.museumaction.org/

MASS Action Toolkit

A compilation of theory, procedures and best practices to create greater equity within the museum field, as well as diagnostic tools to help organizations gauge their readiness for equity work.

https://www.museumaction.org/resources

Museum 2.0

Museum 2.0 is authored by Seema Rao. Her work has mostly been at the edge of experience, inclusion, and technology. From 2006 to 2019, Museum 2.0 was authored by Nina Simon.

http://museumtwo.blogspot.com/

Museums Are Not Neutral

Global advocacy campaign aimed at exposing the myth of museum neutrality and calling for equity-based transformation across museums. Museums can be agents of social change in our communities, and it's up to us to make this happen together.

https://www.museumsarenotneutral.com/

Museum Commons—Gretchen Jennings

This site is intended to be a place of agonistic discussion. A place where differing ideas are considered by equals, and where a serving of disagreement may be considered nourishing

https://museumcommons.com/about-gretchen

Museum Hue

Resources and networking with a focus on community, culture and careers for museum professionals of **color**. Museum Hue is…dedicated to advancing Black, Indigenous, and other POC in the cultural field.

https://www.museumhue.com/

Museums & Race—Transformation and Justice

A movement to challenge and reimagine institutional policies and systems that perpetuate oppression in museums.

https://museumsandrace.org/

The Museums & Race report card.

https://museumsandrace.org/2021/06/09/museums-and-race-report-card-2021-remix/

Project Implicit

Includes implicit bias tests for Blacks, Native Americans, Asian Americans and Arab Muslims, as well as other demographics.

https://implicit.harvard.edu/implicit/selectatest.html

From Jennings and Jones-Rizzi (2017, 2020) and other public sources

Appendix 3.2: The Sciences

We will briefly discuss science museums as a comparison to arts museums. In England, visits to science museums 2008–2019 increased from 4,282 to 5,210 per thousand. These numbers, which match population increase, are encouraging (Statistica, 2020). No differentiation in this data was made by size of museums as does the ASTC. Note that counting there is #/thousand people.

Using yet another form of attendance reporting, ASTC notes that 56% of science center and museum members from 2002 to 2011 had increased attendance. Can we, therefore, surmise that 44% had decreased or static attendance levels. ASTC stated,

> An estimated 73 million visits were made to ASTC's 394 science center and museum members in the United States. [The] median on-site attendance at individual centers was 216,250, with 55.9% of centers reporting an increase over the previous year.
>
> (ASTC, 2013)

When attendance was examined over a ten-year period, however, ASTC reported, "Large centers (> 50,000 square feet of interior exhibit space) had the flattest trend with 2011 median attendance being only 2% higher than 2002" (Russo, 2012). Here reporting was based on the size of the institution.

James Chung, president of Reach Advisors, suggested one reason for a downturn in science museum visitorship:

> The percentage of families with children, who are often science centers' primary audiences, is decreasing in the United States. (currently, more households have more dogs than children)
>
> (Wilkening & Chung, 2009)

And, as in art museums, as we include the more recent international studies, the science museum picture is mixed, both in the United States and in Europe, and inconsistent across categories.

Appendix 3.3: Delpit's "Culture of Power" (1988)

We use Delpit's now more than 30-year-old (1988) analysis of the "culture of power", which critiques both neoliberalist and deficit ideologies by focusing on these aspects: (1) issues of power are enacted in classrooms, or in this case museums; (2) there are rules for participating in power; (3) the rules for participation are a reflection of the rules of the culture in power; (4) those that are not already participants in the culture of power have an easier time acquiring power when explicitly told the rules of the culture; and (5) those with power are the least aware of or the least willing to acknowledge the existence of the power differential, while those with less power are frequently the most aware of the power differential (Delpit, 1988). This taxonomy is fully relevant today.

Appendix 3.4: Levels of Racism

Interpersonal racism *occurs between individuals. These are public expressions of racism, often involving slurs, biases or hateful words or actions.*

Institutional racism occurs in an organization. These are discriminatory treatments, unfair policies, or biased practices based on race that result in inequitable outcomes for whites over POC and extend considerably beyond prejudice. These institutional policies often never mention any racial group, but the intent is to create advantages, for some at the expense of others.

Structural racism is the overarching system of racial bias across institutions and society. These systems give privileges to white people resulting in disadvantages to POC (University of Calgary, 2021).

Notes

1 Part of the research intervention described in Chapter 8.
2 There is an ongoing debate among museum scholars, cultural theorists, government officials and officers in think tanks around the idea of museums being "instrumentalized", which has to do with museums being expected to address policy objectives that have historically existed outside museums—such as propelling innovation (Rodney, 2018).
3 AAM, CFM, ASTC, etc.
4 In their new book, Bevan and Ramos (2021) use theories of social justice, critical pedagogy, culturally relevant pedagogy, critical race theory and others to consider how the museum's dominant cultural structures and norms collide with museum professionals' aspirations for inclusive practices.
5 According to Bingham (2019) using Polaris data for the US…museums are successful at attracting audiences between the ages of 35 and 44 (there was a 16% increase in visitors between 35 and 44 and a 23% decrease in visitors between the ages of 18 to 24 compared to the national average), households with incomes above $200k, and families with one child. On the other hand, they are not attracting young audiences between the ages of 18 and 24, households with incomes below $75k, and larger families with three or more kids. No other demographic, such as race, was included. Interestingly this study, which uses tracking data, does not identify categories for cultural or ethnic origins, thus calling the data into question overall.
6 See also Migration in Museums: Narratives of Diversity in Europe, Network Migration In Europe (http://www.network-migration.org/pr_migration_museum_eng.php)
7 Overall, attendance had declined from 26.5% in 2002 to 23.7% in 2017 but has been picking up since 2012.
8 In 1997, Professor James Clifford proposed the idea of 'museums as contact zones' where different cultures come into contact and collaborate in [an] attempt to create a museum environment conducive to discussion and understanding (Marciano, 2014).
9 From the Gurian website: Turning the Ocean Liner Slowly (1990): "Politically it was a much more optimistic liberal political time then (1990) than now as I upload this paper (2015). The world seems to be universally turning toward the right with power going unevenly to the rich and privileged" (p. 1).
10 See Addendum 3.1.
11 A clarifying frame that reveals a set of common processes and conditions that propagates group-based inequality and marginality (powell & Menendian, 2017, p. 17).
12 The upcoming non-Caucasian majority, the *new mainstream* (Rodriguez, 2009), or the minority majority, in the United Stated, for example, will be a mixed group of cultures, ethnicities and backgrounds, rather than a unified monolith, as it is sometimes portrayed (Rodriguez, 2009).
13 Assimilationism is *normal* in 2020 sociopolitical contexts (Gorski, 2010; Sleeter, 2004), as immigrants are expected to assimilate in order to succeed.
14 Bonnici (2019) noted three aspects of (not) belonging that need to change:

   1. Not seeing yourself, your family or your values reflected in the staff, activities or values of the organization;
   2. Being in spaces with unstated behavior and/or learning
   3. Expectations rooted in dominant culture; and
   4. Having to share low-income status out loud (aka poverty shaming).

15 See Gurian, 1995.
16 Where status quo means slow change.
17 Engeström has been conducting such real-world research for decades; his focus is the Change Lab (1999).
18 These activities may change as museums consider "what '*new-to museum*' consumers may want" and how we might know this information.
19 Which on a personal level includes a shifting self-identity (McDonald et al., 2017).
20 Moore (2014) noted, "[P]roblems concerning communication, normed expectations and cultural conflict can easily overshadow good intentions" (paras 4–5).
21 Others suggesting critical analysis of museum practice have suggested these aspects:

- a critical stance toward old assumptions and ways of working (Ross, 2004)
- critical, self-reflexive and radical reexamination of museums (MacDonald, 2006)
- sustained reflexivity and rigorous deconstruction of museum practice (Shelton, 2013)
- a scientific and academic discipline for the critical and theoretical examination of the museal field
- assist museum workers to become more critical thinkers and moral practitioners, permitting taking control of the future (Teather & Carter, 2009, p. 28–30, adapted from Thistle, 2018, (para. 1).

22 Meanwhile, the Museum of Contemporary Art in Cleveland has had race-related controversies surrounding its board, a new exhibition concerning race and the police, and its internal practices (Litt, 2021)
23 Temporary exhibitions and geopolitical changes continue to serve as key attendance drivers for museums in Europe, the global market leader.
24 Jennings and Jones-Rizzi also presented these combined data regarding four museum associations based in the United States (AAM, ASTC, ACM, CAM and American Association for State and Local History):

- About 12% to 30% of U.S. members of the boards of directors of major U.S.-based museum associations come from minority backgrounds.
- Executive staff and senior leadership at our major museum associations are between 0% and 20% minority. (p. 7)

25 Crenshaw says opportunities are missed when we ignore intersectionality, which "highlight[s] the multiple avenues through which racial and gender oppression were experienced so that the problems would be easier to discuss and understand" (para 4).
26 Differentiating the vertical and horizontal dynamics is an important task, as they are sometimes intermixed (teams, for example); the power inherent in each level matters.
27 The board backed Mr. Campbell's decision to take on a temporary expansion into the Met Breuer. The board also approved Mr. Campbell's efforts to bulk up the museum's digital staff. Clearly then, there are serious contradictions at the top level that impact all the other levels.

References

Ash, D., & Lombana, J. (2019). The reflects model of action: Reflective practice for collaborating with non-dominant populations. In L. Martin, L. U. Tran, & D. Ash (Eds.), *The reflective museum practitioner*. Routledge.

American Alliance of Museums. (2018). *Facing change: Insights from the American Alliance of Museums' Diversity, Equity, Accessibility, and Inclusion Working Group*. https://www.aam-us.org/wp-content/uploads/2018/04/AAM-DEAI-Working-Group-Full-Report-2018.pdf

American Association of Museums. (2019). *Belonging: Co-creating welcoming and equitable museum*. https://www.aam-us.org/2019/11/22/belonging-co-creating-welcoming-and-equitable-museums/

Anderson, G. (2004). *Reinventing the museum: The evolving conversation on the paradigm shift*. Alta Mira Press.

Apple, M. W. (Ed.). (2017). *Cultural and economic reproduction in education: Essays on class, ideology and the state* (Vol. 53). Routledge.

Ash, D. (2014). Positioning informal learning research in museums within activity theory: From theory to practice and back again. *Curator: The Museum Journal, 57*(1), 107–118.

Ash, D. (2018). Cultural conflict: The stories dioramas tell and don't tell. In A. Scheersoi & S. D. Tunnicliffe (Eds.), *Natural history dioramas – Traditional exhibits for current educational themes: Socio-cultural aspects* (pp. 113–130). Springer International Publishing.

Ash, D. (2019). Reflective practice in action research: Moving beyond the "standard model". In L. Martin, L. Tran, & D. Ash (Eds.), *The reflective museum practitioner: Expanding practice in science museums* (pp. 23–38). Routledge. https://doi.org/10.4324/9780429025242-3

Association of Science and Technology Centers. (2013). *2013 Science Center and Museum Statistics*. ASTC. http://www.astc.org/wp-content/uploads/2014/10/2013-Science-Center-Statistics.pdf

Bell, P., Lewenstein, B., Shouse, A. W., & Feder, M. A. (Eds.). (2009). *Learning science in informal environments: People, places, and pursuits*. The National Academies Press.

Bennett, T. (2018). *Museums, power and knowledge: Selected essays*. Routledge.

Bevan, B., & Ramos, B. (Eds.). (2021). *Theorizing equity in the museum integrating perspectives from research and practice*. Routledge.

Bingham, G. (2019, August 19). Are museums still relevant in the digital age? *Ubimo*. https://www.ubimo.com/blog/articles-and-research/museum-attendance-by-visitor-demographics/

Black, G. (2015). Developing audiences for the twenty-first-century museum. *The International Handbooks of Museum Studies*, 123–151. doi:10.1002/9781118829059.wbihms990

Boast, R. (2011). NEOCOLONIAL COLLABORATION: Museum as contact zone revisited. *Museum Anthropology, 34*(1), 56–70. https://doi.org/10.1111/j.1548-1379.2010.01107.x

Bonnici, S. (2019, December 4). *Belonging: Co-creating welcoming and equitable museums*. American Alliance of Museums. https://www.aam-us.org/2019/11/22/belonging-co-creating-welcoming-and-equitable-museums/

California Association of Museums (n.d.). *About CAM*. https://www.calmuseums.org/Public/ABOUT/About/About-CAM/Public/About/About_Us/About.aspx?hkey=cfd1f4e1-8bd0-4b3d-a953-62011df31750.

Callihan, E., & Feldman, K. (2018). Presence and power: Beyond feminism in museums. *Journal of Museum Education, 43*(3), 179–192. doi:10.1080/10598650.2018.1486138

Center for the Future of Museums. (2010). *Demographic transformation and the future of museums*. American Alliance of Museums. https://www.aam-us.org/wp-content/uploads/2017/12/Demographic-Change-and-the-Future-of-Museums.pdf

Center for the Future of Museums. (2014). *TrendsWatch 2014*. American Alliance of Museums. https://www.aam-us.org/wp-content/uploads/2017/12/2014_trendswatch.pdf

Chung, J., & Wilkening, S. (2008). *Museums & society 2034: Trends and potential futures*. Center for the Future of Museums. https://www.aam-us.org/wp-content/uploads/2017/12/Museums-Society-2034-Trends-and-Potential-Futures.pdf

CMA, Cleveland Museum of Art. (2014). *Diversity, equity and inclusion plan.* https://www.clevelandart.org/diversity-equity-and-inclusion-plan

Crenshaw, K. W. (2015 September 24). Opinion: Why intersectionality can't wait. *The Washington Post.* https://www.washingtonpost.com/news/in-theory/wp/2015/09/24/why-intersectionality-cant-wait/

Dailey, T. L. (2006). *Museums in the age of neoliberalism: A multi-sited analysis of science and health museums* [Master's thesis, Georgia State University]. ScholarWorks. https://scholarworks.gsu.edu/anthro_theses/20

Danilova, E. (2014). Neoliberal hegemony and narratives of "losers" and "winners" in postsocialist transformation. *Journal of Narrative Theory, 44*(3), 442–466.

Dawson, E. (2014a). "Not designed for us": How science museums and science centers socially exclude low-income, minority ethnic groups. *Science Education, 98*(6), 981–1008. https://doi.org/10.1002/sce.21133

Dawson, E. (2014b). Equity in informal science education: Developing an access and equity framework for science museums and science centres. *Studies in Science Education, 50*(2), 209–247. https://doi.org/10.1080/03057267.2014.957558

Dawson, E. (2019). *Equity, exclusion and everyday science learning: The experiences of minoritised groups.* Abingdon, Oxon: Routledge.

Delpit, L. D. (1988). The silenced dialogue: Power and pedagogy in educating other people's children. *Harvard Educational Review, 58,* 280–299.

Diaz, C. G. (2019, October). Museum boards must move from tokenism to transformation that only meaningful inclusion can bring. *Grantmakers in the Arts.* https://www.giarts.org/blog/carmen-graciela-diaz/museum-boards-must-move-tokenism-transformation-only-meaningful-inclusion

Dilenschneider, C. (2017). *The key to reaching new audiences for cultural organizations.* Colleen Dilenschneider. https://www.colleendilen.com/2017/11/15/reach-likely-visitors-not-attending-cultural-organizations-data/

Doering, Z. (1995). *Who attends our cultural institutions? A progress report.* Smithsonian Institution Marketing Study.

Dubin, S. (1999). *Displays of power: Memory and amnesia in the American Museum.* New York University Press.

Dubin, S. (2014). *Displays of power: Memory and amnesia in the American Museum.* New York University Press.

Durkin, E. (2015, April 30). Michelle Obama urges cultural institutions to provide free access to children in struggling communities. *Daily News.* http://www.nydailynews.com/news/politics/michelle-obama-urges-museums-kids-free-article-1.2205987

Engeström, Y. (1999). Innovative learning in work teams: Analysing cycles of knowledge creation in practice. In Y. Engeström et al. (Eds.), *Perspectives on activity theory* (pp. 377–406). Cambridge University Press.

Engeström, Y. (2006). Activity theory and expansive design. In S. Bagnara & G. Crampton Smith (Eds.), *Theories and practice in interaction design: Interaction design* (pp. 3–25). Lawrence Erlbaum.

Feinstein, N. W., & Meshoulam, D. (2014). Science for what public? Addressing equity in American science museums and science centers. *Journal of Research in Science Teaching, 51*(3), 368–394. https://doi.org/10.1002/tea.21130

Fernando, C. (2020, November 6). *Museums face calls to better represent people of color.* PBS. https://www.pbs.org/newshour/arts/museums-face-calls-to-better-represent-people-of-color.

Foot, K., & Groleau, C. (2011). Contradictions, transitions, and materiality in organizing processes: An activity theory perspective, *First Monday, 16*(6), doi:10.5210/fm.v16i6.3479

Foot, K. A. (2014). Cultural-historical activity theory: Exploring a theory to inform practice and research. *Journal of Human Behavior in the Social Environment, 24*(3), 329–347. doi:10.1080/10911359.2013.831011

Fota, A. (2019, December 20). What's wrong with this diorama? You can read all about it. *New York Times.* https://www.nytimes.com/2019/03/20/arts/design/natural-history-museum-diorama.html

Gan, A. M., Voss, Z. G., Phillips, L., Anagnos, C., & Wade, A. D. (2014). *The gender gap in art museum directorships.* AAMD. https://aamd.org/sites/default/files/document/The%20Gender%20Gap%20in%20Art%20Museum%20Directorships_0.pdf

Garibay, C. (2009). Latinos, leisure values, and decisions: Implications for informal science learning and engagement. *The Informal Learning Review, 94,* 10–13.

Giroux, H. A. (2002). Neoliberalism, corporate culture, and the promise of higher education: The university as a democratic public space. *Harvard Education Review, 72*(4), 425–464.

Giuliano, C. (2008, January 24), *Philippe de Montebello: Museums why should we care.* https://www.berkshirefinearts.com/01-24-2008_philippe-de-montebello-museums-why-should-we-care.htm

Golding, V. (2013). Collaborative museums: Curators, communities, collections. In V. Golding & W. Modest (Eds.), *Museums and communities: Curators, collections, collaboration* (pp. 13–31). Bloomsbury.

Gopnick, B. (2020, December 31). Museums had better not be planning for a return to the status quo' the. *The Art Newspaper.* https://www.theartnewspaper.com/comment/make-these-meaningful-visits-enduring-ones

Gorski, P. (2010). *Unlearning deficit ideology and the scornful gaze: Thoughts on authenticating the class discourse in education.* EdChange. http://www.edchange.org/publications/deficit-ideology-scornful-gaze.pdf

Gurian, E. (1990). *Turning the ocean liner around slowly: A paper about institutional change.* http://www.egurian.com/omnium-gatherum/museum-issues/community/accessibility/turning-the-ocean-liner-slowly

Gurian, E. H. (1995). *Institutional trauma: Major change in museums and its effect on staff.* American Association of Museums.

Gurian, E. H. (2005). Threshold fear. In S. MacLeod (Ed.), *Reshaping museum space: Architecture, design, exhibitions* (pp. 203–214). Routledge.

Gurian, E. H. (2006). *Civilizing the museum: The collected writings of Elaine Heumann Gurian.* Taylor & Francis.

Gurian, E. H. (2014). Intention civility. *Curator, 57*(4), 473–484.

Gurian, E. H. (2020). Curator: From soloist to impresario. In C. Fiona & L. Kelly (Eds.), *Hot topics, public culture, museums* (pp. 95–111). Cambridge Scholars Publishing.

Haapasaari, A., Engeström, Y., & Kerosuo, H. (2014). The emergence of learners' transformative agency in a Change Laboratory intervention. *Journal of Education and Work, 29*(2), 232–262. https://doi.org/10.1080/13639080.2014.900168

Hajnal, Z., & Baldassare, M. (2001). *Finding common ground: Racial and ethnic attitudes in California.* Public Policy Institute of California.

Harrison, R., Byrne, S., & Clarke, A. (2013). *Reassembling the collection: Ethnographic museums and indigenous agency.* SAR, School for Advanced Research Press.

Harvey, D. (2005). *A brief history of neoliberalism.* Oxford University Press.

Heal, S. (2015). Sharon Heal on the crisis facing regional museums in the UK. *Apollo, 181*(631). Gale Academic OneFile. https://go.gale.com/ps/i.do?id=GALE%7CA414692136&sid=googleScholar&v=2.1&it=r&linkaccess=abs&issn=00036536&p=AONE&sw=w

Henderson, A. F. (2018, August 29). *How one museum is tackling its diversity and equity challenges.* NextCity. https://nextcity.org/daily/entry/how-one-museum-is-tackling-its-diversity-and-equity-challenges

Hooper-Greenhill, E. (2000). Changing values in the art museum: Rethinking communication and learning. *International Journal of Heritage Studies, 6*(1), 9–31. https://doi.org/10.1080/135272500363715

Horrigan, J. B. (2006, November 20). *The internet as a resource for news and information about Science.* Pew Research Center: Internet, Science & Tech. https://www.pewresearch.org/internet/2006/11/20/the-internet-as-a-resource-for-news-and-information-about-science/.

International Council of Museums. (2019, September 1–7). Museums as cultural hubs: The future of tradition. *25th ICOM General Conference*, Kyoto, Japan. https://icom.museum/wp-content/uploads/2020/03/EN_ICOM2019_FinalReport_200318_website.pdf

Jenkins, T. (2016, October 19). *Politics are on exhibit at migration museums, not history.* Foreign Policy. https://foreignpolicy.com/2016/10/19/can-curators-stop-marine-le-pen-migration-museums-europe/.

Jennings, G., & Jones-Rizzi, J. (2017). Museums, white privilege, and diversity: A systemic perspective. *Dimensions, 18*(5), 66–67.

Jones, J. (2017, February 2). The drop in museum visitors reveals a nation without aspiration or hope. *The Guardian.* https://www.theguardian.com/artanddesign/jonathanjonesblog/2017/feb/02/drop-uk-museum-attendance

Jung, Y. (2015). Harlem on my mind: A Step toward promoting cultural diversity in art museums. *The International Journal of the Inclusive Museum, 7*(2), 1–13. https://doi.org/10.18848/1835-2014/cgp/v07i02/44483

Kalshed, D. (2020). *A depth psychological approach to contemporary American culture and political life.* The Retreat at Pacifica Graduate Institute. https://retreat.pacifica.edu/american-culture-and-political-life/.

Karp, I., Kreamer, C. M., & Lavine, S. D. (1992). *Museums and communities: The politics of public culture.* Smithsonian Institution Press.

Kendi, I. X. (2017). *Stamped from the beginning: The definitive history of racist ideas in America.* Bold Type Books.

Kendi, I. X. (2019). *How to be an antiracist.* One World.

Leading with Intent (2021). BoardSource index of nonprofit. In *Leading with intent: BoardSource index of nonprofit board practices.* Washington, DC: BoardSource. https://leadingwithintent.org/

Leading with Intent. (2017). *2017 index of nonprofit board practices.* https://leadingwithintent.org/wp-content/uploads/2017/11/LWI-2017.pdf

Leonardo, Z. (2003). Discourse and critique: Outlines of a post-structural theory of ideology, *Journal of Education Policy, 18*(2), 203–214. doi:10.1080/0268093022000043038

Leung, G. (2020, September 17). *It's time for art museums to address their racist histories.* HYPEBEAST. https://hypebeast.com/2020/9/art-museums-steps-to-address-racism-exclusive-interviews.

Li, S. (2020, December 1). American Museums are going through an identity crisis. *The Atlantic.* https://www.theatlantic.com/culture/archive/2020/11/american-museums-are-going-through-identity-crisis/617221/.

Litt, S. (2021, August). MOCA Cleveland announces new board members, structure following race-related controversies over exhibits, internal practices. *Cleveland.com.* https://www.cleveland.com/news/2021/08/moca-cleveland-announces-new-board-members-structure-following-race-related-controversies-over-exhibits-internal-practices.html

Lonetree, A. (2009). Museums as sites of decolonization: Truth telling in national and tribal museums. In S. Sleeper-Smith (Ed.), *Contesting knowledge: Museums and Indigenous perspectives* (pp. 322–337). University of Nebraska Press.

Lonetree, A. (2012). *Decolonizing museums: Representing Native America in national and tribal museums.* University of North Carolina Press.

MacDonald, S. (2006). *A companion to museum studies.* Blackwell.

Mai, T., & Ash, D. (2012). Tracing our methodological steps: Making meaning of families' hybrid "figuring out" practices at science museum exhibits. In D. Ash, J. Rahm, & L. Melber (Eds.), *Putting theory into practice: Methodologies for informal learning research.* Sense Publishers.

Marciano, O. (2014, April 21). *James Clifford's "Museums as Contact Zones".* RxArt. https://rxart.net/blog/james-cliffords-museums-contact-zones/#:~:text=In%201997%20Professor%20James%20Clifford,conducive%20to%20discussion%20and%20understanding.

McCambridge, R. (2017, May 9). *Museums so white: Survey reveals deep lack of diversity.* Non profit news. *Nonprofit Quarterly.* https://nonprofitquarterly.org/museum-boards-directors-whitest-getting-whiter/.

McDonald, M., Gough, B., Wearing, S., & Deville, A. (2017). Social psychology, consumer culture and neoliberal political economy. *Journal for the Theory of Social Behaviour,* 47(3), 363–379. https://doi.org/10.1111/jtsb.12135

McIntosh, P. (1989). White privilege: Unpacking the invisible knapsack. *Peace and Freedom Magazine,* 10–12. The National SEED Project. https://nationalseedproject.org/Key-SEED-Texts/white-privilege-unpacking-the-invisible-knapsack

Merritt, E. (2016). *Doing diversity in museums.* AAM. https://www.aam-us.org/2016/02/25/do-ing-diversity-in-museums/

Merritt, E. (2014, April 11). *TrendsWatch 2014.* American Alliance of Museums. https://www.aam-us.org/2014/03/18/trendswatch-2014/.

Merritt, E. (2017, March 6). *TrendsWatch 2017: Report helps museums prepare for change in US and Worldwide.* American Alliance of Museums. https://www.aam-us.org/2017/03/06/trendswatch-2017-report-helps-museums-prepare-for-change-in-us-and-worldwide/.

Merritt, E. (2019, March 19). *TrendsWatch 2019 executive summary.* American Alliance of Museums. https://www.aam-us.org/2019/03/19/trendswatch-2019-executive-summary/.

Modest, W., Thomas, N., Prlić D., & Augustat, C. (2019). *Matters of belonging: Ethnographic museums in a changing Europe.* Sidestone Press.

Moore, B. (2013). Understanding the ideology of normal: Making visible the ways in which educators think about students who seem different. [Unpublished doctoral dissertation]. University of Colorado. https://www.semanticscholar.org/paper/Understanding-the-Ideology-of-Normal%3A-Making-the-in-Moore/7a7900fb8e44338c360921fd28d52ca00648f1e9

Moore, P. (2014, January 20). *The danger of the "D" word: Museums and diversity.* The Incluseum. https://incluseum.com/2014/01/20/the-danger-of-the-d-word-museums-and-diversity/

Moore, P. (2016, March 7). *The why of D+I: An [Afro]futuristic gaze at race and museums.* The Incluseum. https://incluseum.com/2016/03/07/afrofuturistic-gaze-race-museums.

Moss, I. D. (2013). *Why aren't there more butts of color in these seats?* Createquity. http://createquity.com/2013/02/why-arent-there-more-butts-of-color-in-these-seats/.

Museum Audience Insight. (2012). *The shifting consumer landscape.* Reach Advisors. https://reachadvisors.com/past-presentations/2012-archive/

National Endowment for the Arts. (2018). The 2017 survey of public participation in the arts. https://artsgovd8.prod.acquia-sites.com/impact/research/arts-data-profile-series/adp-18.

National Landscape Study: DEAI Practices in Museums. (2020). National landscape study: DEAI practices in museums—Welcome to CCLI (Cultural Competence Learning Institute). https://community.astc.org/ccli/about-us/landscape-study.

NBC Universal News Group. (2021, July 9). Nikole Hannah-Jones and Ta-Nehisi Coates on critical race theory and GOP voter suppression efforts. MSNBC. https://www.msnbc.com/all-in/watch/nikole-hannah-jones-and-ta-nehisi-coates-on-critical-race-theory-and-gop-voter-suppression-efforts-116443717982.

Ng, W., Ware, S. M., & Greenberg, A. (2017). Activating diversity and inclusion: A blueprint for museum educators as allies and change makers. *Journal of Museum Education, 42*(2), 142–154. https://doi.org/10.1080/10598650.2017.1306664

Noorani, A. (2019, December 19). *Out of many, one: Immigration, identity and the American dream.* Knight Foundation. https://knightfoundation.org/articles/out-of-many-one-immigration-identity-and-the-american-dream/

O'Mara, J. (2014). *Global diversity & inclusion benchmarks.* The Center for Global Inclusion. https://centreforglobalinclusion.org/wp-content/uploads/2017/09/GDIB-V.090517.pdf

Patrick, F. (2013). Neoliberalism, the knowledge economy, and the LEARNER: Challenging the inevitability of the commodified self as an outcome of education. *ISRN Education, 2013*, 1–8. https://doi.org/10.1155/2013/108705

Pogrebin, R. (2017, August 22). It's a diverse city, but most big museum boards are strikingly white. *The New York Times.* https://www.nytimes.com/2017/08/22/arts/design/new-york-museums-diversity-staff-boards.html

Pogrebin, R. (2020, October 9). Black trustees join forces to make art museums more diverse. *The New York Times.* https://www.nytimes.com/2020/10/09/arts/design/black-trustees-art-museums-diversity.html.

Powell, J., & Menendian, S. (2017, June 29). The problem of othering: Towards inclusiveness and belonging. *Othering and Belonging: Expanding the Circle of Human Concern*, (1), 14–39. https://otheringandbelonging.org/wp-content/uploads/2016/07/OtheringAndBelonging_Issue1.pdf

Reach Advisors. (2013). *Museum audience insight.* Audience Shifts and Meaning Making. https://reachadvisors.com/past-presentations/2013-archive/

Resnick, B. (2017, January 26). White fear of demographic change is a powerful psychological force. *Vox.* https://www.vox.com/science-and-health/2017/1/26/14340542/white-fear-trump-psychology-minority-majority.

Robert, N. (2014). Getting intersectional in museums. *Museums & Social Issues, 9*(1), 24–33. https://doi.org/10.1179/1559689314z.00000000017

Rodney, S. (2018). Art museum attendance declining across the US? *Hyperallergic.* https://hyperallergic.com/421968/is-art-museum-attendance-declining-across-the-us/.

Rodriguez, G. (2009, November 23). *Towards a new mainstream?* Center for the Future of Museums. https://www.aam-us.org/2009/11/23/towards-a-new-mainstream/

Ross, M. (2004). Interpreting the new museology. *Museum and Society, 2*(2), 84–103. https://doi.org/10.29311/mas.v2i2.43

Roth, W. M., Lee, Y. J., & Hsu, P. L. (2009). A tool for changing the world: Possibilities of cultural-historical activity theory to reinvigorate science education. *Studies in Science Education, 45*(2), 131–167. https://doi.org/10.1080/03057260903142269

Russo, A. (2012). The rise of the 'media museum': Creating interactive cultural experiences through social media. In E. Giaccardi (Ed.), *Heritage and social media: Understanding heritage in a participatory culture* (pp. 145–157). Routledge.

Sarubbi, W. (2014, |September 19). Giraffe and elephant fable drives diversity session. Univ. of Central Florida. https://med.ucf.edu/news/giraffe-and-elephant-fable-drives-diversity-session/

Sharpe, E., & Da Silva, J. (2021, April 16). Visitor figures 2020: Top 100 art museums revealed as attendance drops by 77% worldwide. *The Art Newspaper*. https://www.theartnewspaper.com/analysis/visitor-figures-2020-top-100-art-museums.

Shelton, A. (2013). Critical museology: A manifesto. *Museum Worlds Advances in Research*, *1*(1), 7–23.

Simon, N. (2010). Chapter 1: Principles of participation. In *The participatory museum*. Museum 2.0. http://www.participatorymuseum.org/chapter1/.

Simon, N. (2013, October 16). *Who counts? Grappling with attendance as proxy for impact*. Museum 2.0. http://museumtwo.blogspot.com/2013/10/who-counts-grappling-with-attendance-as.html

Sleeter, C. E. (1996). *Multicultural education as social activism*. State University of New York Press.

Sleeter, C. E. (2004). Context-conscious portraits and context-blind policy. *Anthropology & Education Quarterly*, *35*(1), 132–136.

Statistica. (2020). *Museums—statistics & facts*. https://www.statista.com/topics/1509/museums/

Tchen, J. K. W. (2005). *Homeland insecurities: Teaching and the intercultural imagination*.

Teather, L., & Carter, J. (2009). Critical museology now: Theory/practice/theory, *Muse*, *27*(6), 22–33.

The Ralph and Goldy Lewis Center for Regional Policy Studies. (2006). Annual report 2004–2005. *UCLA: The Ralph and Goldy Lewis Center for Regional Policy Studies*. https://escholarship.org/uc/item/0hc935mb

Themed Entertainment Association (TEA) and the Economics practice at AECOM. (2019). *TEA/AECOM 2018 theme index and museum index: The global attractions attendance report*. https://www.aecom.com/content/wp-content/uploads/2019/05/Theme-Index-2018-5-1.pdf.

Thistle, P. C. (2018). *About critical museology miscellanea*. Critical Museology Miscellanea. https://miscellaneousmuseology.wordpress.com/about-critical-museology-miscellanea/.

Turner, V. (2002). The factors affecting women's success in museum careers: A discussion of the reasons more women do not reach the top, and of strategies to promote their future success. *Journal of Conservation and Museum Studies*, *8*, 6–10. DOI: http://doi.org/10.5334/jcms.8022

Ünsal, D. (2019). Positioning museums politically for social justice. *Museum Management and Curatorship*, *34*(6), 595–607. https://doi.org/10.1080/09647775.2019.1675983

University of Calgary. (2021). *Human resources*. https://www.ucalgary.ca/equity-diversity-inclusion

Ward, S. J. (2016). *Understanding contradictions in times of change: A CHAT analysis in an art museum*. [Doctoral dissertation, University of Washington]. ResearchWorks Archive. http://hdl.handle.net/1773/37091

Wilkening, S., & Chung, J. (2009). *Life stages of the museum visitor: Building engagement over a lifetime*. AAM Press.

4
WHO WILL PAY FOR MUSEUMS?

Overview

In Chapter 3 I asked, "Who will come to museums?" or, more precisely, "Who will be invited to participate?" Here I ask, "Who will pay for museums?", analyzing this critical tipping point for museums along the fault line of finances. Here I use a proxy of entrance fees to ground the discussion in the everyday world of art museums.

CHAT tells us that history matters. Thus I begin in the past and then explore ongoing and possible futures involving the financial, cultural and social challenges wrapped up in the interplay of power and money. The central contradiction in this chapter centers on the question of whether the primary role of museums is to be a social/community service or a business-/finance-generating entity and the dialectic between these two. Framing this within CHAT, it becomes relatively easy to recognize the practical historical tension between money and social good. One instance of this is the question of entrance fees. To charge or not to charge?

We focus mainly in this chapter on data from American art museums. The issue of entrance fees is inherently controversial, contentious and visible in the United States. The contradiction between a service/populist vs. 'budget'/finance role (McFelter, 2007) plays out against a deficit/othering vs. resource view of visitors (Feinstein & Meshoulam, 2014; Sleeter, 1996). I discuss several museum pricing models (Rentschler et al., 2004) and variable pricing (Merritt, 2020). I include a critique of the role of neoliberal policies, which specifically promote consumerism and individualism as guiding principles (Apple, 2017; Baltodano, 2012) of the financial effects on educational institutions like museums. I remind the reader that each binary operates as a dialectic. This will help disambiguate the actual function and purpose of museums.

VIGNETTE

At the Metropolitan Museum of Art, New York City

This vignette centers on the often-confusing set of expectations regarding museum entrance fees. The Met in New York is a particularly good example of the contradictions we explore in this chapter. It had recently been unclear what the Mets' entrance fee is. Is the Met free or does it cost $25 to get in? The signs in the atrium of the museum were confusing. The confusion was great enough that the question went to court. Excerpts from the *New York Times* and the *Los Angeles Times* describe the confusion:

> The Metropolitan Museum of Art in New York was being sued over its "recommended" entrance fee of $25. A group of plaintiffs claims that most visitors have no idea that you can get into the museum for free and that paying the $25 is optional.
>
> (Ng, 2013)

> Based on…1893 state law, the suits contend that the museum is required to allow visitors to be admitted at no charge on most days of the week…. This is a case about democracy in New York,…[claimed lawyers for the plaintiffs].
>
> Back in the 1970's…the introduction of the new "Pay What You Wish" policy [created the opportunity to pay]…with simpler sums: many visitors paid less than 25 cents to receive the famous Met buttons.
>
> (Lyall, 2013, New York Times)

In 2013, the New York State Supreme Court dismissed these lawsuits, arguing, in part, that lack of payment to the Met would 'decimate the museum's budget'. Financial need overrode historical precedent.

> The more conventional thinking was supported, that is entrance fees are the most reliable means for generating revenue. Now the policy is that out of NYC visitors pay $25 and NYC residents get in for free. (Lyall, 2013, New York Times).
>
> Cep presented statistics that every visitor "costs the Met $4…. The entrance fee accounts for…16% of the $250 million budget" (Cep, 2014, *The New Yorker*).
>
> (Adapted from Cep, 2014; Grant, 2017; Lyall, 2013; Ng, 2013)[1]

Introduction

"Who will pay for museums?" This is neither a new nor an easy question to answer. In Chapter 3, we explored the conflict between demographics and expectations in museums. Here I focus instead on how demographics and dollars are intimately intertwined. Museums are struggling with how to attract younger and more diverse audiences while maintaining, and often increasing, admissions fees. The inescapable intertwining of the financial and sociopolitical aspects of running museums has been critiqued in the press, museum blogs and research, often unfavorably.

Ekström noted,

> Commercial awareness, which was previously disparaged, is now seen as a legitimate and necessary response to increased competition, enhancing experience, increasing accessibility, broadening inclusivity and sustainable futures with diminishing funding.
>
> (Ekström, 2020, p. 7)

It is not possible to resolve these questions without delving into the fundamentals of museum practice, the underlying ideologies, which in turn, determine how museums view the visitors they wish to attract. In addition, the COVID-19 pandemic has created an unprecedented impact on museum finances, which lays bare the underlying contradictions long present in museums. More than ever before, the most pressing dilemma for museums now, both large and small (Brestovansky, 2020; Tarmy, 2019) is remaining solvent in the age of COVID-19 under rapidly changing social mores and practices while struggling to learn and meet the needs of the 21st century.

Museums have been experiencing financial difficulties for some time (CFM, 2008).[2] Prior to the outbreak of COVID-19, there was "almost no ability to cut the budget in areas that would make a significant enough difference…they're already operating on razor-thin budgets" (Woody, 2019, para. 3–4). Facing such deep financial challenges, contemporary museums have moved pricing from a peripheral issue to one of central importance, with Gombault and Rentschler (2009) suggesting that marketing has become the new holy grail of museums with entrance fees as the lead horse.

Beyond any particular institutional or practical rationale behind marketing, discussions of the financial crisis in museums and possible solutions strongly reflect neoliberal policy and practices of commodification. As with all the other aspects of museums, money is but a proxy for deeper contradictions.

We ask, "What is the intended goal of charging admission and/or increasing entrance fees?" "Are museums budget-first businesses or are they public/community service organizations?" Since at least the 1970s, the question has leaned heavily toward a neoliberal ideology of consumers, commodification and entrepreneurial positioning (Harvey, 2005). A genealogy of admission charges in American art museums looks back over various factors, such as the evolving mission of museums,

Who Will Pay for Museums? **113**

professionalization of the field and [charitable] giving trends, which led to the implementation and expansion of admission charges in the 1970s and 1980s (Cortell, 2011, p. 1; see Cortell, 2011, for a history of admission fees).

The museum entrance fee 'pricing war' is an old dilemma in the museum business, and there have been few new ideas concerning how to move forward. Using CHAT analysis, we can locate where the tensions lie. We will find that the intertwining of money and power is invited and involved at all levels of museum functioning and administration when we go beyond the immediate causes and conditions of pricing practices.

It has been challenging to trace the use of entrance fees in the United States. Cortell's dissertation has helped provide a more coherent history. According to Cortell,

> As early as the 1900s, writings about museums reveal an ongoing dilemma—whether to charge admissions. Some scholars advocated for the museum to become like a public library—open and free of charge. Others suggested that users must be of certain status to enter or enjoy the museum. This philosophical debate, which stretched across the globe and continues today, is deeply connected to the museum's public value.
>
> (p. 10)

Cortell articulated here one of the fundamental contradictions of this chapter: "Are museums open and free of charge or must visitors be of certain status to enter or enjoy the museum?" In the following sections, I break down Cortell's conundrum to expose several secondary contradictions, using the logic of CHAT, deficit views and neoliberalism.

Numerical analyses of dollars and solvency readily capture our attention, but, as elsewhere noted in this book, such surface details serve to hide deeper, often competing, ideological motives which tend to emerge more slowly. Dilenschneider (2014) suggested,

> [M]any organizations have been tasked to maximize earned revenues (often inevitably linked to visitation). Perhaps most concerning of all are attempts to blunt the challenge by proposing half-measures as remedy.
>
> (para. 8)

She implied that the many half-measures, such as *free first Sundays*, are not an adequate remedy. Just as dire demographic projections camouflaged deeper concerns such as *white fear* or other sentiments, we need to search for what is being camouflaged by financial half-measures.

Let us apply CHAT to entrance fees. "Use value can be understood as the direct benefits of an activity's outcomes for the activity's participants, whereas exchange value denotes the worth of something when it is exchanged for something else" (Engeström, 1987, pp. 84–85). *Use* represents *service*, such as teaching, healing or another social good, while *exchange* represents money, monetary gain or other commoditizing. 'Everything has a price'. This oversimplification is a useful way to uncover and study the secondary and tertiary contradictions that arise from questioning museum finances. These contradictions are often shrouded in mystery, history, business as usual or the bottom line, and they drive most current policies and practices, including issues concerning the social good, which are not overtly financial.

Both *othering* and *belonging* and neoliberalism are central here. Neoliberal ideology believes in the exchange value of virtually *everything*, *othering* helps decrease any emphasis on use value, such as social services, in museums and other institutions. Social services are often the first to be eliminated when money is tight in neoliberal institutions that subscribe to *othering* (Feinstein & Meshoulam, 2014).

Follow the Money[3]

Museums across the world have been working mightily to recover from the financial crisis of 2008, yet the damage lingers. It is challenging to make generalizations or correlations of how the past financial crisis affected museums across countries because a large subset of possible differences (geography, rural/urban status, discipline and financial history) between countries confound comparison. Such differences include boards, mission statements, degrees of support from and to the community. Also, unexamined deeper sociopolitical issues such as *othering*/deficit practices, past colonialist practices or increasingly strict structural constraints on staff due to budget cuts render comparisons inaccurate.

Reach Advisors (Chung & Wilkening, 2008) suggested that U.S. museums' financial challenges stem from obvious causes, such as an overly heavy reliance on corporate and individual philanthropy, with 40% of all contributions coming from financial and real estate sectors. Poor investment or overambitious building projects that had been made in times of a booming economy helped lead to the 2008 collapse.

So, what are museums doing to stop the bleeding? Over the past decades, museums, like schools, have become akin to corporate entities, closely tied to budgets, commonization and competition for increasingly scarce resources (Apple, 2017; Tienken & Orlich, 2013). 'Bottom-line' rules have become a driving stance in financial decisions.

Over the past decades, many American museums have experienced decreases in state, city or other local funding. Museums have also lost earmarked funds and have suffered from diminishing core patron support, primarily in the form of memberships. Museums have set higher and higher admissions fees. American museums are more dependent on entrance fees than other countries because far fewer American museums are subsidized. In Europe, public funding is the norm, rather than the exception. Even within Europe, though, it is difficult to find comparative financial data. And, as in the United States, European museums have aspirations to grow financial diversity, often emphasizing consumerism (European Museum Academy, 2019, p. 7).

Museum entry prices around the world differ significantly. A 2019 pre-COVID study suggested the United States had a '$25 club'.[4] Some major American museums have set their standard adult ticket price at $25. Many European museums are free, such as London's British Museum, National Gallery, Tate, Victoria and Albert National Portrait Gallery. Other European museums also charge entrance fees. Yet, "[a] growing number of European museums are engaged in the interesting Museum Depot Shop where de-accessed pieces from the collections are put on sale" (EMA, 2019, p. 7). Still, European museums that are publicly funded tend to be doing better (EMA, 2019, p. 7). As Siegal (2020) noted,

> Institutions supported by government funding are able to weather the storm with a little belt tightening, while those that depend on ticket sales are facing tougher choices. Many are laying off employees and restructuring their business model.
>
> (para. 2)

Overall, entrance fees, where they are charged, have been increasing (Grant, 2017), and these increases range from small to large depending on the geography and discipline. Museum responses to the discomfort of raising fees have tended to center on a sometimes-confusing mixture of temporary fixes that offer access to a wider public, such as family days, and/or evening programs, free days, social Thursday (Grant, 2017; Merritt, 2020; Russeth, 2017).

As museum revenues have been dropping, however, it has been difficult to tease out exactly how much any museum is in the red, even how much of their budget is covered by entrance fees remains murky. This is due to the way museums' financial and demographic data, which has been described as 'creative' by Simon (2017), are not standardized, so do not conform with each other and depend a good deal on who is doing the counting. As with attendance records, Chung and Wilkening (2008) noted a great deal of 'cherry-picking'—that is, selecting and presenting data to preferentially support a particular argument.

Lindqvist (2012) suggested there is little research on the impact of past and present financial crises:

> Economic crises directly and indirectly affect the financial health of museums...[yet] analysing the impact of the economic cycle on museums has not generated much interest among researchers; to date published studies on the recent financial crisis and its reverberations in the museum sector are rare.
>
> (p. 1)

The lack of research on financial distress and its outcomes is consistent with the overall lack of uniform data across museums more generally.

Where there are entrance fees, attracting more visitors means creating more income. On the other hand, greater fees can result in fewer middle-class or minoritized patrons overall and therefore result in lower income and an even more stratified visitor base (Merritt, 2020). This last outcome is the very opposite of what many museums desire.

The significant financial challenges since 2008 have culminated over the past years in a rather significant need to "reorganize the institution and to *retrench* our finances" (Dobnik, 2017) (italics added). Many museums have instituted a variety of *retrenching* efforts such as variable pricing and other financial fix trends, and these are becoming more widespread. I analyze them as tertiary contractions because typically they are 'fixes' borrowed from other institutions to deal with secondary contradictions, such as the dialectic between affordability and profit. Variable pricing, borrowed from airline and ride-share businesses, appears to be working for places such as the Indianapolis Zoo (Merritt, 2020). But does it work as a pricing model for art museums? The phrase 'retrench our finances' is interesting, as it may refer to large and/or small changes. Retrenching has taken many forms, some of which I describe later in this chapter. They include furloughs, entrance fee increases, changes in exhibit selection, and even to deaccessioning art to raise income. If *retrench* means a series of quick fixes or half-measures, they *probably* will not be enough for the structural *reculturing* we need.

More generally, when money is tight, special programming tends to fall off (Feinstein & Meshoulam, 2014); here special refers to programs for minoritized visitors. When and if reeculturing is successful, these programs will no longer be 'special'; they will become the new *norm*. It is important not to lose sight of the long-range goals of museums in times of financial crisis.

Uncovering Ideological Contradictions

To find lasting solutions to these financial challenges, we need to uncover several intertwined ideologically based contradictions. These contradictions are at the heart of museum financial practices at all organizational levels. I take these in turn in the same order as in other chapters.

By first presenting the contradictions as a dialectic, we can examine the underlying ideologies, those deeper preexisting tensions, and discern how they affect museum ethos and practices.

Cultural organizations like museums are increasingly expected to think and run these organizations based on market forces, with visitors seen as customers and exhibits as commodities (Ekström, 2020). Deciding how much to charge for entrance is very much part of this movement; it inevitably involves deeply held ideological stances that can be difficult to tease out (Dawson, 2014; Gurian, 2020; McFelter, 2007). These beliefs are readily given voice, however, when anyone mentions 'going free'. The divisiveness (they won't know what we do here), derision (they can't do the exhibit right) and the discounting (if they don't pay, they won't value the experience) show up on the surface as spontaneous discursive manifestations of deeper tensions. These are both the expression and reflection of the consumerism and deficit ideology within leisure/education, which has been called 'corporate schooling' (Baltodano, 2012) and, by extension then, 'corporate museums' (Ekström, 2020;

Schneider, 2020). Others have situated disagreement as 'entrance fee wars'[5] (Gurian, 2020; McFelter, 2007). In actuality, the financial issues around entrance fees are based on fundamental ideological differences (often implicit) that we explore next.

CHAT analysis predicts that tension between nodes of the activity system is a source of contradiction. Such nodes, include subjects (people), mediational means (tools, artifacts), objects leading to outcomes, division of labor (hierarchy), community and rules. The cases discussed highlighting board members' actions and finances (Halperin, 2019) show how rules and hierarchy can become disturbed in relation to each other, as well as in relation to objects. There may be multiple ways to stay solvent; if, though, solvency is viewed through a consumerist lens, then mediational means/tools chosen will favor entrance fees.

Other actions affecting how to conduct business also reflect this reshuffling of levels of power. We show the emergence of secondary contradictions in the ongoing conflicts in action. In Table 4.1, I highlight some possible nodes in conflict/tension, asked first as a question, as well as some existing tertiary 'fixes', arising when the object of a more developed activity is introduced into the central activity system. These secondary contradictions have already been set in motion, but increasing financial pressure exacerbate and make them more visible.

These possible secondary contradictions are as follows:

1. Bottom line vs. Social Good
   Cortell noted. "This philosophical debate, which stretched across the globe and continues today, is deeply connected to the museum's public value". Danielsen so it is (2008) argues that income is the most significant factor in the likelihood of someone visit[ing] a museum (Cortell, 2011, p. 14).

TABLE 4.1 Secondary contradictions exacerbated by finances

Secondary contradiction	*Nodes in conflict*	*Tertiary contradictions short-/long-term 'fix'*
What is the value/purpose of a visit? **Bottom line vs. social good**	**Object/Mediational means** Tangible goods/diminished operating budget Service vs. monetary	Money gaining/saving actions Deaccession of art/objects Increased entrance fees
When change is essential, who needs to do it? **Us vs. them** Finite resources/zero sum game	**Hierarchy/Rules** Othering vs. resource view	Outreach *Some* deserve to belong *Other*s have deficits
How to position the visitor financially? **Cooperative vs. client logic**	**Hierarchy/Subjects** Money vs. belonging	Free first Saturdays Free family days Coupons/passes to minoritized folks Variable pricing models

2. Us vs. Them
   People must pay for what they get, in order to appreciate it. This *them* view is based on a deficit view, a reflection of *othering* (powell & Menendian, 2017).
3. Cooperative vs. Client
   Do museums view visitors as a source of revenue or as collaborators (Feinstein & Meshoulam, 2014)? The neoliberal commodification of all things positions visitors primarily as a source of revenue.

Bottom Line vs. Social Good

Dilenschneider (2014) noted that organizations are hesitant to acknowledge financial challenges because they want to:

> put the best foot forward, in response to perceived pressure from governing boards…typically comprised [of] businessmen and women whose perspectives may be governed by the bottom-line vs. more populist goals.
>
> (para. 5–6)

The business/budget model and the service/populist model function dialectically. We explore both stances next, querying the purpose of the museum and how entrance fees can relate to that purpose.

Foot (2014) argued that a full examination of contradictions is an excellent example of how CHAT can be useful; in this book, we apply this logic to day-to-day museum life. There is no one simple answer to this contradiction. Some argue that the best answer *may* be a careful and ideologically clear balance between business and service. I argue instead for systemic change based on equity and social justice.

What is meant by value, as in the 'value of a visit'? Aesthetic value does not conform to monetary terms. Entrance fees cannot truly be justified only on the basis of the value of exhibits, even though this is done, especially with specialized, so-called blockbuster exhibits, art exhibits (Van Gogh, King Tut) asking for larger donations. Brown (2020)[6] questioned the notion of mega exhibits and the use of "packed galleries as a metric of success", citing Meta Knol, the director of the Museum de Lakenhal in the Netherlands who said, "We have come out of a decade that celebrated globalism"[7] (para. 6–7).

The end of blockbusters represents a reversal of some neoliberal trends. There is, of course, great value in having more visitors come to the museum on a given day and perhaps return in the future. It is valuable that new visitors become aware of the museum's existence. These ancillary goals cannot be translated into monetary terms either. So why do we feel the need to ask about cost, as if it were valid to put a price tag on social service/responsibility? Tables 4.1 and 4.2 illustrate how to place this contradiction into CHAT theory. These are but some examples of how we can dissect and understand some simple dynamics of

TABLE 4.2 Sample of primary, secondary and tertiary contradictions regarding pricing

Primary contradiction	Secondary contradiction	Tertiary contradiction
Use Value vs. Exchange Value	Museum as a social/community resource vs. museum as a business Nodes of contradiction: Subject/community *[education/curatorial]* The administration needs a certain percentage of income to come from entrance fees; the diversity committee supports frequent free admissions for nontraditional visitors	A compromise experiment is tried: involving variable pricing,[8] which does in fact, increase middle-class visitors but not the first-time minoritized visitors they seek. Additional solutions are sought

(Adapted from Ward, 2016)

potential transformation using activity theory. We must think more clearly about the role of subject, mediational means and objectives, as well as the other nodes of an activity system:

"Tertiary contradictions within an activity system arise when the object of a more "culturally advanced" activity (Engeström, 1987) is introduced into that system…typically to find relief from one or more secondary contradictions and the tensions stemming from them". Table 4.2 shows proposals for *relieving* the tensions from one of the secondary contradictions in Table 4.1, Museum as a social/community resource vs. museum as a business. The hypothetical but not unlikely museum scenario in Table 4.2 involves competing goals; that is, the administration needs a certain percentage of income to come from entrance fees, while the diversity committee wants to have free admission more often for nontraditional visitors. An increasingly common intervention is tried: variable pricing bringing in more middle class but not minoritized first-time visitors. The intervention was only partially successful. As we have suggested, such tertiary contradictions situated as quick fixes are not guaranteed to work and, in fact, can exacerbate the problem. While money is a key factor in limiting the 'previously uninvited', at least as important are more intangible cultural and sociopolitical aspects (e.g., Chapter 3, the giraffe and elephant parable).

Us vs. Them

Many take the position that, if museums are community/public service organizations, then entrance fees should be eliminated, along with ancillary items such as parking (Gurian, 2020; Rosencheck, 2018; Skorten, 2014). Grant (2018), Elaine Gurian (2005, 2006) and Simon (2007a, 2007b, 2017) all take this view, with Gurian asking, "Do museums have a kind of moral obligation, like libraries, to be free?" Simon (2017) referred to Gurian's question when saying,

> Museums provide services that are broad and applicable to everyday life, whose value is variable, and to which entrance (though not necessarily all services) should be free.
>
> (para. 11)

Rosenbaum (2015) also suggested, "A museum needs to be underwritten by the community…more like libraries rather than movie theaters" (Rosenbaum, 2015). Skorten (2014) argued,

> [N]onprofits of all kinds are going to have to be more and more creative in the future…[with] no intention of making the institution less accessible.
>
> (para. 12)

Skorten linked free access to *equitable action to include all*, regardless of cultural, ethnic, racial, "income or residency and immigration status" (para. 13). He equated free admission with enhanced accessibility. Raicovich (2019) argued that the library framework encourages us to envision a different way to use museums through recurring visits, rather than trying to absorb everything all in one day. Raicovich summarized,

> Museums and libraries in the US originated in similar places and via similar patronage models with their foundational collections coming largely from wealthy collectors of books and art objects, sometimes in conjunction with institutions of higher learning.
>
> (para. 8)

The word 'public' remains embedded in what we call the library. Raicovich argued that "clarity around intention and transparency of outlook is an essential aspect of the distinction between museums and libraries and is based in a particular poetics of engagement". She then quoted Jakob Orsoss of the Brooklyn Public Library:

> As a public space our job is about enhancing people's willingness to raise questions and feel uncomfortable. A true public space is constantly negotiating knowledge or the lack of it, rather than presenting a position of expertise. And we in turn have to be open to pushback.
>
> (para. 12)

Raicovich then took the argument further:

> Rather than spaces of abstracted expertise, the cultural sphere should perhaps be perceived by the public as a zone in which to negotiate what we may not agree on.
>
> (para. 13)

This view harkens back to the notion of *contact zone* we noted in Chapter 3, which is "now more or less synonymous with these inclusionist, collaborative programs", as Boast (2011, p. 56) suggested. The basic dialogic and dialectic stance we wish to take at exhibits can only work if they are designed as collaborative *contact zones* rather than competitive or exclusionary viewing halls.

It was almost 15 years ago that Elaine Gurian (2005) foregrounded the public service role of museums, noting the perceived conflict with 'charging'.

> The major and undeniable problem with charging is that it is a means test. In the current situation only those who can afford the cost, and think the experience is valuable enough to pay for, can have access to the patrimony that belongs to us all. We cannot continue to discuss inclusion if we continue to charge for general admission.
>
> (p. 6)

Once again, we have moved into the territory of deficit biases concerning those who have less money or lower socioeconomic or sociopolitical status, in short, the *others* who are often viewed as not having enough *culture* to appreciate museums. Deficit views of *othering* arise in a variety of guises. One example is a heightened sense of ownership of perceived aesthetic norms on the part of those creating museums and exhibits or interpretation of objects for *all* audiences. This hierarchical attitude shows up in concern over 'dumbing down material for *those* people', worries about exhibit breakage or asking "*Why don't they come here?*"

Financial/Business Model

The other side of this tension is represented by the statement: Raising admissions may be the final (and only) solution to balancing a budget, even if that works against your other goals (Grant, 2019, para. 4). This bottom-line approach uses numerous, typically intertwining monetary arguments for paying the bills, with neoliberal ideologies expressed in consumerist language and reflecting deficit/othering attitudes. If a museum is a business, then entrance fees are part of any good business model for generating revenue. In the context of American museums, where entrance fees often are a very important source of discretionary funds, a practical explanation sounds something like this:

> We're all trying to balance our budgets.... You are at the end of the process and coming up a bit short. Should you raise the amount that the trustees are asked to contribute? That may be difficult. Raising admissions may be the final solution to balancing a budget, even if that works against your other goals.
>
> (Grant, 2018 para. 3)

A 'balancing the budget' mindset appears to have become ubiquitous across all levels of responsibility. Researchers have found that "all members of the museum organization appear to believe they have a part in the museums' solvency" (Kundu &

Kalin, 2015, p. 42). How do we know this to be true? Dailey's (2006) research verified this view with finding from 'on the floor' research questioning suggests that educators and curators 'mind the budget' in all they do:

> … people working in museums have a heightened awareness of the economy, and…have a working vocabulary of "economic terms" that is ever present… [they] no longer feel a sense of personal agency, instead they demonstrate feelings of being "controlled by the market".
>
> (p. 5)

The previous quote stems from the perspective of museum workers, highlighting a loss of agency in relation to structural conditions imposed on them by commodification. This is a clear instantiation of neoliberalism in action: with staff agency constrained and institutional financial goals taking precedence. This is a potent example of the structure agency dialectic in action in the practical terms of everyday staff vs. administration caveats based on neoliberal/deficit ideological grounds.

Dailey's research findings are sobering. How much of the everyday staff members' time is now taken up with fundraising? Grant takes an even harsher view, highlighting how entrance fees act to prioritize the middle class and higher as customers:

> Another economic reason to keep high admission prices…is that the principal beneficiaries would…be…the more financially comfortable individuals who ordinarily visit these institutions. That demographic tends to be wealthier and better educated, and its members already have a level of comfort within the walls of art museums.
>
> (Grant, 2019, para. 7)

The deficit-laden question of 'who belongs in museums?' is on full display here. Other deficit arguments include the underlying beliefs that people need to pay for any entertainment, just like they would at Disneyland; 'we have always done things this way'; 'free doesn't attract more people of color on a permanent basis' (AIM, 2016); and, finally, 'visitors need to pay in order to fully appreciate art' (Rosenbaum, 2006). These justifications may not sound particularly ideological; rather, the underlying assumption is simply that someone must pay and that the budget must be a balanced system. If a museum is to remain open, at least in most of the United States, it must pay for itself, rather than be supported within the government/community.

The conundrum is thus made to appear purely financial, without any overt mention of philosophy, equity or the ultimate purpose of museums. Museums as a community resource with free entrance might be nice, but where do we get the money to run the institution without these entrance fees? This is a statement of 'business as usual' in the 21st century. The conundrum appears to be purely financial. This is what Nina Simon (2007a, 2007b) might refer to as *making sausage*, as no one wants to look too closely at the ingredients.

Cooperative vs. Client Distinction

Feinstein and Meshoulam's (2014) dichotomy of "two institutional logics, *client* logic and *cooperative* logic, contain different ideas about the relationship between an organization and its publics" (p. 370). I position the Feinstein and Meshoulam binary with client logic as exchange value and cooperative logic as use value. The client view here is consistent with neoliberal ideas of consumerism.

Feinstein and Meshoulam (2014) suggested that "the tension between them [client vs. cooperative] evokes a broader tension between dissemination and participation in public engagement with science" (p. 371). This view challenges us to query our view on the 'best' or 'highest' purpose of museum visitors. Fraser (2018) invites us all to push on this idea, advocating for staff/visitor agency:

> Artists, museum professionals, and patrons alike must consider whether their specific, personal, artistic, professional, and economic interests in these systems are consistent with their interests as citizens of an open and democratic society.
>
> (p. 189)

Museum Pricing Models

Having explored three secondary contradictions, I here preview five 'nitty gritty' pricing models as tertiary contradictions—positioned as solutions borrowed from other activity systems. I position these experiments not as solutions or even recommendations but as illustrations for how contradictions do indeed breed experimentation and possible expansion. I do not support or oppose them but offer them as example of 'fixes'.

Hybrid Model

Gombault and Rentschler (2009) argued, "Museums have turned from institutions that collect, preserve and exhibit objects to ones subject to market dynamics" (p. 2). They conducted a meta-study of museum pricing strategies in 30 (non-U.S.) contemporary Western museums, and they concluded the most successful used a hybrid model, which included using "free admission within a portfolio logic, which includes ancillary costs such as parking and restaurants" (p. 7).

They found that the "marketization" included a more business-like orientation, with some self-financing, anticipation of consumer behavior and market studies to underpin decisions in pricing, offering multiple kinds of entrance fees. They noted that "other prices" and peripheral offers (as part of a larger portfolio) became increasingly important (services in shops, restaurants, parking, etc.; p. 8).

They found the emergent hybrid pricing strategy to be driven by three kinds of strategic forces:

1. The original ideological approach to price setting (free entry and low prices as a means of access) still shapes the thinking of many museum professionals. Even if pragmatists tend to rule, museum and cultural policy makers remain attached to free admission and low prices as a museum ideal. Even pragmatists most often see admission fees as a 'necessary evil'.
2. At the other end of the scale are the economic models whose application is yet to be proved…[to be] of value to museums. Pricing strategies implement mainly financial strategies of museums. Pricing decisions are based on costs and the search for self-financing. This led to a focus on audience development rather than on segmenting the market.
3. More recently, pricing strategies implement marketing strategies, to reach their various audience goals: democratization, access, social inclusion, attendance, flows regulations.… Price decisions position and target the offer.

(Adapted from Gombault, 2003, pp. 8–9)

They argue that the most dynamic museums chose, depending on social, cultural and political factors, between two main tracks to set their development strategy:

1. No entry charge and the active construction of a commercial enterprise around the museum, as is the case for museums that are heavily subsidized, like the National Gallery of London.
2. Admission fees that are more or less contained within a moderate price range. These museums also benefit from the construction of a commercial enterprise, no less active, nearby.

(Gombault, 2003, p. 10)

This hybrid model of pricing, incorporating politics and marketing motivations, mixes "original access ideology, economic rationality and marketing pragmatism, [and] is a clear marker of museum hybrid identity in transition between what they have historically been and what they are becoming" (Gombault, 2003, p. 10).

Museum Pricing Model

In response to the same pricing tensions, Rentschler et al. (2004) developed a *museum pricing model*, in part due to the lack of marketing research information to guide the development of museum pricing structures. The Rentschler, Hede and Ramsey model, a research meta-study of 23 research studies, proposed four pricing strategies—utilitarian, idealist, integrity, and access, with social responsibility and financial solvency (four quadrants) as end points (see Figure 4.1). These four stances reflect ideologies concerning museum mission. The authors differentiated:

1. "*The Utilitarian view* suggests that entrance fees are not a primary factor in a visitor's decision to attend a museum and that removing admission charges results only in short-term increases in visitation".

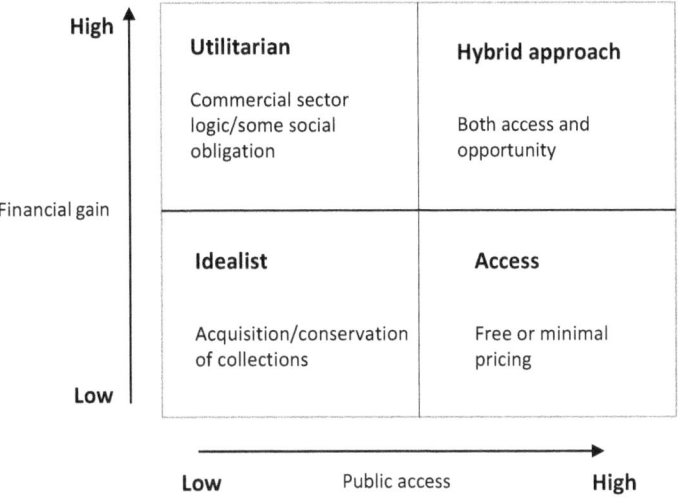

FIGURE 4.1 Adapted museum pricing model developed by Rentschler et al. (2004)

This view was reflected in the Association of Independent Museums' (AIM) study.
2. "*The Idealist view* shows less interest in either the need for financial gain or public access…[focusing] on the care of objects…intellectual heritage…traditions of society…suggesting a requirement to preserve that which is valued from previous generations [and] present and future generations".
This view focused on the material objects being stored and saved for posterity.
3. "*The Integrity strategy* suggests that admission prices can affect specific groups of visitors. 'Drop in' visitors, such as local residents, young people, students, low-income earners, pensioners and children are…affected by pricing due to both actual and perceived restraints…[the] need to segment museum markets… includes…scaling pricing, low income concession rates, free days, local resident passes, and group and school rates".
This view echoes the currently popular variable pricing model I discuss next.
4. "*The Access view* emphasizes the social mission of museums and seeks to impose minimal costs and maximum visitation numbers…high prices perpetuate the idea that museums are for the 'elite',…lowering prices can be viewed as a strategy for initiating future patronage among [noncustomers]".
This socially responsible view is reflected by Gurian, among others cited earlier.

Rentschler et al. (2004) suggested that museums can use different pricing depending on the context; for example,

> museums such as the Guggenheim, operating in different locations in the world and in different markets, may employ different pricing strategies, depending on the product context. Further, any museum may employ more than one pricing strategy, depending on the audience segment targeted.
> (p. 10)

Variable and Dynamic Pricing

This philosophy is not unlike the variable pricing model that follows. The power of this model is that it takes into account the variety of ideological stances we have noted (and others) and fits them into a logical and dynamic model.

Variable and Dynamic Pricing

Variable pricing suggests that entrance fees (and other pricing) be set differently according to the desired public and the goals of the museum. For example, if more visitors are desired in the earlier hours, those fees can be lowered. The model calls for meaningful differential rates that are visible and accessible to target groups. We assume that basic market research has already been done to quantify need. Many museums now practice this type of pricing, for example, holding Thursday evening social events.

Merritt (2020) described two efforts in Indianapolis. The first aimed to attract more lower-middle-class visitors to the Children's Museum of Indianapolis; the second to space visitors to relieve overcrowding at the Indianapolis Zoo. While, thus far, I have focused on art museums, I want to pivot toward solutions (tertiary contradictions) found in other settings to explore other experiments in progress. Lisa Townsend of the Children's Museum of Indianapolis explained their first effort:

> First, they determined (surveys, etc.) that this was a target audience, as they were not attending already…we found that the demographic we were losing most rapidly was lower-middle-income—households earning $35k–$60k/year [who] do not qualify for our Access Pass (which is $2/person), and the museum was concerned about losing them.…We can see that we are attracting people who have never been before, or have not visited in many years, from the middle-income demographic, but attendance from this group is still not as strong as we would like it to be.
>
> (Merritt, 2020, para. 3–4)

These points are telling. First, they did market research to determine who was missing and to know the annual income levels of these groups. They then put a plan into motion. Using a market analysis company and

> using all available data, [the data analysis team] recommends the optimal pricing. Every day at 4 p.m. an automated email from…[this team] gives us new recommended prices for the following week. Staff can approve these recommendations or make changes… Staff have developed a lot of faith in the system.
>
> (para. 4)

One important aspect of this model is that these museums did considerable (survey) market research and determined that lower-middle-class people were hurting the most.

The second pricing experiment Merritt reported on here was described by Dennis Woerner of the Indianapolis Zoo. The Zoo instituted a dynamic pricing model instituted in 2014 that was already used in sports, concerts, etc. In this case, the goal was to space out visitors so the Zoo was less crowded overall. Woerner noted,

> Our ticket price had been $17.50—the new system offers prices from a low of $8 on weekdays in January and February to a high of $29.95 for Saturdays in late June....
>
> Some research…done suggests that lower-income individuals are more likely to buy at the lower rates.... Overall, we didn't see any big change in the demographics of our visitors.
>
> (para. 7)

The Zoo did not experience greater diversity in visitors overall.

These two models addressed different needs. Just as in the *museum pricing model* by Rentschler et al. (2004) and the hybrid model by Gombault and Rentschler (2009), these also had different underlying goals. For the Children's Museum, the goal was attracting more lower-middle-class visitors; for the Zoo, it was providing all visitors with less crowded experiences. Both of these models were in progress before the pandemic. Both models recognized that the visiting public and the museum administration wanted to make sure "those who can't afford the premium are still welcome" during most museum hours (Dobrzynski, 2009, para. 3).

Lastly, we note it is important to do the homework before advancing any model.

One Price for All

In another example, Silvia Filippini-Fantoni and Scott Stulen commented on the Indianapolis Museum of Art policy shifts on how much to charge. This museum went from being free to charging in 2015. Silvia Filippini-Fantoni said this:

> So, instead of charging for the parking, and charging for the exhibitions, we decided to charge for general admission. The general admission included the historic property, includes the museum, includes exhibition, and includes the garden…we wanted to stop nickel and diming people…we got from feedback…that people were tired of always being asked to give money, whether it was for the parking,… I don't think that they were thinking about $18 when they answered that question, but that's the feedback that we got.
>
> (excerpted from Fantoni, 2018, Museum Next talk)

Going Free for All

Another approach has been followed by the Dallas Museum of Art (DMA), which is currently experimenting with free membership and tracking all visits. From the DMA website,

> DMA Friends is a FREE membership program that allows you to earn badges and points to unlock special rewards when you visit the DMA.... What may not be apparent is how the program helps the Museum to know whether we're doing a good job providing engaging experiences with art. In addition to talking one-on-one with our Friends, the DMA uses data collected from DMA Friends to better understand visitor behavior and preferences. DMA has a tracking program and a chart for its "Friends".
>
> (Dallas Museum of Art, 2013 website)

Boards of Directors and Power

Pricing strategies are only one example of tertiary contradictions arising to relieve the secondary contradictions that always arise due to the primary contradiction of service (use) vs. finances (exchange). I would be remiss if I did not include an analysis of power dynamics at the board of directors level of museums.

Decision-making around policy and mission in museums, at least in large American museums, remains in the hands of the boards of directors, who pay large sums for these positions of *power* and *public service*. This pattern links museums with predominantly rich white men and some women as board members, in part because they can afford the expected donation. I note the obvious, that museum boards and the 'new mainstream', which they hope to attract, are not of the same socioeconomic class and may not share similar sociopolitical goals for museums.

Boards by definition[9] have to be concerned with the financial solvency of an organization, especially raising money from other well-off donors. They hold the power and the responsibility. For museums in the United States, "there are no uniform best-practice guidelines to help in appointing board members or deciding what kind of trustees should be accepted or avoided" (Stapley-Brown, 2019). Board members are expected to contribute a major part of the museum budget, up to 20%, which is a great deal more than entrance fees. As Pogrebin et al. (2019) noted, "The price of admission to the boards remains steep, often millions of dollars to enter, and annual donations of six figures to keep a seat" (para. 4).

At the heart of the critique is a call toward structural change. Mallett and Schneider (2019) stated, "Activist groups like *Decolonize This Place* want... [to clean up] what they call a 'closed-door' committee adjudicating the boundary between 'good' and 'bad' money" (para. 6). By 'bad money' they often mean politically fraught investments. Fraser (2018) suggests that "museums [must] clean up their boards by democratizing them, [and] eliminating the pay-to-play contribution requirements" (p. 189).

Neoliberal influences are evident everywhere we examine museum boards in relation to recent decolonizing efforts (Mallett & Schneider, 2019; Shoenberger, 2020; Small, 2021). Over the past decade, the focus on museums' financial and sociopolitical contradictions has gained much traction (Tarmy, 2019), resulting in considerable community pushback (*Decolonize This Place*, *Incluseum*, *The Inclusive Museum*, *Race and Museums*, etc.) through blogs and the press. As a result, directors have been fired, and board members with questionable ties to business and politics have resigned. In one example,

> Warren B. Kanders, a vice chairman of the Whitney Museum of American Art, [was] driven out by a cascading protest over his company's sale of law enforcement and military supplies.
>
> (Pogrebin et al., 2019, para. 5)

The chairman of the board of the Museum of Modern Art (MOMA), Leon Black, recently stepped down in the wake of ties to a known criminal (Greenberger, 2021). Six members of the Detroit Institute of Arts board of directors resigned because of a dispute over its controversial director, Salort-Pons (Rubin & Rahal, 2021), reportedly concerning 'workplace harassment and insular management styles'. Similar criticisms have been levied at the investments of board members at the San Francisco MOMA and other art institutions, calling into question their ethical propriety (Fraser, 2018; Halperin, 2019).

Board Power: The Dialectic in Action

A dialogue between museum directors Glenn Lowry, director of the MOMA, and Philippe de Montebello, past director of the Met (excerpted from Rosenbaum, 2006) during a roundtable discussion published in *Whose Muse: Art Museums and the Public Trust*, actually provides ample discursive manifestations of the dialectic:

> *Glenn Lowry:* I think there are different factors that come into play here. On one level it's almost a moral duty that museums should be free. Our collections are part of everyone's cultural heritage. We should make them available in as broad a way as possible. And an admission fee is one of the greater barriers to attendance.
>
> *Philippe de Montebello:* Wait a minute. Can we be both practical and philosophical? …. Philosophically, what is it about a work of art that makes it mandatory that it should be available for nothing, whereas the C Sharp Minor Quartet Opus of Beethoven should be paid for, that Aida should be paid for, that Ibsen should be paid for? What is [it] about art that it shouldn't be paid for?
>
> *Glenn Lowry* (later in the discussion): Part of me wants museums to be free because there is a sense that our collections and visitors' experiences of them belong to the public at large and should be available to anyone regardless of

cost. Another part of me, though, says, why should it be free? Why should this treasured experience be free, especially for an entity that gets virtually no government funding? And by making it free, are we inadvertently devaluing it.

(paras. 12–14)

Lowry's argument sits on the edge of the dialectic. He wants admission to be free but he doesn't want to devalue art (de Montebello's idea).[10] Subtle and not so subtle deficit views are in the undertow as the two directors debate whether art should be free. Lowry even appears to have changed his views in the face of deMonebellos's assertion of *high art* linked to *high music*.

Dialogues such as this are important to recognize and decode for hidden meanings, as they reveal biases concerning worth, being aesthetically cultured enough and belonging. In this dialogue, high art aesthetics won out.

Such views reflect the intertwining of power, money and sociopolitical status. This point was made by the book *Museums, Money, and Politics* by Andrea Fraser (2018), which examines the intersection of electoral politics, money and private nonprofit arts organizations ("prominent hubs of political finance") in the United States.

Retrenching Efforts

The pandemic has changed the museum world. Before COVID-19, we had conflicting predictions for museums, some optimistic (Bell, 2013) and some darker (Chung & Wilkening, 2008; Reach Advisors, 2013). The present-day crisis rendered that dialogue moot, adding a whole new layer of concern onto a field already teetering on the edge. As Woody (2019) said, "It's no secret that…museums…struggle to keep their doors open. There is almost no ability to cut the budget in areas that would make a significant enough difference" (para. 6). No country has been immune. The challenge is global. UNESCO and the International Council of Museums (ICOM) have both said

> 90% of the planet's museums—some 85,000 institutions—have had to shut at least temporarily [and]…nearly 13% of museums around the world may never reopen,…those in poorer countries faced a greater risk.
>
> (UNESCO, 2020)

The Network of European Museum Organizations, NEMO reported in April (2020),

> While some museums have found their budget minimally impacted as of yet, some museums, especially the larger museums and the museums in touristic areas, have reported a loss of income of 75–80%, with weekly losses adding up to hundreds of thousands of Euros.
>
> (NEMO, 2020)

Similarly in the United States, the AAM noted,

> One in every six American museums faces "significant risk" of closing permanently because of financial duress exacerbated by the COVID-19 pandemic.
>
> (Vankin, 2020, para. 2)

The Metropolitan Museum of Art in New York announced "projected losses of $100–$150 million…decisions made in the next year could determine the accessibility of their objects for the next century" (O'Donnell, 2020, para. 4).

The AAM (2020) reacted to the financial crisis of the pandemic by producing a laundry list of long and short-term financial retrenching efforts, including furloughing staff, diminishing reserves, re-opening with reduced staff, expected cutbacks on educational programs, as well as deaccessioning. There is real uncertainty concerning how to operate post-COVID. O'Donnell even queried, "[W]hat do they actually want to accomplish when the Covid-19 crisis subsides and the lockdowns end?" (O'Donnell, 2020, para. 2). How can museums stay solvent? In the face of this dire financial wasteland, how are museums responding? This next section reviews specific examples of *retrenching efforts*.

Quick Fixes: Consolidation, Reorganization, Furloughs, etc.

Museum personnel are typically the largest part of any institution's budget, and therefore the place for cutting costs. Before the pandemic, museums had already begun laying off workers, furloughing staff, reducing staff benefits, relying more on volunteers and deferring the hiring of new workers (Smith, 2016). Museums were already relying to a greater extent on existing museum collections and deferring routine maintenance. There were shifts in emphasis from externally procured expensive exhibitions to those created from existing museum collections. Museums had begun selling parts of the physical plant, selling art and objects (deaccession), delaying or canceling new shows and programs and shutting down satellite centers, among other cost-saving strategies. Famous museums, such as the San Francisco Exploratorium, the Bishop Museum in Honolulu, the Philadelphia Museum of Art (Itzkoff, 2009) and the Carnegie Museum of Art (Coyn, 2015), among others, had begun such measures even before COVID.[11]

Because personnel costs are always the largest budget item, the pay disparity in many museums between staff and directors looms larger. Pogrebin suggested,

> The pay disparity issue, already simmering in the museum world last year, has bubbled up since the pandemic as critics question whether museums should further curtail executive pay and draw on their endowments to keep their staffs employed.
>
> (Pogrebin, 2020, para. 4)

Some museum directors have taken voluntary pay cuts during the COVID-19 crisis. Pogrebin (2020) reported,

> Many of New York's museum leaders have taken pay cuts.... But at a time when museums are facing their most severe financial downturn in decades... critics are questioning whether such reductions go far enough.[12]
>
> (para. 4)

For example,

> the Metropolitan Museum of Art laid off 79 employees and furloughed an additional 181. That brings the Met's total layoffs to about 20 percent of their staff since March, when COVID-19 shutdowns began.
>
> (Conrardy, 2020, para 1)

Such layoffs are all too common; we find similar numbers in 2020 for the Museum of Natural History in New York, the Huntington in Los Angeles and Philadelphia Museum of Art, just to name a few. Some are dipping into their endowments, as allowed. It is problematic that museums often cannot use their sometimes-large endowment for salaries because "the paradox of endowments is that their primary function is not to be spent but to grow" (Di Liscia, 2020, para. 2).

In addition, scandals concerning money management have become increasingly frequent. In a series of *Chicago Tribune* articles focusing on the Field Museum in Chicago, there were claims of bad financial management and an upcoming balloon payment, as well as "[impending] layoffs and a massive restructuring" (Miner, 2013).

Sometimes museums have been forced to merge, as Woody (2019) described:

> Once a museum has reached a point where it can no longer afford to operate, it has few choices to consider, the main two being to close completely or attempt to merge. With sad irony, to close the museum will most likely involve an element of selling and disbursing its collection anyway.
>
> (para 8)

These cost-saving and sometimes desperate strategies give a general idea of the financial pressure museums have endured over the past decades. Although many have made strides through retrenching toward stability, others were already in the process of restructuring when COVID-19 added to their financial problems.

Deaccessioning Art

Possibly the most controversial measure museums are turning to in order to make money is *deaccessioning* paintings and art objects, as well as selling buildings to raise money for other projects. Such deaccessioning comes with many tensions (Blair, 2014; O'Donnell, 2020; Smith, 2013).

One such crisis in Detroit involved creditors requesting the Detroit Institute for Arts (DIA) to *sell off* its art. The court settled that this would be illegal (Kennedy, 2014) because the art was held by DIA in public trust, "meaning it couldn't be used for other purposes like paying off city debt" (Smith, 2013 para 3). This important legal precedent, that it is illegal to sell off art held in public trust, may have an impact on future contested *provenances* (ownership history) in the museum lexicon and of the legality of possession of some objects (see also Chapter 6). In the meantime, the ban on deaccessioning is shifting with the COVID-19 crisis. As O'Donnell (O'Donnell, 2020) noted,

> In normal times museum associations—the AAMD in particular…have sanctioned [frowned upon] selling art]…[Recently] The AAMD issued temporary guidelines allowing the spending of income earned on such proceeds…but it remains very much to be seen how great an impact that can have. And like many crises, it is hard to imagine the old rules sliding neatly into place afterwards.
>
> (para 2)

This has not occurred without fierce debate. The AAMD recognized that the

> financial disruption caused by the pandemic could be so severe that museums might need to take extraordinary measures…amid the pandemic and Black Lives Matter protests, there's a perfect storm of self-analysis, self-examination at museums…huge amounts of money, and core principles, are at stake in many of these battles.
>
> (Russeth, 2021, para 4)

Deaccessioning has generated much anxiety, basically concerning the rights of original donors, as well as the public mission to keep art for future generations (Riley, 2011). What was once unthinkable, "the notion of selling off a Claude Monet or two to plug a budgetary hole—or to fend off a total financial meltdown—is suddenly something to contemplate" (Smee & McGlone, 2020, para 3). Some museums, such as the Corcoran and the Newseum, both in Washington, D.C., have considered selling off part or all their physical properties (Mullins, 2012). As we saw in Table 4.1, the underlying contradiction is larger than the idea of selling art. There is a fundamental conflict between a museum's social/public goals and monetary concerns. *Deaccession* marks the dialectic.

There are trade-offs in all retrenching efforts; museums know they can raise revenue using entrance fees, but it must be balanced against other cost-cutting efforts. For example, as one museum director in England said after the 2008 crisis, "The worst option is for museums and public collections to start selling works to pay the bills; he opted for entrance fees instead." (Jones, 2011, para 3)

Power and Neoliberalism

Money is power in corporate entities.

Increasingly we have come to realize the degree to which neoliberalism and structural rigidity have come to undergird much of museum infrastructure and the actions of board members, especially their business affiliations. Kundu and Kalin (2015) have argued that "the so-called public space of the museum is being replaced by market logics, cloaked in ideals of humanism, inclusion, participation, public good, value, and citizenship" (p. 39) while concealing neoliberal goals. Dailey (2006) argued the same for science and health museums, suggesting "people working in museums have a heightened awareness of the economy, and…have a working vocabulary of 'economic terms' that is ever present" (p. 3). Both Dailey's and Kundu and Kalin's research detail how neoliberal tendencies play out on the museum floor, as staff members understand very well the demands to meet the bottom line. This has deeply affected their work and diminished their agency. Clearly, the SAD plays a role here as well.

The Future of Museums and Libraries: A Discussion Guide (Pastore, 2009) intended to predict thinking into the 21st century, suggesting (ten years ago), "Traditional power structures and notions of authority in the transference of knowledge and information may no longer characterize the museum and library experience" (p. 7). This has been made quite clear this past decade with criticism from many quarters, not the least of which strongly critiques existing museum power (primarily boards and directors) and their intertwined financial concerns. Some transformation has begun. The question is, "*How fast and how fully*" can change happen? While there has been change, it has, in most cases, been only piecemeal and cannot be called reculturing.

Summary

The opening vignette illustrates the increasing need for money by one of art museums' most famous institutions, the Met in New York City. This was followed by various examples of belt-tightening, both general and specific budget cuts, across countries, museum disciplines and size (Merritt, 2010). Such conflicts have been a quiet part of museum literature but, in more modern examples such as the Met vignette at the beginning of this chapter we see the larger ideological contradictions concerning balancing the budget vs. service, and their origins emerge more clearly.

Following the global financial crisis in 2008 and now especially in the time of COVID, museums are desperate for revenue streams. Finances are forcing museums to restructure, retrench, reculture, revise and/or review their core missions and practices (see also Cortell, 2011). Every partial solution comes with a cost. Increasing admission fees, for example, exacerbates the existing problems museums are having in failing to attract a sufficient market share of the 'new mainstream' (Rodriguez, 2009). I described five pricing strategies that attempt to help in the short term.

We have discussed some intertwined ideologically based contradictions apparent in this chapter. The most obvious three were

- the service/populist vs. budget/finances view of mission (Gurian, 2020),
- the deficit vs. resource views of visitors (Sleeter, 1996) and
- the collaborator vs. client views of visitors (Feinstein & Meshoulam, 2014).

I examined the dynamics at the highest levels of the museum hierarchy, describing primary contradictions at play when organization service goals for the public good have their functioning determined by directors following bottom-line principles.

Appendix 4.1: Pricing Details

There are conflicting views of the impact on entrance fees on visitor attendance overall. Danielsen's research (2008) has shown income has the most significant effect on the likelihood of a person visiting a museum (Cortell, 2011. p. 14). But a 2016 AIM (2016) report claimed that of the 311 independent museums they surveyed,

> what a museum charges has no effect on the diversity of its audience—both charging and free-entry museums have similar demographic profiles for their visitors....The research is timely as an increasing number of museums are thinking about introducing admission charges, in response to reductions in local authority funding.
>
> (para. 6)

How can both be true? This disagreement in the field serves to illustrate again how little we know of minoritized visitors and their relationship, if any, to museums as well as how ill-defined data gathering measures are. The AIM study is a counterargument to populist claims that money makes all the difference and runs counter to most other findings. Without clear theoretical foundations and analytic guidelines, research will not provide reliable information for policy making.

Appendix 4.2: Museum Executive Pay in New York City

Executive Pay at New York City Museums

1. **Glenn D. Lowry, Museum of Modern Art**
   Total director compensation: $5.1 million*
   Total museum expenses: $267 million
2. **Ellen V. Futter, American Museum of Natural History**
   Total director compensation: $1.8 million
   Total museum expenses: $215 million
3. **Richard D. Armstrong, Solomon R. Guggenheim Foundation**
   Total director compensation: $1.4 million**

Total museum expenses: $74.6 million
4. **Daniel H. Weiss, Metropolitan Museum of Art**
   Total director compensation: $1.25 million
   Total museum expenses: $491 million
5. **Adam D. Weinberg, Whitney Museum of American Art**
   Total director compensation: $1.1 million
   Total museum expenses: $89.4 million
6. **Josette Sheeran, Asia Society**
   Total director compensation: $937,000
   Total museum expenses: $32.7 million
7. **Ian Wardropper, The Frick Collection**
   Total director compensation: $851,000
   Total museum expenses: $41.9 million
8. **Lisa Phillips, New Museum of Contemporary Art**
   Total director compensation: $768,000
   Total museum expenses: $17.5 million
9. **Louise Mirrer, New York Historical Society**
   Total director compensation: $715,000
   Total museum expenses: $43.3 million
10. **Colin B. Bailey, Morgan Library and Museum**
    Total director compensation: $648,000
    Total museum expenses: $27.7 million

Source: *Museum federal tax returns (Pogrebin, 2020)*
★ *Compensation includes one-time retirement plan payout earned in earlier years.*
★★ *Compensation for 2018.*

Notes

1 Admission fees represent about 16% of the Met's total $297 million revenue, according to its most recent annual report.
2 Museums are most often supported by meta museum organizations dedicated to their particular community, sponsoring meetings, providing written documents, surveys and other aspects of museums when looked at as a collection of like-kind entities. Science museums, for example, look to the ASTC, children's museums to the Association of Children's Museums, art museums to the AAMD. Such associations are also organized geographically; there is, for example, the Florida Association of Museums, the California Association of Museums and, internationally, the Network of European Museum Organizations (NEMO).
3 Halperin (2019) echoes the original tipping point argument saying, "When academics look back, it's possible that 2019 will be remembered as an inflection point in the history of museums and their relationship to money….[M]ajor art institutions—and more specifically the people who fund and run them—have come under unprecedented scrutiny". (para. 3)
4 Metropolitan Museum of Art, Museum of Modern Art, Whitney Museum of American Art, Guggenheim Museum, SFMOMA, LACMA and the Art Institute of Chicago.

5 People in the lowest income bracket [in Germany] regard entrance fees as a barrier almost five times as much as people in the highest income bracket.... Closely related to income are education and occupation as variables influencing this assessment. An explanation for the impact of these variables on the assessment of museum entrance fees as a barrier can be found in the sociological models of lifestyle or milieu identifications. A visit to a museum is more than an economic decision; it is an expression of a lifestyle (Kirchberg, 1995, p. 10).
6 Brown (2020) argued that the age of blockbuster is over, due at least part to the pandemic, saying, "In short, as museums begin to slowly reopen, they are looking at a landscape that has changed completely, and the blockbuster trend—the product of a heavily trafficked world—faces an uncertain future" (para. 5).
7 Which staged "Young Rembrandt", a major exhibition, in 2019.
8 Setting entrance fees according to usage patterns, such as airlines do.
9 It is not typical for museum boards to advertise their funding shortfalls or the financial mismanagement of boards of directors, but these times are not normal, and museums are being more open about distress.
10 Sometimes museums are labeled playgrounds for the middle class and more educated but not for others. The argument then becomes, Why should such costs be underwritten by the public?
11 In New York City, the Guggenheim furloughed 92 staff members, the Whitney laid off 76 employees a week prior. MoMA terminated all freelance educator contracts, acknowledging that it could be years before the museum returns to "budget and educator services." (Di Liscia, 2020, para 4)
12 "The salaries of museum directors have to be listed on the institution's tax returns, which show that leaders of a half-dozen major institutions in New York received annual pay packages last year of $1 million or more, even as low-level employees earned as little as $35,000". (Pogrebin, 2020)

References

AAM (American Association of Museums). (2020, October). *National snapshot of COVID-19 impact on U.S. museums*.

Apple, M.W. (Eds.). (2017). *Cultural and economic reproduction in education: Essays on class, ideology and the state* (Vol. 53). Routledge.

Association of Independent Museums (AIM). (2016). *Taking charge—evaluating the evidence: The impact of charging or not for admissions on museums*. https://www.aim-museums.co.uk/wp-content/uploads/2017/04/Executive-Summary-Taking-Charge-%E2%80%93-Evaluating-the-Evidence-The-Impact-of-Charging-or-Not-for-Admissions-on-Museums.pdf.

Baltodano, M. (2012). Neoliberalism and the demise of public education: The corporatization of schools of education. *International Journal of Qualitative Studies in Education, 25*(4), 487–507. https://doi.org/10.1080/09518398.2012.673025

Bell, F. (2013). *How are museums supported financially in the United States?* GPA Publications. http://iipdigital.usembassy.gov/st/english/pamphlet/2012/05/201205155699.html#ixzz3

Blair, E. (2014, August 11). *As museums try to make ends meet, 'Deaccession' is the art world's dirty word*. NPR. http://www.npr.org/2014/08/11/339532879/as-museums-try-to-make-ends-meet-deaccession-is-the-art-worlds-dirty-word

Boast, R. (2011). Neocolonial collaboration: Museum as contact zone revisited. *Museum Anthropology, 34*(1), 56–70. https://doi.org/10.1111/j.1548-1379.2010.01107.x

Brestovansky, M. (2020). Officials warn of dire consequences if state cannot get outbreak under control. *Hawaii Tribune-Herald.* https://www.hawaiitribune-herald.com/2020/08/05/hawaii-news/officials-warn-of-dire-consequences-if-state-cannot-get-outbreak-under-control/

Brown, K. (2020, July 1). Is the age of the blockbuster exhibition over? A perfect storm of challenges suggests it may be a thing of the past. *Artnet News.* https://news.artnet.com/art-world/the-end-of-blockbusters-1890212.

Center for the Future of Museums. (2008). *Museums & society 2034: Trends and potential futures.* American Association of Museums. https://www.aam-us.org/wp-content/uploads/2017/12/Museums-Society-2034-Trends-and-Potential-Futures.pdf.

Cep, C. N. (2014, February 7). The case for free admission. *The New Yorker.* http://www.newyorker.com/business/currency/the-case-for-free-admission

Chung, J., & Wilkening, S. (2008). *Museums & society 2034: Trends and potential futures.* Center for the Future of Museums. aam-us.org/upload/museumssociety2034.pdf

Conrardy, A. (2020, August 10). Museums layoffs continue amid ongoing COVID-19 shutdowns. *Nonprofit Quarterly.* https://nonprofitquarterly.org/museums-layoffs-continue-amid-ongoing-covid-19-shutdowns/

Cortell, S. (2011). *The cost of free admission: A comparative study examining the feasibility of eliminating museum admission charges.* [Master's thesis, Ohio State University]. OhioLINK. https://etd.ohiolink.edu/

COVID-19: UNESCO and ICOM concerned about the situation faced by the world's museums. UNESCO. (2020, June 2). https://en.unesco.org/news/covid-19-unesco-and-icom-concerned-about-situation-faced-worlds-museums.

Coyn, J. (2015, February 12). Carnegie Museum of Art announces restructuring, layoffs. *Pittsburgh Business Times.* https://www.bizjournals.com/pittsburgh/news/2015/02/12/carnegie-museum-of-art-announces-restructuring.html

Dailey, T. L. (2006). *Museums in the age of neoliberalism: A multi-sited analysis of science and health museums* [Master's thesis, Georgia State University]. ScholarWorks. https://scholarworks.gsu.edu/anthro_theses/20

Dallas Museum of Art. (2013). Dallas Museum of Art announces $9 million gift to support free general admission and free online access to its entire collection. https://dma.org/press-release/dallas-museum-art-announces-9-million-gift-support-free-general-admission-and-freehttps://dma.org/.

Danielsen, A. (2008). The persistence of cultural divides: Reflections on the audience for culture and the arts in Norway. *International Journal of Cultural Policy, 14*(1), 95–112.

Dawson, E. (2014). Equity in informal science education: Developing an access and equity framework for science museums and science centres. *Studies in Science Education, 50*(2), 209–247.

Di Liscia, V. (2020, April 16). Why museums can't always fall back on endowments. *Hyperallergic.* https://hyperallergic.com/556133/why-museums-cant-always-fall-back-on-endowments/.

Dilenschneider, C. (2014). *Signs of trouble for the museum industry (DATA).* colleendilenschneider. https://www.colleendilen.com/2014/12/03/signs-of-trouble-for-the-museum-industry-data/

Dobnik, V. (2017, May 15). *Metropolitan Museum of Art works to rebound from money woes. AP News.* https://apnews.com/article/c11725a6bb8645f6a627b95577a7f78c

Dobrzynski, J. (2009, April 27). Variable prices for museums. *Forbes.* https://www.forbes.com/forbes/2009/0427/024-opinions-museums-lifestyle-on-my-mind.html

Ekström, K. M. (Eds.). (2020). *Museum marketization: Cultural institutions in the neoliberal era.* Routledge.

Engeström, Y. (1987). *Learning by expanding: An activity-theoretical approach to developmental research*. Helsinki: Orienta-Konsultit. http://communication.ucsd.edu/MCA/Paper/Engeström/expanding/toc.htm

European Museum Academy (EMA). (2019). *Annual report*. http://europeanmuseumacademy.eu/wp-content/uploads/2020/01/EMA-ANNUAL-REPORT-2019-.pdf

Fantoni, S. F. (2018, February 5). Film: Should museums charge for admission? *MuseumNext*. https://www.museumnext.com/article/to-charge-or-not-to-charge-museums-and-the-admission-dilemma/

Feinstein, N. W., & Meshoulam, D. (2014). Science for what public? Addressing equity in American science museums and science centers. *Journal of Research in Science Teaching*, *51*(3), 368–394. https://doi.org/10.1002/tea.21130

Foot, K. A. (2014). Cultural-historical activity theory: Exploring a theory to inform practice and research. *Journal of Human Behavior in the Social Environment*, *24*(3), 329–347. doi:10.1080/10911359.2013.831011

Fraser, A. (2018). *2016. In museums, money, and politics*. The MIT Press.

Gombault, A. (2003). The new organizational identity of museums. *Revue française de gestion*, *1*(142), 189–203.

Gombault, A., & Rentschler, R. (2009, June 28–July 1). Museum pricing in contemporary museums: A hybrid model. *AIMAC 2009: Proceedings: 10th International Conference on Arts & Cultural Management*, SMU, Dallas, Texas.

Grant, D. (2017, March 14). The admission fees are too damn high. *Observer*. https://observer.com/2017/03/rising-admission-fees-museums-moma-met/

Grant, D. (2018, January 4). With admission fees, the question is: What should a museum be? *Observer*. https://observer.com/2018/01/met-museums-new-admission-policy-why-do-museums-charge-entry-fees/

Grant, D. (2019, July 23). How much is too much? *The New Criterion*. https://newcriterion.com/blogs/dispatch/how-much-is-too-much.

Greenberger, A. (2021, March 26). Amid Jeffrey Epstein fallout, Leon Black will step down as MoMA board chair. *ARTnews*. https://www.artnews.com/art-news/news/leon-black-moma-board-chairman-steps-down-1234588009/.

Gurian, E. H. (2005). Free at last: A case for eliminating admissions charges in museums. *Museum News*, *84*(5), 33–66.

Gurian, E. H. (2006). *Civilizing the museum: The collected writings of Elaine Heumann Gurian*. Taylor & Francis.

Gurian, E. H. (2020). Curator: From soloist to impresario. In C. Fiona & L. Kelly (Eds.), *Hot topics, public culture, museums* (pp. 95–111). Cambridge Scholars Publishing.

Halperin, J. (2019, July 17). In an age of political division and dirty money, can museum boards ever be immaculate? Some think they have found a solution. *ArtNet News*. https://news.artnet.com/art-world/boards-museums-money-2019-1600507

Harvey, D. (2005). *A brief history of neoliberalism*. Oxford University Press.

Itzkoff, D. (2009, February 25). Budget cuts bring layoffs to museums. *The New York Times*. http://www.nytimes.com

Jones, J. (2011, July 21). Museums should feel free to charge admission. *The Guardian*. https://www.theguardian.com/artanddesign/jonathanjonesblog/2011/jul/21/museums-charging-admission-entry-fee

Kennedy, R. (2014, November 7). 'Grand bargain' saves the Detroit Institute of Arts. *The New York Times*. http://www.nytimes.com

Kirchberg, V. (1995). Entrance fees as a subjective barrier to visiting museums. *Journal of Cultural Economics*, *22*(1), 1–13.

Kirchberg, V. (1998). Entrance fees as a subjective barrier to visiting museums. *Journal of Cultural Economics*, 22, 10.

Kundu, R., & Kalin, N. M. (2015). Participating in the neoliberal art museum. *Studies in Art Education*, 57(1), 39–52. https://doi.org/10.1080/00393541.2015.11666281

Lindqvist, K. (2012). Museum finances: Challenges beyond economic crises. *Museum Management and Curatorship*, 27(1), 1–15. https://doi.org/10.1080/09647775.2012.644693

Lyall, S. (2013, October 7). Seeking clarity on fees at the metropolitan museum. *The New York Times*. https://www.nytimes.com/2013/10/08/arts/design/seeking-clarity-on-fees-at-the-metropolitan-museum.html.

Mallett, W., & Schneider, K. (2019). Ranking New York's most toxic museum boards. *Vulture*. https://www.vulture.com/2019/08/new-york-most-toxic-museum-boards.html

McFelter, G. (2007). The cost of free. *Museum News*, 86(1), 60–67.

Merritt, E. (2010, December 22). *The path to sustainability—working together*. Center for the Future of Museums Blog. https://www.aam-us.org/2010/12/22/the-path-to-sustainability-working-together/

Merritt, E. (2020). *Where do we go from here: A call to action*. Demographic Transformation and the Future of Museums. https://www.aam-us.org/wp-content/uploads/2017/12/Demographic-Change-and-the-Future-of-Museums.pdf

Miner, M. (2013, December 9). Hammered by the *Chicago Tribune*, the Field Museum recovers. *Chicago Reader*. https://www.chicagoreader.com/Bleader/archives/2013/12/09/hammered-by-the-chicago-tribune-the-field-museum-recovers

Mullins, L. (2012, November 27). Crisis at the Corcoran. *Washingtonian*. https://www.washingtonian.com/2012/11/27/crisis-at-the-corcoran/

Network of European Museum Organizations (NEMO). (2020) *Survey on the impact of the COVID-19 situation on museums in Europe*. https://www.ne-mo.org/fileadmin/Dateien/public/NEMO_documents/NEMO_Corona_Survey_Results_6_4_20.pdf

Ng, D. (2013, March 7). Metropolitan Museum of Art is sued over 'recommended' admission. *Los Angeles Times*. https://www.latimes.com/entertainment/arts/culture/la-et-cm-metropolitan-museum-of-art-sued-20130306-story.html.

O'Donnell, N. (2020). How far can museums go to stay afloat during the current crisis? *Apollo Magazine*. https://www.apollo-magazine.com/museums-coronavirus-crisis/

Pastore, E. (2009). *The future of museums and libraries: A discussion guide (IMLS-2009-RES-02)*. Institute of Museum and Library Services. https://www.imls.gov/publications/future-museums-and-libraries-discussion-guide

Pogrebin, R. (2020, August 2). Museum boss salaries: Reduced but still an issue amid wider cutbacks. *The New York Times*. https://www.nytimes.com/2020/08/18/arts/design/museum-leader-salaries-pay-disparity.html

Pogrebin, R., Harris, E. A., & Bowley, G. (2019, October 2). New scrutiny of museum boards takes aim at world of wealth and status. *The New York Times*. https://www.nytimes.com/2019/10/02/arts/design/whitney-art-museums-trustees.html.

Powell, J., & Menendian, S. (2017, June 29). The problem of othering: Towards inclusiveness and belonging. *Othering and Belonging: Expanding the Circle of Human Concern*, (1), 14–39. https://otheringandbelonging.org/wp-content/uploads/2016/07/OtheringAndBelonging_Issue1.pdf

Raicovich, L. (2019). Why libraries have a public spirit that most museums lack. *Hypoallergenic*. https://hyperallergic.com/author/laura-raicovich/

Reach Advisors. (2013). *Museum audience insight*. Audience Shifts and Meaning Making. https://reachadvisors.com/past-presentations/2013-archive/

Rentschler, R., Hede, A.-M., & Ramsey, T. (2004). Pricing in the museum sector: The need to balance social responsibility and organisational viability. *Australian & New Zealand*

Marketing Academy. Conference (2004: Victoria University of Wellington), Wellington, New Zealand. http://hdl.handle.net/10536/DRO/DU:30.

Riley, G. (2011, February 1). *When museums sell art: A better way*. Broad Street Review. http://www.broadstreetreview.com/theater/when_museums_sell_art_a_better_way.

Rodriguez, G. (2009). *Towards a new mainstream?* Center for the Future of Museums. futureofmuseums.org/events/lecture.

Rosenbaum, L. (2006, July 6). *Lowry and de Montebello on admission fees*. CultureGrrl. http://culturegrrl.blogspot.com/2006/07/lowry-and-de-montebello-on-admission.html

Rosenbaum, L. (2015, September 7). The brave new museum sputters into life. *The Wall Street Journal*. https://www.wsj.com/articles/the-brave-new-museum-sputters-into-life-1441657298.

Rosencheck, M. (2018, January 8). Museums should be free to everyone, regardless of where they live or how much they earn. *Philadelphia Enquirer*. https://www.inquirer.com/philly/opinion/commentary/new-york-the-met-admission-pay-what-you-can-museum-20180108.html

Rubin, N., & Rahal, S. (2021, March 29). Detroit Institute of Arts board members resign in dispute over controversial director. *The Detroit News*. https://www.detroitnews.com/story/news/local/detroit-city/2021/03/29/detroit-institute-arts-board-members-resign-dispute-over-director/7050624002/

Russeth, A. (2017). *At the art museum ticket office, how much is too much? Artnews*. https://www.artnews.com/art-news/news/at-the-art-museum-ticket-office-how-much-is-too-much-8707/

Russeth, A. (2021, February 8). As museums push to sell art, competing ideas about deaccessioning are playing out in public. *Artnews*. https://www.artnews.com/art-news/market/museum-deaccessioning-coronavirus-pandemic-1234583143/

Schneider, T. (2020, November 23). The gray market: Why corporate collections are thriving while museums starve (and other insights). *Artnet News*. https://news.artnet.com.

Shoenberger, E. (2020). *What does it mean to decolonize a museum?* MuseumNext. https://www.museumnext.com/article/what-does-it-mean-to-decolonize-a-museum/

Siegal, N. (2020, April 29). Many museums won't survive the virus. How do you close one down? *The New York Times*. http://www.nytimes.com

Simon, N. (2007a, March 20). *Hierarchy of social participation*. Museum 2.0. http://museumtwo.blogspot.com/2007/03/hierarchy-of-social-participation.html.

Simon, N. (2007b, June 19). *Book club part 1: Free at last*. Museum 2.0. http://museumtwo.blogspot.com/2007/06/book-club-part-1-free-at-last.html

Simon, N. (2017, August 16). *Guest post by Seema Rao: How museums can resist racism and oppression*. Museum 2.0. http://museumtwo.blogspot.com/2017/08/guest-post-by-seema-rao-how-museums-can.html

Skorten, D. (2014). The demands of running a 21st-century museum. *The Atlantic*. http://www.theatlantic.com/national/archive/2014/10/david-skorton-on-the-smithsonians-future/382117/

Sleeter, C. E. (1996). *Multicultural education as social activism*. State University of New York Press.

Small, Z. (2021, February 9). After a year of reckoning, US museums promised to implement diversity policies. Workers are still waiting to see what that means. *Art News*. https://news.artnet.com/art-world/dei-initiatives-museums-1941407

Smee, S., & McGlone, P. (2020, December 6). A Baltimore museum tried to raise money by selling three pricey artworks. It backfired stupendously. *Washington Post*. https://www.washingtonpost.com/entertainment/museums/baltimore-museum-warhol-sale/2020/12/04/1643859e-3317-11eb-8d38-6aea1adb3839_story.html

Smith, J. (2016). Museum of modern art to offer employee buyouts. *The Wall Street Journal*. http://www.wsj.com/articles/museum-of-modern-art-to-offer-employee-buyouts-1461975639

Smith, R. (2013, September 10). In Detroit, a case of selling art and selling out. *The New York Times*. http://www.nytimes.com.

Stapley-Brown, V. (2019). Philanthropy, but at what price? US museums wake up to public's ethical concerns. *The Art Newspaper*. https://www.theartnewspaper.com/news/what-price-philanthropy-american-museums-wake-up-to-public-concern

Tarmy, J. (2019). The latest attacks on private philanthropy remove one of the only methods museums have to survive. *Bloomberg News*. https://www.bloomberg.com/news/features/2019-08-15/the-american-museum-is-in-crisis

Tienken, C. H., & Orlich, D. C. (2013). *The school reform landscape: Fraud, myth, and lies*. Rowman and Littlefield.

Vankin, D. (2020). Pandemic could close some museums forever. *The Columbus Dispatch*. https://www.dispatch.com/story/entertainment/arts/2020/07/26/pandemic-could-close-some-museums-forever/42101519/

Ward, S. J. (2016). *Understanding contradictions in times of change: A CHAT analysis in an art museum*. [Doctoral dissertation, University of Washington]. ResearchWorks Archive. http://hdl.handle.net/1773/37091

Woody, R. C. (2019, March 16). *Museums in financial trouble: Sell, close, or plan a museum merger?* Lucidea. https://lucidea.com/blog/museums-in-financial-trouble-sell-close-or-plan-a-museum-merger/.

5
WHOSE STORY IS IT?

Overview

This chapter asks, "*Whose story is it?*" We review the stories museums tell and don't tell, as well as the contradictions such stories make visible.[1] Both in public life and in museums, people are implicitly and explicitly pressed to accept narratives or stories about origins, meaning and import. I address here the tensions surrounding the social, cultural and historically informed stories museums do tell, as well as those they do not tell—that is, counter-narratives. There are different ways to tell narratives, as well as multiple ways to interpret and value them. Exploring these we can glimpse ideological contradictions.

Contradictory views of history, sociopolitics and culture affect the selection and *translation*[2] of stories on the museum floor, on websites, in publications and in the surrounding communities. I focus in this chapter on contradictions in natural history and cultural museums, specifically those portraying Native Americans in the United States, and Indigenous people across the world, to stand in for other contested histories.

Wherever there is a master narrative, by which I mean the dominant *story* that contains and constrains alternative/counter-narrative in order to counteract any resistance (Bamberg & Andrews, 2004, p. 185), we must ask: *who owns it*, and *what happens when it is challenged by counter-narratives*? Braddock and Horgan (2015) define narratives as "any cohesive and coherent account of events with an identifiable beginning, middle, and end about characters engaged in actions that result in questions or conflicts for which answers or resolutions are provided". Opposing positions to such narratives are called "counter-narratives" (p. 383). In order to delve into the central contradiction in this chapter, I use a proxy from Native American histories. By focusing on one large cultural group, I hope to delineate some main points of contention and how these may or may not transfer to other contested

DOI: 10.4324/9781003261681-5

histories in other times and places. Contested history refers to how different ideologies represent certain 'historical' events, for example, Western expansion vs. destruction of Native societies (cultural genocide).

> **VIGNETTE**
>
> At the University of Michigan natural history museum, situated near dinosaur bones, fossils and taxidermy, 14 miniature 3D scenes illustrated Native Americans' ordinary life before European contact. The scenes were typical of the kinds of displays common in many natural history museums. Native American faculty members, students and others who visited these dioramas voiced their dissatisfaction, suggesting these dioramas were out of place in this museum:
>
>> We are living, breathing, contemporary human beings.... Many of us felt it was wrong that we had been represented so long as little dolls in the context of a natural history museum.
>> (Margaret Noori, a professor of Ojibwe language and literature at the University of Michigan; Capriccioso, 2009, para. 3)
>
> A member of the Sault Ste. Marie Tribe of Chippewa Indians [said]: "I never really felt good about it", adding "she would "sometimes come to stare at the dioramas, wishing they would be removed". She had come to the University of Michigan to learn the Ojibwe language. These dioramas disturbed her: "it's just an odd idea to see what are supposed to be my people in a tiny box" (para 4).
>
> When Amy Harris became director of this museum in 2001, a Native American Committee soon asked her to 'improve the situation'. Labels and timelines were added; some contemporary explanations were included, and new displays, for example one on powwows were added.
>
> These efforts did not satisfy the Committee, however. They suggested removing the dioramas altogether. "Indians, after all, were still being represented as tiny miniatures in boxes, sort of like hamsters", some said. Director Harris removed the dioramas in 2010, arguing that Native American representations did not belong in the museum. "We were concerned that we were leaving the impression that Native Americans are extinct, just like the dinosaurs on the second floor," said Harris (Capriccioso, 2009, para.5).
>
> Since 2001 Harris has met regularly with a range of constituents, including UM faculty, students and Native Americans from around the state. Her goal has been to gauge the effectiveness of exhibits. Harris responded appropriately as she learned that and how dioramas were offensive and perpetuated negative attitudes.
>
> (Excerpted from Capriccioso, 2009; University of Michigan website; Brown, 2009; Diep, 2014)

Introduction

Echoing this vignette, current literature is filled with debates concerning the stories museums tell about Native Americans and other Indigenous and enslaved peoples, and why they tell them the way they do. I focus on such narratives because they are such a crucial way we learn and make sense of complex phenomena (Bedford, 2001). I call into question unexamined "master narratives that have dominated stories about the past…in light of emerging alternatives" (Cox & Stromquist, 1998, p. 12). Philosophers and linguists suggest that *master* narratives inform all stories that are told.

The central contradiction I propose here focuses on the disjuncture between narratives told about Native peoples, which are often couched in versions of lore and anti-lore; master narrative; and counter-narrative. I particularly ask, "*Who owns the story?*" We have all experienced the effect of a master narrative at work when we go to the movies. Within the genre of 'the western', we recognize the European American hero to be the one in the white hat. No number of local stories of resilient American Indians can easily wipe away the power of this symbol of westward expansion.

Bamberg and Andrews (2004) have suggested that master narratives are, in fact, "sociocultural forms of interpretation…meant to delineate and confine the local interpretation strategies…[for] individual subjects as well as in social institutions" (p. 287). By delineating and confining local interpretations, the master narrative becomes and remains the dominant story. Counter-narratives, then, "offer resistance, either implicitly or explicitly, to dominant cultural narratives" (Bamberg & Andrews, 2004, p. 4).

Wherever we find a master narrative, we need to ask, "*Who owns it, and what happens when they are challenged by counter-narratives?*" Carpio has argued that the master narrative's power comes from

> the absence or deliberate exclusion of the "other's" history…to reify the master narrative, as does the utilization of a historical "presence" or inclusion that only benefits the dominant narrative.
> (Carpio, 2008, in Lonetree & Cobb, 2008, p. 291)

Counter-narratives, then, are "the stories which people tell and live which offer resistance, either implicitly or explicitly, to dominant cultural narratives" (Bamberg & Andrews, 2004, p. 4). Decolonizing invokes counter-narratives, counter-history, counter-policies and offers resistance (Jaime & Stagner, 2019). The current challenges to dominant European American master narratives by Native Americans throughout the United States are thus being mirrored in museums by demands for representing counter-narratives alongside or instead of the master narrative of Western expansion.[3]

One secondary contradiction we see in the vignette is how it is possible to position Native American people in diorama exhibits as frozen in the time of European contact rather than as they are now. This was the source of some personal embarrassment for modern Ojibwe in the vignette. This chapter focuses on several contradictions as potential focuses for transformation. As just one example, Lonetree (2009) linked the colonization process to the museum's master narrative, arguing that museums, by and large, historically received a great deal of their goods, the objects that are on display, via the colonization process. Decolonization, therefore, can act as a partial undoing of previous damage done to oppressed peoples and their counter-narratives (Akers, 2014; Chinn, 2007; Lonetree, 2009, 2012). I discuss decolonizing in more detail in this and the next chapter.

I discuss the stories museums tell, I highlight competing ideologies and the contradictions they invoke, all the while paying attention to how master and counter-narratives interact dialectically.

In the mini-dioramas of the vignette, historical, primarily primitive representations stood in for real people living in the here and now, who have much to say about their own culture, objects, signs and messages. In the vignette, though, the museum chose what would be conveyed about tribal history and culture. Here is also a clear secondary contradiction between creating interesting objects for schoolchildren to look at and documenting a modern living culture, a tension in this case between subjects and tools. These small dioramas had been in the museum since 1969[4]; they had not been brought up to date. Sensibilities in 1969 were very different from now. As David Penney suggested in 2006, confirming the actions of Director Harris in the vignette,

> Today, when museums consider organizing an exhibition with an American Indian topic, there are nearly always three major agents at work: the institution of the museum and the representatives of living American Indian communities…both of whom address the third agent, the "object" of the exhibition.
> (Penney, 2006, p. 49)

By object he means the intended outcome, following activity theory, in this case a new negotiated object.

This is not exclusively a North or South American phenomenon; similar struggles occur in Australia, South Africa, New Zealand and many other places where Indigenous peoples have been targeted by colonial enterprises.

Lonetree (2006a) argued that "shared authority" between Native people and museum curators has changed the way Indian history and culture are represented. We certainly saw the clash of authority in the mini-dioramas. Lonetree warns, however, that shared authority is complex: "[W]hile collaborative efforts on the surface appear to be a positive direction—and there are certainly success stories to note—these successes are uneven at best" (2006, p. 635).

Even in situations of shared authority, it is still the museum's work/responsibility to deal directly with narrative, history and controversy in order to help visitors interpret what they *see*. In helping visitors interpret any person, object or event in history, it is often unclear whose values, history, stories, ethos and ideologies/epistemologies are being represented. Conflicts of interest and perspective are inevitable;

it is uncertain that the ideological conflicts in these two points of view can be resolved to some supposed impartiality.

Counter-Narrative as Resistance

Narratives are multisided, dynamic and often contradictory, rather than linear, chronological or fossilized. They always convey power. Counter-narratives offer resistance *either explicitly or implicitly* to the power of master narratives (Andrews, 2002; Ender, 2018). Scholarship exploring the concepts of *decolonizing* (Lonetree, 2009; Tuck & Yang, 2012) and *settled expectations* (Bang et al., 2012) and structures (Glenn, 2015) show how both function as powerful ways to counter and resist the sociopolitical, historical colonialist narratives that have been prevalent in museums and society in the past.

Once *decolonializing* has analyzed the ideologies behind words, actions and products considered *normal* or orthodox in our society more generally, and in museums in particular, then museums can 'see and do' things differently. As always with contradictions, we need to pay attention to who is involved, what the motivation and goal may be, the use of mediational means, the dynamics of power and hierarchy and explicit and implicit rules. We are particularly interested in how power and hierarchy are used and the rules that follow from these in constructing and using master narratives.[5]

Historical examples may help clarify this issue. Was Russia the victor that saved the world in World War II, or does the United States have that honor or do they both? (Rozhnov, 2005)[6] Was the Enola Gay, the airplane that dropped the atomic bomb on Japan, a blessing or an act of murder? (Dubin, 1999). Was westward expansion a boon to mankind or an agent of genocide (Lonetree, 2009; Robbins, 1989)? These are contentious issues for historians (Crosby, 1986) and much more so for the museums responsible for *accurately* interpreting these historical activities. For each master narrative, counter-narratives abound, and the notion of accuracy, or even impartiality, becomes quite opaque, perhaps even impossible (Bennett, 2018).

If the story happens to be about one's own family history or group history and is being represented in a particular exhibit (Russian, American Indian or Japanese, for example) one may or may not agree with the way the 'story' is being told. In the vignette, Native Americans felt strongly that their 'story' was not being told *accurately*.

What do we mean by *accurately*? How do we view 'western expansion'?

> [N]othing wrong had transpired in the course of U.S. history. On the contrary, it had all been a noble undertaking, carried out by a combination of gallant leaders and brave settlers forging a better future.
>
> (Churchill, 2010, para. 5)

Or was it more along these lines?

> The Columbian Legacy, now 510 years and counting, is by many accounts genocidal…the bodies and beliefs of the Indian peoples of the Western

> Hemisphere, along with their possessions and their lands, were plundered and debased.
>
> (Lonetree, 2006a, p. 632)

These two 'stories' directly contradict each other. When we delve into how competing stories describe the very same event, object or culture, we gain insights into the dilemma museums face every day. Where do they find *accuracy*? History is notoriously fickle in this regard.

More recently, museums, with strong prodding from Indigenous cultures and/or other nondominant communities, are becoming more receptive to counter-narratives, partly because they must. As we noted before, such efforts are often cosmetic or partial fixes to deeply structural problems. A few examples in this chapter show the early effects of reculturing. Sometimes this starts with inviting minoritized groups to take part in special *listening sessions*,[7] where the museum staff listens and then collaborates on exhibit design. Unfortunately, invited participants sometimes complain of tokenism rather than real structural change (Lonetree & Cobb, 2008).

The Power of Stories

The master narrative is the big story from which other smaller stories emanate, telling how the world works, as viewed and validated by society (Blades, 2007). Dominant or master narrative means just that: the power relationship between the story and those in power in the society is openly named, providing what is assumed to be a normative position. Andrews suggests "wittingly or unwittingly we become the stories we know and the master narrative is reproduced" (Andrews, 2002, p. 1). Thus, power is reproduced.

Dubin argues,

> Power and patrimony are always on display when we examine competing interpretations of history, its objects and people because so much emphasis is placed on telling the *accurate* story and representing the accurate ideologies, historical perspectives and sociocultural views of *power* dominant in the moment.
>
> (Dubin, 2014, p. 12)

Dubin, Blades and others suggest that power and privilege maintain the perpetuation of master narrative. Therefore, from their perspective "the master narrative reinforces the 'natural order' of the privileged position of the dominant by virtue of their class, race, gender, religion and nation" (Blades, 2007, para. 2).

For all these reasons, stories are powerful mediational means for persuasion. We may frame narratives within CHAT as either the mediational means for achieving a certain object or outcome or as the outcome itself if it is under negotiation. Using CHAT analysis helps us relate master and counter-narrative dialectically, as mutually negotiated objects. Counter-narrative efforts to decolonize museums and create new museums designed by American Indians (see Lonetree, 2009) stand, therefore, as resistance to past master museum narratives. Native-designed museums tell a different story. As Andrews (2002) might say members of 'outgroups' consciously go against the grain.

Historically, the *accurate* story was the one told by the museum and its educators, through signs, videos, docents or other public relations efforts. History (including natural history) predictably describes events from the point of view of the conquerors. For example, the narrative frames society has constructed of westward expansion stands in stark contrast to the lived experience of American Indians. This conflict illustrates the biases of history and reveals several important subordinate themes, all of which arise from and inform the master narrative, including depersonalizing objects and dioramas, relying on artifacts[8] as proxies and viewing inconvenient truths at arm's length through the wrong end of the telescope.

Because narratives and counter-narratives are key elements of all social, cultural and historical work that museums do, museums have assumed implicitly the right and power to interpret science, history, art and other disciplines, and to determine the chronology of events through which stories are told at exhibits, via signs, video or trained educators. Moreover, the master narrative informs smaller derivative narratives that trace their lineage back to the master story. For example, one aspect of manifest destiny might argue that any time before Western contact was unimportant. Until recently, this *story dominance* has been tacitly accepted by the power majority public.

Because narrative is also the hidden and not-so-hidden ideologically based mediational means by which *selected* histories, cultures and beliefs are promulgated, stories are not neutral, nor can they ever be. Both Dubin and Blades have argued that we need to more ably interrogate the role of *power* in telling any story, understand the role of master narratives and the abbreviated smaller versions that spring from them, as well as the fallout from unequal power relationships, either overt or covert.

Because history, science and art are created by people, the stories told of history, science and art must also characterize the people associated with such activity. Given the mandate under which museums function, master and counter-narratives become significant for many reasons: first and foremost, they reflect the logic and ideology a museum has selected or inherited regarding their mission, educational efforts and public relations, as well as their contributions to the public good. The way stories are told reveals the underlying forces behind the storytelling.

A cursory review of current newspapers or TV news reveals how dominant narratives are used. In 2019–2020, one dominant political narrative concerned immigrants; both in the United States and Europe, as well as in some other countries, the status of immigration had become unclear and politically fraught. News programs and documentaries have flooded print and airwaves telling narratives and counter-narratives, either demonizing or lauding immigrants and immigration. This is but one example where master and counter-narratives meet dialectically and are current, active and volatile in countries across the world (Ekman, 2019; Feinstein & Bonikowski, 2019; Mehta, 2019; Sahin Mencutek, 2020).

Story spills into all areas of the museum. Consider the power of storytelling for museum educator teaching (see Chapter 8). In the past, museum educators were explicitly trained to deliver specific 'story' content points, i.e., thus, being less tuned to listening and more to telling (Ash, 2014; Ash et al., 2012; Tran, 2008). Museums may argue that it is difficult and costly to allow space and time for the public to join in telling stories, as there is so much disciplinary content for educators, curators and exhibits to deliver.

Museums are in the business of telling; the hope is that the "story form generates personal connections between visitors and content" (Bedford, 2001). Roberts (1997) argued, though, that museums need to listen to the narrative of visitors and, as we noted in Chapter 3, to position nondominant, minoritized cultures as resources. As Black (2018, 2021) noted, museums claim to be

> adopting both the mind-set and infrastructure to do what it takes to make visitors want to come, to feel welcome when they arrive, cared for and engaged during their stay.
>
> (Black, 2018, p. 302)[9]

The above is a lovely aspiration, but it remains aspirational. Secondary contradictions arise with shifts away from didacticism; the individual agency of educators is limited by educational structural constraints. We study this aspect of structure/agency dialectic in Chapter 8. We mention it here as it exemplifies a particular structure/agency dialectic; also it is but one of the more obvious aspects in telling *true* narratives at the ordinary level of the visitor/educator/exhibit interface. Another more subtle aspect involves uncovering the core values of the museum that inform what the educators are expected to convey and how and whether they are trained to be critical consumers of that message. We address this next with the question, "*How is the master narrative constructed in museums and what are the underlying ideologies/epistemologies informing it?*"

Ideological Contradictions and Master Narratives

CHAT allows us to examine how underlying contradictions of narrative evolve, transform and take form as narratives in museums. Remember the value of the primary contradiction in activity theory—the difference between *use and exchange* values, where use emphasizes the use to which something can be put, while exchange emphasizes its exchange or monetary value. Pragmatically, the vignette at the beginning of this chapter presents exactly how this primary contradiction gives rise to secondary contradictions. The museum chose to create *interesting* objects for schoolchildren at the expense of being true to a modern living culture. Now, with societal shifts in values, there is active pressure to reculture away from an old dominant narrative of 'westward expansion' and 'manifest destiny' toward questioning the acceptability of collateral damage and the calculated indifference' (Whyte, 2017) to humans and nature. All such shifts in storytelling perspectives signal contradictions at work.

Museums have long been thought of as exhibitors of truth, but truth isn't universal. Past master narratives in our museums have often served *deficit* ideologies, *othering*, neocolonialism and commoditization. The stories museums tell are not neutral because people in power create museums.[10] Yet, museums are trusted as arbiters of truth (Reach, 2018). I examine some examples in the following section.

Conflicting Ideologies: Settler Colonialism/Westward Expansion vs. Decolonization/Native Rights

I use an exploration of the historical dialectical tension between *westward expansion/settler colonialism* vs. the more recent views of *decolonizing* (Lonetree, 2014) and Native rights (the latter as interpreted by federal laws such as the Native American Graves Protection and Repatriation Act) in present-day museums as a *proxy* for examining contested histories across the world. As contradictions are *levers for transformation* (Engeström, 2001), we use that lens to understand the origins and underpinnings of both settler colonialism and decolonization.

Decolonizing in museums means facing their colonialist origins, recognizing the resulting policies and practices and then *changing* them, acknowledging history in its fullness, not just Western versions, making explicit the underlying epistemologies of colonialist collectors (Lonetree, 2012). We discuss settler colonialism and decolonizing here and in the next chapter.

Settler colonialism, Barker and Battell Lowman (n.d.) argued, "is not an historical event tucked safely away in the past, but rather a constantly evolving structure that seeks allies in modern economies" (para. 6).[11] The term *settler colonialism* means "a distinct type of colonialism that functions through the replacement of indigenous populations with an invasive settler society that, over time, develops a distinctive identity and sovereignty" (Barker & Battell Lowman, n.d.; Barker, 2012). Kidman expanded on this view, arguing that "neo-settler-colonialism progresses the colonial project by drawing on a neoliberal toolkit of free-market ideas and practices in ways that disguise contemporary forms of imperial logic" (Kidman, 2019, p. 248). Such disguises are common in *helping* developing countries, where Taneja (2020) argues that "neo-colonialism is colonialism in disguise".[12] Speaking from the perspective of Indigenous academics, Joanna Kidman argued that there has been and still is "a continuity between European settler-colonialism and contemporary forms of neoliberalism" (Lloyd & Wolfe, 2016, in Kidman, 2019, p. 249). The power of settler colonialism, according to Barker (2012), has in part been because it is largely invisible.

Native American Story Power

The Indigenous people of North America have been a large part of narrative history, viewed primarily from a colonialist perspective in the past and a neocolonialist/neoliberalism position now.[13] As Kidman points out, the neo refers to adapting 20th- and 21st-century neoliberal principles onto historical approaches. Such neoliberal interpretations have wide-ranging implications for land use, sacred and material goods, power and sovereignty.[14]

Any narrative, master or counter, begets certain phrases and words that identify them (Lakoff & Ferguson, 2006). Generally, the victors get to choose the value-laden words, by claiming, for example, that westward expansion was a heroic event, where courageous pioneers believed in America's divine obligation, and manifest destiny reflected beliefs of cultural and racial superiority. The word *expansion* reflects a positive view—something is growing, getting bigger and better in the name of building a new country. 'Westward expansion' is 'settler colonialism', and a helpful focus for our discussion of a master narrative now being questioned (Jacobi & Tzfadia, 2017).

Westward expansion involves particular historical markers in time, often depicted in textbooks, popular culture and movies as involving cowboys and armies. The very real collateral damage of Native people being dislocated, looted, killed and almost eradicated has been excluded or minimized. What are these historical markers of settler colonialism? Public documents of the 1800s are quite explicit. The so-called benefits of the Indian Removal Act of 1830 (see Appendix 5.1) are one facet of the westward expansion narrative.

If we were instead to tell a more accurate story of Indigenous peoples' genocide, a different set of thoughts, words, intentions and actions comes to mind. A counter-narrative would include these *facts*: 'westward expansion', as it was carried out, involved "the annihilation of peoples, their property, plants and animals, the American bison, plains grasses, plains animals, and what we now recognize as the genocide of the American Indian" (Lonetree, 2009, p. 327).

Manifest destiny is a deficit ideology taking 'an us vs. them' position consistent with modern interpretations of neoliberalism. Othering and dehumanization are the rallying cry of all such efforts (Kendi, 2017). In distinct contrast to many of the 'words of destiny', Bang et al. (2012) commented on desettling *settled expectation* and 'disarming' normed narratives, knowing that both are built on historically situated socioculturally and politically racist foundations. *Norms* and *settled expectations* are the stuff of master narratives carried over generations and institutions as basic lore.

There are similar tensions in museums across the globe in geographic areas representing Indigenous peoples. The Indigenous Peoples and Museums Network[15] and the Association of Tribal Archives, Libraries, and Museums (ATALM), among others,[16] provide powerful counter-narratives for decolonizing and refuting *settler colonialism*.

Expansive Learning: Altering the Colonist Narrative

External pressure has encouraged museums to begin to decolonize, or at least renegotiate unintended consequences and disputed interpretations, as well as create more access to sacred materials. Museums are also being asked to *alter a narrative* and use it as the centerpiece of new exhibitions highlighting decolonizing efforts (Smith, 2005). One such example occurred with the American Museum of Natural

History diorama of 'Early New York' representing Dutch and Native history. In this case, the AMNH self-corrected the many mistakes present in an existing and inaccurate diorama depicting Dutch settlers and Native Lenape Indians interacting. The current AMNH website says,

> This 1939 diorama depicts Dutch leader Peter Stuyvesant receiving a delegation of Lenape, including Oratamin, a sachem (leader) of the Munsee branch. But the depiction of the Lenape reflects common clichés and a fictional view of the past that ignores how complex and violent colonization was for Native people.... Large-scale labels added in 2018 offer a layer of context and highlight misrepresentations in this scene.
>
> (AMNH, 2018)

In the original, Native customs were inaccurately portrayed, the placement of boats was wrong, Native clothing was incorrect, the minimization of women's power was incorrect, the placement of the main actors was Eurocentric and so on. At the root of the misrepresentation was a then *normed* view of power and Western cultural superiority, that matched the view of colonists then and neocolonialists now.

After a long discussion, the AMNH team decided not to take the diorama down. Instead, they kept the diorama and added critically reflective comments. This allowed the team to forefront these inaccuracies alongside the original picture, noting exactly where misappropriations were made on the original representation, thereby inviting public dialogue about misrepresentation of Native cultures.[17]

The point of contact between the Lenape and the Dutch gave rise to the question, "*Whose story are we to believe?*" Were the rich and well-dressed Dutch bestowing their knowledge on the primitive Indians? Or were the proud Indians bestowing their knowledge on the ignorant Dutch? Two master narratives were in conflict and the revised exhibit showed clearly how the diorama had originally served as the mediational means for the Dutch version, for the desired object of showcasing the Western narrative. We could not hear the Lenape version in story or diorama, as many were killed by disease, or by the Dutch and English, and not yet represented in the museum.

I suggest several ways to use CHAT to analyze two conflicting narratives of one moment in historical time. Relying again on the primary contradiction, the exchange aspect concerns the Dutch and the English stated goals that included land, money and ownership; *they bought the land*. The Native Indians, in this case the Lenape, had a collective view of how land is managed and owned and had management agreements with nearby tribes. Buying land was not understood, but land use rights were.

Using third-generation CHAT, we note the two communities share a contested object, which is land use. If we analyze only the museum activity system using second-generation activity theory, we note tensions between several nodes, including mediational means (an out-of-date narrative) and object (intended outcome of understanding history a certain way) and between mediational means and the Native Indians as subject, reflecting the misrepresentation of culture.

Another secondary contradiction, not often quoted directly, stems from the act of portraying the diorama more accurately. Doing so, museums run the risk of losing their long-time supporters (e.g., core patrons who may believe in manifest destiny). We can use CHAT to analyze how and under what conditions adjustments are and are not made.

Similar dioramas across the country (Dartt-Newton, 2009; Lonetree, 2014) represent how power, hegemony and money (Golding, 2009) were portrayed in early meetings between cultures. Many museums still contain such dioramas with contested master narratives and a lack of neutrality in designing and interpreting Native cultural history (Dartt-Newton, 2009).

Museums believe that these stories are powerful mediational means for visitors to "access [the story] on their own terms, their own choice and within their own place and time" (Kelly, 2003, p. 7). However, in Lisa Roberts (1997) words, this would comprise trusting visitors *enough* to place meaning into their hands. But how can the visitor make sense of it all when the picture, the signs and the story are wrong? Such an object of activity is at best misleading and, at worst, damaging for both visitors and educators.

In the terminology of CHAT, we can also say that altering the master narrative of early New York was an example of expansive learning. In this case, the staff questioned the diorama's narrative and representation, analyzed its shortcomings, created a new narrative model for understanding and disseminated it publicly. Seo and Creed (2002) described how the best-case scenario for reculturing efforts involves embedded social actors, museum staff, acting as change agents within the institution. In this Early New York diorama example, it appears the collective agency of curators, educators and other staff was instrumental in expanding the local system. School curriculum materials were also rewritten to match the revised narrative. The representation, the original mediational means, became the object of activity and was transformed into a new and different mediational means (Ash & deGregoria Kelly, 2013). This is representative of possibilities within the expansive learning cycle as entire systems change.[18]

I apply the same rationale of contradiction as transformative force and expansive learning for the remainder of this and other chapters. Viewed from a CHAT perspective, alternative master narratives eventuate as a contested object of negotiation, both informed by and informing all other nodes of the activity system, that is, its subjects, rules, division of labor, mediational means (tools), and community. A 'story' with different elaborations and outcomes depends on the specific master narrative (e.g., colonialism was good). If we accept the settler colonial narrative, then the resulting objects of so-called hegemony would be prized as trophies. By this we would mean Native headdresses, jewelry and so on. This was the spirit of collection by many private collectors in the 1800s.

If instead, we believe that the things that were collected are in fact sacred objects, then our elaborations and outcomes and subsequent analysis are quite different and would refer back to the origins and context of traditional cultural, historical value. This changes the narrative and, also, moves away from settler colonialism and

Whose Story Is It? **155**

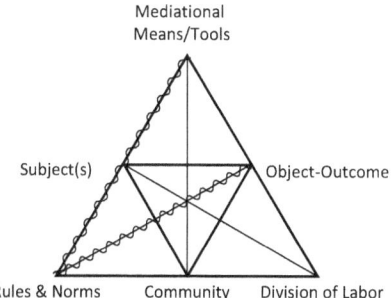

FIGURE 5.1 Activity system showing secondary contradictions in tension

toward decolonizing. Just as we noted in the revised version of old New York in the AMNH, the renegotiated object reflected Native traditions, influences and origins

I represent the aforementioned secondary contradiction (colonialism vs. neo-colonialism) in more practical ways using representation such as Figure 5.1, which offers insights into how an activity system experiences specific tensions.

The wavy lines indicate the tensions (secondary contradictions) following from the primary one. In Figure 5.1, we see the tensions between rules and objects as one possible tension, reflecting the contradiction of *how to view objects* of colonialism—that is, as trophies or sacred? Historically speaking, we note that some of the forces involved in these views may include both the Indian Removal Act of 1830, which changed the dynamic in the collecting/colonialism direction, and NAGPRA, which moved the dynamic in the other direction—that is, toward decolonizing, protection and preservation.

We also see a wavy tension between rules and mediational means in Figure 5.1, which represents another tension, here between rules and the tools they might be allowed to use. If Native artifacts are stored away, the Native people do not have access, spiritually or otherwise.[19] Further, the tension between mediational means and hierarchy might include the notion that educators may not be allowed to voice concerns about the master narrative the museum chooses to tell. In this case, the mediational means are constrained according to the hierarchical power relations between different roles within the museum (see Chapter 8) (Table 5.1).

Master Narrative Revisited: Ideological commitments

Bruner and Lucariello (1989) argued that ideologically driven dominant narratives often become taken-for-granted metaphors of how things were or became, and narratives alternative to the dominant one are then ignored or discounted as having no weight. This is an important corollary, suggesting master narratives tend to override other interpretations. Social, cultural, historical beliefs, power, deficit thinking and more come together when we consider the master narrative as a reflection of ideological commitments. For example, if we view Native Americans

TABLE 5.1 A representation of some possible secondary contradictions

Nodes in tension	Instantiation	Fixes/Tertiary contradictions
Rules/object	Colonizing vs decolonizing	Diorama @AMNH, recultured,
Tools/object	NAGPRA vs. Indian Removal Act	exhibits taken down, Univ. of Michigan
Mediational means/ div of labor	Land grabs, vs. preservation/respect for land	AMNH teaching conservation of land, species Research on indiv. vs. collective ownership
Mediational means / object	Slavery, rape, material goods financial political vs spiritual, cultural worth	Reculturing the story, repatriating the goods

or African Americans as less than human, then logically it is acceptable to enslave or annihilate them.

By ideological commitments, I refer to the underlying belief systems present in anything we see or do. Master narratives are consistent with such ideological commitments, manifested on a grand scale. The master narrative stance of many large older museums began and was perpetuated by elite European American buyers and owners, who collected items for display purposes (Yanni, 2005). We saw with both the AMNH and the University of Michigan museum that change can happen as museums critically reflect on their narratives for reinterpretation in current times. In a critique of the NMAI master narrative, Lonetree & Cobb suggested that while things are changing, the master narrative 'hurt' has long and deep roots. This is especially problematic when the change and the historical interpretation are in the hands of the institutions controlled by the successors of the original 'wound'. They argued:

> The story is not that simple. The historical legacy of the relationship between American Indians and museums is difficult to overcome. We suffered great injustices in the colonization process and in the name of Western science—both of which are intimately linked with the museum world.
> (Lonetree & Cobb, 2008, p. 307)

A culture's ideologically informed master narrative may be implicit and remain unquestioned as a *norm* or ' things are always done this way'. It then serves as a script we can use to reflect our expectations. We may not even be aware of the master narrative underlying our logic and beliefs. Bruner and Lucariello (1989) suggested that it is hard to change master narratives once "they have entered the social, cultural and historical mainstream" (p. 73). Even when conflicting data and competing stories exist, these alternatives can then be ignored entirely or expected to quietly go away. Such a pattern of belief and disbelief is all too familiar in our current social media-centric culture.[20] We might also wonder if museums can afford to critically reflect when many of the core donors come from the monied classes (Mayer, 2010).[21]

To place tensions regarding 'narrative truth' in a larger context, we note that Natural History museums were created in the late 19th century.[22] Sheets-Pyenson (1987), among others, considered them to be "monuments to colonialism, where "reputations…depended upon the number of specimens amassed, with considerable cachet attached to the acquisition of exotic foreign materials" (p. 280). Precisely because of their origin, the master narrative has necessarily reflected colonialist ideals even centuries later.

Another, perhaps competing narrative in natural history museums now, centers on a conservation message[23]—namely, that it is mankind's job to keep these objects, animals, plants, etc., safe and that the visitor also has a role to play in advocating for conservation efforts. Such a narrative affirms the importance of the institution and the important role a visitor can play. It is difficult to disagree with the latter argument; keeping animals and ecosystems safe from annihilation is critical, both for plants and animals and the human species. These are some of the same museums, however, that place Natives next to dinosaurs and retain inaccurate dioramas. There is sometimes merely a fragile truce between past colonial and current conservation narratives.

This is especially true as neoliberalism has co-opted environmental narratives (Cousins et al., 2009). This has been labeled the 'commodification of nature' (Büscher et al., 2012) or, as McAfee (1999) suggested, 'selling nature to preserve it'. We need to carefully choose which version of the conservation narrative we adopt.

Any commodified view of nature makes it even harder for museums of natural history to move away from their 1800s' 'collect at all cost' roots (Bennett, 2018). We indicate this in Table 5.2. The two subjects appear antithetical because if the object of collecting is commodified, conservation efforts disappear and ownership and power retain their primacy.[24]

Whichever aspect of this particular dialectic we believe, museums have the job of listening to and interpreting *multiple* voices of history for the public, and for this, underlying ideological/epistemological stances matter. In the case of the Michigan dioramas, we noted that the view of the museum director changed, and the exhibit was taken down. In coming to this decision, the director conferred with both Smithsonian experts and with her own community. We can appreciate that colonialist/conservationist narratives may no longer comfortably coexist, as we now understand that colonists often destroyed animals and plant habitats, as well as Indigenous peoples, while simultaneously collecting from them (Crosby, 1986).[25]

TABLE 5.2 Commodification vs. conservation

Secondary contradiction			*Tensions*
Colonialist collecting Commodification of nature	vs.	Conservation Nature as social/ common good	Collecting/selling objects/ nature Everything has a price

158 Whose Story Is It?

TABLE 5.3 Controversies at three levels

	Location	Level
Controversy 1	Sutter Buttes, California	Local
Controversy 2	*Californio* Indians, Central California	State-wide
Controversy 3	National Museum of the American Indian	National

American Indian Narratives: Secondary Contradictions

When museums position controversy as the central subject of an exhibit and step back from taking sides, they move closer to accepting that visitors are capable of making their own meanings of the presented events. This requires trusting the activity system, people, mediational means and object to self-adjust, perhaps with optimal scaffolding.[26] Visitors can handle controversy. To explore this, I examine the contested meanings of three controversial areas (Table 5.3).

Controversy 1: Whose Story on a Local Scale: The Sutter Buttes as an Example of the Public/Private Dialectic

This case considers three different stories about land 'ownership' in California, specifically across the conflicts between public and private use of land. This exposes the competing ideologies behind the meaning of land. The overarching conflict concerning best "use of simultaneously state-owned, sacred, [and] privately contested land resonates with larger environmental issues" (Baker, 2013, para. 4).

The Oakland Museum of California's (OMCA) relatively new natural history gallery (Baker, 2013) used the mountains in the Sacramento Valley of central California, known as the Sutter Buttes or 'Middle Mountain', as it was named by the Maidu (Figure 5.1)[27] to ask about land management and ownership. As the OMCA explains on its website,

> The *Sutter Buttes*...were chosen as remnants of the vast number of habitats and species now largely eliminated in this area, and a context for presenting contemporary issues of land management and ownership.
>
> (OMCA, n.d.)

The innocuous-sounding phrase *contemporary issue of land management and ownership* reflects one of the many contradictions emerging about land use in central California and elsewhere. The focus of the exhibit was twofold—providing a detailed history of the area and presenting the current *contested* meaning of land management and ownership. One secondary contradiction then involves money

FIGURE 5.2 The Sutter Buttes (Photo from Alamy)

and land use. The OMCA exhibit includes stories from three points of view: Native Americans, private landowners and the State of California. Using the personal stories, history and pictures of the Sutter Buttes, the exhibit asks the visitor to consider different narratives in conflict (Figure 5.2).

Native Americans: Sacred

The Native American narrative of "Middle Mountain" appears to be a simple story, encapsulated by this sentence, "The Sutter Buttes hold both ceremonial and mythical significance to both the Maidu and the Wintun" (Milliken, 2011).[28] Indigenous peoples ask us to consider land as sacred.[29] The Sacred Land Project, an organization dedicated to preserving the Buttes, has suggested the following in relation to sacred land and Indigenous people:

> To the Western ear, "sacred" may be synonymous with "sacrosanct"—inviolably holy—but to an indigenous culture, a place labeled as "sacred" may instead mean something spiritually alive, culturally essential, or simply deserving of respect. This Western conception of emphasis on "sacredness" often leads indigenous groups to accept the label, however ill-fitting it may be, because protection efforts might otherwise be ignored.
>
> (Blair, 2014; Sacred Land Project, 2020)[30]

This view of land being "*a special place to be revered…not a place to live*" is still not well understood in the modern Western European–oriented United States, which values and legally protects private ownership. Because both tribes view the spot as a sacred space, neither permanently lived there, instead held it as "a special place to be revered" (Milliken, 2011). Collective ownership, especially by Indigenous peoples, has always presented a challenge to Western concepts of legal and ethical rights.[31]

The Private Landowners: Stewardship

The private landowner view about the Sutter Buttes is as follows:

> About a dozen families own the majority of land in the Sutter Buttes, much of which is still used as ranchland…[creating] a family relationship with the land that spans more than 100 years. They are proud of their ranching heritage and their private stewardship of the land and want to see it remain undeveloped.
>
> (sacredland.org)

Stewardship was the justification for private landowners, who felt a threat when the State of California acquired a parcel of the land.

> These long-time landowners feel a special kinship for this land, have allowed the Maidu Indians to worship and use the Buttes for their own purposes, and believe they have been good stewards of this valuable property for many years.
>
> (OMCA, n.d.)

The State of California: High-Quality Recreation

On April 8, 2005, the State Park and Recreation Commission reclassified the Sutter Buttes, naming the Sutter Buttes property a state park. Part of the State's impetus for acquiring Sutter Buttes is that the

> property represents these resource values and potential for high-quality recreational experiences…[which in turn] would likely provide the park system with an as yet untapped and lucrative opportunity.
>
> (Milliken, 2011, para. 3)

> At the time of writing, the site remains closed to the public, as access to the area is limited.
> (California State Parks, The Sutter Buttes Project, para. 4)

The OMCA faced a challenge in creating this exhibit. Do they choose one or all three versions, or focus on the natural beauty of the land? It would have been simpler to step away from the controversy, yet they decided to tell all three stories. They gathered the requisite information and trusted visitors to make sense for themselves. The exhibit offered engagement to 'work the dialectic' between these three relationships to land—that is, Native-spiritual, private ownership-stewardship and state-public use.[32]

"*What do we mean by private ownership?*" "*How does that translate into an Indigenous framework?*" And, "*Where does the public view of the state fit in?*" These questions arise here and are echoed in the next two controversies. Sutter Buttes is a local story. It has national and international implications because, as we already noted, land use (and land grabbing) has been an essential challenge for almost all Indigenous peoples, all over the world, including in Hawaii, Australia, Indonesia, Canada and New Zealand.

Controversy 2: Two Views of the Californio Indians in California

Dartt-Newton (2009) explored competing dominant narrative structures in her study of museum exhibits on the history of the Californio Indians. She based her research on interviews and observations within Central Coast Indian/mixed heritage communities and the museums situated in those communities, conducted over a three-year period. Dartt-Newton followed Bruner and Lucariello (1989), who argued,

> [In] the 1930s and 1940s…. [Indian narrative] is characterized by these themes: the present as disorganization, the past as glorious, and the future as assimilation…. A decade after World War II, the narrative changed dramatically to…: the past as exploitation, the present as resistance, and the future as ethnic resurgence [and] there is little continuity between the two dominant stories.
> (Bruner & Lucariello, 1989, p. 139, in Dartt-Newton, 2009, p. 6)

Dartt-Nelson found both themes in her research. She also found "a delay of two to three decades for the museums she studied to establish the second, 'new' narrative, and some have *never* shifted from the pre-World War II narrative" (p. 7). Dartt-Newton reaffirmed ever-present underlying ideologies regarding westward expansion, deficit views and uneven power relations. I have extrapolated four different themes regarding how Californio Indians were viewed from Dartt-Newton's research. I treat them as secondary contradictions; that is, each theme reflects a tension between different nodes of the activity system. I list these with signifying discursive traces in Table 5.4.

TABLE 5.4 Secondary contradictions in the Californio narrative (Dartt-Newton, 2009)

Secondary contradictions	Nodes in tension	Discursive manifestation
Frozen in time vs. Dynamic Time/space warps	Subjects/Rules of time Subjects/Object	"the continuity of our people" Eurocentric eras—e.g., mission
Primitive vs. advanced	Subjects/Mediational means (ideology)	[we are]—"very animalistic, with all the other animals" "I'd like to see us taken from the animal museum and put into the human museum"
Dehumanized vs. humanized	Subject/Mediational means (ideology)	"As a people, they literally do not count"
Romanticized vs. real	Subject/ Mediational means	"without reference to a thriving modern culture"

Frozen in Time vs. Dynamic

Often, museum narratives present American Indians as primitive people, 'discovered' by Europeans. This lack of accurate time keeping is a common example of *deficit/othering* in action, suggesting that Indigenous people's past lives don't matter. The *story* begins at the point of contact. This Western chronological bias ignores life from the Native peoples' perspective, which began long before European 'discovery'. Being denied living history or continuous development obliterates Indian history and the ways Indians have informed and changed all our lives.

The vignette at the beginning of this chapter illustrated this secondary contradiction, arising out of a colonialist master narrative that presented only "the static or frozen representation devoid of dynamism, without reference to a thriving modern culture" (Dartt-Newton, 2009). Once again ideology forces us to focus on the relationship between object and story. The dead or disappeared object and people tell a static story that warps the time/space continuum (Bang & Marin, 2015). This is an important argument of *desettling 'settled expectations'*,[33] which demands greater consciousness of the way in which the time and space[34] are portrayed when considering American Indians (Bang et al., 2012; Smith, 2012). In fact, from Indigenous perspectives, an accurate portrayal of time-space relations is completely missing. This is not only "a story of domination; it is also a story which assumes that there was a 'point in time'...[that] [T]raditional indigenous knowledge ceased...when it came into contact with 'modern' societies, that is the West" (Smith, 2012, in Bang et al., 2015, p. 113).[35]

Questioning the Western space/time continuum, Dartt-Newton (2009) claimed that California museums use Eurocentric eras, such as the Spanish/Mission,

Mexican/Rancho and American/Gold Rush to organize the Indian exhibits.[36] She argued that museums perpetuate the 'discontinuities' between the stories conquerors tell vs. the stories Indian people tell. The museums "fail to pierce the 'collective amnesia,' of painful historical realities, such as rape, which played a significant part of the history of Central Coast people, [and was] a biological reality in many of their family trees" (Dartt-Newton, 2009, p. 261).[37]

Dartt-Newton reported that Chumash (central California) parents experienced the same embarrassment as the parents viewing the Michigan exhibit, not wanting their children to see these museum exhibits that either inaccurately portray the history of American Indian culture or, even worse, did not portray modern American Indians at all. Dartt-Newton's research suggests that the ongoing experience of modern-day American Indians has been almost completely absent. As a Chumash woman in Dartt-Newton's study said, "To over-focus on one period of time is misrepresentative and depressing" (Dartt-Newton, 2009, p. 162).

Primitive vs. Advanced

Traditionally, if the culture under study was not European American, if, for example, it was Alaskan, Hawaiian, Apache, Hopi, Ojibwe, African American or Asian American in origin, it was considered to be 'less civilized', not holding up culturally to European standards. This is another form of *othering*. Furthermore, such Indigenous cultures were often situated alongside natural history collections (Hadal, 2013) and dioramas where "less civilized nations and peoples not appreciating the role of art, history, culture, etc., [are] placed...next to the natural history collections, rather than with the culture collections" Forrest, 2007, p. 223).[38] As one Chumash respondent in Dartt-Newton's research said,

> Here, in the Natural History Museum...[we are]—very animalistic, with all the other animals. I'd like to see us taken from the animal museum and put into the human museum.
>
> (Dartt-Newton, 2009, p. 163)

This is yet another stark instance of deficit ideology, which classifies the Natives with non-humans. This view can permeate a museum's educational materials and activities and informs the "forms of pedagogy...[and] perspectives of the docents...and staff charged with interpreting them for the public" (Dartt-Newton, 2009, p. 245). Even when Native consultants were available to help museums understand cultural differences, Dartt-Newton found the cultural competence of museum interpreters to be questionable, advising that it is

> unwise to avoid...cultural competency training for staff and docents. I experienced more cultural ignorance, racism and insensitivity in the field than I can recount here, most often among docents.
>
> (p. 248)

Once again, objects are given more importance than the people who made and used them. Also, the very real events of slavery and rape of Natives (and slaves) at the hands of colonists are avoided "because they fear it is too controversial. But, to do this is to erase the aboriginal history of California" (Dartt-Newton, 2009, p. 123).

Dehumanized vs. Humanized

The doctrine of manifest destiny expresses the norm of settled expectations based in whiteness and remains deeply embedded in our culture (Bang et al., 2012). *"How does any country justify mass removals, elimination and enslavement?"* Humans have always had a way to justify this: consider the *other* less than human. As Bang et al. (2012) noted,

> settled expectations...based in whiteness gave "legitimacy" to settler colonialism....gradation of human beings [Smith, 1999]..."not fully human"... mass removals, elimination, and enslavement of indigenous peoples of North America and Africa.
> (Lee, 2004, 2007, in Bang et al., 2012, p. 30)

The American Indians lost 90% of their population, from an estimated 12 million in 1500 to an estimated 237,000 in 1900 (Lewy, 2004). This has rightly been called genocide. The worldview that encourages barbaric actions is the belief that the 'other' is less than human and innately 'savage'. Newcomb (2012), quoted Helen Hunt Jackson's famous 1884 book, which examines how whites were allowed to treat American Indians at that time[39]:

> Once the Indians were depicted in a dehumanizing manner, they were also effectively silenced because the views of those who are less than human do not have to be taken into account. As a people, they literally do not count.
> (Jackson, 1884, in Newcomb, 2012)

Jackson documented how whites were allowed to treat American Indians.[40] Not being human became an excuse for barbarism, internment, concentration camps, rape and slavery, as well as forced labor.[41] Even a drastic reduction of numbers was generally accepted. An entire people were *almost* exterminated, using their dehumanization as an excuse. The story of the colonization of American Indians is only one example in a history full of dehumanization of the 'other'. It is difficult to view representations without seeing clearly just what the Indian Removal Act actually entailed (Figure 5.3).

Romanticized vs. Real

A fourth contradiction in Native American and other Indigenous stories (and slavery lore) at museum exhibits is the romanticization of Indian artifacts instead of

FIGURE 5.3 Little BigHorn diorama at the Monroe County Historical Museum in Monroe, Michigan, U.S.A. (Photo from Alamy)

reflection on the reality of removal. Dartt-Newton (2009) refers to this as "cultural appropriation and misrepresentation" and a preference for telling "a romantic Indian past", rather than looking at real events (p. 18). The telling and retelling of a romantic American past misrepresents the horrors experienced by the American Indians and their descendants. Dartt-Newton noted that the romanticization of Indigenous people, and the way in which objects (artifacts) are used as representations, deliberately mask the uglier aspects of history.

From the colonialist's perspective, the noble savage had obscure cultural and social values, and obscure but collectible symbolic cultural items such as peace pipes, basketry, pottery and headdresses. These objects in glass cases have been treated as oddities or commodities, even though they have spiritual value (Dartt-Newton, 2009). Interpreting a community's values and beliefs and the role of objects in their lives is always an imperfect process. The results depend on the ideological commitments of the interpreter.

Dartt-Newton's interpretations suggest that even though research and theory in recent decades have challenged the romanticization of the 'Native narrative', its symbols, objects and representations of the 'noble savage', some museums remain "uninformed by this scholarship". They have not revised that narrative, as Bruner and J. Lucariello have suggested (Bruner & Lucariello, 1989). These museums continue to perpetuate public misunderstanding and stereotypes of Native life (see Kaplan, 1994; Karp & Lavine, 1991; Karp et al., 1992, in Dartt-Newton, 2009, p. 18).

166 Whose Story Is It?

Appendix 5.1 describes two exhibitions that focused on the romanticization of Indian artifacts but also referred to the Indian Removal Act. These exhibitions and the dialogue about them foreground the fetishization of Indian art or everyday or sacred objects as art. They are accompanied by a 'collective amnesia' concerning the larger societal, cultural costs of historical events (Gray, 2008). Any exhibition that focuses mainly on the imagery and objects of a dislocated, 'removed' people does a disservice to Indians' history, culture and societal presences in modern times. In both of these exhibitions *settled expectations* (Bang et al., 2015; Marin & Bang, 2015) become part of the accepted narrative of the time, with the implications of the Indian Removal Act fading behind pretty pictures and objects.

Controversy 3: NMAI, Achieving Decolonization

Lonetree (2009, 2012) has challenged the NMAI about its truth-telling (Figure 5.4). Many Indian museums do not even hint at the Holocaust suffered by Native Americans. Lonetree pointed out the irony that "the Smithsonian's National Museum of the American Indian, the self-proclaimed 'Museum Different,' reflects this still complicated Western representation that has been so intimately linked to the colonization process" (Lonetree, 2006b, p. 632). Lonetree recommended that all contemporary museums 'speak the hard truths of colonization within exhibition spaces'. She noted,

FIGURE 5.4 A display of vintage advertising showing stereotypes of Native Americans at the National Museum of the American Indian in Washington, D.C., U.S.A. (Alamy photo)

I am profoundly disappointed about this missed opportunity to truly challenge the American Master Narrative—a narrative that has silenced and even erased the memory of the genocidal policies of America's past and present.

(Lonetreeb, 2012, p. 311)

Lonetree argued that just as the Holocaust museums directly portray the Jewish Holocaust in stark detail, American Indian museums need to portray the Native American Holocaust. She castigated the NMAI for not even hinting at this. She upbraided such willful "ignorance of history" and the museum's silence concerning an aspect of American history that constitutes genocide through the Indian Removal Act of 1830 and similar acts.

Lonetree (2009) has suggested ways that museums, curators and educators could deal more effectively with 'centuries of unresolved trauma'; beginning certainly with recognition of worldviews different from Western ones (Sleeper-Smith, 2009). Some new Native-led museums do honor American Indian worldviews, narratives and ways of knowing; they actively challenge the misrepresentation of Indigenous people's history, values and daily and spiritual lives that have prevailed.

Museums have collected many contested objects and their stories, either from other collectors or more directly; historically they have made it difficult for American Indians and other Indigenous and enslaved people to access, handle or even see their sacred objects (see Chapter 6). Lonetree describes this challenging relationship as missed opportunities. Museums have retained objects of colonization and, more importantly, have maintained their power to interpret them to the public. To put this in context, it is the equivalent of presenting modern America solely through the colonial times, omitting completely what modern American life actually looks like today. Dartt-Newton pointed out that damage is done by museum docents. Although they may be well-intentioned, they have not been adequately trained, and so they continue to overly romanticize the subjects of the exhibits and completely omit the brutal facts of Indian/Western contact.

Counter-Narratives in New Museums

Modern researchers promoting decolonization call for creating alternative master narratives, instead of portraying American Indians solely either as less than human or as victims (Lonetree, 2009, in Coleman, 2015, and in Shannon, 2014). Lonetree (2012) wrote of several new museums that are deeply influenced by Indian spirituality, culture and history and have found ways to tell their story differently, as a counter-narrative. Lonetree did 'narrative walk-throughs and reviews' of three Native-oriented museums.[42] She has recognized the Ziibiwing Center[43] of Anishinabe Culture and Lifeways as a successful example of a decolonized museum. The Ziibiwing Center was tribally developed and is a tribally controlled museum that gives a powerful example of resilience: ["An]...unflinching treatment of colonization [that] provides the context that makes the survival of the Saginaw Chippewa so amazing and worthy of celebration" (Lonetree, 2014, p. 133).

The Ziibiwing Center tells the Saginaw Chippewa story, but unlike many other mainstream Indian exhibitions, the Ziibiwing Center uses oral history as its centerpiece and relies on seven prophecies to underpin its master narrative:

1. Written in stone (wisdom in stone, petroglyphs),
2. Teaching lodge (spiritual, lifelong learning),
3. The laws/rules made by the government (U.S. policies),
4. When the promises were made (how a treaty may have looked),
5. Great illness and death (result of U.S. government policies),
6. Blood memory (the inherent connection to spirituality, ancestors and all of Creation, and
7. The reburial of the Anishinabe of long ago (ancestors remain undisturbed).

The Ziibiwing Center puts American Indian survival into a colonial context, directly challenging the classic western narrative of American Indian disappearance after westward expansion. The Center delves into a discussion of diseases, murder, land theft, poverty, violence and forced conversion by Christian missionaries. It promotes the Anishinabe language, making all text bilingual, and actively works to raise awareness of the trauma of the boarding school days when American Indian children were forced to move away from home, speak only English and adopt Western ways.

Foregrounded here is the recognition that Native communities have been forcibly separated from knowledge of their own language and cultural practices. The museum has also included an exhibit on repatriation, a topic addressed in the next chapter on objects.

Lonetree remained hopeful that, through these efforts to decolonize and indigenize, museums can be transformed from "sites of colonial harm into sites of healing and restoring community well-being" and "from sites of oppression…into sites of revitalization and autonomy" (Shannon, 2014, from Lonetree p. 173).

Lonetree argued that the decolonization process must go beyond "merely collaborating with Indigenous peoples"; it must extend to telling "hard truths" about colonialism. These hard truths are of course the decimation of people. She used the term Holocaust to refer to the 90% of Indigenous people who died post-contact. She also requested that museums create "healing spaces", where visitors can sit quietly and compose themselves after witnessing and reflecting on this scale of death and destruction.

Summary

I began this chapter by asking how contradictory views of history and culture affect what is said on the museum floor and in the surrounding community. Master narratives reflect the philosophical cultural stance underlying the stories that are told; counter-narratives offer resistance to master narratives. We focused on natural history and cultural museums, specifically those portraying Native Americans in the United States and Canada because they provide a stark study of inevitable contradictions.

As we saw in the vignette, debates abound regarding how stories are told about Indigenous people and their artifacts, both in museums and in society. The very names of two museums, the Smithsonian's National Museum of the American Indian and the National Museum of African American History and Culture signal a shift in emphasis, language and historical interpretation in the 21st century. We invoked the dialectic between narratives of westward expansion vs. cultural genocide as a way to examine ideological positions informing these narratives. We studied three examples of local, statewide and national representation of American Indians in the United States and identified secondary contractions in their narratives. We examined a powerful example of counter narrative in an American Indian designed and led museum, the Ziibiwing Center.

I have pointed out the more subtle ways that contradictory goals eventuate in museum floor practices and beyond. Neoliberal-influenced pressures of sponsorship, funding and ownership are all related to income sources, as well as to the disparate linguistic, cultural and historical concerns of those in power vs. those disenfranchised.

From the vignette to the Ziibiwing Center, interpretations are changing as Native Americans become increasingly involved in discussions of museum exhibits in the United States, as well as in Canada, Australia and South Africa. A warning here: while many museums do in fact invite Native Americans to help inform their storytelling, this can devolve into another form of tokenism if full collaboration is not offered.

This discussion remains incomplete without a deeper discussion of the tools or mediational means that have acted as representatives of such contradictions. Stories and artifacts inform, regenerate and complete each other. These artifacts are, in fact, the spoils of genocide, whether they are the spiritual objects, such as bones, or everyday objects, such as a spinning wheel. These artifacts are the focus of the next chapter.

Appendix 5.1: Two Recent Exhibitions About Controversy

Controversial topics for museums include slavery, war, ethnic cleansing, ownership of artifacts and, more generally, the processes of decolonization after colonization.[44] The horror of slavery is conveyed by a museum display of rare decorative silverwork with which a slave was shackled (in an exhibit on Maryland's economic dependence on slavery (Birchall, 2012, p. 12)), or the presentation of an exhibit on the history of the Jews of Bologna in the Bologna Jewish Museum (Museo Ebraico di Bologna), or by the depiction of the history of Rapa Nui in the Museo Padre Sebastián Englert (Kales, 2015) or by attempts at an overview of slavery in the Museum of the African Diaspora. These museums and their stories are relatively recent global phenomena.

Two recent exhibitions about controversy offer us insight into the role of narrative in shaping understanding. The first exhibition, called *Imprinting the West: Manifest Destiny, Real and Imagined*,[45] argued that "printed imagery played an important role in the dissemination of knowledge and understanding about the West and those who inhabited it". Beautiful displays of 'printed imagery' were designed to

> explore the potent imagery of the time that shaped how the American Indians and the west were understood.... The migration westward and settlement of white Americans only accelerated territorial tensions, which often culminated in bloodshed.
>
> (para. 3)

The exhibit appears to have been designed to reposition manifest destiny for modern times, relying on the visitor to interpret the conflicts. Its centerpiece was the Indian Removal Act of 1830, the infamous policy of the American government that forcibly removed many tribes from their lands at great financial and moral cost to the nation. The exhibit sent the romanticized work of artists like George Catlin around the world and across the United States.

The printed media embellished the Indian Removal Act, replacing genocide with more ordinary language. Precisely because the art was beautiful, it hid the ugly underbelly of ethnic destruction. In response to the much-praised exhibition, some critics pointed out that "the idea of conquering the west is understood and implicit, with the printed media of the times…, thus hiding the true story" (MAAA, 2021). We know that printed media, a mediational means, is both a reflection of and also a proactive voice for particular values or beliefs; thus, we question whether this exhibit could foster dialogue about the main contradiction or challenge the master story of expansion without presenting the counter-narrative in any form.

Another similar exhibition called *"Americans"* was presented at the Smithsonian's NMAI in Washington (Fonseca, 2018). This exhibit used imagery *and* objects of Native Americans, again referring to the 1830 Indian Removal Act; again, "people say the exhibit, and its website, fail to capture the violence and horror of the Act" (Shand, 2018). There has been significant critical pushback on this exhibit as well; Native Americans objected to using genuine *artifacts* in these ways. As Ben Barnes, second chief of the Shawnee Tribe[46] said,

> It made it seem like it was a *trivial* matter that turned out best for everyone…. I cannot imagine an exhibit at the newly established African-American museum that talked about how economically wonderful slavery was for the South.
>
> (Fonseca, 2018, para. 5)

In both exhibits, the Indian Removal Act was positioned historically as a fact, perhaps having the effect of normalizing it. Exhibit organizers may have meant to suggest that the imagery of the time was used as propaganda to 'sell' massive relocation and destruction to the American and global public of the time, but the 'prettiness' of the objects diffused their point and further concealed the underlying contradictions. Fonseca argued further,

> Two centuries ago, some people imagined a country free of American Indians. Others thought the removal of the Indians would lead to expanded wealth from cotton fields, where millions of blacks worked as slaves.
>
> (2018, para. 6)

Fonseca was exposing here how the U.S. government planned to completely replace one enslaved population for another. This quote links the two most oppressed people of that time, African Americans and American Indians. Socially, politically and, most importantly, economically, they were linked. This vision of an Indian-free west filled with cotton-picking African Americans is as startling as it is accurate. The Indian Removal Act has been treated in these exhibitions as a given, rather than as contested history.

According to Jewish scholars, Hitler was guided by the Native American Holocaust (Mandelbaum, 2013). Hitler studied the ways European settlers forcibly moved, killed, enslaved and consigned American Indians to reservations or missions in order to subdue and slowly eradicate them by starvation, work and disease. He too claimed Jews were less than human. Hitler knew how to hide concentration camps from the public. According to Mandelbaum,

> Hitler's concept of concentration camps as well as the practicality of genocide owed much…to his studies of English and United States history. He admired the camps for Boer prisoners in South Africa and for the Indians in the Wild West; and often praised to his inner circle the efficiency of America's extermination—by starvation and uneven combat—of the red savages who could not be tamed by captivity.
>
> (Mandelbaum, 2013)

Some museums highlight the controversies themselves, so we can hold competing worldviews in a dialectic relationship. This gives visitors room to shift beliefs and to change our understanding within a more dynamic depiction of history.

Notes

1 In Chapter 6, we focus on the role of objects used to tell these stories.
2 By translation we mean the cultural and social norms within which a story is told.
3 Lisa Roberts (1997) was among the first to call attention to narrative in museums, suggesting, among other things, that museums use a narrative approach to explain exhibits to visitors. Roberts also suggested that museums don't hold all the narrative power because visitors bring their own resources to a narrative. This was an important change of emphasis toward an increasing multiplicity of voices.
4 Robert Butsch, who directed the museum years ago, completed them in 1969. They showed eight Indigenous cultures of North America, of which six were from the Michigan area. Four of the Michigan tribes were represented as they would have looked at colonial contact and two depicted even more ancient times (Capriccioso, 2009).

5 "Due to such shifting sociopolitical currents and decolonizing efforts over the last few decades, the relationship between Native Americans and museums experienced a major shift since the 1970s. When a groundswell of Native American activism in museums sought to challenge these objectifying and exploitative practices… [this] led to the establishment of tribal museums, the passage of the Native American Graves Protection and Repatriation Act (1990), Indigenous involvement in mainstream institutions, and the creation of the Smithsonian's National Museum of the American Indian (NAGPRA"; Lonetree & Cobb, 2008, p. xvii).

6 "In the West, for some time…public opinion has taken the view that the Soviet Union played a secondary role", says the Russian historian Valentin Falin. "On the other hand, opinion polls show that two-thirds of Russians think the Soviet Union could have defeated Hitler without the Allies' help, and half think the West underestimates the Soviet contribution" (Rozhnov, 2005, para. 5).

7 Minnesota Museum of American Art (n.d.), Listening Sessions: Tell Us About the Arts in Your Community, https://mmaa.org/listening-sessions-we-the-people/.

8 Artifacts can only represent a static essentialist view; no object can by itself tell anything about how it is used; about its significance, either practical or sacred; or about its place in history.

9 "People are thinking about the experience of culture differently than in the past, placing value on a more immersive and interactive experience than is possible through mere observation" (Brown & Novak-Leonard (2011, reprinted 2014, in Black, 2021, pp. 2–3).

10 It is difficult to overstate how much the American public trusts museums. Respondents to a 2018 survey conducted by analytics firm Reach Advisors had more confidence in museums than in any other institution on its list, including local newspapers, the U.S. government and academic researchers (Reach Advisors, 2018).

11 "People are thinking about the experience of culture differently than in the past, placing value on a more immersive and interactive experience than is possible through mere observation" (Brown & Novak-Leonard (2011, reprinted 2014, in Black, 2021, pp. 2–3).

12 Neocolonialism and neoliberalism are not identical, but there are important overlaps.

13 As Ghosh, 2020 noted, "One feature that is less remarked upon…is the role that neoliberal policies have played globally, in reinforcing contemporary imperialism…in developing countries, including in so-called "emerging markets. Current global economic structures impose constraints upon developing countries that are so severe that they are actually quite similar to the constraints that are characteristic of the period of direct colonial control. Neoliberalism has created a revamped form of neocolonialism" (para. 8).

14 Other contested historical contexts, based on cultural, historical or social othering, may not always involve Indigenous people (for example, slavery in the United States, Jews in Germany in the 1900s and 1940s), but they are also characterized by loss of individual and collective rights, livelihood, dehumanization and similar characteristics.

15 The Indigenous Peoples Muse.

16 "Whose collective mission aims at improving relations between museums and Indigenous peoples, supporting Indigenous peoples working in both tribal and mainstream museums; and improving communication…recognizing, respecting, and welcoming the value of Indigenous peoples and their cultures" (ATALM, Association of Tribal Archives, Libraries, and Museums website, n.d.).

17 See the AMNH website.

18 Other examples might include the reconciliation that occurred in South Africa after the fall of formal apartheid. Instead of hardening positions, a softening occurred through an opening up to healing dialogue and the potential for mutually negotiated goals. Essentially, these actions reveal a belief in the basic goodness and humanity of others and

a process of forgiveness (Tutu & Tutu, 2018). Such efforts at reconciliation have been rare in the past, yet this methodology may inform us of how to make them more common and successful in the future.
19 If Native peoples experience the return of the objects as per NAGPRA, then scientists don't have access. We discuss this in two case studies in Chapter 6, Kennewick man and *Iwi Kūpuna*, bones of the ancestors, case studies.
20 For example, in the United States, a dominant xenophobic sociopolitical narrative has taken firm hold in major parts of the country; … to protect citizens from the 'immigrant invasion', or what can be called our "national reality disorder" (Kalshed, 2020, p. 1). This presupposes that immigrants are dangerous and an invading force, a logic that is part of the particular master narrative being promulgated (von Spakovsky, 2019).
21 Even history textbooks are not immune; in a recent review of texts, Ignacio Brescó de Luna (Brescó, 2018) argued "that Spanish textbooks present a 'rosy' picture of colonialism…[and] tend to downplay the role of Spain as a former colonizing country…to uncritically convey a rosy story about colonialism in general" (p. 89). Similarly, regarding a Zimbabwean textbook, de Lukna found "little trace of the 'postcolonial turn' and its attention to the ambiguities, contradictions, tensions, nuances, and hybridities characterizing the colonial project" (pp. 193–194).
22 "By 1910…no fewer than two thousand scientific museums [were] in existence" (Sheets-Pyenson, 1987, p. 279).
23 The AMNH, founded by Theodore Roosevelt, is based on the notion of conservation.
24 Starn noted, "Since the 1970s, history in the museum has become a thriving branch of public history, with publications and training programs aimed at museum work in public or corporate settings; academic historians, by and large more recently, have done important work on the cultural history of the museum" (Starn, 2005, p. 69).
25 Many museums simultaneously find themselves considering the repatriation of cultural objects bought or stolen just 100+ years ago. These challenges are discussed in more detail in Chapter 6.
26 We can label such effort as seeking *hybrid meaning making*, discussed later in Chapters 7 and 8.
27 "The Buttes are in a circular configuration with a diameter of 10 miles, covering an area of about 75 square miles" (www.sacredland.org).
28 California State Parks website.
29 According to Sacredland.org, the Maidu and Wintun refer to this land as *Esto Yamani* and *Onolai-tol*, respectively, both of which mean "Middle Mountain" (www.sacredland.org).
30 See https://sacredland.org/tools-for-action/ for a deeper discussion of sacred land.
31 It is not a part of any Judeo-Christian ethic of possession, which was based on a doctrine known as the Doctrine of Discovery (Banner, 2005), which basically allowed Europeans and their descendants to usurp land as they saw fit.
32 Generally, Indigenous peoples have a *collective* view of land, while private owner stewardship centers on property rights, with some public use allowed, and state, *public* stewardship focuses on common use, with some possible private and/or spiritual use. Each of these views of the land is underpinned by different ideologies, which are not always apparent.
33 Following Cheryl Harris's writings on racial hierarchies, these are "the set of assumptions, privileges, and benefits that accompany the status of being white…that whites have come to expect and rely on" across the many contexts of daily life (Harris, 1995, p. 277, in Bang et al., 2012).
34 "Different orientations towards time and space…underpin notions of past and present, of place and of relationships to the land" (Smith, 2012).
35 This view echoes the Americanization exhibit (see Appendix 5.1) where exceedingly beautiful objects and paraphernalia were displayed without dynamism, as if Indian culture

never entered the modern world. This lack of dynamism in museum exhibits, along with the implicit lack of power of Native peoples to tell their own stories, is characteristic of the representations of many oppressed peoples.
36 Dartt-Newton followed a family through these periods, discussing how "the ways of their lives were impacted by newcomers, including negative impacts" (p. 270).
37 In addition, "slavery in the Missions is downplayed or ignored and never referred to as slavery" (p. 226). These actions deny present-day American Indians their place in the modern world and "don't speak" to Native ways of representing culture and group identity (Dartt-Newton, 2009).
38 A related troubling tendency highlighted by Dartt-Newton suggests that "visitors [are] deficient if they don't understand the exhibit, which may have few signs or labels" (Dartt-Newton, 2009, p. 170).
39 "Historical narratives written from the European perspective… grant privilege to those who referred to themselves as fully human because they were historically "white" and "Christian"" (Newcomb, 2012).
40 "Genocide is the mass extermination of a whole group of people, an attempt to destroy an entire group and wipe them out of existence…. The term…coined in 1943…combined the Greek word "genos" (race or tribe) with the Latin word "cide" (to kill)" (BBC News, 2016).
41 Similarly, the Koisan in South Africa were not considered human, and American blacks were not considered human.
42 The Mille Lacs Indian Museum, a 'hybrid tribal museum' created in collaboration with the Minnesota Historical Society; the NMAI in Washington, D.C.; and the Ziibiwing Center of Anishinabe Culture and Lifeways in Michigan (Shannon, 2014).
43 The Ojibwe Museum & Cultural Center (in Lac du Flambeau, Wisconsin) also has been developing presentations that are truer to the American Indian master narrative.
44 McConnell and Hess (1998) provided a time line of the controversies addressed by museums from 1913 to 1998 in the United States. Similarly, the 'contested sites' project, a study in Australia by Kelly and colleagues, investigated "how institutions can deal effectively with the challenge of developing exhibitions on controversial issues and sensitive topics" (Kelly et al., 2002, p. 11).
45 Curated by Dr. Randall Griffey, associate curator of Modern American Art at the Metropolitan Museum of Art, New York. Exhibits U.S.A.
46 The IRA…"led to the deaths of thousands of people who were marched from their homes without full payment for the value of their land. And it affected far more tribes than the five described on the museum's website" (Fonseca, 2018).

References

Akers, D. L. (2014). Decolonizing the master narrative: Treaties and other American myths. *Wicazo Sa Review, 29* (1), 58–76. doi:10.5749/wicazosareview.29.1.0058

Andrews, M. (2002). Counter-narrative and the power to oppose. *Narrative Inquiry, 12*(1), 1–16.

Ash, D. (2014). Positioning informal learning research in museums within activity theory: From theory to practice and back again. *Curator: The Museum Journal, 57*, 107–118. http://dx.doi.org/10.1111/cura.12054

Ash, D., & deGregoria Kelly, L. (2013). Thoughts on improvable objects, contradiction and object/tool reciprocity in a study of zoo educator professional development. *Cultural Studies in Science Education, 3*, 587–594.

Ash, D., Lombana, J., & Alcala, L. (2012). Changing practices, changing identities as museum educators: From didactic telling to scaffolding in the ZPD. In E. Davidsson & A. Jakobsson (Eds.), *Sociocultural theory and museum practices* (pp. 23–44). Sense Publishers.

Association of Tribal Archives, Libraries, and Museums. (ATALM). (n.d.). *Advancing Indigenous Cultural Organizations*. https://www.atalm.org/node/401

Baker, K. (2013, May 26). Oakland Museum of Calif.: Grand reopening. *SFGATE*. http://www.sfgate.com/art/article/Oakland-Museum-of-Calif-Grand-reopening-4543144.php.

Bamberg, M. G., & Andrews, M. (2004). *Considering counter narratives: Narrating, resisting, making sense?* John Benjamins Publishing Company.

Bang, M., Faber, L., Gurneau, J., Marin, A., & Soto, C. (2015). Community-based design research: Learning across generations and strategic transformations of institutional relations toward axiological innovations. *Mind, Culture, and Activity*, *23*(1), 28–41. doi:10.1080/10749039.2015.1087572

Bang, M., & Marin, A. (2015). Nature-culture constructs in science learning: Human/non-human agency and intentionality. *Journal of Research in Science Teaching*, *52*(4), 530–544. doi:10.1002/tea.21204

Bang, M., Warren, B., Rosebery, A. S., & Medin, D. (2012). Desettling expectations in science education. *Human Development*, *55*(5–6), 302–318. https://doi.org/10.1159/000345322

Banner, S. (2005). *How the Indians lost their land: Law and power on the frontier*. Harvard University Press.

Barker, A. J. (2012). Locating settler colonialism. *Journal of Colonialism and Colonial History*, *13*(3). https://doi.org/10.1353/cch.2012.0035

Barker, A. J., & Battell Lowman, E. (n.d.). *Settler colonialism*. Global Social Theory. https://globalsocialtheory.org/concepts/settler-colonialism/#:~:text=Settler%20colonialism%20is%20a%20distinct,a%20distinctive%20identity%20and%20sovereignty.

BBC News. (2016, March 17). How do you define genocide? *BBC News*. https://www.bbc.com/news/world-11108059.

Bedford, L. (2001). Storytelling: The real work of museums. *Curator*, *44*(1), 27–34.

Bennett, T. (2018). *Museums, Power and Knowledge: Selected Essays*. Routledge

Birchall, D. (2012). *Institution and intervention: Artists' projects in object-based museums*. [Master's thesis, Birkbeck College, University of London]. Creative Commons. https://museum-cultures.files.wordpress.com/2012/12/dannybirchall_institutionandintervention.pdf

Black, G. (2018). Meeting the audience challenge in the 'age of participation'. *Museum Management and Curatorship*, *33*, 302–319. doi:10.1080/09647775.2018.1469097.

Black, G. (2021). *Museums and the challenge of change: Old institutions in a new world*. Routledge.

Blades, M. (2007, September 9). Reinventing the 'Master Narrative' of America. *Daily Kos*. http://www.dailykos.com/story/2007/09/09/382746/-Reinventing-the-lsquo-Master-Narrative-rsquo-of-America.

Blair, E. (2014, August 11). As museums try to make ends meet, 'Deaccession' is the art world's dirty word. NPR. https://www.npr.org/2014/08/11/339532879/as-museums-try-to-make-ends-meet-deaccession-is-the-art-worlds-dirty-word.

Braddock, K., & Horgan, J. (2015). Towards a guide for constructing and disseminating counternarratives to reduce support for terrorism. *Studies in Conflict & Terrorism*, *39*(5), 381–404. https://doi.org/10.1080/1057610x.2015.1116277

Brescó, I. (2018). A rosy foreign country: Examining modern colonialism in Spanish history textbooks (1964–2015). In J. Pires, & K. Van Nieuwenhuyse (Eds.), *Representations of colonial pasts in (post)colonial presents: Historical and social psychological perspectives through textbook analysis* (pp. 71–93). Information Age Publishing.

Brown, A. S., & Novak-Leonard, J. L. (2011). *Getting in on the act: How arts groups are creating opportunities for active participation*. James Irvine Foundation. https://irvine-dot-org.s3.amazonaws.com/documents/12/attachments/GettingInOntheAct2014_DEC3.pdf

Brown, K. (2009, October 6). Removing dioramas provokes debate. *Arts & Culture*. https://arts.umich.edu/news-features/dioramas-debate/.

Bruner, J., & Lucariello, J. (1989). Monologue as narrative recreation of the world. In K. Nelson (Eds.), *Narratives from the crib* (pp. 73–97). Harvard University Press.

Büscher, B., Sullivan, S., Neves, K., Igoe, J., & Brockington, D. (2012). Towards a synthesized critique of neoliberal biodiversity conservation. *Capitalism Nature Socialism, 23*(2), 4–30. doi:10.1080/10455752.2012.674149

California State Parks. (2005). *Sutter Buttes: Maidu's spirit mountain*. Department of Parks and Recreation. http://www.parks.ca.gov/?page_id=23786

Capriccioso, R. (2009, September 12). *Museum to remove CONTROVERSIAL Native AMERICAN DIORAMAS*. Indian Country Today. https://indiancountrytoday.com/archive/museum-to-remove-controversial-native-american-dioramas.

Carpio, M.V. (2006). (Un)disturbing exhibitions: Indigenous historical memory at the NMAI. *The American Indian Quarterly, 30*(3), 619–631. https://doi.org/10.1353/aiq.2006.0018

Carpio, M.V. (2008). (Un)disturbing exhibitions: Indigenous: Historical memory at the NMAI. In A. Lonetree & A. Cobb (Eds.), *Understanding the NMAI*. University of Nebraska Press.

Chinn, P.W. U. (2007). Decolonizing methodologies and indigenous knowledge: The role of culture, place and personal experience in professional development. *Journal of Research in Science Teaching, 44*(9), 1247–1268. https://doi.org/10.1002/tea.20192

Churchill, W. (2010, June 26). Movies convey "America's master narrative". *Newspaper Rock*. http://newspaperrock.bluecorncomics.com/2010/06/movies-convey-americas-master-narrative.html.

Coleman, E. (2015, March 3). *Decolonizing museums*. Museum Studies at IUPUI. https://mstdiupui.wordpress.com/2015/02/23/decolonizing-museums/.

Cousins, J. A., Evans, J., & Sadler, J. (2009). Selling conservation? Scientific legitimacy and the commodification of conservation tourism. *Ecology and Society, 14*(1). https://doi.org/10.5751/es-02804-140132

Cox, J., & Stromquist, S. (Eds.). (1998). *Contesting the master narrative: Essays in social history*. University of Iowa Press.

Crosby, A. W. (1986). *Ecological imperialism: The biological expansion of Europe, 900–1900*. Cambridge University Press.

Dartt-Newton, D. D. (2009). *Negotiating the master narrative: Museums and the Indian/Californio Community of California's Central Coast* [Unpublished doctoral dissertation]. University of Oregon.

Diep, R. (2014). The passing of the Indians behind glass. *The Appendix: Futures of the Past 2*(3). http://theappendix.net/issues/2014/7/the-passing-of-the-indians-behind-glass.

Dubin, S. (1999). *Displays of power: Memory and amnesia in the American Museum*. New York University Press.

Dubin, S. (2014). *Displays of power: Memory and amnesia in the American Museum*. New York University Press.

Ekman, M. (2019). Anti-immigration and racist discourse in social media. *European Journal of Communication, 34*(6), 606–618. https://doi.org/10.1177/0267323119886151

Ender, T. (2018). Counter-narratives as resistance: Creating critical social studies spaces with communities. *The Journal of Social Studies Research, 43*, 22–31.

Engeström, Y. (2001). Expansive learning at work: Toward an activity theoretical reconceptualization. *Journal of Education and Work, 14*(1), 133–156. https://doi.org/10.1080/13639080020028747

Feinstein, Y., & Bonikowski, B. (2019). Nationalist narratives and anti-Immigrant attitudes: Exceptionalism and collective victimhood in contemporary Israel. *Journal of Ethnic and Migration Studies*, 47(3), 741–761. https://doi.org/10.1080/1369183x.2019.1620596

Fonseca, F. (2018, February 19). New exhibit examines Native American imagery in US culture. *The Seattle Times*. https://www.seattletimes.com/nation-world/native-images-in-exhibit-questions-how-america-is-defined/.

Forrest, M. E. (2007). Action research. *Health Information and Libraries Journal*, 24(3), 222–226. https://doi.org/10.1111/j.1471-1842.2007.00725.x

Ghosh, J. (2020). *Neoliberalism as neocolonialism*. Dollars & Sense. http://dollarsandsense.org/archives/2020/0520ghosh.html.

Glenn, E. N. (2015). Settler colonialism as structure. *Sociology of Race and Ethnicity*, 1(1), 52–72. https://doi.org/10.1177/2332649214560440

Golding, V. (2009). *Learning at the museum frontiers: Identity, race and power*. Ashgate.

Gray, C. (2008). Instrumental policies: Causes, consequences, museums and galleries. *Cultural Trends*, 17(4), 209–222. doi:10.1080/09548960802615349

Hadal, K. A. (2013). *Why Native American art doesn't belong in the American Museum of Natural History*. Indian Country Today. https://indiancountrytoday.com/

Harris, C. I. (1995). Whiteness as property. In K. Crenshaw, N. Gotanda, G. Peller, & K. Thomas (Eds.), *Critical race theory* (pp. 276–291). The New Press

Jackson, H. H. (1884). *Ramona*. Originally serialized in the *Christian Union*, now Random House.

Jaime, A. M., Stagner, T. (2019). Decolonization, counter-narratives and education of two native women in higher education. In S. Sharma & A. Lazar (Eds.), *Rethinking 21st century diversity in teacher preparation, K–12 education, and school policy. Education, equity, economy* (vol. 7). Springer, Cham.

Kales, S. (2015). *Representation of contested narratives in the anthropological museum: Case studies on Rapa Nui (Easter Island) and the Northern Paiutes of Central Oregon* [Unpublished honor's thesis]. University of Oregon. http://hdl.handle.net/1794/19140

Kalshed, D. (2020). *A depth psychological approach to contemporary American culture and political life*. The Retreat at Pacifica Graduate Institute. https://retreat.pacifica.edu/american-culture-and-political-life/.

Kaplan, F. S. (1994). *Museums and the making of 'ourselves': The role of objects in national identity*. St Martin's Press.

Karp, I., Kreamer, C. M., & Lavine, S. D. (1992). *Museums and communities: The politics of public culture*. Smithsonian Institution Press.

Karp, I., & Lavine, S. D. (1991). *Exhibiting cultures: The poetics and politics of museum display*. Smithsonian Institute Press.

Kelly, L. (2003). *What does learning mean for museum visitors?* The Australian Museum. https://publications.australian.museum/what-does-learning-mean-for-museum-visitors/.

Kelly, L., Savage, G., Landman, P., & Tonkin, S. (2002). *Energised, engaged, everywhere: Older audiences and museums*. The Australian Museum. https://media.australian.museum/media/dd/Uploads/Documents/2591/fullreport.baa24bf.pdf

Kendi, I. X. (2017). *Stamped from the beginning: The definitive history of racist ideas in America*. Bold Type Books.

Kidman, J. (2019). Whither decolonisation? Indigenous scholars and the problem of inclusion in the neoliberal university. *Journal of Sociology*, 56(2), 247–262. https://doi.org/10.1177/1440783319835958

Lakoff, G., & Ferguson, S. (2006, May 19) The framing of immigration. *The Blog, Huffington Post*. http://www.huffingtonpost.com/george-lakoff-and-sam-ferguson/the-framing-of-immigration

Lee, C. (2004). *The role of boundary negotiating artifacts in the collaborative design of a museum exhibition*. [Doctoral dissertation, University of California, LosAngeles]. doi:10.1080/09647770701470427

Lee, C. P. (2007). Reconsidering conflict in exhibition development teams. *Museum Management and Curatorship*, 22(2), 183–199. https://doi.org/10.1080/09647770701470427

Lewy, G. (2004). *Were American Indians the victims of genocide?* History News Network. https://historynewsnetwork.org/article/7302.

Lloyd, D., & Wolfe, P. (2016). Settler colonial logics and the neoliberal regime. *Settler Colonial Studies*, 6(2), 109–118. https://doi.org/10.1080/2201473x.2015.1035361

Lonetree, A. (2006a). Missed opportunities: Reflections on the NMAI. *The American Indian Quarterly*, 30(3), 632–645. https://doi.org/10.1353/aiq.2006.0029

Lonetree, A. (2006b). Continuing dialogues: Evolving views of the National Museum of the American Indian. *The Public Historian*, 28(2), 57–62. https://doi.org/10.1525/tph.2006.28.2.57

Lonetree, A. (2009). Museums as sites of decolonization: Truth telling in national and tribal museums. In S. Sleeper-Smith (Ed.), *Contesting knowledge: Museums and indigenous perspectives* (pp. 322–337). University of Nebraska Press.

Lonetree, A. (2012). *Decolonizing museums: Representing Native America in National and Tribal Museums*. University of North Carolina Press.

Lonetree, A., & Cobb, A. J. (2008). *The National Museum of the American Indian: Critical conversations*. University of Nebraska Press.

Mandelbaum, L. (2013). *Hitler's inspiration and guide: The Native American Holocaust*. Jewish Journal. https://jewishjournal.com/

Marin, A., & Bang, M. (2015). Designing pedagogies for indigenous science education: Finding our way to storywork. *Journal of American Indian Education*, 54(2), 29–51. https://www.jstor.org/stable/pdf/10.5749/jamerindieduc.54.2.0029.pdf

Mayer, J. (2010, August 30). Covert operations the billionaire brothers who are waging a war against Obama. *The New Yorker*. https://www.newyorker.com/magazine/2010/08/30/covert-operations.

McAfee, K. (1999). Selling nature to save it? Biodiversity and green developmentalism. *Environment and Planning D: Society and Space*, 17(2), 133–154. https://doi.org/10.1068/d170133

McConnell, M., & Hess, H. (1998). Too hot to handle? Museums and controversy; a controversy timeline. *Journal of Museum Education*, 23(3), 4–6. https://doi.org/10.1080/10598650.1998.11510383

Mehta, S. (2019, August 27). Immigration panic: How the west fell for manufactured rage. *The Guardian*. https://www.theguardian.com/uk-news/2019/aug/27/immigration-panic-how-the-west-fell-for-manufactured-rage.

MAAA (Mid-America Arts Alliance). (2021). *Imprinting the west: Manifest destiny, real and imagined*. EUSA. https://eusa.org/exhibition/imprinting-the-west-manifest-destiny-real-and-imagined/.

Milliken, T. (2011). *Sutter Buttes: The middle mountain controversy*. Indigenous Religious Traditions. http://sites.coloradocollege.edu/indigenoustraditions/sacred-lands/sutter-buttes-the-middle-mountain-controvery/.

MMAA (Minnesota Museum of American Art). (n.d.). *Listening sessions: We the people*. https://mmaa.org/listening-sessions-we-the-people/.

Newcomb, S. (2012, June 20). On historical narratives and dehumanization. IndianCountry Today. https://indiancountrytoday.com/archive/on-historical-narratives-and-dehumanization-HsG1bI-YSkCHU93o2Gd3Bw.

Oakland Museum of California (OMCA): A Bay Area Art, History & Science Museum. (n.d.). https://museumca.org/.

Old New York Diorama. American Museum of Natural History. (2018). https://www.amnh. org/exhibitions/permanent/theodore-roosevelt-memorial/hall/old-new-york-diorama.

Penney, D. W. (2006). The poetics of museum representations: Tropes of recent American Indian Art Exhibitions. In National Museum of the American Indian, Smithsonian Institution & University of Washington Press (Authors), *The changing presentation of the American Indian: Museums and native cultures* (pp. 47–66). University of Washington Press. http://www.jstor.org/stable/j.ctvcwnp35.6

Reach Advisors. (2018). *Future-proofing museums*. Ecological Society of America. https://reachadvisors.com/

Robbins, W. G. (1989). The western lumber industry. In G. D. Nash & R. W. Etulian (Eds.), *The twentieth-century west: Historical interpretations* (pp. 233–256). University of New Mexico Press.

Roberts, L. C. (1997). *From knowledge to narrative: Educators and the changing museum*. Smithsonian Institution Press.

Rozhnov, K. (2005, May 5). Europe Who won World War II? *BBC News*. http://news.bbc.co.uk/2/hi/europe/4508901.stm.

Sacred Land Film Project. (2020). *Our Story Lives Forever*. https://sacredland.or

Sahin Mencutek, Z. (2020). Refugee community organisations: Capabilities, interactions and limitations. *Third World Quarterly, 42*(1), 181–199. https://doi.org/10.1080/01436597.2020.1791070

Seo, M. G., & Creed, D. (2002). Institutional contradictions, praxis, and institutional change: A dialectical perspective. *The Academy of Management Review, 27*(2), 222–247. doi:10.2307/4134353

Shand, S. (2018, February 23). *Show examines native American imagery in US culture*. VOA. https://learningenglish.voanews.com/a/show-examones-native-american-imagery-in-us-culture/4264250.html.

Shannon, J. (2014). Review of the book *Decolonizing Museums: Representing Native America in National and Tribal Museums* by Amy Lonetree. *Great Plains Quarterly, 34*(2) 194–195. doi:10.1353/gpq.2014.0032.

Sheets-Pyenson, S. (1987). Cathedrals of science: The development of colonial natural history museums during the late nineteenth century. *History of Science, 25*(3), 279–300. https://doi.org/10.1177/007327538702500303

Sleeper-Smith, S. (2009). *Contesting knowledge: Museums and indigenous perspectives*. University of Nebraska Press.

Smith, A. (1999). *Indigeneity, settler colonialism, white supremacy*. https://www.calfac.org/sites/main/files/file-attachments/andy_smith_indigeneity_settler_colonialism_white_supremacy.pdf

Smith, C. (2005). Decolonising the museum: The National Museum of the American Indian in Washington, DC. *Antiquity, 79*(304), 424–439. doi:10.1017/S0003598X00114206

Smith, L. T. (2012). *Decolonizing methodologies research and Indigenous peoples* (2nd ed.). Zed Books.

Starn, R. (2005). A historian's brief guide to new museum studies. *The American Historical Review, 110*(1), 68–98. https://doi.org/10.1086/ahr/110.1.68

Taneja, M. (2020). *Neo COLONIALISM is colonialism in disguise*. Independently Published.

Tran, L. U. (2008). The work of science museum educators. *Museum Management and Curatorship, 23*(2), 135–153.

Tuck, E., & Yang, K. W. (2012). Decolonization is not a metaphor. *Decolonization: Indigeneity, 1*(1), 1–40.

Tutu, D., & Tutu, M. (2018). *The book of forgiving: The fourfold path for healing ourselves and our world*. Harper One.

University of Michigan. (n.d.). https://umich.edu/.

von Spakovsky, H. (2019, September 3). *Crimes by illegal immigrants widespread across U.S. – Sanctuaries shouldn't shield them*. The Heritage Foundation. https://www.heritage.org/crime-and-justice/commentary/crimes-illegal-immigrants-widespread-across-us-sanctuaries-shouldnt

Yanni, C. (2005). *Nature's museums: Victorian science and the architecture of display*. Princeton Architectural Press.

6
WHO OWNS THE ARTIFACT?

Overview

This chapter asks, "*Who owns the artifact?*", and "*What ideologies inform our thinking?*" To some degree, these questions and their answers impact what is considered to be 'ownership of history' (Wilcox, 2009, p. 12). In Chapter 5, we challenged master narratives; here we examine the meaning and use of artifacts bought, stolen or traded from nondominant peoples in colonial times. I focus especially on Indigenous artifacts that *mark* or signify social, spiritual, cultural or historical importance, for example, Kwakwaka'wakw masks, Sioux headdress, *iwi kūpuna* (skulls), Hopi Katsina or slave chains.

Historically, artifacts have been used for a variety of purposes in museums, one we explore here ties to Chapter 5 discussions about 'pretty distractions' from the hard truths of colonialism. As the second vignette that follows shows, objects carry great significance, culturally and spiritually. The role of artifacts in and for museums deserves to be examined in its own right; in this chapter, we do that.

Collecting was originally a rich man's sport; objects and art were organized in cabinets of curiosities or in private galleries. They were then sometimes donated to larger museums, whose aim was to "put the natural world in a rational order" (Fortey, 2008, p. 10). Victorians envisioned a steady progression of social evolution, placing "their society at its pinnacle. ... In such circles, collecting goods from graves, primitive cultures or local workers was the norm" (Dartt-Newton, 2009, p. 114).

Exploring the role of objects allows us to re-examine core ideological commitments; to query the processes of collecting, exhibiting and interpreting; and to uncover fundamental contradictions regarding contextualized and contingent meanings and ownership of artifacts. The primary contradiction as always concerns the use vs. exchange value. The secondary contradictions are numerous—for example, secular vs. sacred significance and uses, and cultural vs. monetary importance.

DOI: 10.4324/9781003261681-6

182 Who Owns the Artifact?

I examine two prominent cases of ancestral bones, the 8,500-year-old Kennewick Man in Washington State in the United States and the Hawaiian *iwi kūpuna*, originally held in a London museum. Both directly concern the artifact itself as our focus of attention, knowing full well that the narrative and the artifact are intertwined.

We ask now whether artifacts, often acquired in the heat of colonialist empire-building, ought to be made available for commoditization, for science or any other purpose other than what was originally intended for them. I focus here on spiritual artifacts, as I focused on land ownership in Chapter 5.

TWO VIGNETTES

Unlike other chapters, I include here two vignettes, one focusing on financial concerns of collection of Indigenous artifacts, the second on sacred uses.

The Sale of Kwakwaka'wak Masks (From the Northwest) in Chicago

At an antique roadshow in Chicago, a man brought in a collection of north-western masks crafted on the north end of the island of Vancouver in Canada. The masks were made by carvers in the Native American group once called the Kwakiutl, who are now known as the Kwakwaka'wakw. These masks raise an important question for all collectors of Native American objects: When is it legal for non-Native individuals to buy and sell, or even own, such Native American objects? The financial interest is at the surface when we hear one collector suggest to another,

> Make sure to get paperwork by a reputable seller so you have something to stand on if it blows up in your face.... If the guy says it's not a problem to buy it, have him put it in writing. If there is a problem, you can take him to court and say you want your money back.
>
> (Sharp, 2015, para. 3)

Clearly, the concern being addressed was protecting the collector's financial rights. This example highlights the contradiction between monetary and cultural value.

The Repatriation of a Sacred Item From Scotland to Canada

Neil Curtis, the director of the Marischal Museum at the University of Aberdeen, described a ritual transfer of sacred bundles (headdress) to the ookaan, held in Canada.

> A spectacular double tepee was put up in the centre of the circle. Horses, blankets, shawls and money filled the circle, all given by the people receiving a bundle to those who had cared for them in previous years. For most of the day the members of the Horn Society were hidden from sight within the tepee, but as dusk fell the fire inside the tepee started to cast silhouettes of people, some wearing horned headdresses.
>
> Eventually, lit by the car headlights, they emerged…. This was the first time that the headdress had been brought out since its return, completing the group of four that are at the heart of the ocean. It ended with the distribution of traditional foods, including fried bread and delicious hot sweet Saskatoon berry soup…. Without knowing the "meanings" of the headdress, I now have more understanding of its importance and why the repatriation mattered, as well as a richer perspective on the historical contact between Europeans and the native people of North America.
>
> (Curtis, 2005, p. 43)
>
> This vignette highlights the contradiction between sacred and secular.

Introduction

Stories and objects are inextricably intertwined. We explored how stories carry ideological worldviews in Chapter 5. These two vignettes concerning the stolen Kwakwaka'wakw masks and the ookaan headdresses set the tone for our explorations in this chapter, which highlight examples of contested sacred artifacts and contexts where Indigenous and Western cultures come into contact and conflict, where power and money are always in play and where heritage and ownership are sometimes made a matter of debate. The very nature of what is held sacred and what is secular is an important recurring theme in positioning our discussion of objects. I examine here alternative realities and norms as they impact the ways we interpret objects, incorporating aspects of past colonialist narratives examined in the previous chapter.

Steven Conn argued that much of the 19th museum century was about collecting, "'classifying and cataloging'…[an] encyclopedia of knowledge and the storehouse of objects" (Conn, 2010, p 58). While the collection aspect may have slowed down, the uses to which artifacts are put and their interpretation have remained contentious. In fact, the uses and fates of objects have become more significant. Shoenberger (2019) noted, "[T]he very meaning of decolonizing is being debated" (para 4) because multiple interpretations for objects have been suggested, including context, use, place in the spiritual realm and history behind the artifact. In many cases, the contested (histories) behind the objects have now become 'the story'.

Only recently have Indigenous and previously enslaved peoples been able to contest the rules of provenance, especially by explicating the private spiritual practices, understandings and power of particular objects, appealing to Indigenous epistemologies rather than relying on curators and scientists from museums to do so.

It is now vital to examine the disrupted connections that have impacted both the spiritual and financial values of objects, where *value* is a mutable, contingent and contested topic. I compare colonizing and decolonizing ideologies and perspectives in relation to objects, as well as the power dynamics inherent in negotiating the meaning of a shared outcome involving different interpretations of value.

Here again, we use objects as a proxy to highlight existing contradictions in museums where misunderstandings arise from starkly opposing value systems (Lynch & Alberti, 2010). Such misunderstandings have been particularly tense in the United States for Native American and Native Hawaiian populations and African American slaves (Bennett, 2018). Similar contradictions abound in Europe, South Africa, New Zealand, Canada and many other countries.

At issue is not merely the return of masks or headdresses but also the recognition of the cultures within which they are historically situated and spiritually bound. I discuss how objects have been portrayed in ways that are historically inaccurate (Fota, 2019); static rather than dynamic (Dartt-Newton, 2009); 'as seen by' the victors (Phelan, 2019), in narratives told by settler colonizers (Allain Bonilla, 2017); and stripped of their essential spiritual nature.

As this book goes to press, the world is in an especially raw, turbulent, potentially transformative era, due partially to the worldwide COVID-19 pandemic. You might want to ask me what old bones and headdresses have to tell us when the here and now is so challenging? Historically, as Harrison noted, "the richness and diversity of the cultures of the colonized peoples were of little interest to the colonial powers" (Harrison, 1997, p. 46). Now though, in the 21st century, these cultures and their artifacts *are* of interest to us, especially because in the past, the 'richness and diversity of the cultures' was often reduced to the culture's objects. Now though, surrounded as we are by suffering and death, we may find deeper significance ourselves in the bones of the ancestors and sacred objects from Indigenous cultures. As with so many other conflicts in reculturing museums, contradictory views are in transition, being tested and morphing before our eyes, as societal and cultural norms shift toward an evolving, decolonizing, postcolonialist stance.

Hawaiians, Polynesians, Native Americans in Canada, the United States and Central America; Maori in New Zealand; Aborigines in Australia; and the Koi and the San in South Africa are all concerned about their ancestors' physical and cultural remains. For this reason, we explore the repatriation of bones, a process that reflects the powerful contrasting meaning of any *object's* past, present and possible futures. As Indigenous and previously enslaved people take a more significant role in interpreting their own history and how their cultural/spiritual objects are 'seen' or valued, they are in a position to determine exhibit content and insist on the actions underlying such concepts as unsettling *settler colonialism, decolonizing, and resistance as counter-narrative*. Many museums increasingly recognize their white racist pasts, and new museums are being created to fill the cultural void.[1] Discussions of sacred and secular have increased recently, in part because more sacred artifacts have made their way to Western museums but also because of ideological shifts surrounding object interpretations. As Glenn (2018) has noted,

> Religion is difficult—it lies at the heart of who we think we are, and how we understand the universe we live in....I don't really believe any object "speaks for itself"...visitors should also be helped and encouraged to understand the religious significance of the object.
>
> (para. 2)

Glenn referred to the changing mores of museums, and the increasing emphasis on contextualizing objects.

Kalshed (2020) noted, "We all live in an interpretive reality...[and] we examine alternative realities". Those realities are projected onto the objects we see and notice in museums. The moving description in the second vignette of the ritual return of a missing *ookaan* headdress, allowing the completion of the group of four sacred headdresses, and using them in the intended fashion, allows the reader to more fully recognize the impact of cultural reunification of sacred objects. With this in mind, collecting objects for compensation from outside one's own cultural community provokes questions across a variety of axes, among them cultural appropriateness, monetary value and legality, among others. The collector's discursive trace "blowing up in your face" from the first vignette reflects how questionable collector's rights are coming to be viewed in an age increasingly more attuned to cultural rights and misappropriation.

Misappropriation has been ubiquitous in the world of museums. Stanford's anthropologist and American Indian Wilcox (2009) delineated the burden Native tribes have had in working with professional experts, suggesting that

> Indian people must demonstrate connections to a past that has been created by a professional and theoretical dialogue that has explicitly excluded them.... The web of interests and claims enveloping these shards, bones, sculptures and masks is dense indeed. Law, the legacy of colonialism, aesthetics, human history, property... it's not easy to sort out.
>
> (p. 12)

He suggested that those who bore the burden of colonialism continue to do so as they attempt to repatriate their artifacts. The Indigenous cultures who created and maintained these objects still have little to say about how they are used, displayed or interpreted, much less the right to own them. Many objects considered sacred have important places in world history, culture and practice, aspects sometimes not conveyed by museums. Often, because objects are sacred, the knowledge behind them has been kept secret from everyone, except to those who need to know. Such limited access to sacred knowledge seems appropriate; modern religious practices have similar caveats (Chalice, Bible, Quran, Ketubah, Thanka, etc.). The dilemma then was how to convey meaningful context about an object's spiritual significance and

It is helpful here to remind ourselves of the *contingent* nature of objects, using the historical, cultural and social language of CHAT to apply the ever-present critique of the neoliberal stance of commodification and representation using the presentation of objects of the 'other' in museums as touchstones. Having introduced the topic enough to understand the main issues we face in regard to bones, provenance and ownership, I touch base briefly again on theoretical underpinnings I use throughout this book.

CHAT and neoliberalism work together in highlighting the centrality of individualism, marketization and commodification as central organizing themes for museums as institutions.[2] CHAT helps uncover the historically bound, contradiction-rich, ritualized contexts and norms ubiquitous in museums of the past. These tensions have also led to secondary and other contradictions I will explore. Neoliberalism is invoked continuously as I refer to monetary, cultural, spiritual, historical and other values. When we question museum ownership or custodianship, I interpret exchange value (market value) as an enhanced ability to attract visitors, fame and scientists to the museum and also to advance the institution's worth.

The analysis can lead to ways to allow a multiplicity of meanings in objects, which more accurately represent and speak to the lived experiences of culture in our 21st century world (Ash, 2014; Foot, 2014).

Ownership

Museums started as 'cabinets of curiosity' used to house unusual historical-cultural pieces and made "available to the limited gaze of high society"—that is, for the aristocracy. In the 19th century, collectors "opened their doors to the general public… [an act] essential to a display of power" (Bennett, 2018, p 23). Bennet has argued that "the exhibitionary complex[3] is a context for the *permanent* display of power/knowledge" (p. 30). Power and objects have often been conjoined in museum critical literature (Dubin, 1999; Kapuni-Reynolds, 2015).

Museums are increasingly aware of the mistakes of settler colonists, but as Harrison noted, "representation of the 'other' has fundamentally altered very little from its historical posture" (Harrison, 2007, p.41). Colonialist customs had allowed and, in fact, encouraged "collecting, 'borrowing' and looting from the disenfranchised" (i.e., people of color; Landry, 2009).[4] As we move away from the settler colonialist[5] (Kidman, 2019) 'cabinets of curiosities' to the museums of today, we uncover unacknowledged 'historical truths', raising contradictions that carry into the 21st century. One of these is *ownership*.

What *ownership* actually means varies a good deal across history, cultures and society. Due to decolonizing and related efforts,[6] the notion of *ownership* has become more complicated for museums and private collectors around the world. A tipi can be considered a home or a church; a headdress or feather cape can be an adornment, a sacred ceremonial object or a symbol of an endangered species. We can view skulls as bones to be buried or burned, tested for DNA or as objects that hold the spirit of one's ancestors. Finally, as we saw in the Sutter Buttes example in Chapter 5, there is the notion of collective community claims of ownership rather than individual claims.

Museums pride themselves on being able to track the legal trail of ownership, what they term the *provenance* of a painting, bones, pottery and other objects. Rules and paper trails accompany most objects. Provenance is primarily about proving the trail of ownership. Yet ownership for a museum is often at odds with the sensibilities of Native Americans whose graves were robbed, of European Jews whose art was confiscated in World War II (see Appendix 6.3), or the spoils of enforced slavery.

In museums, *provenance* typically is a chain of verified and written past ownership.[7] Provenance is not only the concern of the museum art and culture departments, provenance is also the concern of the scientists wishing to use the objects for research. But what does provenance possibly mean for Indigenous peoples, whose ideas of 'ownership' do not map onto Western ones? Provenance is especially challenging when discussing Indigenous people's skeletons.

The 'significance' of objects, their power and their *best* use are often deeply embedded in the particular activity systems (contexts) that are or were responsible for their design, maintenance and subsequent contextualized interpretations. Artifacts may be vases, taxidermied animals, paintings, dioramas, sculptures, pottery, skulls, bones or many other physical and abstract representations of *things* and ideas with historical, social, spiritual and cultural value to a particular society.

Societal perceptions of the purpose of artifacts can be skewed toward the sacred or the monetary, to power or lack of it or altogether other ideologies. In the case of who owned the ookaan headdress or the masks, whose belief system do we refer to in making that judgment? Campfens (2020) suggested that "any object/artifact, whether sacred or practical, everyday or historical, or all of these, is given meaning by its 'continuing cultural link'" (p. 256); in other words, its meaning is *contingent* on its cultural context, how and when it was used and for what purpose. The second of the two vignettes gives us a clearer idea of what *contingent* means for the *ookaan* headdress.

Campfens (2020) argues, "[O]riginal owners should still be able to rely on a 'heritage title' if there is a *continuing cultural link*". The concept of a continuing cultural link is designed

> to capture the legal bond between cultural objects and people, distinct from ownership, and is informed by international cultural heritage and human rights law norms…whilst ownership interests are accounted for in national private law, legal tools are lacking to address heritage interests and identity values that are acknowledged in international law.
>
> (p. 257)

This view is in direct contradiction to most private law and to provenance settled on the basis of ownership. Moreover, ownership rights pass across national boundaries because such objects are so often transported away from their original place of use.

Competing Ideologies Regarding Ownership of Indigenous Artifacts

In the 19th century, and even into the mid-20th century, there was little understanding of the role or importance of a particularly revered object, such as a skull, partially out of ignorance of their meaning for others. Skulls were considered inanimate, static objects, viewed purely as scientific material to be measured and compared with other skulls, used for potential DNA studies and so on. Alternative views were either unknown or rejected as sentimental and unscientific.

The pervasive patterns of the past are changing. As Dawson (2014), Garibay (2009), Hooper-Greenhill (2009), Macdonald (2006), MacLachlan (2012), Moore (2014), Lonetree (2009), Feinstein and Meshoulam (2014) and others have suggested, museums are beginning to collaborate within their communities, opening up their objects to new meanings and pluralistic views, treating nondominant visitors as collaborators rather than clients, and curtailing the 'othering' of the original creators of the objects on display.

We must ask, "*Do objects represent the culture and use which gave birth to them, or do they serve as evidence to prove various theories about science or history or both?*" The starkly contrasting arguments of Hutterer and Meighan that follow illustrate the two extreme positions within the conflict. Karl Hutterer, previously of the Museum of Anthropology, University of Michigan, suggested in 1980,

> The act of collecting ethnographic specimens must be seen as an act of taking possession, both physically and symbolically, of some of the essence of individuals as well as whole societies and cultures.
>
> (Hutterer, 1980, p. 7)

Archaeologist Meighan (1999) stated an opposing view of returning and reburying American Indian bones to their tribes as

> the equivalent of the historian burning documents after he has studied them…it is impossible for scientists to carry out a genuinely scientific study of American Indian prehistory…. An entire field of academic study may be put out of business.
>
> (para. 7)

Such diametrically opposing views regarding how objects should be treated by archaeologists, anthropologists, historians and curators have led to court battles, contested history and both legal and illegal *appropriation*. In the two vignettes, we saw the clear contradictions between the spiritual vs. scientific, monetary vs. cultural value, private ownership vs. tribal and other lenses museums have used. We see similar controversial contradictions in places like Philadelphia, in the United States, where bones of slaves were used to prove controversial and false race narratives (Schuessler, 2021).

McMullen (2008) argued that museums often tend to portray a *literal, rather than symbolic*, understanding of objects, which "reduces Native culture to its physical products, often permanently separated from related knowledge" (p. 83). Numerous commentaries concerning *sacred* objects convey the strong reactions such reductionism evokes. Lonetree (2010) argued that the "Indigenous people's worldview often considers objects, especially bones, as living entities, representing many layers of meaning, precisely because they are 'deeply connected to the past, present, and future of Indigenous communities'" (Lonetree, 2010, p. 176).

TABLE 6.1 Secondary contradictions of uses of artifacts

Secondary contradiction	Affected nodes	Discursive traces
Scientific purposes vs. spiritual/utilitarian	Mediational means/rules	"Like burning up a resource after using it" "How would you feel if a Native American dug up your grandmother?"
Monetary value/vs. cultural (priceless)	Division of labor/ mediational means	"Make sure to have the paperwork" "Bones are living entities" Enslaved peoples' bones used to support the now-discredited "race science"
Contextualized meaning vs. decontextualized meaning	Rules/ mediational means	"It was the old woman and her hut and her fields of cotton (that gave meaning)"

The conflicts we see regarding how artifacts are 'used' in these examples typically reflect underlying neoliberal and deficit ideologies. This was explicit in the first vignette regarding selling masks, showing up as an emergent secondary contradiction in Table 6.1. The *othering* and disempowerment of Indigenous, previously enslaved and Native people represented in museums (Lonetree, 2010; Reagan, 2015) is also overt in the first vignette.

Morrissey (2015) has argued that "institutions become increasingly *econo-centric* in designing for the 'public good', but actually use 'the logic of the market'" (Morrissey, 2015, p. 619, in Kidman, 2019, p. 251). This means that *public good* can be morphed into economic terms. In this way, market values can come to dominate and override individual or collective cultural goals. Thus, all things are commodified, including rare and significant sacred items, like bones. We represent such tensions between nodes as secondary contradictions in Table 6.1.[8]

These tensions continually exert power in the process of changing sociopolitical and sociohistorical perceptions of the essential value or purpose of artifacts. Just as with sacred land in Chapter 5, the contradictions are strikingly obvious, especially if we ask, "*How much is it worth?*" To accentuate so-called *ownership* differences, I focus especially on complex dilemmas involving human remains. To introduce this dilemma, I quote Strauss who asked in 2016, "*When Is It Okay to Dig Up The Dead?*"

> The objections often stem from religious beliefs and historic grievances, but the outrage is also driven by perceptions of indecency—the discomfort of disturbing a person's final resting place to satisfy idle curiosity.... And there's the most heated issue…repatriating and reburying human remains that are now held in museums or research labs.
>
> (Strauss, 2016, para. 3)

While we might bridle at terms like *idle curiosity*, we must also recognize the ideological bias that prioritizes scientific purposes over the sacred nature of bones of the dead, especially from Indigenous cultures.[9] Commenting after a raid in the four corners, one tribal leader asked, "How would you feel if a Native American dug up your grandmother and took her jewelry and clothes and sold them to the highest bidder?" (Sharp, 2015, para. 7).

In North America, the conflict surrounding bones and funeral objects centers on American Indians and the 1990 federal Native American Graves Protection and Repatriation Act (NAGPRA), "under which certain objects with 'cultural affiliation' to certain descendants and tribes must be returned by museums" (Brodie et al., 2009, p. 12). With NAGPRA, *cultural affiliation* and a *reasonable relationship to artifacts must be established* in regard to human remains or cultural items, but "closest cultural affiliation can be complex" (Brodie et al., 2009, p. 13). NAGPRA does not require DNA testing to determine this, and tribes[10] often use a percentage of Indian blood, rather than DNA, as proof of membership (Conn, 2010; see Appendix 6.2, NAGPRA).[11]

I use the two vignettes at the beginning of this chapter and two to come, the *Ancient One* in Washington State, U.S.A., and the *Iwi* of Hawaii and London, as examples of contingency, provenance and ownership in conflict. These cases serve as a template for considering other similar controversies across the globe, including famous cases such as the Elgin marble, Buddhist manuscripts from Afghanistan or skulls from South Africa, Polynesia or North America, many of which are in European museums.

Contradictions: Positioning Ideologies as Mediational Means

The primary contradiction is always the use vs. exchange value. We saw new tensions between nodes in the activity system in Figure 5.1. Such secondary contradictions reflect, exacerbate or amplify existing underlying, competing ideologies. In the first case, the scientist and the Native discursive manifestations mark a tension between the mediational means (artifact) and rules (who is allowed). As Foot and Groleau (2011) noted,

> CHAT refers not only to what we traditionally understand as tools, *i.e.*, material entities which we manipulate, transform and create, but also includes signs, language, symbols, and abstract constructs such as models and epistemologies.
>
> (para. 3)

In the case of bones, abstract constructs and ideologies mediate the subject–object relationships, in this case regarding how objects such as bones are used, valued, traced and sold. We can view bones as the mediational means, but we may also locate ideologies in this position. Positioning ideologies as mediational means makes sense, as deep-seated beliefs inform how we value objects, and they are inbred; that is, they are part of an inviolate master narrative that does not question itself. With regard to the question of bones, the scientific vs. sacred use of an artifact creates tensions between division of labor, rules and mediational means, with each tension involving different nodes.

Power is always embedded in such tensions. Certainly, there are unequal power differentials between scientific and sacred constituencies; power is not equally shared, across many different axes, including money, prestige, narratives, and historicity. We have referred to power inequalities in every chapter; here though, at the heart of a museum's authority over collections, curators and discourses, we see power clearly manifest, shaping social, moral, political and ideological values as the institution wields an instrument of power to decide the fate of people's sacred bones (Rodrigues & Smith, 2014). Such decision-making exacerbates existing tensions, for example, between subject and community and divisions of labor (hierarchy) and rules. There is also a related secondary contradiction that centers on competing views of the monetary value of artifacts, one axis of which can be called cultural/functional and the other monetary/trade value. This resembles the contradictory ideologies concerning landownership we discussed in Chapter 5. So here again, we can note the tension over objects caused by cultural beliefs that center on collective rather than individual determination of ownership.

Contingency and Context

Objects frequently symbolize the spiritual aspects of the world for non-Western cultures; therefore, their *value* is misunderstood by museums and by museum visitors. Artifacts are treated by most Indigenous cultures as having a social life of their own (Dudley, 2012).[12] Underlying competing ideologies show themselves in the meanings we create from and with objects, and always remain *contingent on the social, historical and cultural contexts* within which the objects emerged and were created (Gosden & Marshall, 1999, p. 169).

To set the frame for seeing *contingent* meaning from the museum professional's perspective, I turn to Richard Kurin, who wrote on the Smithsonian blog (2014) his reflection on an experience of buying a spinning wheel from an old woman in India in order to explain his change in view on the role of objects in museums:

> [I]t was the spinning wheel, but more than the object, it was also the old woman, and her hut and her fields of cotton and her family and her children and her grandchildren. It was the entire experience. I've now spent the better part of four decades working on making those connections between people and artifacts, and telling the backstories, and providing the context to material culture—that which makes "stuff" so interesting.
>
> (para. 8)

Kurin said that many years later when he saw the spinning wheel on a museum website, it was completely devoid of any contextual information. He reflected,

> The sanitized image of the spinning wheel and the clinically precise metadata used to describe it stripped away all of the significant backstory of its history and the last woman who used it.
>
> (para. 9)

Kurin may have called it *backstory*, but it entails an entire social, historical, political and cultural context. Such stories of meaning in context are vital; every *object has a context*, a story, a past, present and future. The British Museum and other museums now contextualize or create biographies for their objects in order to

> consider the history of their collections in exhibitions. This approach highlights the ways in which objects were exchanged and collected and so how their meanings are contingent on context, will change over time and may be contradictory.
>
> (Curtis, 2006, p. 6)[13]

Note that Curtis included the secondary contradiction concerning meaning and context in the statement.

Throughout this book and chapter, I have assumed that contradictions tell us where along the ideological/epistemological lines the conflicts lie. However, with the spinning wheel example, the masks and the *ookaan* headdress, objects are often separated from their context, made devoid of their original cultural meaning or appreciated merely for their artistry or workmanship. In addition, if they are sacred, as are many materials in pre-Western times, such as the *ookaan* headdress, then we may remain ignorant of their significance.

Imagine for a moment an exhibit representing our own 21st-century history to future generations. This exhibit might highlight iPhones, iPads and computers as stand-alone objects, suggesting these tell the story of who we were and what we did. Or perhaps, the exhibit shows pictures of tall buildings in large cities or mountains of plastics in the oceans and other destructive waste. Or, again, the exhibit might include malas, crucifixes, rosaries or the Quran. Does any of this represent our civilization or in any way satisfy us? It is a humbling prospect to recognize how inaccurately we have done this, most especially with disenfranchised Indigenous peoples.

Ideally, we would situate artifacts within a social, cultural, political and historical context, rather than as remote, beautiful, ugly or abstract entities that speak for themselves. We would claim that ownership is always *contingent on context*, which, in turn, depends on current values, cultural norms (P. Moore, 2014), political and personal ideologies and 'settled expectations' (Bang et al., 2015). We would keep in the forefront the discourse of resistance, *desettling settled expectations* and decolonizing and what they bring to the meaning and context of contested objects.

In order to analyze contradictions inherent in the conflict surrounding artifacts, I provide some background before we turn to two cases that bring these issues alive.

Decolonizing/Colonizing

Learning to step out of the colonialist mindset is a difficult and humbling experience. The NMAI, meant to represent a change in how museums represent American Indians, has been challenged for its 'deafness' and failure to grapple actively with the slaughter of Indians (Lonetree, 2010; MacLachlan, 2012). Brady (2009) suggested that some artifacts there have been treated 'without honor' or without reference to history, cultural or historical context.

Despite current awareness of and attempts at decolonizing, examples abound of how the social and cultural history of peoples can be subsumed by the material artifact, by 'cultural appropriation', the borrowing from someone else's culture without their permission, without acknowledgment of victim culture's past (Wood, 2017, p. 1). Grabbing artifacts with a lack of concern for past hurts and imposing hefty prices on the objects are emblematic of neoliberalism's lack of concern with collateral damage and emphasis on 'calculated indifference' (Whyte, 2017) and commoditization.

It remains, therefore, extremely challenging for Indigenous people to 'fit into' (Contreras, 2017) a public school or university (Kidman, 2019) or a museum's authoritative history. Indigenous objects, privately or museum owned, have almost always been placed outside of their original spiritual/cultural context (often out of ignorance) and held away from the efforts and interests of tribal or community members. Artifacts often may only be viewed by special request, or, sometimes, they are locked in cabinets, to be viewed only by scientists.

As Kootenai medicine man Pat Lefthand said,

> I see a lot of things that are just sitting on tables, being tossed around, that to my people are sacred. The very people who are scientists haven't got the foggiest idea what they are handling, and yet they won't go back to tribes to find out what it is, how those things should be handled. And when the tribes ask for those things back, they say "no you don't have the proper facilities to take care of them".
>
> (Parker, 1990, p. 43, in MacLachlan, 2012, p. 39)

We saw some of this 'treatment of the sacred' reflected in the vignette at the beginning of this chapter. The *ookaan* headdress was finally seen *in its proper context* for the first time by the Scottish museum administrator only after repatriation (Curtis, 2008). Curtis had the humility to admit his earlier ignorance. The story of the Kwakwaka'wakw masks being bought and stored away as commodities and then offered for sale with little regard to owner, context or purpose beyond money never overtly mentions any cultural concerns. The only concern expressed was that federal regulations might make the masks difficult to sell.

Decolonizing Actions

Decolonizing relates to practice, leadership and virtually all aspects of museology. Decolonizing, this very public current movement, may help museums

- to face their colonialist origins and the resulting practices, and to *change* them;
- to acknowledge history in its fullness, not just Western versions; and
- make explicit the underlying epistemologies of colonialist collectors, which were

- theories about the inferiority of non-whites (Strauss, 2016),
- dehumanizing non-whites so as to justify stealing sacred and everyday objects, and
- claiming that the cultures and peoples are disappearing, so objects should be collected now.[14]

In carrying out decolonizing, Lonetree argued that the interpretation of objects should include

- their original purposes, context and/or historical use[15];
- interpreting spiritual and cultural objects, [as] the complex amalgam created by the object/artifact/bone/tipi/headdress, etc.; and
- the humans using the object in any interpretation of the object.

These suggested actions may seem reasonable and practical strategies, yet lurking beneath them are very intense and often unnoticed effects on the sensibilities of the people most directly involved. Lonetree argued again that

> every engagement with objects in museum cases or in collection rooms should begin with this core recognition…[we are not] viewing the native objects…as interesting inert, static pieces of material from the past, but instead that "we are privileged to stand as witnesses to living entities that remain intimately and inextricably tied to their descendant communities".
>
> (2010, p. xc)[16]

Such issues are not limited to American Indian peoples. For many Indigenous cultures, Polynesian, South African, Australian and New Zealand, for example, the user typically imbues part of his/her spirit into the object with use. Most importantly, bones are sacred, on the assumption that the spirit of the owner still resides there (Elliott, 2010; Lonetree, 2010). Colonialist Western Europeans discounted such beliefs. Colonial collectors' practical interpretation wiped out the history, the spirituality and all ways of understanding from the original owner's perspective. Notice, though, that colonial collectors never included the bones of their own people in any collections. Those bones remain interred in the ground.

Repatriation: Who Gets the 'Old Bones'?

The return of bones from museums to tribes typically rests on the notion of repatriation, a term typically used for people returning to their home countries. More recently, it has also been applied to objects, often disputed objects that are no longer in their original cultural context. These objects have been moved, borrowed, stolen or bought so that they could appear in private and public places such as museums and collections. We now are learning the capacity to view bones, for example, as "deeply connected to the past, present, and future of Indigenous communities"

(Boorn, 2016) or sacred (Elliott, 2010).[17] We may wonder, then, how we could not return them to their original lineal descendants! I review two case studies next, noting that the return of bones is still highly contested. These two cases of repatriation involve Indigenous bones: a recently resolved NAGPRA case involving the 8,500-year-old skeletal remains of *Kennewick Man* in Washington State, U.S.A., and the *Iwi Kūpuna* (bones of the elders from Hawaii) that were housed in London.

Case 1: Kennewick Man

Two college students stumbled across a human skull in 1996 on public land along the Columbia River in Kennewick, Washington, U.S.A. The provenance of the 8,500-year-old remains of Kennewick Man, the *Ancient One*, was disputed for years (Ziimmer, 2015). The case involved disagreement, errors in claims of origin and patrimony and, finally, controversial DNA testing to determine the 'closest cultural affiliation'. The *Ancient One* was eventually awarded to the Colville tribe of Washington to bury in 2017 (Rosenbaum, 2017).[18]

Over the course of researching and writing this book, the bones have changed hands from a Washington museum to DNA tests by European scientists to Native Americans and a ceremonial burial. It serves as a bell-weather for future cases. Decisions regarding the final resting place for bones reflect rapidly shifting sociopolitical views. Howard (2015) succinctly summarized the two sides of the debate in this way:

> On one side are scientists eager to continue to study the skeleton. On the other side are Native Americans who consider the skeleton [to be] the sacred remains of an ancestor to be reburied. The scientists won the [first] court case that gave them the right to study the skeleton…but members of Northwest tribes continue[d] to press for Kennewick Man's reburial.
>
> (Howard, 2015, para. 2)

Then, in 2014, as reported by *Science* magazine,

> DNA testing finally confirmed the remains were of Native American ancestry, clearing the way for the skeleton to be reburied—after years of scientific study—in a secret location in the Columbia Basin of the Pacific Northwest.
>
> (Preston, 2014, para. 3)

What Happened?

I retrace the steps as they occurred over the past 20 years because they are interesting markers of shifting ideologies. The Burke Museum in Washington, where the bones were being housed, originally said on their website,

> Under U.S. law, human remains cannot be "owned" by anyone. However, the *Kennewick Man* remains were recovered from federal land and are thus…

> controlled by the US Army Corps of Engineers and are housed in the Burke Museum.
>
> (Burke Museum, 2017)

The process from 1996 to 2017 was anything but smooth.

1. In 2004, the Ninth Circuit upheld a ruling that Kennewick Man is not related to any of the present-day tribes and therefore can remain at its current location at the Burke Museum of Natural History and Culture in Seattle (Burke Museum, 2017).[19]
2. In September 2014, Dr. Douglas Owsley, Smithsonian physical anthropologist and one of the plaintiffs in the case, shared his morphology-based findings that indicated that the skeleton was not of Native American affinity and may have been more closely related to circumpacific groups, such as the Ainu and Polynesians (Burke Museum, 2017).
3. In June 2015, University of Copenhagen geneticist Dr. Eske Willerslev…after sequencing the genome of Kennewick Man…compared DNA extracted from a hand bone to worldwide genomic data, including the Ainu and Polynesians. They found that *The Ancient One* is more closely related to modern Native Americans than any other living population[20] (Joyce, 2015, para. 3).
4. President Barack Obama signed legislation passed by Congress authorizing the return of the Ancient One to the tribes, and on February 20, [2017] he was buried in a secret location not far from where he was found (Tchenkmedyian, 2017, para. 6).

It is important to note that genomic testing was not a factor for Dr. Owsley but became so after Dr. Willerslev became involved (Klinkhammer, 2017).

The Burke website now says,

> The Burke Museum provided secure and respectful curation of *The Ancient One* from 1998–2017, under contract to the US Army Corps of Engineers, the government agency that controlled the remains until they were repatriated. The return of the *Ancient One* to the tribes is the right decision and was long overdue.

This case raises a number of questions. First, with respect to time, *How long or short a period constitutes lineal descent or cultural affiliation?* Further, questions on the best use of DNA evidence, and how to weigh and balance historical evidence (e.g., how people came to North America) vs. sacred views on the burial remain. We note that NAGPRA uses cultural affiliation rather than DNA, yet DNA settled this particular dispute, as nothing else could.

It is ironic that DNA testing only occurred because the Burke (due to the court's decision) held onto the bones long enough for them to go to Europe for DNA testing.

Overall, this case teaches us a few important lessons. First, cultural affiliation can be difficult to resolve when competing enterprises have what seem to be valid reasons for 'ownership'. This case reminds us how fraught these conflicted histories can be because it took so many years to settle. There is, in fact, still debate over this and similar cases.[21] Scientists argue that there is yet too much "to learn about where Kennewick Man came from to bury him now" (Joyce, 2015 para. 2). As *Nature* magazine's *This Week* editorialized in 2016,

> [M]any scientists will lament the loss. But there are hopeful signs that disputes such as this between researchers and Native Americans will themselves become a relic of the past. A new generation of geneticists is more likely to involve Native Americans in their research, for instance, by drafting plans for the handling of human remains before they are discovered.
>
> (p. 7)

Case 2: Hawaiian Iwi Kūpuna: Long Journey Home

While the legal status of Kennewick Man had to be settled over a period of 20 years in court, the next case study involves a 2013 negotiated repatriation between two countries (the United Kingdom and the United States). This case was settled by joint *repatriation* of the *iwi kūpuna*, mostly skull bones of Hawaiian ancestors,[22] which had been housed in the British Natural History Museum in London and were returned to Hawaii. The following text was taken from the Kai Wa Ola website (2013):

> In late August, Hui Mālama i Nā Kūpuna o Hawai'i Nei (Hui Mālama) and the Office of Hawaiian Affairs sent a small team on assignment to bring home 144 kūpuna from the Natural History Museum (NHM) and one kūpuna from the Wellcome Trust, both located in London.
>
> (Kai Wa Ola, 2013)

A 2014 newsletter article, video and public talk sponsored by Hui Malama I Na Kūpuna O Hawai'i Neil (Group Caring For the Ancestors of Hawai`i), created in 1988 and sponsored in part by the Office of Hawaiian Affairs, described the "23 year process of repatriating the bones (iwi) of the elders (Kūpuna), mostly skulls designated for scientific research, from the Natural Museum of History in London" (Hui Malama, Abad, 2013).[23] In this case, as in that of Kennewick Man, the *iwi kūpuna* ask us to reconsider the ownership, meaning and purpose of specific ancestral bones, physical remains that matter deeply to the original cultures.

Native Hawaiians believe ancestral burial sites must be left in place and undisturbed; it is a taboo in Native Hawaiian society to do otherwise. The following paragraph conveys the essence of Native Hawaiian beliefs regarding the bones of the ancestors *(iwi kūpuna)*:

> Hawaiians believe…iwi (the bones) to be the primary physical embodiment of a person. Following death…iwi were considered sacred, for within the bones resided the person's mana (spiritual essence)…. Native Hawaiians spent their lives maintaining and enhancing their mana…. Ancestral bones were guarded, respected,…and even deified. It was believed that the 'uhane' (spirit)[24] of a person hovered near…iwi. Desecration of…iwi resulted in an insult to the 'uhane' and trauma and harm to living descendants.
>
> (Ayao, 2000, p. 3)

The public news announcements at the time included a picture of Edward Halealoha Ayau, executive director of Hui Malama at that time, signing an agreement with Margaret Clegg of the NHM. Clegg was an expert in the provenance of human remains collections and on the effects of human activity on a skeleton during life and after death. She was a key facilitator in negotiations between Hui Malama and her museum. Ayau is a lawyer and activist who has worked to release *iwi kūpuna* from many museums, including the AMNH, the Field Museum and others.[25]

We might ask how Hawaiian skulls came to be housed in the NHM in London in the first place. In fact, during the time of colonial collections, many museums gifted or bought from each other so-called primitive peoples' collections from all over the world. Sometimes the ownership trace (provenance) is impossible to follow. Dusty old storerooms and labels can be hard to decipher and manage, as is evident from the repatriation of many of Hui Malama's acquisitions over the last 26 years.[26]

Hui Malama's retrieval of the *iwi kūpuna* of the ancestors from dusty old storerooms for reburial in their original homeland echoed the *Ancient One experience*. Both cases required decades and much effort. The positive outcomes for the Colville Indians and for Hui Malama and Native Hawaiians carry deep significance for present and future generations. In both cases, we are dealing with materials in the 21st century from centuries ago. These examples also underscore the cultural hegemony that allowed for the original 'harvesting' and nonsacred treatment of human remains.

One question remains though, "*When is it ok for archaeologists to dig up the dead?*" (Alex, 2018).[27] Alex's short answer is, "There's no blanket answer". As Alex also noted of one of her archaeological digs:

> Banana was code for human bones, on one archaeological dig where I've worked. We were excavating a cemetery, several thousand years old, and had permits from the appropriate authorities. However, certain religious groups in the area had a history of protesting any destruction of burials, so we kept our work discrete.
>
> (Alex, 2018, para. 3)

The Danish DNA expert, Eske Willerslev countered,

> For many tribal groups, human remains from the Americas are considered ancestors whether or not there is evidence of cultural or genetic links.... Ignoring tribal consultation can no longer be explained by lack of awareness. It's a decision, and must be considered a statement.
>
> (Balter, 2017, para. 4)

Three Themes: Sacred/Contingent/Monetary

In 1997, Julia Harrison discussed the ways that neocolonialism is embedded in museums; she moved the dialogue of the time in the direction of historicity, highlighting alienation, both intellectual and material, as a core aspect of early museums and their buildings, arguing,

> Almost by default colonialist ideology infused the institutional hegemony of 19th century museums, and largely continues into the late 20th century… [allows the] perpetuation of the metanarrative of the 'other'. (p. 42.) In the end the museum's discourse of representation of the 'other' fundamentally altered very little from its historical posture.
>
> (p. 41)

This is disheartening but consistent with Lonetree (2009, 2010) and others' analysis of NMAI. For example, Harrison argued further that alienation (see Appendix 6.5) is a critical aspect of *othering* and not *belonging*. Harrison isolated three main themes "as a heuristic device, [which] overlap and intertwine and cannot fully be separated…containment, objectification and reduction".[28]

The identification of these three themes is insightful and helps clarify the themes we have discussed throughout. In the following, I integrate Harrison's themes with three dialectical secondary contradictions from this chapter.

1. Secular vs. Sacred
2. Contingent vs. Solidified
3. Selling/Deaccessioning vs. Culture

Secular vs. Sacred: (Reduction and Objectification)

Grimes (1992) has suggested that there is probably no culture where everything is sacred or where nothing is sacred. The definition of sacred very much depends on context. NAGPRA is a secular law dealing with sacred objects, as well as the sacred/spiritual elements of Native Americans' belief systems. MacLachlan (2012) has suggested that even when repatriation of sacred items does occur, this decision is being made through a secular lens where the understanding of the concept of "sacred items" creates difficulties. Western sensibilities typically overwhelm Native American ones.[29]

In relation to NAGPRA and other reparative actions, it matters very much what counts as sacred because of different interpretations of that word by different nations, institutions and, of course, museums. It is the definition of *sacred* that is challenging because differences between Western and Indigenous classification systems of belief differ diametrically. In the Western anthropological lexicon, "the terms 'sensitive' and 'culturally significant' are typically associated with sacred and are generally used as adjectives connoting esteem or deference to the supernatural" (MacLachlan, 2012, p. 40). Typically, we defer to anthropologists and curators, and more recently to Native Americans, to interpret this term. Compare this with "[A museum's] collection, in Maori terms, is not just the collection; it's also the Maori viewpoint. They're not just collections; they're ancestors" (Clavir et al., 2019, para 5). The Government of Canada suggests sacred objects are "sacred or holy pieces used in ritual…[and] include materials that are culturally restricted; for example, those seen or handled only by specific people such as initiates or medicine keepers, or by one gender only" (Clavir, 2002; Clavir et al., 2019; Government of Canada website, 2019; Moses, 1993).

Intermingling the sacred and secular is not new to the Western world; we need only look at places like the Asian Art Museum in San Francisco or the Cloisters and the Rubin Museums in New York City and others that have included or emphasized the sacred or intermixed the sacred and the secular. This is true for museums incorporating Christian, Asian, Confucian, Taoist and Buddhist art. Typically religious statuary, Thankas or paintings (think of all the early works of Christian art originally intended for churches) are the centerpieces of such collections.

Remember, as well, the Native American belief that each owner imbues something of themselves into an object, like a poi pounder in Polynesian societies. The object becomes filled with the intentions and use of its previous owners. The question then, is how do we treat sacred objects centuries later, especially if they have been stripped of context and locked in museum cabinets for future scientific research?

Given multiple interpretations,[30] it is nearly impossible to create a universal definition of sacred, and we need to ask if it is even necessary to create such a definition. Only our ingrained Western and White ways of thinking demand this kind of *precise* taxonomy. Our insistence on a definition may also keep us stuck in a colonialist mindset rather than challenging (reculturing) ourselves to negotiate a more explicit anti-racist stance.

Eakin (2006) argued that sacredness can also have many different meanings among different Native American tribes. If the term *sacred* is elastic and contextualized and is interpreted differently by different tribes, both of which are wholly appropriate, then it becomes more challenging for the average European American to comprehend and to create and enforce *laws* to protect multiple meanings of sacred objects. In this situation, when there is an intermingling of sometimes incommensurate ideas about what is deemed to be sacred or *legal*, we must ask ourselves what processes must we engage in to distinguish and disambiguate them. Accepting the validity of lived experience, we may yet come to believe a culture's delineation of sacredness of its objects and practices. The process is challenging.

One of the unintended outcomes of NAGPRA may have been to diminish the meaning of the word *sacred*, as experienced in Native American cosmologies and belief systems, into a more quantifiable Western secular term. An overemphasis on the difficulty could become simply another manufactured act of neocolonialism imposed on people with less power.

One alternative approach has developed a compromise between Indigenous traditions and museum practice by designating museums as 'keeping places' (e.g., Kreps, 2003). The Government of Canada has a carefully worded website written by anthropologists. One section considers the following:

> Traditional care can take many forms. In its private, behind-the-scenes aspect within collections storage, it may involve the periodic smudging of objects or the ritual feeding of selected items such as masks.... Ritual feeding might involve the application of vegetable oil or foodstuffs to the surfaces of objects.
> (Clavir et al., 2019, para. 5)

The Museums Australia document *Continuous Cultures, Ongoing Responsibilities* (2005) highlights the importance of 'custodianship and care taking rather than ownership' and a 'recognition of the value of stories and other intangibles associated with objects' (Museums Australia, 2005). As a result of this shift in understanding, the National Museum of Australia demands that "any research undertaken on ancestral remains held on behalf of communities must have the prior consent of traditional custodians or those authorised by them", as well as from the museum (National Museum of Australia, 2005, p. 4; see Appendix 6.5).

Contingent vs. Solidified: (Objectification and Containment)

In the field of museum studies as well as elsewhere, the tensions among the underlying ideologies are now changing (Leonardo, 2003), and our understanding of objects and the stories we tell about them are also changing. Thus, reliance on *artifact meaning and relevance in context*—that is, seeing the contingent rather than fixed ideological interpretations—has become more common. Because everything concerning decolonization also points toward contingency, the norms or settled expectations (Bang et al., 2015; Kidman, 2019) regarding social, cultural, political, historical artifacts are in a state of flux. This is reflective of Kalshed's (2020) notion of interpretive realities, rather than codified rules written in stone.

By *adopting a contingent context*[31] (Christen, 2007; Swan & Jordan, 2015) stance, we can come to discover the meaning(s) people create regarding museum objects. We can influence how institutions select, present and group objects into exhibitions, how museum educators interpret/explain them and how other media convey the official message to the public. As noted by Dan Contreras, a Stanford anthropologist,

> Ownership, context and use add up to a very interesting pattern of behavior that tells us about trading, culture, society, gender and so on. One pot out of context doesn't tell us that.
>
> (Wilcox, 2009, p. 11)

This view strikes some as being dangerously relativistic (Browarny, 2010). But context has often been determined by the designated 'owner' or a trail of the provenance of an item, separate from its true cultural significance. Is this not also dangerous? (see also Browarny, 2010; Dartt-Newton, 2009).

To explore the idea further, we ask ourselves, then, what it means for the 21st-century museum to make the shift toward 'contingent ownership in context', toward interpretive realities in art galleries, museums of anthropology, natural history and science, and other similar informal settings, where trails of provenance formerly ruled. Since the late 20th century, such questions have been asked with increasing frequency and intensity in public forums, writings, books, and museum circles, increasingly and with respect to Indigenous populations and other nondominant cultural groups wishing to repatriate sacred items, as well as regarding war reparations and restitution to besieged communities (see also Ash, 2018).[32]

We know the significance of a thing is often linked to its previous ownership or provenance—who made it, out of what, when and where. But ownership *stories* matter too. In fact, who owned and used a thing can completely alter our perception of it, as well as its story. We already noted this in the previous spinning wheel example.

Even when there are newer intentional, contextualized, story-based and contingent interpretations in exhibits of Indigenous people's objects, there are *still* contradictions. We already noted Brady's (2009) critique of the NMAI, for "commodification and voyeuristic treatment of Native American objects [which] helps to create an assumption that material culture is more important than the people, their customs, and their ways of being" (p. 136). Here is the primary contradiction reflected again in the tension between commodification and the authentic custom-laden purpose of a thing.

Selling/Deaccessioning Vs. Culture: (Commodification and Objectification)

As noted in Chapter 4, museums have been selling (*deaccessio*ning) art and artifacts from permanent collections to make money; the cultural significance is deemed less important than the financial goals of the museum. There have been many *deaccessions* by notable museums.[33] There is a darker side of deaccessioning when we consider the sale of bones, in terms of their spiritual vs. financial value. Bones attract visitors and therefore make money for museums.

While deaccessioning is allowed, museums have created rules of acceptable practice, and the breaking of these rules has, in some cases, caused public outcry (Riley, 2011).[34] When deaccessioning turns to bones though, perhaps with the exception of relics in Christian history, the same monetary rules exacerbate any perceived desecration of the sacred. Di Domenico (2015) argued that beyond outright sales of artifacts, there is another side to the corporate thinking of museums, that

> bones bring in people, more visitors, and therefore more money.... The delicate issue of human remains has caused UK public museums, among others, to debate, probe and defend their functions and identities.... The overt display of human remains, in order to attract the public, has led these public museums to re-examine their ethical approaches and codes in light of changed public understandings.
>
> (p. 3–4)

Outside of museums, many Native American sacred objects continue to be sold on the open market by private owners, especially in Europe. The legality of such collecting is being contested as well. There is no NAGPRA in Europe. Take the example of the Hopi Katsinam, offered for sale in Paris in the early 2010s:

> Hopi tribal leaders and Arizona's members of Congress are asking U.S. law enforcement to stop the sale of about a dozen sacred Hopi artifacts at a Paris auction house in June (2015).... This is the sixth time the French auction house...has sold objects sacred to Native American tribes. It has argued that the items legally belong to collectors, and a Paris court has ruled that such sales are legal.
>
> (Keaten, 2015, para. 5)

The Hopi Tribe considers selling these sacred items to be sacrilegious and offensive. Despite such objections, the sale went through in June 2015. According to the *Wall Street Journal*,

> Six masks—known as the Hopi Katsina Friends—crafted about a century ago using combinations of leather, wood, cotton and feathers—sold Monday for €40,500 ($44,000).
>
> (Masidlover, 2015, para. 2)

This situation may seem merely unfortunate, yet it is more than that:

> Hopi Katsina friends are among the most sacred Hopi ritual objects.... When worn during Katsina ceremonies, the friend—the spirit of Katsina—is united with the spirit of man.
>
> (Ganteaume, 2013, para. 2)[35]

While we may be dismayed over French actions,[36] we also need to remember that in the United States, despite NAGPRA, there are still sales that are questionable or difficult to monitor. When a cache of Native American artifacts was found in a warehouse in Utah (Mozingo, 2014; Sharp, 2015) a federal agent discovered tens of thousands of looted objects recovered in a massive sting.... In one suspect's home, a team of 50 agents and archaeologists spent two days cataloging more than 5,000 artifacts.... At another house, investigators found some 4,000 pieces. They also discovered a display room behind a concealed door controlled by a trick lever. In all, they seized some 40,000 objects—a collection so big it now fills a 2,300-square-foot warehouse on the outskirts of Salt Lake City and spills into parts of the nearby Natural History Museum of Utah.

(Sharp, 2015, para. 5)

This is not unlike the Nazi loot found in Gurlitt's house (see Appendix 6.3) in 2015. Similar issues exist in Australia where the remains of Indigenous peoples, mostly bones, are in store cases in large museums like the National Museum of Australia, and scattered, as well, among other museums across Europe and America.[37]

Summary: What Now?

"Should we view bones as scientific artifacts to be held in perpetuity?" "Who gets to decide?" "Must every decision go to court?"

Scientists and collectors argue they need to keep bones and skulls for the future, for measurement, comparisons and contrasts, or to extract DNA when necessary. DNA extraction, as we saw, has proven quite useful. But we cannot predict how these bones, many of which have been in museum storages for centuries, often far from their origins, might be used. Ongoing storage tends to be favored to allow future potential scientific research; typically this tends to outweigh the rights of the original owners, especially for sacred objects, such as bones. Museums often viewed this as provenance, legal ownership. This is changing.[38]

One of the most visible aspects of this change is the decolonizing process. Here *reculturing means* promoting the decolonizing process and repatriating the objects. We know from the many examples we have explored that the process has not been smooth or comfortable and is as yet incomplete. Pluralism has its price. Museums are hierarchies, and the official view still tends to align with those holding financial power, academic power or other forms of hegemony. As such, it is very difficult to change the museum ethos from within. Yet, this is exactly what is required for successful *reculturing*. There are an increasing number of books, dissertations, articles, blogs and other written and oral sources that discuss these controversies. There will be many more in the coming decades. The shift from financial hegemony to cultural respect and collaboration is proceeding. I have selected some of the key issues that lie at the heart of the current dialogues. It is my hope that this exploration of the role of objects in modern museums in the 21st century has helped clarify this change process and will help facilitate future progress.

Appendix 6.1: Repatriation In the United States: NAGPRA

U.S. museums have been struggling with what repatriation means in our postmodern, decolonizing context. Museums in the United States are now moving to return funerary remains and related sacred objects to Native American peoples in large part due to NAGPRA passed in 1990 and revised in 1996. NAGPRA has been a game changer for object repatriation in the United States, and it has had repercussions around the world. What does NAGPRA actually ask of museums? NAGPRA legislated that

> institutions that receive federal funding to inventory their collections, consult with federally recognized Native American tribes, and repatriate human remains or cultural items that meet certain criteria…prioritizes a principle termed "cultural affiliation" which means a reasonable relationship can be demonstrated between an identifiable earlier group and a present-day federally recognized tribe or tribe.
>
> (NAGPRA, 2021)

With this act, *cultural affiliation* and a *reasonable relationship to artifacts* must be established in questions regarding human remains or cultural items. NAGPRA raised a number of complex issues for the museum because "the matter of closest cultural affiliation can be complex".

Appendix 6.2: DNA Testing

It was determined that the 'ancient one's' skeleton: "[D]oes share a close genetic affinity with members of the Confederate Tribes of the Colville Reservation" (Rasmussen et al., 2015). As Rasmussen et al. asserted in 2015,

> His population affinities have been the subject of scientific debate and legal controversy. Based on an initial study of cranial morphology it was asserted that Kennewick Man was neither Native American nor closely related to the claimant Plateau tribes of the Pacific Northwest, who claimed ancestral relationship and requested repatriation under the Native American Graves Protection and Repatriation Act (NAGPRA). These tribes stem from the Pacific Northwest, and are among several Native American groups that demanded custody of the skeleton (Joyce, 2015, NPR). As per NAGPRA guidelines (lineal descent), *the ancient one* belongs with the Confederate Tribes of the Colville Reservations.
>
> (Rasmussen et al., 2015, p. 3)

Appendix 6.3: Who Owns Nazi Loot?

To better understand the contexts within which 'ownership' discussions have taken place, we look to the language and the underlying epistemologies that support 'normed' practice. Terms such as *provenance, reparation* and *repatriation* can act as sanitized language for the uglier sides of ownership of objects/artifacts in museums. There are two main ownership issues: *reparations* as in the return of Nazi war loot (Jewish-owned artwork, either taken, bought or traded and permanently held after World War II, all of which have questionable provenance) and the *repatriation* of American Indian remains following the enactment of the NAGPRA. The two words—reparation and repatriation—have similar etymologies for restoration. Both have, now simultaneously, reached increasingly fractious levels of attention in public forums as well.[39]

We can define reparation as,

> the making of amends for a wrong one has done, by paying money to or otherwise helping those who have been wronged, [for example] *the courts required a convicted offender to* **make** *financial* **reparation to** *his victim* .1.1 (**reparations**) The compensation for war damage paid by a defeated state.
>
> (Oxford English Dictionary)

In the museum world, the case for reparation typically rests on questions of provenance. We note that questions of provenance are interpreted through the lens of Judeo Christian, Western, European legal notions of what it means to own and/or to prove that one has owned something in terms of written documentation. This presupposes the existence of written language and records and an epistemology that embraces individual ownership, all of which are socially constructed.

We *do* know what provenance means to most art museums. According to the International Foundation for Art Research, provenance

> derives from the French *provenire* meaning "to originate".... The provenance of a work of art is a historical record of its ownership...(e.g.) provides a documentary record of owners' names, dates of ownership, and means of transference, i.e., inheritance, or sale through a dealer or auction; and locations where the work was kept, from the time of its creation by the artist until the present day.
>
> (Flescher et al., n.d.)[40]

But what does provenance mean if artwork and or other material goods were stolen or obtained in an unscrupulous manner? It is difficult to parse the meaning of the term unscrupulous during wartime when many civil rules do not apply. When your home and lives are endangered and overtaken, cherished objects tend to disappear. Does the victor keep the spoils, even when the victor is widely recognized as evil?

Granted, the 1940s recede farther and farther from our memories, yet the wounds run deep and are not handled well within an adversarial legal system, where the victims are dead and dying and the state is slow. In many cases, the *real* story was too ugly to reveal—that is, genocide and dehumanization and mass pillage.[41] In the case of the Nazis, we note that time is of the essence in making reparation. It is now the second and third generations who are fighting this battle, as the many original traces of paperwork, memories and 'provenance' have disappeared. Much knowledge will be lost if the ownership of illegally gained objects is not challenged by reparative actions in the next few years before legal time limits expire.

> There is some hope, according to a report (Lane, 2014) in the *Wall Street Journal*. Germany is setting up an independent center to comb museum collections for art looted by the Nazis, [according to] the country's culture minister…the Gurlitt case has revealed weaknesses in Germany's restitution system. Others claim that the process has been entirely too slow: The two organizations…studying the identification of Jewish artwork and historical artifacts stolen by the Nazis for the past 15 years…have come to the conclusion that the majority (2/3) of countries who had signed on to Jewish art reparation agreements have done "little or nothing" to implement the requirements of these agreements.
>
> (Jewish Virtual Library, 2014)[42]

We may wonder why it has taken so long for reparation and restitution to occur? This question brings us back to the meaning of the term *ownership*. Does ownership imply money, time, history, squatter's rights or another worldview? There are widely divergent opinions on this subject. These matters cross jurisdictions and derive from painful history many do not even wish to acknowledge.

Appendix 6.4: Alienation

Harrison located alienation in the larger meta-story of how museums were first built: "glass cases, shelves and drawers in museums confined the material evidence of the colonized peoples into new and unusual configurations" (Harrison, 1997, p. 44). The overarching 'structure of containment' of these configurations was the museum buildings themselves, be it the ethnographic museums in Europe or the natural history museums in the United States.

> Alienation, I would suggest, could thus be operationalized at both an intellectual and material level. Intellectual alienation, I might suggest, of the 'other' in the nineteenth century was profoundly reinforced to the museum visitor, by the mere fact that museums were large imposing edifices filled with the material wealth of this "new cultural subject." Museums and public exhibitions were powerful exemplifications of "material" alienation—both in the sense of what had been alienated from colonial subjects, and in the separation that visitors would feel from these objects due to their unfamiliar nature. This process of "coming to know" was heavily determined by the nature of the museum which, as Hooper-Greenhill suggests, directly reflected the rules and structures of that colonial milieu.
>
> (Harrison, 1997, p. 45)

Appendix 6.5: Australia

From the Western Australian museum http://museum.wa.gov.au/referendum-1967/aboriginal-rights:

> Please be advised: this website may contain names, images and voices of people who are now deceased. Some material may include language or views from the period in which it was written/recorded that today we consider inappropriate or even offensive. The Western Australian Museum does not endorse this language of the past and apologises for any distress caused.
>
> The usage of the term 'Aboriginal' within historical records is used to denote all peoples of Aboriginal and Torres Strait Islander descent. Across this website, the term "Aboriginal" may also be taken to encompass those who identify as Torres Strait Islander.

As a result of this shift in understanding, in the National Museum of Australia, "any research undertaken on ancestral remains held on behalf of communities must have the prior consent of traditional custodians or those authorised by them", as well as from the museum (National Museum of Australia, 2005, p. 4).

Notes

1. The NMAI offers one example; new and local Native American–designed and operated museums, such as the Ziibiwing Center, described at the end of Chapter 5, are other examples (see also Lonetree, 2012).
2. O'Connor (2010) refers to neoliberal coercive competition, which forces lasting architectural and behavioral change on nations, firms, and workers (p. 696).
3. By which he means, among other things, notions of spectacle, for example tours of the slaughterhouse, as controlled vision (Bennett, 2018, p. 30).
4. There is also controversy concerning how items were acquired into collections, such as the Parthenon Marbles at the British Museum, London, and Zodiac of Dendera in the Louvre, Paris (Shoenberger, 2019).
5. Over 20 years ago, Julia Harrison (1997) foreshadowed the current critique of neoliberalism in her description of neocolonialsim in modern museums.
6. And NAGPRA, Native American Graves Protection and Repatriation Act.
7. This interpretive difference has a significant impact on the Indigenous peoples of most countries, including Canada, Mexico, Europe and Asia.
8. It is not clear what the monetary loss is for museums due to NAGPRA, but clearly if the Elgin marble is returned, for example, there would be financial damage to the British Museum.
9. There are few cases of digging up non-Indigenous or non-enslaved peoples' bones.
10. To be considered enrolled members, they must in turn meet various criteria for tribal membership, which vary from tribe to tribe and are typically set forth in tribal constitutions approved by the U.S. Bureau of Indian Affairs (Thornton, 1996).
11. NAGPRA has made decisions somewhat easier for American museum committees and other similar institutions. However, there have been claims that when museums do return sacred items, other than bones, they place conditions on their subsequent use, making their use temporary.

12 In contrast, Simon (2010) defined objects in this way: "[A]n object is a physical item that is accessible to visitors, either on display, shared through educational programming, or available for visitors to use. I'm talking about artifacts that cultural institutions collect, preserve, and present".

13 This is not an entirely new idea.

In 1976 at the Folklife Festival…on the National Mall… one of the formative secretaries here at the Smithsonian, who in response to what he saw as the stuffy, dusty, artifact-crowded museums of the day, ordered curators to 'Take the instruments out of their cases and let them sing'.

(Kurin, 2014, para. 10).

14 This is one way that museums came to be filled with sacred, secular, valuable and also very ordinary American Indian and other Indigenous peoples' objects during colonialist times. Museums acquired materials in altogether legitimate ways as well, through purchase and donation. For a brief discussion of this, see Shoenberger (2019).

15 Similarly, as another unintended outcome, MacLachlan noted, "[I]tems that were created as tradition were now created commercially to suit colonialists…traditional items that were central to religious and spiritual belief systems amongst Native Americans became for the colonialist, curiosity items to be collected" (Maclachlan, 2012, p. 28).

16 Walker (2013), for example, has argued, "From a decolonialist perspective then (and there are more than one) we see such Colonialist spoils of aggression and war representing a basic dehumanization of the other" (Bhabha, 2001, p. 17).

17 These remains were collected by explorers and anthropologists between 1788 and 1948 in what most Aborigines consider a glorified grave-robbing campaign, when bodies and parts were plucked from trees and ripped from riverbanks, dug up from burial sites and stolen from hospitals, asylums and prisons. Zoologist Eric Mjoberg, who led the first Swedish expedition into the Kimberley in 1910, followed Aborigines on ceremonies, only to later raid their sites, smuggling the remains out of Australia as "kangaroo bones". Publication of Mjoberg's diaries, in which he describes "skeleton hunting" and depicts Aborigines as cannibals, outraged Swedes and led, in 2004, to the voluntary return of 18 boxes of bones by Stockholm's Museum of Ethnography (Elliott, 2010).

18 Friday [2.18.17], the Colville, Yakama, Nez Perce, Umatilla and Wanapum sang traditional songs during a day-long inventory and transfer of the remains by the U.S. Army Corps of Engineers at the Burke Museum in Seattle.

19 The plaintiffs and their colleagues made three visits to the Burke Museum to carry out scientific research on the remains. Representatives of some of the tribes involved in the case also visited the remains to conduct ceremonies and remained committed to having *The Ancient One* repatriated (Burke Museum, 2017).

20 In 2014, the Danish scientists who retrieved the DNA said, "We can see very clearly that Kennewick Man is more closely related to present day Native Americans than he is to anybody else…. We probably will never be able to say who is, in fact, the closest living relative of Kennewick Man" (Joyce, 2015, para. 5).

21 In contrast to the Ancient One "in which scientists have consulted tribal peoples and obtained their blessings before extracting DNA from ancestral Native American remains, the researchers (with bones from the AMNH) are only now discussing their results with tribal groups…the American Museum of Natural History (AMNH), which has held these ancient Puebloan remains in its collection since they were first excavated in the late 1890s…[said] that the bones were "culturally unidentifiable"—that is, they could not be linked directly to any living tribal group…. The AMNH apparently made little or no attempt to bring its 2000 review up to date…[even now] if the AMNH fulfilled the letter of the law, the question remains whether it fulfilled the law's spirit of respect for tribal

cultural traditions. ... The AMNH's explanation for not consulting with the tribes before granting the team permission to do its research is 'unacceptable' given NAGPRA's long history, says Kurt Dongoske, the tribal historic preservation officer for the Pueblo of Zuni in northwest New Mexico" (Balter, 2017, para. 3).

22 To clarify, the Hawaiians are not Native Americans, but of Polynesian origin, having migrated originally from northern China to spread throughout Australasia, ultimately inhabiting all the Polynesian islands and beyond (Jiao, 2012, personal communication).

23 Ayau recalled, "Bishop Museum [in Honolulu] explained that they gave the Mo'omomi kūpuna to the Cranmore Ethnographic Museum in Kent, England, and that it had since closed. Its collections were split among several institutions" (Abad, 2013, para. 6).

24 "'Uhane' soul, spirit, ghost; dirge; or song of lamentation *(rare)*; spiritual. 'Uhane role, without a soul; shameless, like a beast. Lele ka 'uhane, the soul leaves [death]. Kuʻu i ka ʻuhane (Kin. 35.29), to give up the ghost. Pili ʻuhane, spiritual. ʻUhane ʻololī, thin, shriveled soul or ghost". Hawaiian dictionaries, Wehewehe wikiwiki, (n.d.), hilo.hawaii.edu/wehe/glossary.

25 See https://vimeo.com/102279162 for a complete explication of Hui Malama's efforts.

26 As noted earlier, bones from colonial transactions typically were placed in the natural history collections. See Ash (2018) for a discussion of the role of natural history museums in keeping human remains and other artifacts rather than history museums.

27 It wasn't until the 1960s and 1970s that professional archaeologists established comprehensive ethical guidelines (Strauss, 2016).

28 [In] containment...ideas and understandings are objectified and reduced. In reduction, subjects are often contained and objectified. Objectification implies reduction and containment. (Harrison, 1997, p. 45)

29 MacLachlan suggests that NAGPRA acknowledges that Native American belief in the boundaries between the secular and the supernatural realm are not as defined as in Western thought and that items can hold supernatural qualities with their own classifications of Indigenous belief (MacLachlan, 2012, NAGRA compliance, 2021).

30 Michael F. Brown (2003a) suggested that to outsiders, sacredness can be elastic—that is, "stretched to include all kinds of things that wouldn't be sacred or religious" (p. 10). Others have suggested sacred is tied to social unification because sacredness can also be embodied within the group.

31 Christen (2007): This is an..."examination of the strategic and tactical alliances involved in the development of museums...a form of cultural production...[a] detailed discussion of the implications of collaborations that incorporate community values and protocols as major tenets of the partnership (...development of an Aboriginal community's cultural center in east central Australia) uses the term "contingent collaborations" to describe the complex sets of interrelationships involved" (pp. 107, 114).

32 It was not uncommon in the 1800s, for example, for collectors to loot "fresh Native American graves and burial platforms. They dug up corpses and even decapitated dead Indians lying on the field of battle and shipped the heads to Washington for study" (Preston, 2014).

33 Deaccessioning is not specific to art museums. The same phenomenon routinely occurs with privately owned Native American or Nazi-obtained objects, which were typically purchased years before, borrowed or taken with or without the full understanding of the owner.

34 In 2011 "the Cleveland Museum of Art put up 32 old-master paintings for auction and the J. Paul Getty Museum offered 15. Meanwhile, the Pennsylvania Museum of Fine Arts and the Carnegie Museum of Art are selling five paintings each, and the Art Institute of Chicago is selling two Picassos, a Matisse and a Braque at Christie's in London" (Riley,

2011). For example, the Delaware Museum of Art had made plans to pay for its multimillion dollar building expansion debt and rebuild its endowment by selling its art. That's not permitted, according to the Association of Art Museum Directors, an umbrella organization of more than 200 members that wrote the current guidelines. Also Deaccession is often opposed by museum administrators and art critics on the grounds that art is held in the public trust…[according to current guidelines] deaccession is only to be used to buy other works of art (Blair, 2014).

35 Respecting non-Western sacred objects. http://blog.nmai.si.edu/main/2013/04/respecting-non-western-sacred-objects.html-non-western-sacred-objects.html

36 "Here we see different spiritual values pitted against each other as though spirituality is the same to both Catholic and Native systems. American politicians and museums petitioned President Hollande to block the sale, arguing that: The sale of such objects violates various federal, state and tribal statutes that protect the United States' cultural resources and tribal property. In response, the selling agency said: …it would be tough to establish special rules to cover the masks, noting that religious objects from the Catholic Church are routinely sold at auctions in France despite objections from some Catholics" (Masidlover, 2015).

37 Daley (2014) noted: "The skull belongs to Kanabygal, an Aboriginal warrior who died when troops shot and beheaded him in New South Wales in 1816… among the remains of 725 Aboriginal people held here. …victims of frontier violence between tribesmen – defending traditional lands on the past … frontier – and colonial troops, paramilitary police forces, settler militia and raiding parties. Their bodies were cut up for parts that became sought-after antiquities in colonial homesteads across Australia and in cultural, medical and educational institutions across the US, Britain and continental Europe".

38 DiDomenico suggested a new hybrid model for museums, meaning a shift in organizational identity that museum go through when ethos, belief systems and ownership are challenged. Hybridization may result in a "merger of public and private sector [organizational] features by seeking 'the best of both worlds: public accountability and private efficiency' features" (Kopell, 2006, p 1, in Di Domenico, 2015, p. 12).

39 The heated debate is likely another marker of the larger cultural shift toward decolonization within museums, signaled by NAGPRA actions. This shift questions the meaning of the word 'ownership'.

40 See International Foundation for Art Research (IFAR) https://www.ifar.org/provenance.php for an excellent discussion of Nazi era art restitution.

41 O'Connor (2013) argued that matters are unlikely to change quickly, as German laws have statutes of limitations, and that those holding Nazi-stolen art are simply waiting for them to expire.

42 We must remind ourselves that Nazi-looted art remained up for grabs because Jews, like the American Indians, (Australian Aborigines, South African Koi, American slaves, etc.) had no power to represent their own interests; they were dehumanized and robbed of their objects. Crimes were based on the faulty logic that the victims were less-than human, a deep strain running through power-laden institutions. Slavery was based on the same faulty logic (Kendi, 2017).

References

Abad, K. (2013, October). *The long journey home*. Kamakako'i: The Cutting Edge. https://www.kamakakoi.com/longjourneyhome.

About. Hui Mālama Ola Nā 'Ōiwi. (n.d.). https://hmono.org/.

Alex, B. (2018, September 7). When is it OK for archaeologists to dig up the dead? *Discover Magazine*. https://www.discovermagazine.com/planet-earth/when-is-it-ok-for-archaeologists-to-dig-up-the-dead.

Allain Bonilla, M.-L. (2017). *Issues*. ONCURATING. https://www.on-curating.org/issue-35-reader/some-theoretical-and-empirical-aspects-on-the-decolonization-of-western-collections.html#.X_lbwthKhyw.

Ash, D. (2014). Positioning informal learning research in museums within activity theory: From theory to practice and back again. *Curator: The Museum Journal, 57*, 107– 118. http://dx.doi.org/10.1111/cura.1205

Ash, D. (2018). Cultural conflict: The stories dioramas tell and don't tell. In A. Scheersoi & S. D. Tunnicliffe (Eds.), *Natural history dioramas – Traditional exhibits for current educational themes: Socio-cultural aspects* (pp. 113–130). Cham: Springer International Publishing.

Ayao, E. H. (2000). Native burials: Human rights and sacred bones. *Cultural Survival Quarterly Magazine*. https://www.culturalsurvival.org/publications/cultural-survival-quarterly/native-burials-human-rights-and-sacred-bones.

Balter, M. (2017, March 30). *The ethical battle over ancient DNA*. Sapiens. https://www.sapiens.org/archaeology/chaco-canyon-nagpra/#:~:text=Researchers%20who%20study%20the%20DNA,still%20more%20sensitivity%20.

Bang, M., Faber, L., Gurneau, J., Marin, A., & Soto, C. (2015). Community-based design research: Learning across generations and strategic transformations of institutional relations toward axiological innovations. *Mind, Culture, and Activity, 23*(1), 28–41. doi:10.1080/10749039.2015.1087572

Bennett, T. (2018). *Museums, power, knowledge: selected essays*. Routledge Taylor & Francis Group.

Bhabha, H. (2001). Introduction: The subjunctive mood of art. In L. Rothfield (Ed.), *Unsettling "sensation": Arts policy lessons from the Brooklyn Museum of art controversy*. (pp. 93–95). Rutgers University Press.

Blair, E. (2014, August 11). *As museums try to make ends meet, 'deaccession' is the art world's dirty word*. NPR. https://www.npr.org/2014/08/11/339532879/as-museums-try-to-make-ends-meet-deaccession-is-the-art-worlds-dirty-word.

Boorn, A. L. (2016). *Interpreting the transnational material culture of the 19th-century North American plains Indians: Creators, collectors, and collections*. [Doctoral dissertation, Kansas State University]. http://hdl.handle.net/2097/34472

Brady, M. J. (2009). A dialogic response to the problematized past: The National Museum of the American Indian. In S. Sleeper-Smith (Ed.), *Contesting knowledge: Museums and indigenous perspectives* (pp. 133–155). University of Nebraska Press.

Brodie, N., Contreras, D., Merryman, J., Harrison, P., Seligman, T., & Meskell, L. (2009, January 28). *Buying, selling, owning the past*. Interaction. https://news.stanford.edu/news/multi/features/heritage/images/paper_heritage.pdf.

Browarny, L. (2010). *Art, artifact, anthropology: The display and interpretation of Native American material culture in North American Museums* (Publication No. 736). [Master's Thesis, Seton Hall University].

Brown, M. (2003a). *Who owns Native Culture?* Cambridge: Harvard University Press.

Brown, M. (2003b). *Stunning Nazi-looted art find reignites question of German restitution guidelines for treatment of sacred objects*. http://www.nytimes.com/2006/08/10/arts/design/10sacr.html?_r=0

Burke Museum. (2017, February 17). *Statement on the repatriation of the ancient one*. https://www.burkemuseum.org/news/ancient-one-kennewick

Campfens, E. (2020). Whose cultural objects? Introducing heritage title for cross-border cultural property claims. *The Netherlands International Law Review, 67*, 257–295. https://doi.org/10.1007/s40802-020-00174-3

Christen, K. (2007). Following the Nyinkka: Relations of respect and obligations to act in the collaborative work of aboriginal cultural centers. *Museum Anthropology, 30*(2), 101–124.

Clavir, M. (2002). *Preserving what is valued: Museums, conservation and first nations.* University of British Columbia Press.

Clavir, M., Moses, J., & Evans, R. (2019, September 24). *Caring for sacred and culturally sensitive objects.* Government of Canada. https://www.canada.ca/en/conservation-institute/services/preventive-conservation/guidelines-collections/caring-sacred-culturally-sensitive-objects.html

Conn, S. (2010). *Do museums still need objects?* University of Pennsylvania Press. http://www.jstor.org/stable/j.ctt3fh6rd

Contreras, D. (2017, January). Buying and selling, owning the past. *Interaction, Stanford Report* (11).

Curtis, N. G. W. (2005). A continuous process of reinterpretation: The challenge of the universal and rational museum. *Public Archaeology, 4*(1), 50–56. https://doi.org/10.1179/pua.2005.4.1.50

Curtis, N. G. W. (2006). Universal museums, museum objects and repatriation: The tangled stories of things. *Museum Management and Curatorship, 21*(2), 117–127. https://doi.org/10.1080/09647770600402102

Curtis, N. G. W. (2008). Thinking about the right home- repatriation and the University of Aberdeen. In M. Gabriel & J. Dahl (Eds.), *Utimut: Past heritage – future partnerships – discussions on repatriation in the 21st century* (pp. 44–55). IWGIA/NKA.

Daley, P. (2014, June 13). The bone collectors: a brutal chapter in Australia's past. *The Guardian.* https://www.theguardian.com/world/2014/jun/14/aboriginal-bones-being-returned-australia.

Dartt-Newton, D. D. (2009). *Negotiating the master narrative: Museums and the Indian/Californio Community of California's Central Coast* [Unpublished doctoral dissertation]. University of Oregon.

Dawson, E. (2014). "Not Designed for Us": How Science Museums and Science centers socially exclude low-income, minority ethnic groups. *Science Education, 98*(6), 981–1008. https://doi.org/10.1002/sce.21133

Di Domenico, M. L. (2015). Evolving museum identities and paradoxical RESPONSE strategies to identity challenges and ambiguities. *Journal of Management Inquiry, 24*(3), 300–317. https://doi.org/10.1177/1056492615569885

Dubin, S. (1999). *Displays of power: Memory and amnesia in the American Museum.* New York University Press.

Dubin, S. (2014). *Displays of power: Memory and amnesia in the American Museum.* New York University Press.

Dudley, S. H. (2012). *Museum objects and Experiencing the properties of things.* Routledge.

Eakin, H. (2006, August 9). Museums establish guidelines for treatment of sacred objects. *The New York Times.* http://www.nytimes.com/2006/08/10/arts/design/10sacr.html?_r=0.

Elliott, T. (2010, March 12). Jealous keepers of the sacred bones. *The Sydney Morning Herald.* https://www.smh.com.au/national/jealous-keepers-of-the-sacred-bones-20100312-q48m.html.

Feinstein, N. W., & Meshoulam, D. (2014). Science for what public? Addressing equity in American science museums and science centers. *Journal of Research in Science Teaching, 51*(3), 368–394.

Flescher, S., Duffy-Zeballos, L., Goldman, V. S., & Boddewyn, J. M. (n.d.). *Provenance guide*. International Foundation for Art Research (IFAR). https://www.ifar.org/provenance.php.

Foot, K., & Groleau, C. (2011, June 6). Contradictions, transitions, and materiality in organizing processes: An activity theory perspective. *First Monday, 16*(6). https://firstmonday.org/ojs/index.php/fm/article/view/3479/2983.

Foot, K. A. (2014). Cultural-historical activity theory: Exploring a theory to inform practice and research. *Journal of Human Behavior in the Social Environment, 24*(3), 329–347. doi:10.1080/10911359.2013.831011

Fortey, R. A. (2008). *Dry storeroom no. 1: the secret life of the Natural History Museum*. Vintage Books.

Fota, A. (2019, December 20). What's wrong with this diorama? You can read all about it. *New York Times*. https://www.nytimes.com/2019/03/20/arts/design/natural-history-museum-diorama.html

Ganteaume, C. (2013, April 15). *Respecting non-western sacred objects: An A:shiwi Ahayu:da (Zuni war god), the Museum of the American Indian–Heye Foundation, and the Museum of Modern Art*. Smithsonian National Museum of the American Indian. https://blog.nmai.si.edu/main/2013/04/respecting-non-western-sacred-objects.html

Garibay, C. (2009). Latinos, leisure values, and decisions: Implications for informal science learning and engagement. *The Informal Learning Review, 94*, 10–13.

Glenn, J. (2018, July 27). *Religious objects in museums: An interview with Crispin Paine*. Glencairn Museum. https://glencairnmuseum.org/newsletter/2017/3/27/religious-objects-in-museums-an-interview-with-crispin-paine.

Gosden, C. & Marshall, Y. (1999). The cultural biography of objects, *World Archaeology, 31*(2), 169–178.

Government of Canada website (2019). *Caring for sacred and culturally sensitive objects*. https://www.canada.ca/en/conservation-institute/services/preventive-conservation/guidelines-collections/caring-sacred-culturally-sensitive-objects.html#a1

Grimes, R. L. (1992). Sacred objects in museum spaces. *Studies in Religion/Sciences Religieuses, 21*(4), 419–430. https://doi.org/10.1177/000842989202100404

Harrison, J. (1997). Museums as agencies of neocolonialism in a postmodern world. *Studies in Cultures Organizations and Societies, 3*(1), 41–65. doi:10.1080/10245289708523487

Harrison, P. (2007). "How Shall I Say it …?" Relating the nonrelational. *Environment and Planning A: Economy and Space, 39*(3), 590–608. https://doi.org/10.1068/a3825

Hawaiian Dictionaries. (n.d.). *'uhane*. http://wehewehe.org/gsdl2.85/cgi-bin/hdict?d=D19758&l=en&e=d-11000-00---off-0hdict--00-1----0-10-0---0---0direct-10-ED--4--text pukuielbert%2Ctextmamaka-----0-1l--11-haw-Zz-1---Zz-1-home-Uhane--00-3-1-00-0--4----0-0-11-00-0utfZz-8-00

Hooper-Greenhill, E. (Ed.) (2009). *Cultural diversity: Developing museum audiences in Britain*. Leicester University Press.

Howard, J. (2015). Mystery of ancient 'Kennewick Man' skeleton may soon be solved. *Huffington Post*. http://www.huffingtonpost.com/2015/01/22/kennewick-man-dna-test_n_6516562.html

Hutterer, K. (1980, June 8–12). *The sharing of anthropological collections: Cooperation with Third World Museums*. Annual meeting of the American Association of Museums and the Canadian Museums Association, Boston, USA. https://anthrosource.onlinelibrary.wiley.com/doi/pdf/10.1525/mua.1980.4.5.5

Jewish Virtual Library. (2014). *Holocaust restitution: Recovering stolen art*. https://www.jewishvirtuallibrary.org/recovering-stolen-art-from-the-holocaust.

Joyce, C. (2015). *DNA confirms Kennewick man's genetic ties to Natives Americans*. NPR. http://www.npr.org/sections/health-shots/2015/06/18/415205524/dna-confirmskennewick-Mans-genetic-ties-to-native-americansxlvii

Kalshed, D. C. (2020). *A depth-psychological approach to the current malaise in American social, culture and political life*. Retreat, Pacifica Graduate Institute.
Kapuni-Reynolds, H. M. K. (2015). *Curating Ali`i collections: Responsibility, sensibility, and contextualization in Hawai'i-Based Museums* [Doctoral dissertation, University of Denver]. Electronic Theses and Dissertations. https://digitalcommons.du.edu/cgi/viewcontent.cgi?article=2062&context=etd
Keaten, J. (2015, June 1). Paris auction of Hopi artifacts decried in US stir protest. *AP News*. https://apnews.com/article/63b272d72b8a491aa85ad72bf1187c00
Kendi, I. X. (2017). *Stamped from the beginning: the definitive history of racist ideas in America*. Bold Type Books.
Kidman, J. (2019). Whither decolonisation? Indigenous scholars and the problem of inclusion in the neoliberal university. *Journal of Sociology*, *56*(2), 247–262. https://doi.org/10.1177/1440783319835958
Klinkhammer, A. (2017, February 21). Kennewick man's bones reburied, settling a decades-long debate. *Discover Magazine*. https://www.discovermagazine.com/planet-earth/kennewick-mans-bones-reburied-settling-a-decades-long-debate
Kopell, J. (2006). *The politics of Quasi-government: Hybrid organisations and the dynamics of bureaucratic control*. Cambridge University Press.
Kreps, C. (2003). *Liberating cultures: Cross-cultural perspectives on museums, curation and heritage preservation*. Routledge.
Kurin, R. (2014, December 17). For every object, there is a story to tell. *Smithsonian Magazine*. https://www.smithsonianmag.com/smithsonian-institution/for-every-object-there-is-story-to-tell-180953589/#AzFr6CKHb5g51qBq.99
KWO, KaWai Ola (2013, October 1). The long journey home. *Issue*, *30*(10). https://issuu.com/kawaiola/docs/kwo01013_web/18
Landry, D. (2009). The Ottoman origins of English modernity, on the hoof. *Turkish Area Studies Review*, 39–46.
Lane, M. M. (2014, February 12). Germany to comb museums for Nazi-looted Art. *The Wall Street Journal*. http://www.wsj.com/articles/SB10001424052702304104504579377181476479324
Leonardo, Z. (2003). Discourse and critique: Outlines of a post-structural theory of ideology, *Journal of Education Policy*, *18*(2), 203–214, doi:10.1080/0268093022000043038
Lonetree, A. (2009). Museums as sites of decolonization: Truth telling in national and tribal museums. In S. Sleeper-Smith (Ed.), *Contesting knowledge: Museums and Indigenous perspectives* (pp. 322–337). University of Nebraska Press.
Lonetree, A. (2010). *Decolonizing museums: Representing Native America in national and tribal museums*. University of North Carolina Press.
Lynch, B. T., & Alberti, S. J. M. M. (2010). Legacies of prejudice: Racism, co-production and radical trust in the museum. *Museum Management and Curatorship*, *25*(1), 13–35. https://doi.org/10.1080/09647770903529061
MacDonald, S. (2006). *A companion to museum studies*. Blackwell
MacLachlan, N. (2012). *Sacred and secular: An analysis of repatriation of native American Sacred Items from European Museums*. [Unpublished doctoral dissertation]. University of Aberdeen. https://www.academia.edu/2624865/
Masidlover, N. (2015). Native American Artifacts sold at Paris auction despite opposition. *The Wall Street Journal*. http://www.wsj.com/articles/native-american-artifacts-sold-at-paris-auction-despite-opposition-1433189811
McMullen, A. (2008). The currency of consultation and collaboration. *Museum Anthropology Review*, *2*(2), 54–87. https://scholarworks.iu.edu/journals/index.php/mar/article/view/88

Meighan, C. W. (1999). Native Americans and Archaeologists: Debating NAGPRA's effects – burying American Archaeology. *Archaeology Magazine Archive*. https://archive.archaeology.org/online/features/native/debate.html.

Moore, P. (2014, January 20). *The danger of the "D" word: Museums and diversity*. The Incluseum. https://incluseum.com/2014/01/20/the-danger-of-the-d-word-museums-and-diversity/

Morrissey, J. (2015). 'Regimes of performance: Practices of the normalised self in the Neoliberal University'. *British Journal of Sociology of Education*, 36(4), 614–34.

Moses, J. (1993). First nations traditions of object preservation. In *First people's art and artifacts: Heritage conservation issues* (pp. 1–11). Conservation Program, Queen's University.

Mozingo, J. (2014, September 21). A sting in the desert. *Los Angeles Times*. https://graphics.latimes.com/utah-sting/.

NAGPRA compliance. Association on American Indian Affairs. (2021). https://www.indian-affairs.org/nagpra-compliance.html.

National Museum of Australia. (2005). *Continuous cultures, ongoing responsibilities: Principles and guidelines for Australian museums working with Aboriginal and Torres Strait Islander cultural heritage*. Museums Australia Inc. https://www.amaga.org.au/sites/default/files/uploaded-content/website-content/SubmissionsPolicies/continuous_cultures_ongoing_responsibilities_2005.pdf

O'Connor, A. M. (2013, December 19). The Nazi art theft crisis in Europe. *Time*. https://ideas.time.com/2013/12/19/the-nazi-art-theft-crisis-in-europe/.

O'Connor, J. (2010). Marxism and the three movements of neoliberalism. *Critical Sociology*, 36(5), 691–715. https://doi.org/10.1177/0896920510371389

Oxford English Dictionary. (n.d.). Home. Oxford English Dictionary. https://www.oed.com/.

Parker, P. (1990). *Keepers of the treasures: Protecting historic properties and cultural traditions on Indian lands: A report on tribal preservation funding needs submitted to congress by the National Park Service, United States Department of the Interior*. The Branch.

Phelan, M. (2019, November 27). "History is written by the victors" was not written by the victors. *Slate Magazine*. https://slate.com/culture/2019/11/history-is-written-by-the-victors-quote-origin.html.

Preston, D. (2014, September 1). The Kennewick man finally freed to share his secrets. *Smithsonian Magazine*. https://www.smithsonianmag.com/history/kennewick-man-finally-freed-share-his-secrets-180952462/.

Rasmussen, M., Sikora, M., Albrechtsen, A., Korneliussen, T. S., Moreno-Mayar, J. V., Poznik, G. D., ... Willerslev, E. (2015, June 18). The ancestry and affiliations of Kennewick man. *Nature News*. https://www.nature.com/articles/nature14625.

Reagan, S. (2015, June 26). In mainstream museums, confronting colonialism while curating Native American art. *Hyperallergic*. https://hyperallergic.com/217807/in-mainstream-museums-confronting-colonialism-while-curating-native-american-art/

Riley, G. (2011, February 1). When museums sell art: A better way. *Broad Street Review*. http://www.broadstreetreview.com/theater/when_museums_sell_art_a_better_way.

Rodrigues, P. S., & Smith, L. (Eds.). (2014). *Museums, discourse and power*. MIDAS. https://journals.openedition.org/midas/623.

Rosenbaum, C. (2017, March 9). Ancient one, also known as Kennewick man, repatriated. *Tribal Tribune*. http://www.tribaltribune.com/news/article_aa38c0c2-f66f-11e6-9b50-7bb1418f3d3d.html.

Schuessler, J. (2021, April). *What should museums do with the bones of the enslaved?* https://www.nytimes.com/2021/04/20/arts/design/museums-bones-smithsonian.htm

Sharp, K. (2015, November 1). An exclusive look at the greatest haul of Native American artifacts, ever. *Smithsonian Magazine*. https://www.smithsonianmag.com/history/exclusive-greatest-haul-native-american-artifacts-looted-180956959/.

Shoenberger, E. (2019, December 11). *What does it mean to decolonize a museum?* MuseumNext. https://www.museumnext.com/article/what-does-it-mean-to-decolonize-a-museum/.

Simon, N. (2010). Chapter 1: Principles of participation. In *The participatory museum*. Museum 2.0. http://www.participatorymuseum.org/chapter1/.

Strauss, M. (2016, April 7). When is it okay to dig up the dead? *National Geographic*. https://news.nationalgeographic.com/2016/04/160407-archaeology-religion-repatriation-bones-skeletons/.

Swan, D. C., & Jordan, M. P. (2015). Contingent collaborations: Patterns of reciprocity in museum-community partnerships. *Journal of Folklore Research*, *52*(1), 39–84.

Tchenkmedyian, A. (2017, February 21). After two decades, the Kennewick man is reburied. *Los Angeles Times*. https://www.latimes.com/nation/la-na-kennewick-man-reburial-20170220-story.html.

Thornton, R. (1996). *Tribal membership requirements and the demography of "Old" and "New" Native Americans, changing numbers, changing needs: American Indian demography and public health*. National Academies of 'Science, 'Engineering and Medicine, National Academies Press.

Walker, R. (2013). *On objects, and storytelling*. Future of Museums. http://futureofmuseums.blogspot.com/2013/04/on-objects-and-storytelling.html

Whyte, J. (2017). Human rights and the collateral damage of neoliberalism. *Theory & Event*, *20*(1), 137–151. https://www.muse.jhu.edu/article/646849

Wilcox, M. (2009). *Buying, selling, owning the past*. InterAction. https://news.stanford.edu/news/multi/features/heritage/images/paper_heritage.pdf

Wood, M. (2017). Cultural appropriation and the plains' Indian headdress. *The Journal of Undergraduate Research and Creative Scholarship*. Virginia Commonwealth University.

Ziimmer, C. (2015, June 18). New DNA results show Kennewick man was Native American. *The New York Times*. http://www.nytimes.com

7
WHERE IS THE LEARNING, AND WHO GETS TO LEARN?

Overview

In this chapter, I explore how learning theory and learners have been viewed in museums. Museums more generally have emphasized individuals interacting with phenomena at exhibits; a sociocultural view of learning suggests this is an incomplete analysis. I discuss two main contradictions. First, I deliberately return to the robust debate of the late 1990s that informs our current theoretical understanding; that debate concerns where 'learning is located', posing the question of primacy between social vs. individual views. That era, sometimes described as ushering in 'the social turn', has significantly shifted the focus in learning theory and practice. I briefly review the key points of that crucial debate because it informs current policy and practices and because history matters in CHAT.

I then revisit past debates, specifically comparing deficit and resource-based ideologies concerning how visitors are situated as learners. Both of these dialectically-based debates are critical to how we position learning in museums and elsewhere in the 21st century and beyond. As with other chapters that precede and follow, the individual vs. social learning comparison may not be an entirely accurate representation of the current nature of the field, yet, it serves well as a proxy in my discussion of ideology. Similarly, as we have been discussing throughout this book, we use the dialectic of resources vs. deficit views to frame policy, practice and ideological debates. We know we cannot do justice to this topic of inequitable distribution of power around the globe. We can, however, mark the critical contradictions underlying this state of affairs.

VIGNETTE

"What do we do here?" "Sylvester", an African American father in his mid-30s asked his wife "Ana", also mid-30s, as they approached the DINO-Saurus exhibit with their two sons, "Jaylen" (8) and "Jamal" (6).

The DINO-Saurus exhibit included a structurally large (3ft x 5ft) dinosaur head with an open mouth and detachable plastic teeth, surrounded by two tables displaying samples of meat-eating and plant-eating animals' teeth.

ANA: "Um, I don't know, let's read. Probably just put the teeth in".
JAYLEN: "This is going to be easy! All you have to do is just put them in".

Jaylen proceeded to place the teeth in the dinosaur's mouth while his younger brother Jamal followed him to a table, picked up a tooth and walked toward the dinosaur head.

JAMAL: "This probably goes here".

The two boys figured out the exhibit together and were at times puzzled as to why the teeth did not fit properly. At the same time, the mother went to the nearby display tables to read for clues or instructions. She came upon a display of different animal's teeth and attempted to draw the others' attention, while the father proceeded to impersonate a dinosaur by holding up two pointed teeth to his mouth and talking in a "dinosaur tone". All laughed at his impersonation and then went back to doing their own activities.

As Ana and her sons continued to work on tooth placement, Sylvester climbed into the dinosaur's mouth from behind and playfully impersonated the dinosaur.

SYLVESTER: "Hello.... My name is Brutus, the happy dinosaur.... As you can see, I'm just a little old, my teeth are falling out. Would you please help me?"
Ana: "They're all rotten".
Sylvester: "It's been quite a while since I went to the dentist. This is what you look like when you skip brushing!"
Ana: (laughs) "All your teeth fall out all over, all over the floor. You got it in [Jaylen]?"
Jaylen: "Yeah, you look like an old man who has no teeth!"

This family conversation evolved into a discussion of the consequences of improper oral hygiene—that is, your teeth will fall out. Rather than investigating the relationship between a dinosaur's tooth size and shape and its diet (as was the goal of the exhibit designers), the family used dental hygiene as their motif for engaging with the exhibit.

(Adapted from Mai & Ash, 2012)

Introduction

In this chapter, I discuss the two historically important questions concerning learning. The first is: "*Should learning be positioned as an individual act or as a social activity?*" The second question asks: "*How are deficit orientations and learning theory intertwined?*" Both questions require researchers and practitioners to be critically reflective of ideologies and historicity. These fundamental questions have been part of educational systems, including museums since their inception.

I have delved into deficit ideologies in all the preceding chapters; here I explicitly intertwine deficit ideologies with learning theory. In museums, the notion of deficit might translate to *not expecting* a family from a nondominant group or 'new to museums' to know 'how to do' hands-on learning. Upon reflection, knowing how 'to do museums', of course, is a *learned* social and cultural skill (Mai & Ash, 2012).

Throughout this chapter, I emphasize that almost all activities in museums are connected to how we situate learners and understand learning. This includes teaching, greeting, assessing, advertising, listening and lecturing. Whatever is defined as learning or learner in any educational space informs related activities, such as educator professional development, exhibit design and signage and, less directly, mission statements, public relations, community outreach and board agendas.

The Braydon family, an African American group of four who were not regular museumgoers, made up their own curriculum in the context of the dinosaur exhibit. There were numerous social interactions occurring between the members of the family, eventuating in something that no one member of the group could have done alone. The family appeared to "learn" together, especially in the ways they interacted with the exhibit objects, such as the teeth and dinosaur head.

The father played with the idea of dental hygiene, making it a focal point for fun dialogue. Together, family members made up their own agenda, choosing to follow the father's lead. The underlying 'curriculum' of the exhibit related tooth shape to food-eating categories, such as carnivore or herbivore. The Braydons demonstrated not only how much fun it is to play at exhibits; they let us 'watch' *in situ* learning as it occurs. More subtly, they also displayed a competent and quiet resistance to the museum agenda. The many museum practitioners who have watched this collective activity agree that it constitutes 'social learning in action' and 'hands-on learning', with family members using their own resources, language and background knowledge to create it (Ash, 2014a).

Tishman (2005) argued that no matter which version of learning theory one holds, and no matter how one views learners' abilities, museums are excellent places to view *learning theory in action*. What do we mean when we say *learning theory in action*? McDermott (2015) complained that "the word 'learning' has fallen in with a bad crowd…[because] 'learning' is a contested term that must always report to considerations of how and when it is used and with what intentions and consequences" (p. 335). Dawson (2014b) noted that European American epistemologies get in the way of our interpretations of what is happening in museum settings; she feared we are blinded to the things we are not in the habit of noticing. I argue further that we expect to see so-called typical, i.e., 'white', behavior, rather than what is actually happening. Exactly because of this issue, we analyze the Braydon episode more fully so that we do not discount different interpretations of learning.

Museums have been working to pursue a better understanding of learning theories in order to promote *best* teaching practices for minoritized visitors like the Braydons. But which learning theories do museums rely on? Will these theories satisfy our critiques of *norms* and *othering*? Can these theories serve all the visitors we hope to have in our museums of the future?

From the vantage point of the 21st century, we have witnessed a dizzying array of learning theories. I cannot review the entirety of the history of learning theory here, but I will trace how learning theory has generally morphed over the past 40-plus years, first with regard to the individual vs. the social tension and second by analyzing how the deficit vs. resource contradiction is now shifting.

Numerous scholars addressed individual and social/participatory aspects of learning in the late 1980s and the 1990s. It was a fertile time. Brown and Palincsar published work on reciprocal teaching, collaborative learning and knowledge acquisition in 1986. Jean Lave and Etienne Wenger wrote their seminal text *Situated Learning. Legitimate Peripheral Participation* in 1991. Yrjö Engeström and Reijo Miettinen wrote *Perspectives on Activity Theory (Learning in Doing: Social, Cognitive and Computational Aspects)* in 1999. Wenger wrote *Communities of Practice. Learning, Meaning and Identity* in 1998. Chaiklin and Lave edited the volume *Understanding Practice: Perspectives on Activity and Context*, in 1993, and the seminal *How People Learn*, edited by Bransford et al., appeared in 1999. All of these texts addressed the individual vs. social tension (Cole, 1988; Engeström, 1987; Vygotsky, 1978).

For Vygotsky (1978), all learning was social, but more importantly, his view relied on the primacy of cultural mediation. Vygotsky argued that individual thought processes originate in social interaction (Brown & Palincsar, 1986, p. 8). By returning to Vygotsky, we can use his original work to reconsider internal and external processes. As John-Steiner and Mahn (1996) argued, "The power of Vygotsky's ideas lies in his explanation of the *dynamic interdependence* of social and individual processes" (p. 192).[1]

An Intertwining of Equity and Learning Theories

I am concerned with learning and with equity. My question "*How are deficit orientations and learning theory intertwined?*" allows me to treat learning theory and deficit/othering in tandem by considering them to be reciprocally intertwined. Therefore, I not only explore how learning theory is used in museums but also consider how deficit orientations, *othering* expectations and ideological stances inform how both learning and learners are viewed, interpreted and misunderstood.

While we now take for granted the social perspective that looks carefully at what is actually happening, this was not so when such family-centered research first began in the mid-1980s (see Appendix 7.2). The relevance of social vs. individual aspects of learning was loosely queried by such early family-oriented researchers in the late 1980s as Minda Borun, Judy Diamond, Lynn Dierking and Paulette McManus. Such research was in its infancy then but contained the glimmerings of a socially situated perspective for research in informal settings.

Frank Oppenheimer, the founder of the Exploratorium science center, famously said, "Nobody ever flunked a science museum" (Exploratorium, 2013). Dawson (2014b) disagreed: "[T]here are grounds to seriously question the claim made by Oppenheimer, because minoritized visitors can be seen to fail if they do not 'do the museum' in expected, normative, orthodox, assimilated ways" (p. 982).

Over the decades, this early research has appropriated a more robust theoretical framework. Combining social/participatory learning theories with concerns of equity has been important to the field. It is only more recently, however, that researchers have begun to rely on CHAT (deGregoria Kelly, 2009; Rahm, 2012; Ward, 2016; Yamagata-Lynch, 2010). I use it here, along with deficit/othering and focusing on contradictions, to examine the dialectical, historically situated, culturally bound, nonbinary learning contexts and then to more accurately understand the tensions surrounding equity and social justice in museums.

Building on the work of Vygotsky, Leont'ev and others, I use CHAT in educational settings because it looks at systems rather than at individuals or small groups. It builds on sociocultural theory by answering a different set of questions. CHAT tells us that *historicity* and *the dialectic* matter. These are factors that have been left out in some sociocultural analyses of activity in educational settings (Engeström & Sannino, 2010). By definition, CHAT learning activity systems include tools, practices and habits of mind that are developed through the social *process*; they are "continually evolving [and] brought about through the dialectical contradictions between the different levels and elements of the system" (Timmis, 2014, p. 13).[2] I rely here on both the history of learning and a perspective centered on equity and the dialectical contradictions that inform and are informed by the interaction between learning and equity historically.

Changing and evolving learning theories and their resultant teaching practices show us an ever-shifting landscape. Gutiérrez and Rogoff (2003) identified "linguistic and cultural-historical repertoires…[by which] we mean the ways of engaging in activities stemming from observing and otherwise participating in cultural practices" (p. 22). A decade later, Vossoughi and Gutiérrez (2014) had broadened the scope, suggesting that we "unsettle normative definitions of learning, to move beyond reductive dichotomies and…focus on the multiple activity systems in which people develop repertoires of practice" (p. 605). This concept of *repertoires of practice* helps us reconsider what we count as 'learning' and to connect it to an analysis of the tensions arising between the established institutions with many preset norms and stories, and the visitors new to such institutions, who also have stories to tell. Those most accustomed to visiting museums know that there is an expected way to 'do them'; we know the rules of the road, what to do and what not to do. Those without these experiences spend a good deal of time trying to 'figure out' what they are expected to do (Mai & Ash, 2012).

It is a further step to recognize that families who differ from the *norm* by race, ethnicity, culture, language, physical ability, gender, age or in other ways may create their own *repertoires of discourses and practices*, sometimes using humor. These repertoires may vary from those considered the *norm* for museum educators and curators (Ash, 2014a; Dawson, 2014b). Watching the Braydons, we discover that following the specific and contextualized experiences of nontraditional, minoritized families making sense of an exhibit with words (jokes), gestures (welcoming) and their own ideas (dental hygiene) stretches our perspective of what constitutes the learning process.

Repertoires of Practice

Those unfamiliar with museums may not know whether it is permitted to touch materials, talk loudly or question authority. The Braydon family found no explicit guidance as to what particular actions or nonactions, such as *don't touch*, were expected of them. This relates to the signage, typically only in one language. A whole process is involved in becoming acclimated to a strange new place that has its own special rules and ways of behaving.

The Braydons acted as a cohesive social group with shifting leadership. By paying attention to, and not discounting, the affective realm of talk, fun and jokes, we are able to discern these visitors' resources. We have only to recognize them as such. Simply because the intent of the exhibit designer and curator was difficult to recognize in their exchanges does not mean they did not learn. They learned something different.

Looking for *activities* different from the expected recognizes that families from nondominant backgrounds intentionally and legitimately overlay their cultural resources, content themes and social patterns onto unfamiliar exhibits (Ash, 2019). This is what Vossoughi and Gutiérrez (2014) meant by *repertoires of practice*. Vossoughi and Gutiérrez (2014) refer to "cultural repertoires that are necessarily co-constituted and leveraged across places, spaces, and time scales" (p. 605) in home, school or museum. They note that "to draw on the full range of linguistic, intellectual, and cultural tools within one's repertoires of practice may involve varying degrees of risk and vulnerability" (p. 611). Citing risk and vulnerability includes the psychological perspective in the analysis of learning, which is important because *othering* and the deficit view create real potential for shame and blame of visitors in the social setting of a museum. In this case, the Braydons *took a risk* in exposing their *repertoire of practice* in the absence of other meta information, such as signs or educators telling them how to engage with this particular exhibit.

Families develop *repertoires of practice* in the course of their communal lives, and these practices are aspects of the unrecognized *resources* families bring with them to new museum experiences. As we observe the Braydons' behavior at the exhibit, we could analyze it as developing an alternative dialogue, resisting the dominant narrative of canine/herbivore/omnivore in favor of family fun. Some have argued that the family was just playing around and not learning important content because they did not talk about the intended curriculum of tooth structure and function. They weren't 'doing the exhibit right'! I have heard such criticisms of family interactions at museums when showing similar video episodes at conferences and professional development workshops. Social learning practitioners and researchers, when viewing the same segment, have commented on the unique resources the Braydon family brought by discussing the importance of dental hygiene, thus making the exhibit their own. So, which version is true?

The answer depends on your view of learning and on what learners bring to the learning setting. The viewer's stance on individual vs. social learning and on deficit vs. resource views of learners matters deeply. Some argue that resources are difficult things to uncover and so we should stick to the standard curriculum. When I have done that, I have found that I miss a lot. Also, getting to the root of what constitutes typical or normal or orthodox is complex, and this normative perspective's relationship to learning theory and its outcomes is also socially, culturally, politically and historically bound.

It is often claimed that hands-on learning helps to level the playing field for *all* learners when adequate scaffolding is available (R. Gutiérrez, 2002, 2007). Yet, research suggests that this is problematic when families are faced with the dilemma of how 'to do' exhibits without guidance. Further, ideology matters and plays a role in how any event, dialogue or action will be interpreted. If we look for 'wrong', we can generally find it; the same is true if we look for 'normed' behaviors.[3] In fact, we may overattribute background knowledge and learning success when learners appear to know their way around exhibits by using scientific jargon, for example.

How can researchers gain flexibility in recognizing what visitors and educators do and don't recognize? The oldest strategy, as ethnographers know, is to watch everything closely. Many important conversations, for example, occur in the 'off times', for example, while going for a snack. Newly developed and older repurposed socially oriented research methods, which aim at accurate capture of what is actually occurring at such exhibits, have upgraded our ability to 'see'. Most notably, video offers a rich account of interaction and provides nuance and flexibility. Typically, I have used sophisticated audio and video technology to capture interviews and reflections, as well as actions and talk at exhibits. Later, I spend significant time dedicated to analyzing the themes and the discourse moves, such as questioning, turn taking, leadership and more (Anderson & Ellenbogen, 2012; Ash, 2004, 2014a; Ward, 2016). Video is not essential for museum professionals on the floor. I have worked now with many educators who have trained themselves to be accurate ethnographic notetakers.

Moving beyond data collection, the analytic methodological practices, such as coding, units of analysis, transcription for *interpreting* learning, are as diverse as the theories that undergird them. Similarly, the ideological stances of the particular researchers or analysts matter. Do the analysts recognize both dialectics of individual vs. social and deficit vs. resource? To paraphrase Jean Lave, we always wear glasses when we do research, these glasses are colored; we should know what color

(J. Lave, personal communication, 1990). In short, we carry our biases with us when doing research. Especially as white researchers of nondominant populations, it is vital to know and be critical of our own ideological stances. Such critical reflection is essential if we wish to deal honestly with contradictions, historicity and resistance and their consequences in museums. We can counter such biases, to some extent, by constant reflection on our own choices and by regular outside checks and balances from knowledgeable advisers. Toward that end, some museums are conducing critical reflection on 'whiteness', for example, the Delaware Art Museums, Minnesota Museum of Science, the Smithsonian National *Museum* of African American History and Culture and the Oakland Museum of California in the United States, and the Art Gallery of Ontario in Canada, among others.[4]

The 'Individual/Social Turn' Treated Historically

Salomon and Perkins (1998) claimed more than 30 years ago that "social learning is in the air" (p. 1). In the 1980s and 1990s, the debate concerning individual vs. social fully dominated questions about learning theory and the practices that eventuated. Many theorists were challenged to integrate their previous cognitive/constructivist views with social-centric/practice/participatory models. Salomon and Perkins suggested that until the 1990s, social learning was largely considered background information because of its 'gestalt-like nature', and it was "ignored by psychologists over the years, relegated at best to the study of background context, not really on a par with the learning of the individual" (Gardner, 1985 in Salomon & Perkins, 1998, p. 1). Salomon and Perkins asked,

> If we can raise the question of whether social learning is a valid and viable phenomenon, the opposite question might equally well be raised: Is it not possible that solo learning is simply a figment of the traditional laboratory-based psychology, on the one hand, and of a socially shared respect for the individual qua individual, on the other?
>
> (p. 1)

So, which is the background, and which is the foreground? Similarly, in 1998, Sfard asked, "Is the learner to be understood primarily as an individual or as a community?" This is a strong articulation of the social vs. individual tension. This question was debated extensively in the late 1980s and early 1990s. Sfard's positioning of the debate asked us to compare and contrast what we know about individual-oriented cognitive/constructivist and socially based theories. As Sfard noted, each view of learning has its own metaphor:

> — the individual learner [view],
>   ...emphasiz[es] the acquisition of knowledge and cognitive skill as transferable commodities.
>
> (e.g., Anderson et al., 1996, p. 323)

On the other hand, we have the sociocultural conception of learning as a collective participatory process of active knowledge construction emphasizing context, interaction, and situatedness.

(e.g., Cole & Engeström, 1993, p. 491)[5]

Sfard argued that when using the acquisition interpretation, we 'see' learning as a commodity that can be hoarded, where people who have knowledge might be seen and valued as "superior to others". This positions the human mind as a container to be filled with certain valuable materials and the learner as the owner of these valuable commodities.[6]

Scholars have cited Sfard as an inspiration and a starting point for their own research, as her multimetaphor approach is a powerful model for viewing learning in any context. We note, for example, that the acquisitional aspect of individual learning potentiates the creation of inequities in learning contexts reflected in the attitudes: more is better, mastery means learning and commodities can be hoarded. These inequities are consistent with various interpretations of a deficit stance. Of course, any mention of the word *commodity* evokes neoliberal ideology. All these connections have been and are currently being made (McDermott, 2015).

Ray McDermott asked similar questions in the 1980s and 1990s, railing against learning interpreted as "isolated cognitive skills, stockpiled knowledge" [and] achievement by zero-sum competition, and citing neoliberal governance as one of the causes for this skewed interpretation. McDermott (2015) argued, "[A]ll these aspects are correlated with race and class differentials" (p. 335). Both Sfard and McDermott argued that if our goal is to create equity, we would do well to choose collective and participatory learning theories as our foundation.

Paul Cobb, in a seminal article called "Where Is the Mind?: Constructivist and Sociocultural Perspectives on Mathematical Development" (Cobb, 1994), argued that these two views are actually complementary, saying,

> These constructivist and sociocultural perspectives at times appear to be in direct conflict, with adherents to each claiming hegemony for their view of what it means to know and learn.... I contend that the two perspectives are complementary.
>
> (p. 13)

On the other hand, Hodkinson et al. (2008) argued, "[T]he debate...[is] between two paradigmatically different and largely incompatible ways of understanding learning (p. 30). Which is it?

To complicate the question further, it can be almost meaningless to ask if learning is individual or social, depending on how we define individual learning and socially situated learning. For all these reasons, it is important to be clear on the *roots* of learning theory. Table 7.1 summarizes the three main traditions suggested by Case (1996), a taxonomy similar to one also proposed by Greeno et al. (1996).

TABLE 7.1 A taxonomy of learning

Roots	Empiricist	Rationalist	Sociohistoric
Theorists	Watson, Thorndike, Hull, Skinner	Descartes, Kant, Piaget, Baldwin, Kuhn	Hegel, Marx, Vygotsky
Based upon	Structure of the objective world, sensory experiences	Structure of the subject and spontaneous cognition [Piaget: how one interacts with the objective world]	Social and material history of culture
Origin/development of thoughts on knowledge acquisition	Didactic, behavioral, with standardized tests within a sequential logical curriculum. Knowledge structures are logical and/or system-wide (not domain specific)	Knowledge is acquired from the organization of sensory data. Learning takes place from inside out *and* outside in. Intellectual development of preexisting domain-specific structures (mental structures/order-imposing devices) Knowledge has a unique internal structure modified endogenously	Dependent on social, cultural and physical contexts. Language is the important factor. Community of practice—apprenticeship, exposure to and interaction with experts (teachers)
Children learn by	Direct instruction and practice	Engage natural curiosity, exploratory, model-building. Reflection, 'guided discovery'. Content focused exploratory instruction [not direct instruction]	Social interactions, ZPD. Notational systems Scaffolding
Additional terms	Behaviorist	Constructivist, Cognitive	Cultural, Situated, Activity Theory

(Adapted from Case, 1996; input from Greeno et al., 1996)

I have relied on this standard taxonomy in my own research and share it here to ground our continuing discussion.

The importance of this taxonomy is that it locates the prevailing theories in three discrete categories: empiricist, rationalist and sociohistorical. Note that constructivism is in the rationalist column, while sociocultural theories, such as a community of learners, are included in the sociohistoric column.

Looking at the three roots, empiricist, rationalist and sociohistoric, we see that both empiricist and rationalist learning have tended to be interpreted as individual endeavors.[7] While activity theory is not mentioned in Case's taxonomy, it is represented in the sociohistorical category in Greeno et al. (1996).

Note also that Piaget is listed as a rationalist and Vygotsky sociohistoric. These seemingly separate fundamental categorizations might make us think Piaget and Vygotsky were diametrically opposed in terms of social vs. individual. Cole and Wertsch (1996) argue that both Piaget and Vygotsky addressed the ongoing *contradiction* of the individual vs. the social. Further, they claim that while this was important, *this was not* the main theoretical point that substantially separated Piaget and Vygotsky. I will return to this point later in our discussion.

Over the decades, the social turn has been subject to different theoretical interpretations, including Vygotsky's mediated action in the ZPD (Vygotsky, 1987), Dewey's experience-based learning (Dewey, 1916), Lave and Wenger communities of practice (Lave & Wenger, 1991) and Engeström (1987) and Wetsch's view of activity theory (Engeström, 1987; Wertsch, 1991).[8] Not all social learning theories are new; some have been around for quite some time. John Dewey, for example, wrote in 1926 in *Democracy and Education*:

> A being whose activities are associated with others has a social environment.... A being connected with other beings cannot perform his own activities without taking the activities of others into account.
>
> (p. 14)

As Dewey acknowledged over 100 years ago *the social environment and taking the activities of others into account* are part of normal learning research and practice.

Schools and museums have for the most part eschewed behaviorist views of learning in favor of constructivist, cognitivist and sociocultural orientations (Bransford et al., 1999; Hein, 2014). Since the late 1960s, many museums, such as the Exploratorium and other science centers, have come to rely on constructivism and experiential 'learning by doing', often framed as inquiry.

Museums have more recently embraced the social, participatory museum model (Simon, 2010), shifting toward valuing social participation, sometimes framing it as social constructivism, because such theories provide the grounding for analyses of collective activity in museums and classrooms (Brown, 1992; Resnick, 1992).

Over the past several decades, researchers have been designing and testing new methodologies for tracing collaborative groups, such as families and school groups, at exhibits emphasizing social participation (Callanan, 2012; Ash, 2014a; Ellenbogen et al., 2004; Palmquist & Crowley, 2007; Rahm, 2012; Rowe & Bachman, 2012). Beyond social learning theory per se, a growing area of research in the U.S.A. and abroad (Ash, 2004, 2014a; Dawson, 2014a; Garibay, 2009; Gurian, 2009, 2019; Golding, 2013) has featured collaborating with visitors from nondominant, minoritized or culturally and linguistically diverse populations to expand our understandings of *the intersection of equity and learning*. This latter research informs the arguments in this chapter.

Learning Theories in Mission Statements of Museums

We can find learning theories more publicly reflected in the mission statements of museums. Common echoes of constructivist learning theory are recognizable in such phrases as *hands-on learning experiences, learning by doing* or *interacting with exhibits*. For example, a statement from the 'about us' section of the Exploratorium website (2021) states,

> Our mission is to create inquiry-based experiences that transform learning worldwide. Our vision is a world where people think for themselves and can confidently ask questions, question answers, and understand the world around them.

The Exploratorium was founded on constructivist principles in the late 1960s (Hein, 1995, 2014). By constructivist I mean here the more Piagetian notion that Hein (1991) explained as

> learners need to be active…in hands-on involvement in participatory exhibits and programs. But the more important point, I believe, is the idea that the actions which we develop for our audience engage the mind as well as the hand.
> (Exploratorium, 2021)[9]

As I have already argued, assumptions about what constitutes learning inform exhibit design, educator professional development (i.e., how to teach the public), written guidelines (treasure hunts, teacher's guides, etc.), fundraising, mission statements and board agendas. Learning theory is designed to trickle up and down from exhibit design to the evaluation studies that follow from exhibit design. If 'learning by doing' is the prime directive, then exhibit design and evaluation, and what we recognize as learning, necessarily follow.

The Exploratorium explicitly notes how these aspects interact:

> We create tools and experiences that help you to become an *active explorer*: hundreds of *explore-for-yourself exhibits*…We also create *professional development programs* for educators and are at the forefront of changing the way science is taught.
> (Exploratorium, 2021, italics added)

It is clear here that a constructivist view of learning permeates exhibit design and professional development, and is intended, as they say, to "change the way science is taught". I take up this last theme in Chapter 8, where I consider professional development and how visitors are 'taught'.

How we view learning also impacts how we 'see' learners. One assumption appears to be that *all* learners will benefit from the hands-on approach. This may or may not be true; more research is needed.[10] If we believe hands-on activities are the most important aspect of learning, we might discount the usefulness of a docent lecturing at an exhibit. Conversely, if we believe that receiving direct information from an expert teacher is more important, we may disapprove of visitors loosely 'messing about'. These contradictory views can even exist simultaneously when learning theory is not adequately articulated.

What might this mean to us when interpreting the hands-on activities in the Braydon example? We could say that they didn't seem to learn about 'teeth structure and function', the leading content of the exhibit. That would be a deficit view. In point of fact, the Braydon mother actually did read and relay information about tooth structure and function from a separate table near the dinosaur head later on. In addition, the father may well have been motivated to use jokes and banter to make this a fun occasion to lighten the pressure of being videotaped. There was a lot more going on than 'hands-on' activity.

Reducing this activity to hands-on then limits everything we do and see as practitioners, researchers, evaluators, educators, designers and administrators. Our judgments determine what we look at, how we measure it, how we communicate these findings to others, and what we believe is happening.

Assimilation and Resistance

Minoritized families such as the Braydons bring a rich world of social, linguistic, cultural and other knowledge as resources with them when they visit a museum. Museums, though, still may not know of, value, look for or understand these resources (Ash, 2014a; Carpenter, 2019; Dawson, 2014a). "Our epistemologies get in the way...of what might actually be happening in museums" (Dawson, 2014b, p. 201). This is true everywhere in art, science and natural history museums (Grant & Price, 2020). We don't look for what we don't know and thus can't see. When we begin to acknowledge the resources families bring to the setting, we can begin to understand how such resources evolve, mingle and hybridize with formal science content (Ash, 2014a; Gutiérrez et al., 1999; Moje et al., 2004). Notice I brought in the concept of hybridity. Hybrid spaces are

> safe, comfortable environments that allow learners to draw on their everyday knowledge and merge it with more formal or academic knowledge. [These] are often called hybrid spaces. The concept of "hybridity" captures the "messiness" often involved when merging different ways of "doing".
>
> (Gutiérrez et al., 1999; Moje et al., 2004, in Ash, 2014a, p. 536)

As we study what actually occurs in museums, we expand our technical vocabulary to encompass what we find, what CHAT theorists would say what 'we don't yet know'. In the process of the unfolding interactions, we often find hybridization of museum expectations and families' realities.

Researchers and practitioners are surrounded by the sequelae of deficit thinking, the supremacy of evaluation, concepts of superiority and inferiority, melting pot/color blindness and other forms of denial of the diversity of humanity; "stereotypes of intellectually, morally, and culturally deficient or deviant" (Gorski, 2010, pp. 4–5). To understand how such biases affect our attitudes and findings, I turn to underlying ideologies, the master narratives of what constitutes learning and the artifacts or methodologies learners are currently expected to use.

But What Is the Contradiction?

With the primary contractions expressed always as use value vs. exchange, one secondary contradiction positions minoritized visitors as passive, untutored learners, needing to be filled up, as Sfard noted, or commoditized as McDermott argued or shamed and blamed "by pointing to the supposed deficiencies within disenfranchised individuals and communities" (Gorski, 2010, p. 3). This latter attitude blames visitors for 'not being able to or not wanting to' take advantage of what museums have to offer, not knowing how to use exhibits correctly, not asking the right questions, not speaking English correctly or just not 'fitting in'. Here we are back with the giraffe and the elephant from Chapter 3, 'shrinking' in order to 'fit in', becoming more like the 'norm', in museums, schools, work, stores and other social settings, losing the capacity to be ourselves.

Minoritized populations have rarely been a major part of most museum research data sets in the past. My research group and I have collaborated for over two decades with minoritized families in museums and aquariums, looking past the overarching master narrative of 'fitting in, or shrinking to fit in', and have come to analyze the activities we observe from a strong resource perspective (Dawson, 2014b). At first, it can be challenging to see the *adjustments* museums require of *others* because we are habituated museumgoers. My research team and I observed educators expecting *assimilation* time and time again (Ash & Lombana, 2012). When we do become aware of the pressures requiring others to change to fit in, we can look for and find those changes and the personal costs and consequences they exact from people (Ash, 2014b; Dawson, 2014a, 2014b; Garibay, 2009; Hooper-Greenhill, 2009).

In contrast to this stance of seeing visitors as passive and meant to assimilate to a new, possibly unfamiliar, way of being and doing, the Braydons maintained control of the agenda. They risked changing the focus of their activity to their own humorous play with the theme of dental hygiene. This is an instantiation of culturally congruent *repertoires of practice* involving humor (Ash, 2014a; Ash et al., 2005). Using humor lightened the mood, but more subtly allowed the Braydons to remain in control. Such subtle resistance allowed them to comfortably enter the repertoire of practice called "hands-on activity" of 'doing museums' and establish a degree of agency. Such *repertoires of practice* as humor and alternative everyday curriculum directly resist (R. Gutiérrez, 2007) unfounded expectations that minoritized populations should already know how to navigate exhibits in the ways educators expect.

Recent research findings indicate that museum educators should expect minoritized families to work with their own culturally congruent repertoires of practice that are not necessarily consistent with the past 'norm'. This turnabout caused a good bit of tension in at least one larger museum activity system (see Chapter 8, Ash & Lombana, 2015).[11] As socially/culturally congruent *repertoires of practice* factors are recognized and become more familiar, our museum educators can become better ambassadors for museums. Imagine, for example, what might have happened if a museum educator had corrected the Braydon family, telling them they were talking about the 'wrong thing'. The experience of being told *you are 'wrong'; do it this way* is inherently shaming. Would you return to a museum where people treated you this way?[12]

As I and my team learned to 'look and see' what was actually occurring during minoritized family visits, we noticed that 'learning to do' as an activity necessarily preceded any 'learning' of disciplinary material the exhibit offered (Mai & Ash, 2012; Ash, 2014a, 2014b). Just as with any other family, when those new to museums become familiar with the environment, they ask many questions, try out ideas and frequently express their eagerness to learn more (Ash et al., 2005; Ash, 2014a). It is an embarrassment that we have missed this in the past.

Placing museum *belonging* into a CHAT framework allows us to position 'knowing norms and not knowing norms' as a tension or secondary contradiction, within which museum educators typically favor those who already know the norms. Once my team and I recognized the 'figuring out' behaviors (Mai & Ash, 2012), we were able to reposition them as 'finessing the norm'. We researchers just needed to learn to 'see' these transformations. Out of this can emerge effective ways to signal to visitors that they are welcome (Garibay, 2009) to not know, to ask for help or to figure it out for themselves. The tertiary contradictions in this case involved training educators and researchers to use their ethnographic skills and to scaffold activity more carefully.

Over decades of such research, my team and I observed collaborating minoritized families repeatedly 'finessing the norm', often creating their own social context for their visits (Mai & Ash, 2012), creating new content themes and intertwining them in sophisticated ways (Ash et al., 2008). For example, one father used jokes at every exhibit, seeming both to keep his family involved and to frame the content (e.g., "Does that fish eat carne asada?"; Ash, 2014a; Ash et al., 2005). He spoke little English, while one of his three children was fully bilingual. We did not fully grasp this pattern of joking about content with questions until we carefully analyzed the hours-long transcripts. Once we considered his joking to be a resource, leaving behind deficit thinking, we could notice the social bonding benefits of his strategy. Using examples like these, museum educators, administrators and curriculum developers can work toward a more meaningful hybrid agenda at exhibits (Mai & Ash, 2012). Actively seeking out hybrid interactions and the unknown allows visitors to take up museum content that aligns with existing resources so that they can 'belong' and 'do the exhibit right'. Isn't that the essence of museum visits for all of us?

Putting Theory into Practice: The Role of Mediational Means

Two key voices in the debate between the social and individual points of view have been Jim Wertsch and Mike Cole. In 1996, they together laid out their thinking in an important paper called "Beyond the Individual-Social Antinomy", specifically comparing Piaget and Vygotsky. By antinomy they meant a "contradiction between two beliefs or conclusions that are in themselves reasonable; a paradox". In that paper, they started by suggesting,

> According to the canonical story, for Piaget, individual children construct knowledge through their actions on the world: *to understand is to invent*. By contrast, the Vygotskian claim is said to be that understanding is social in origin.
>
> (p. 253)

There are some difficulties with this account.

> First Piaget did not deny the co-equal role of the social world in the construction of knowledge.... Second, Vygotsky, contrary to another stereotype, insisted on the centrality of the active construction of knowledge.
>
> (p. 256)

Cole and Wertsch's interpretation of the individual-social antinomy reminds us that the essentials of sociocultural theory may be missed if we focus only on the individual vs. social divide. For Cole and Wertsch, culture plays a crucial mediating role in the process of human development. I again quote from that seminal paper:

> [B]y and large commentators on the differences between these two thinkers [Vygotsky and Piaget]…have placed too narrow an emphasis on their ideas about the primacy of individual psychogenesis versus sociogenesis of mind, while neglecting what we believe is a cardinal difference between them: their views concerning the importance of culture, in particular, the **role of mediation of action through artifacts, on the development of mind**.
>
> (p. 257)

> A year before his death Vygotsky said: "the central fact about our psychology is the fact of mediation".
>
> (Vygotsky, 1982, p. 62)

Wertsch and Cole recognized that the individual-social divide, while important, often leads educators to overlook other pressing aspects that define the sociocultural approach.

They summarized four key aspects to note:

> *First*, **artifacts help transform mental functioning** in fundamental ways…they do not simply facilitate mental processes, they fundamentally shape and transform them.
> *Second*, all psychological functions begin, and to a large extent remain, **culturally, historically, and institutionally situated and context specific**.
> *Third*, making cultural mediation central to mind and mental development means that the **meaning of an action and of its context are not independent** of each other.
> *Fourth*, the implication that **mind is no longer to be located entirely inside the head**; they also include the cultural mediational artifacts and the culturally structured social and natural environments of which persons are a part.
> (Adapted from Cole & Wertsch, 1996, p. 260; bold added)

Applying Cole and Wertsch to the Braydon Visit

How might Cole and Wertsch's four aspects of sociohistorical theory manifest in the Braydon family interactions?

> *Point 1.* Cole and Wertsch suggested that **artifacts** do not merely **facilitate mental processes**, but rather they **fundamentally shape and transform them**. This vignette certainly demonstrates this. The artifacts played an integral part in the unfolding of the interaction. If the artifacts had not been there, the pattern of logical reasoning started by the father and subsequently followed by the mother and sons could hardly have emerged. The opportunity would not have presented itself.
>
> As Cole and Wertsch suggested, it is not the artifacts (teeth) per se that created the interaction; it is how the 'artifacts transform mental functioning'. The mental functions of the participants shifted and adapted with tactile use and mediation of the artifacts; the players (the family) and the artifacts (teeth and head) became inextricably intertwined in the narrative the Braydons created together. This is what Wertsch (1998) might have called the subject-tool dyad, in which we can consider united/inseparable pairs linked in activity. Werstch's examples include pole and pole vaulter. Other examples include the horse and rider in a horse-jumping competition. In the sense that the pole is essential to *pole-vaulting* or the horse to the rider, so too the teeth are also essential to the dental hygiene discussion. Neither is complete without the other; the pole is useless without the vaulter and vice versa (see also Yamagata-Lynch, 2010). In Wertsch's (1998) example,
>
> > pole-vaulting as a mediated activity cannot be understood without the individuals engaging in the sport, their interaction with the pole, and the type of pole-vaulting experience that the pole material introduced

to the activity. This example can help social science researchers start to see how individuals taking part in a mediated activity and the sign reaction that tools introduce to individuals are inseparable.
(Wertsch & Rupert, 1993, in Yamagata-Lynch et al., 2016, p. 4)

One way to picture this relationship is the standard first-generation activity theory triangle. The Braydons (subjects) and the dinosaur (mediational means) and making sense (object) are related in this way.

Point 2. Here Cole and Wertsch suggested that all psychological functions begin, and to a large extent remain, **culturally, historically and institutionally situated and context specific**. In the past, research concerned with individual cognition has ignored context. Many scholars have discussed the implications of this in recent decades (Brown, 1992; Rogoff, 1995; Wertsch, 1998). In the Braydon vignette, the social and historical background, existing dialogic patterns, prior experiences and cultural norms, as well as distributed expertise, all interacted with artifacts explicitly designed by museum curators for specific learning outcomes in an intended learning sequence. The artifacts and the people interacted to create the causes and conditions for a lesson on oral hygiene. Every aspect was essential to the creation.

In research on learning, we also need to pay attention to the family and the contexts that brought the family to this moment of interaction with exhibit materials and ideas. Concurrently, we need to explore the views of past exhibits, as well as the embedded views of learning that led to the design and testing of this particular exhibit. The exhibit design cannot be considered a 'neutral' or 'ahistorical' act of creating material; it is a curricular tool created within a specific context, intended to promote specific outcomes. It actively reflects the views of its designer, the administrators and the institution. An exhibit originates with designers following the museum's guidelines. Once the Braydons and the exhibit came together, the Braydon's cultural background and previous experiences, while not matching the museum's exhibit designers, provided a novel interpretation of the exhibit for family members.

Let us assume for a moment that these two different systems, that of the family and that of the exhibition's designers and purveyors meet like rivers in a space that becomes their interaction. I have labeled the space where family and exhibit meet as a hybrid space and the activities they create as 'hybrid interaction'.[13] I have argued that the cultural-historical interpretation of the museum, as well as the more local interpretations of the family, can both be situated historically and culturally in a hybrid space (Ash, 2014a). "Hybridity is understood as a theoretical 'in-between-ness' or a liminal arena in which we apply, evaluate, and/or adjust our knowing, doing, and being to approaching different situations" (Moje et al., 2004, p. 40).

Point 3. Cole and Wertsch suggested that **the meaning of an action and its context are not independent**. This makes a great deal of sense when we observe the Braydon family's activities. Their talk and actions about dental habits and teeth were inextricably intertwined with the exhibit's "falling out teeth", the historical past of the family, their ways of joking and making fun of potentially serious topics (braces, dental costs, etc.) and the ease with which they interacted. They were having fun! There would be no meaning without the artifacts, just as there would be no meaning without the dialogue that narrated their actions.

They were not typical museumgoers as per Hood's (1991) criteria but neither were they neophytes to educational opportunities. They made the most of their interaction at this exhibit, both following the exhibit's curriculum later in the same episode and not following it at this time. The point is that this particular dialogue might not have occurred without the exquisite intertwining of people, artifacts and context. We can say that context and event are mutually constituted (Scollon & Scollon, 2007). More recent research on the role of contextualization in learning (Tolbert, 2015) has reaffirmed such a linkage in classroom settings. My own research findings over the past decade have also borne this out.

Point 4. Cole and Wertsch pointed out "the implication that **mind is no longer to be located entirely inside the head**; higher psychological functions are transactions that include the biological individual, the cultural mediational artifacts, and the culturally structured social and natural environments of which persons are a part" (p. 251). The knowledge within the activity is distributed. Cobb clarified this issue well in his "where is the mind" question (Cobb, 1994). Historically, this has been a contentious subject, as learning theories and theorists have usually been concerned with the knowledge in the head. But, as Cole and Wertsch (1996) argued,

> In short, because what we call mind works through artifacts it cannot be unconditionally bounded by the head nor even by the body, but must be seen as distributed in the artifacts which are woven together and which weave together individual human actions in concert with and as a part of the permeable, changing, events of life.
>
> (p. 263)

Cole and Werstch noted that Vygotsky (1987) suggested that introducing new artifacts (tools, mediational means) helps the distribution and quality of what is done 'within and beyond the skin'. The Braydons acted as if the exhibit's artifacts became part of their extended family and used them as seamlessly as they used their hands and voices.

Summary

The Braydon vignette illustrates a typical family with nondominant status taking time to talk, argue, tease, tell stories and jokes, interrupt, tell each other how to do

TABLE 7.2 Individual vs. social views of learning through a neoliberal lens

	Individualistic	*Social*
Learning theory perspective	Cognitive/constructivism behaviorism	Sociocultural/CoP/CHAT
External characteristics	Neoliberal	Collective
	Competition	Participation
	Knowledge acquisition	Collaboration
	Indiv. testing and metrics	Projects
	Efficiency	Shared sense of purpose
	Meritocratic	Cohesion
	Sorting	Community

things, ask questions and watch each other as part of a science museum research project (Ash, 2019; Ash & Lombana, 2012; Mai & Ash, 2012). They demonstrated well the successful conjoining of social cohesion, purpose and camaraderie with seeming joy in each other's company. They appeared to be learning collectively and collaboratively.

I have linked here two dialectic relationships not always specifically connected in the learning and teaching literature or in actual practice. The first dialectic, a historical perspective, compares situating learning as an individual activity *vs.* viewing learning as a social activity. The second dialectic compares learning from a deficit model (learners lack fundamental skills or knowledge) to viewing learners as having fundamental resources (skills or knowledge). I have treated the two dialectical relationships in tandem. I reviewed the historical treatment of the individual vs. social interpretations of learning while simultaneously examining the deficit/othering orientation that often is embedded in how learning theories are interpreted.

We saw that individualism, competition and evaluation have been strongly promoted as part of neoliberal ideologies. In schools, this has eventuated in large-scale individual tracing, national testing, sorting and ranking (Apple, 2017; Au & Ferrare, 2015), as well as competition, isolation and a praxis crisis among teachers (Tolbert et al., in preparation). In the chart we highlight some differences in viewing individual vs. social views of learning with a neoliberal lens (Table 7.2).

In short, neoliberal tendencies have led to increased hierarchical stratification, lack of cohesion, meritocratic morphing of educational systems at the expense of teachers and students. Nondominant populations particularly have been left out and blamed for their 'lack' of success. Museums are not far from the school's scenario.

Appendix 7.1: Learning Research Pragmatics

Research since the 1990s suggests that learning generally involves social as well as physical and mental activities (Brown, 1992; Piaget, 1929; Vygotsky, 1978). People engage with words, with objects, with other people and with ideas, but seldom do we actually know what exactly is going on inside their minds. We use proxies such as survey, interview, reflection and digital media as ways to approximate mental activities.

This is the perpetual challenge of all learning research. We typically conduct member checks to verify our interpretations. Such assessments give us a superficial view, at least of what people *think* they learn or remember. Post interviews and surveys cannot really tell us how interactions actually occurred. We have come to rely on physical behavior (pointing, gesturing, etc.) and speech behavior (often captured digitally in single instances or over time), as the most concretely traceable indicators of what may be occurring in people's minds.

Our strategies have become more numerous and more nuanced over the decades. The terms we use and the ways in which we characterize the learning process more generally reflect the theory we know best or have been trained to use. Each descriptive learning word or phrase signifies areas of special importance, as well as reveals something of the nature of the underlying epistemologies of their users. Certain code words mark our stance; for example, *participation*, *learning by doing* or *negotiation* may flag communities of practice, constructivism and sociocultural theories by turn.

It is important to be explicit and reflective about the particular learning theories and the words we use to describe them, as well as the practices arising from them. We work under the assumption that it is never one term or phrase that matters most, but rather the practices arising from the underlying theoretical assumption that most inform our interpretations. Assuming that each word or set of words/ideas connotes an underlying ideology, we can say, for example, that the phrase *hands-on learning*, meaning individuals interacting with phenomena, is rather clear in intent and strongly reflects constructivist assumptions. Every theory has such hallmark constructs and signifying words.

Evaluation studies have helped us uncover some aspects of discovering underlying assumptions; increasingly now, we are coming to rely on more detailed, ethnographically based research studies. What we have not used until recently is a comprehensive theory within which to combine many of these complex aspects: the social, the cultural, the cognitive, the participatory, the hands-on or other research foci. This overarching comprehensive theory can allow more complexity and more precision in our analyses. This is particularly true for research with nondominant populations, which introduces further aspects of cultural, linguistic and economic diversity. CHAT and sociocultural theory, more generally, offer us this powerful tool.

Appendix 7.2: Some Origins of Social Learning Research in Museums

Tracing this work historically, we look first to the work of Paulette McManus in the United Kingdom who began describing family learning behaviors in the late 1980s (1986, 1987; 1996). Linda Blud (1990) published work concerning family social learning interactions, and Theaano Moussouri published her dissertation on family learning in hands-on museums in 1997 in the United Kingdom. In many ways, McManus's and Blud's work was the forerunner of the social learning movement.

In the United States, Lynn Dierking published a family-centered dissertation in 1988, and Judy Diamond (1986) wrote of family learning experiences in the late 1980s, both women putting such research on the map in the United States. Minda Borun's PISEC research (Borun & Dritsas, 1997) focused on making exhibits user-friendly, using family-friendly criteria. This research also noted learning markers of family activity. Later, Ash (2004), Crowley and Callanan (1998), Ellenbogen et al. (2004) and others have continued this work. It is interesting to note that up until the mid to late 1990s, most scholars conducting this research were women. Family museum learning research paralleled features of research also being undertaken in classrooms in the late 1980s and early 1990s (Brown et al., 1993; Newman et al., 1989; Tharp & Gallimore, 1988) in that it expanded units of analysis (i.e., the focus of research attention) beyond the individual.[14]

These early researchers 'followed the family' as a social group to see what eventuated over time, noting the importance of social dynamics and the 'group', as well as the individual. This was an early move toward social learning research in museums. In fact, this was the incipient positioning of families within a sociocultural context. Paulette MacManus, for example, was quite clear in the 1990s about the social interaction of families, especially how members individually and collectively depended on each other to make sense (see McManus, 1986, 1987, 1996). For all these reasons, I originally focused on families as well in my earlier museum research (Ash, 2002, 2004).

In the early days, more generally, museum research was grounded in a loosely interpreted constructivist theory (Hein, 1991), with emphasis on the individual making sense of natural phenomena, rather than being told concepts or ideas. The Exploratorium is a prime example of such an epistemology. Founded in the 1960s, it is one of the birthplaces of 'learning by doing, inquiry-based and hands-on' interpretations of constructivist ideas in museums often, compared with behaviorism (Hein, 1995). Educators and administrators rightly point out that it is important to guide learners to construct meaning using the tools and ideas that the museum presents.

Taken together, this body of work has gradually built up a larger framework within which we can explore both individual and socially based interactions. It turns out the family is an excellent group within which to explore negotiation of meaning, discourse, and sense making, as well as all the other social interactions that occur between members of any group of people who know each other well, have learned how to take turns, speak openly with each other and have a common purpose. Families are willing to do all this under the scrutiny of researchers and evaluators, as well as cameras and microphones.

Appendix 7.3: What's in a Name?

We review some of the terms used to describe learning in informal settings, knowing full well that any term reveals underlying ideologies. The main point to make here, concerning meaning and naming or thought and speech as intimately intertwined, as Vygotsky (1987) might say, is that our thoughts and ideas are revealed in the particular words we use to convey them. Clarity in such matters is critical when designating and designing virtually anything in a museum—curriculum, exhibits, community days, free days, etc., and especially when attempting to collaborate with nondominant groups. Such groups are often unfamiliar with the context, culture, social mores, even typical dialogic forms, such as repetitive questioning, that characterize the typical visitor of the past.

Some of the terms currently used (a list that is not yet complete) for museum learning contexts include designed environment, informal environment, out-of-school time (OST) and the participatory museum (Simon, 2010). Some of the names used for studying how people make sense and interact in museums include active learning, free-choice learning, intent participation, informal learning, interest-driven collaborative learning, learning in informal environments and participatory learning, among others.

I offer here a brief discussion of only some the terms surrounding learning in informal settings.

Examining learning in informal settings such as museums, gardens, clubs and similar contexts is challenging. Chief among the reasons for this is agreeing on what we mean by learning and then locating instances that prove our point.

In using the phrase *informal learning*, we are still left with the implication that there is something fundamentally different about *informal* learning. Certainly, the contexts and reward systems between formal and informal settings are different, but every student has seen informal-looking classrooms and formally structured museum exhibit docenting. The term *learning in informal environments* typically connotes an interest in the social and contextual aspects of learning, as these environments tend to connote sociability, mediational means and the like. *OST* specifically connotes something opposite from school time learning. The emphasis is on the difference, perhaps suggesting that alternatives to school approaches are expected.

The phrase 'designed environment' is a newer expression, harkening to the use of design experiments (Brown, 1992). Simon's (2010) participatory museum reveals clues as to her own theoretical framework—perhaps akin to community of practice theory (Lave & Wenger, 1991) involving actions of the collective. Simon helped to open the museum world to the notion of social participation.

According to Rogoff et al. (2003), intent participation, where learning occurs by observation that may not involve direct action or even words, is firsthand learning. These authors define intent participation by Indigenous children as the ability to observe and listen with "intent concentration and initiative and [that]…collaborative participation is expected when they're ready to help and share endeavors" (p. 177).

In the view of many researchers, none of these informal, free-choice or participatory models are perfect. For now, I will use the phrase *informal learning* as a fallback that we all know is imperfect. The emphasis for me has always been on the reciprocal exchange between learners and teachers, the use of design to support learning and an emphasis on context as something that matters (A. Brown, 1992).

Free-choice learning (Dierking, 1987; Dierking & Falk, 1994) emphasizes the freedom to choose, perhaps reflecting a strong individualist sensibility of taking action in order to make sense of the surrounding environments. "'*Free-choice learning*' is all about what you choose to do in your learning time" (Gilles, 2012); it suggests that, in the museum setting, people perhaps have more choice than in other learning settings, specifically formal schools. Is that really the case? Exhibits are a form of curriculum, and according to the criteria for full inquiry (Exploratorium, 2021), the topic, the questions, and the materials are determined by the museum in advance. The visitor's choice, then, involves only how and in what order to engage with them.

The often-used phrase *informal learning* from the 1970s connotes "the lifelong process by which every person acquires and accumulates knowledge, skills, attitudes and insights from daily experiences and exposure to the environment—at home, at work, at play" (Coombs & Ahmed, 1974, p. 8) and perhaps signals a different kind of learning than that which occurs in formal classroom settings. For decades now, learning researchers have dichotomized *formal* and *informal* environments, specifically synthesizing comparisons. Vadeboncoeur and Murray (2014, p. 246) argued,

> Some authors explicitly challenge the usefulness of the formal/informal dichotomy in relation to learning and argue for using labels such as "incidental" and "implicit" to better describe the types of learning (Eraut, 2000). "There is no consensus about what informal learning might be".
> (Sefton-Green, 2003, p. 40, in Vadeboncoeur and Murray, 2014, p. 246)

Often, museums are positioned in opposition to formal schooling. Such perceived differences in informal and formal learning environments over the past decade were commonly offered at least in part to validate the importance of learning activity in informal learning settings. Such validation and such strong dichotomies are less necessary now, as a more robust body of museum learning research literature has emerged over the past several decades.

Interestingly, there has been a diminishing demarcation between schools and museums, especially as they both promote the adoption of the Next Generation Science Standards or Common Core (Ng-He, 2015; Short, 2014). This collaboration reveals an interest in working on jointly selected (hybrid) curriculum content. Such a sharing and overlap of practices has grown in part, no doubt, from the many experimental collaborations across informal and formal communities of practice (see also Bevan et al., 2012; Kisiel et al., 2012).

Notes

1 Vygotsky conceptualized development as the transformation of socially shared activities into internalized processes (John-Steiner & Mahn, 1996).
2 Timmis noted that although CHAT is increasingly being used for researching educational settings, "it is often employed only descriptively or as a set of guiding principles

and the dialectical method, which focuses on emergent contradictions and tensions, is not always fully explored" (Timmis, 2014, p. 7).
3 The stance of looking for different kinds of skills, practices and content has been long known as *funds of knowledge* (González, 2005).
4 See https://canadianart.ca/features/a-crisis-of-whiteness/ for a review of Canadian museums leadership.
5 Sfard was primarily concerned with the term *acquisition* and related terms such as "knowledge, concept, conception, idea, notion, misconception, meaning, sense, schema, fact… representation, material, contents, reception, acquisition, construction, internalization, appropriation, transmission, attainment, development, accumulation, grasp…cognitive structure, conceptual change". Conversely, with participation, she referred to learning as a "legitimate peripheral participation…or as an apprenticeship" (Sfard, 1998, p. 5–6).
6 Wholly in the participatory metaphor, the "talk about private possessions [is replaced] with discourse about shared activities" (p. 8). Sfard later suggested 'metaphorical pluralism'—i.e., citing the danger of choosing but one view, possibly inviting bricolage (Lawler, 1985).
7 Views such as distributed cognition, Salomon and Perkins (1998) and situated cognition, Lave (1991).
8 Roth and Jornet (2014) framed experience in this way, pulling together many strands concerned with a more holistic sense of social: "Experience…a minimal unit of analysis that includes people (their intellectual, affective, and practical characteristics), their material and social environment, their transactional relations (mutual effects on each other), and affect. Thus, experience…extends in space and time across individuals and setting in the course of temporally unfolding societal relations, which themselves are perfused with affect" (Vygotsky, 1935, p. 107, in Race et al., in preparation, p. 28).
9 https://www.exploratorium.edu/education/ifi/constructivist-learning
10 See Tang et al. (2017), inquiry as a starting point for equity.
11 As the museum educators began to listen and scaffold more while talking less, other educators and their mid-level managers were not ready to change the 'norm'; that is, they were unwilling to rock the boat of the 'status quo" (Ash & Lombana, 2012).
12 Beyond having signs in multiple languages, non-English speaking families often first need specialized information beyond simple observation in order to understand what the exhibit expects of them. Museums need to move beyond the expectation that hands-on activity, without scaffolding, is equally efficacious for all (Yoon et al., 2013).
13 In past research, I have taken special note of such an intermixing or hybridizing when family members use new mediational means of tools (exhibit, signs, videos, etc., presented by the museum), as well as their own available resources (prior knowledge, gestures, language) to negotiate meaning (Mai & Ash, 2012).
14 We learned a good deal about learning in museums in the '80s/'90s. We have long recognized that we should design multiple entry points—that is, different pathways into the content and skills an exhibit promotes (Borun & Dritsas, 1997) to accommodate different levels of expertise.

References

Anderson, D., & Ellenbogen, K. (2012). Learning science in informal contexts—epistemological perspectives and paradigms. In B. Fraser, K. Tobin, & C. J. McRobbie (Eds.), *Second international handbook of science education* (pp. 1179–1187). Springer.

Anderson, J. R., Reder, L. M., & Simon, H. A. (1996). Situated learning and education. *Educational Researcher, 25*, 5–11.

Apple, M. W. (Ed.) (2017). *Cultural and economic reproduction in education: Essays on class, ideology and the state* (Vol. 53). Routledge.

Ash, D. (2002). Negotiation of thematic conversations about biology. In G. Leinhardt, K. Crowley, & K. Knutson (Eds.), *Learning conversations in museums* (pp. 357–400). Lawrence Erlbaum Associates.

Ash, D. (2004). Reflective scientific sense-making dialogue in two languages: The science in the dialogue and the dialogue in the science. *Science Education, 88,* 855–884. https://ashresearchassociates.com/wp-content/uploads/2014/12/ash-2004-reflective-sm.pdf

Ash, D. (2014a). Creating hybrid spaces for talk: Humor as a resource learners bring to informal learning context. *National Society for the Study of Education, 113*(2), 535–55.

Ash, D. (2014b). Positioning informal learning research in museums within activity theory: From theory to practice and back again. *Curator: The Museum Journal, 57,* 107–118. http://dx.doi.org/10.1111/cura.12054

Ash, D. (2019). Reflective practice in action research: Moving beyond the "standard model". In T. Martin & Ash (Eds.), *The reflective museum practitioner: Expanding practice in science museums* (pp. 23–38). Routledge. https://doi.org/10.4324/9780429025242-3

Ash, D., Crain, R., Brandt, C., Loomis, M., Wheaton, M., & Bennett, C. (2008). Talk, tools, and tensions: Observing biological talk over time. *International Journal of Science Education, 29*(12), 1581 – 1602.

Ash, D., & Lombana, J. (2012). Methodologies for reflective practice and museum educator research. In D. Ash, J. Rahm, & L. M. Melber (Eds.), *Putting theory into practice. New directions in mathematics and science education* (pp. 107–122). Sense Publishers. https://doi.org/10.1007/978-94-6091-964-0_4

Ash, D., & Lombana, J. (2015). Reculturing museums: Working toward diversity in informal settings. *Journal of Museum Education, 38*(1), 69–80. https://doi.org/10.1080/10598650.2013.11510757

Ash, D., Loomis, M., & Hohenstein, J. (2005). ¿Qué come? Preguntas para la significación de conceptos científicos. Academia.edu. https://www.academia.edu/14895185/_Qu%C3%A9_come_Preguntas_para_la_significaci%C3%B3n_de_conceptos_cient%C3%ADficos.

Au, W., & Ferrare, J. A. (Eds.) (2015). *Mapping corporate education reform: Power and policy networks in the neoliberal state (critical social thought).* Routledge.

Bevan, B., Bell, P., Stevens, R., & Razfar, A. (Eds.) (2012). *LOST opportunities: Learning in out-of-school time* (Vol. 23). Springer Science & Business Media.

Blud, L. M. (1990). Social interaction and learning among family groups visiting a museum. *Museum Management and Curatorship, 9*(1), 43–51. https://doi.org/10.1080/09647779009515193

Borun, M., & Dritsas, J. (1997). Developing family-friendly exhibits. *Curator: The Museum Journal, 40*(3), 178–196. https://doi.org/10.1111/j.2151-6952.1997.tb01302

Bransford, J., Brown, A. L., Cocking, R. R., & National Research Council (U.S.). (1999). *How people learn: Brain, mind, experience, and school.* National Academy Press.

Brown, A. L. (1992). Design experiments: Theoretical and methodological challenges in creating complex interventions in classroom settings. *The Journal of the Learning Sciences, 2*(2), 141–178.

Brown, A. L., Ash, D., Rutherford, M., Nakagawa, K., Gordon, A., & Campione, J. C. (1993). Distributed expertise in the classroom. In G. Salomon (Ed.), *Distributed cognitions: Psychological and educational considerations* (pp. 188–288). Cambridge University Press.

Brown, A. L., & Palincsar, A. S. (1986). Reciprocal teaching of comprehension strategies: A natural history of one program for enhancing learning. In J. Borkowski & J. D. Day (Eds.), *Intelligence and cognition in special children: Comparative studies of giftedness, mental retardation, and learning disabilities* (p. 8). Ablex.

Callanan, M. A. (2012). Conducting cognitive developmental research in museums: Theoretical issues and practical considerations. *Journal of Cognition and Development, 13*(2), 137–151. https://doi.org/10.1080/15248372.2012.666730

Carpenter, M. (2019, August 23). *View from the field: The challenges to being inclusive in museum collections.* The Inclusive Historian's Handbook. https://inclusivehistorian.com/view-from-the-field-the-challenges-to-being-inclusive-in-museum-collections/.

Case, R. (1996). Changing views of knowledge and their impact on educational research and practice. In D. Olson & N. Torrance (Eds.), *The handbook of education and human development* (pp. 75–99). Blackwell.

Chaiklin, S. & Lave, J. (1993). *Understanding practice: Perspectives on activity and context.* Cambridge University Press.

Cobb, P. (1994). Where is the mind? Constructivist and sociocultural perspectives on mathematical development. *Educational Researcher, 23*(7), 13–20.

Cole, M. (1988). Cross-cultural research in the sociohistorical tradition. *Human Development, 31,* 137–151.

Cole, M., & Engeström, Y. (1993). A cultural-historical approach to distributed cognition. In G. Salomon (Ed.), *Distributed cognitions: Psychological and educational considerations* (pp. 1–46). Cambridge University Press.

Cole, M., & Wertsch, J. V. (1996). Beyond the individual-social antinomy in discussions of Piaget and Vygotsky. *Human Development, 39*(5), 250–256. https://doi.org/10.1159/000278475

Coombs, P. H., & Ahmed, M. (1974). *Attacking rural poverty: How non-formal education can help.* John Hopkins University Press.

Crowley, K., & Callanan, M. A. (1998). Identifying and supporting shared scientific reasoning in parent-child interactions. *Journal of Museum Education, 23,* 12–17. https://upclose.lrdc.pitt.edu/articles/1998%20Crowley%20&%20Callanan.pdf

Dawson, E. (2014a). "Not designed for us": How science museums and science centers socially exclude low-income, minority ethnic groups. *Science Education, 98*(6), 981–1008. https://doi.org/10.1002/sce.21133

Dawson, E. (2014b). Equity in formal science education: Developing an access and equity framework for science museums and science centres. *Studies in Science Education, 50*(2), 209–247.

deGregoria Kelly, L. A. (2009). Action research as professional development for zoo educators. *Visitor Studies, 12*(1), 30–46.

Dewey, J. (1916). *Democracy and education: An introduction to the philosophy of education.* Macmillan.

Diamond, J. (1986). The behavior of family groups in science museums. *Curator: The Museum Journal, 29*(2), 139–154. https://doi.org/10.1111/j.2151-6952.1986.tb01434.x

Dierking, L. (1987). *Parent-child interactions in a free choice learning setting: An examination of attention-directing behaviour.* [Dissertation University of Florida].

Dierking, L. D., & Falk, J. H. (1994). Family behavior and learning in informal science settings: A review of the research. *Science Education, 78*(1), 57–72. 199.

Ellenbogen, K. M., Luke, J. J., & Dierking, L. D. (2004). Family learning research in museums: An emerging disciplinary matrix? *Science Education, 88*(S1). https://doi.org/10.1002/sce.20015

Engeström, Y. (1987). *Learning by expanding: An activity-theoretical approach to developmental research.* Orienta-Konsultit.

Engeström, Y., Miettinen, R. & Punamäki-Gitai, R. L. (1999). *Perspectives on activity theory (Learning in doing: Social, cognitive and computational aspects).* Cambridge University Press.

Engeström, Y., & Sannino, A. (2010). Studies of expansive learning: Foundations, findings and future challenges. *Educational Research Review, 5,* 1–24. http://dx.doi.org/10.1016/j.edurev.2009.12.00

Eraut, M. (2000). Non-formal learning and tacit knowledge in professional work. *The British Journal of Educational Psychology, 70* (1), 113–136.

Exploratorium. (2021, September 24). *About us.* https://www.exploratorium.edu/about-us.

Exploratorium founder Frank Oppenheimer. (2013, April 17). *Exploratorium.* https://www.exploratorium.edu/press-office/press-releases/exploratorium-founder-frank-oppenheimer.

Gardner, H. (1985). *The mind's new science.* Basic Books.

Garibay, C. (2009). Latinos, leisure values, and decisions: Implications for informal science learning and engagement. *The Informal Learning Review, 94,* 10–13.

Gilles, N. (2012). What makes people want to learn? Free-choice learning research comes of age. *Confluence, 1*(3), 3–7. https://seagrant.oregonstate.edu/sites/seagrant.oregonstate.edu/files/confluence/confluence-1-3.pdf

Golding, V. (2013). Collaborative museums: Curators, communities, collections. In V. Golding & W. Modest (Eds.), *Museums and communities: Curators, collections, collaboration* (pp. 13–31). Bloomsbury.

González, N. (2005). Beyond culture: The hybridity of funds of knowledge. In N. González, L. C. Moll, & C. Amanti (Eds.), *Funds of knowledge: Theorizing practices in households, communities, and classrooms* (pp. 29–46). Routledge.

Gorski, P. (2010). *Unlearning deficit ideology and the scornful gaze: Thoughts on authenticating the class discourse in education.* EdChange. http://www.edchange.org/publications/deficit-ideology-scornful-gaze.pdf

Grant, C., & Price, D. (2020). Decolonizing art history. *Art History, 43*(1), 8–66. https://doi.org/10.1111/1467-8365.12490

Greeno, J. G., Collins, A. M., & Resnick, L. B. (1996). Cognition and learning. In D. C. Berliner & R. C. Case. Changing views of knowledge and their impact on educational research and practice. In D. Olson & N. Torrance (Eds.), *The handbook of education and human development* (pp. 75–99). Blackwell.

Gurian, E. H. (2009, February 11). *Curator from soloist to impresario.* Curator. http://www.egurian.com/omnium-gatherum/museum-issues/collections/acquisition-deaccession-and-ownership/curator-from-soloist

Gurian, E. H. (2019, December 22). Elaine Heumann Gurian on the importance of and museum next. https://www.museumnext.com/article/the-importance-of-and/

Gutiérrez, K. D., Baquedano-Lopez, P., & Tejeda, C. (1999). Rethinking diversity: Hybridity and hybrid language practices in the third space. *Mind, Culture and Activity, 6*(4), 286–303.

Gutiérrez, K. D., & Rogoff, B. (2003). Cultural ways of learning: Individual traits or repertoires of practice. *Educational Researcher, 32*(5), 19–25.

Gutiérrez, R. (2002). Beyond essentialism: The complexity of language in teaching mathematics to Latina/o students. *American Educational Research Journal, 39*(4), 1047–1088. https://doi.org/10.3102/00028312039004 1047

Gutiérrez, R. (2007). (Re)defining equity: The importance of a critical perspective. In N. Nasir & P. Cobb (Eds.), *Improving access to mathematics: Diversity and equity in the classroom* (pp. 37–50). Teachers College Press.

Hein, G. (1991, October 15–22). *The museum and the needs of people* [Conference presentation]. *CECA (International Committee of Museum Educators) Conference,* Jerusalem, Israel. https://www.exploratorium.edu/education/ifi/constructivist-learning

Hein, G. (1995). The constructivist museum. *Journal for Education in Museums, 16,* 21–23.

Hein, G. (2014, May 26–127). Museum: Knowledge, democracy and transformation conference on organizational change within participating institutions related to the citizenship project, Helsingor, Denmark. https://silo.tips/download/kronburg-castle-and-danish-maritime-museum-helsingr-denmark-may-2014-museums-kno

Hodkinson, P., Biesta, G., & James, D. (2008). Understanding learning culturally: Overcoming the dualism between social and individual views of learning. *Vocations and Learning* 1, 27–47, https://doi.org/10.1007/s12186-007-9001-y

Hood, M. G. (1991). Significant issues in museum audience research. *A Journal of Visitor Behavior*, 6(4), 18–23. https://www.informalscience.org/sites/default/files/VSA-a0a1y3-a_5730.pdf

Hooper-Greenhill, E. (Ed.). (2009). *Cultural diversity: Developing museum audiences in Britain*. Leicester University Press.

John-Steiner, V., & Mahn, H. (1996). Sociocultural approaches to learning and development: A Vygotskian framework. *Educational Psychologist*, 31(3–4), 191–206. doi:10.1080/00461520.1996.9653266

Kisiel, J., Rowe, S., Vartabedian, M. A., & Kopczak, C. (2012). Evidence for family engagement in scientific reasoning at interactive animal exhibits. *Science Education*, 96(6), 1047–1070. https://doi.org/10.1002/sce.21036

Lave, J. (1991). Situating learning in communities of practice. In L. B. Resnick, J. M. Levine, & S. D. Teasley (Eds.), *Perspectives on socially shared cognition* (pp. 63–82). American Psychological Association.

Lave, J., & Wenger, E. (1991). *Situated learning*. Cambridge University.

Lawler, R. W. (1985). *Computer experience and cognitive development: A child's learning in a computer culture*. John Wiley & Sons

Mai, T., & Ash, D. (2012). Tracing our methodological steps: Making meaning of families' hybrid "figuring out" practices at science museum exhibits. In D. Ash, J. Rahm, & L. Melber (Eds.), *Putting theory into practice: Methodologies for informal learning research*. Sense Publishers.

McDermott, R. (2015). Does "learning" exist? *WORD*, 61(4), 335–349. https://doi.org/10.1080/00437956.2015.1112956

McManus, P. (1986). Reviewing the reviewers: Towards a critical language for didactic science exhibitions. *International Journal of Museum Management and Curatorship*, 5, 213–226.

McManus, P. (1987). It's the company you keep…: The social determination of learning related behavior in a science museum. *International Journal of Museum Management and Curatorship*, 6, 263–270.

McManus, P. (1996). Frames of reference: Changes in evaluative attitudes to visitors. *The Journal of Museum Education*, 21(3), 3–5. Retrieved July 26, 2021, from http://www.jstor.org/stable/40479067

Moje, E. B., Ciechanowski, K. M., Kramer, K., Ellis, L., Carrillo, R., & Collazo, T. (2004). Working toward third space in content area literacy: An examination of everyday funds of knowledge and discourse. *Reading Research Quarterly*, 39(1), 38–70. https://doi.org/10.1598/rrq.39.1.4

Newman, D., Griffin, P., & Cole, M. (1989). *The construction zone: Working for cognitive change in school*. Cambridge University Press.

Ng-He, C. (2015). Common goals, common core: Museums and schools work together, *Journal of Museum Education*, 40(3), 220–226. doi:10.1179/1059865015Z.00000000098

Palmquist, S., & Crowley, K. (2007). From teachers to testers: How parents talk to novice and expert children in a natural history museum. *Science Education*, 91(5), 783–804. https://doi.org/10.1002/sce.20215

Piaget, J. (1929). *The child's conception of the world*. Kegan Paul Trench & Trubner.

Rahm, J. (2012). Science in the making at the margin: A multi-sited ethnography of learning and becoming in an afterschool program, a garden, and a math and science Upward Bound program. In E. Davidsson & A. Jakobsson (Eds.), *Understanding interactions at science centers and museums*. Sense Publishers.

Resnick, L. (1992). Learning in school and out. *Educational Research, 16* (9), 13–54.

Rogoff, B. (1995). Observing sociocultural activity on three planes: Participatory appropriation, guided participation, and apprenticeship. In J. V. Wertsch, P. del Rio, & A. Alvarez (Eds.), *Sociocultural studies of mind* (pp. 139–164). Cambridge University Press.

Rogoff, B., Paradise, R., Arauz, R. M., Correa-Chávez, M., & Angelillo, C. (2003). Firsthand learning through intent participation. *Annual Review of Psychology, 54*(1), 175–203. https://doi.org/10.1146/annurev.psych.54.101601.145118

Roth, W.-M., & Jornet, A. (2014). Toward a theory of experience. *Science Education, 98*(1), 106–126. https://doi.org/10.1002/sce.21085

Rowe S., & Bachman J. (2012). Mediated action as a framework for exploring learning in informal settings. In D. Ash, J. Rahm, & L. M. Melber (Eds.), *Putting theory into practice* (pp. 143–162). New Directions in Mathematics and Science Education, 25. SensePublishers. https://doi.org/10.1007/978-94-6091-964-0_14

Salomon, G., & Perkins, D. N. (1998). Individual and social aspects of learning. *Review of Research in Education, 23*, 1–24.

Scollon, R., & Scollon, S. W. (2007). Nexus analysis: Refocusing ethnography on action. *Journal of Sociolinguistics, 11*(5), 608–625. https://doi.org/10.1111/j.1467-9841.2007.00342.x

Sefton-Green, J. (2003). Informal learning: Substance or style? *Teaching Education, 14*(1), 37–51. https://doi.org/10.1080/10476210309391

Sfard, A. (1998). On two metaphors for learning and the dangers of choosing just one. *Educational Researcher, 27*(2), 4–13. https://doi.org/10.3102/0013189x027002004

Short, J. (2014). How can museums help teachers with the NGSS? *Dimensions.* https://cadrek12.org/sites/default/files/Short_NovDec2014.pdf

Simon, N. (2010). Chapter 1: Principles of participation. In *The participatory museum.* Museum 2.0. http://www.participatorymuseum.org/chapter1/.

Tang, G., El Turkey, H., Cilli-Turner, E., Savic, M., Karakok, G., & Plaxco, D. (2017). Inquiry as an entry point to equity in the classroom. *International Journal of Mathematical Education in Science and Technology, 48*(suppl. 1). https://doi.org/10.1080/0020739x.2017.1352045

Tharp, R. G., & Gallimore, R. (1988). *Rousing minds to life: Teaching, learning, and schooling in social context.* Cambridge University Press.

Timmis, S. (2014). The dialectical potential of cultural historical activity theory for researching sustainable CSCL practices. *The International Journal of Computer-Supported Collaborative Learning, 9*, 7–32. https://doi.org/10.1007/s11412-013-9178-z

Tishman, S. (2005). *As museums broaden their missions, learning is becoming a fresh and central concern for institutions as a whole.* Harvard Graduate School of Education. https://www.gse.harvard.edu/news/uk/05/09/learning-museums-0

Tolbert, S. (2015). Because they want to teach you about their culture: Analyzing effective mentoring conversations. *Journal of Research in Science Teaching, 53*(10), 1325–1361.

Tolbert, S., Spurgin, C., & Ash, D. (in preparation). Toxic individualism and other neoliberal forces in science teacher professional development.

Vadeboncocur, J. A., & Murray, D. (2014). Imagined futures in the present: Minding learning opportunities. *National Society for the Study of Education, 113*, 633–652.

Vossoughi, S., & Gutiérrez, K. D. (2014). Studying movement, hybridity, and change: Toward a multi-sited sensibility for research on learning across contexts and borders. *Teachers College Record, 116*(14), 603–632.

Vygotsky, L. S. (1935). *Umstvennoe razvitie detei vprotsesse obucheniia [The mental development of the child in the process of instruction].* Uchpedgiz.

Vygotsky, L. S. (1978). *Mind in society: The development of higher psychological processes.* Harvard University Press.

Vygotsky, L. S. (1982). *LECTURE 16: Vygotsky*. https://www.massey.ac.nz/~wwpapajl/evolution/lect17/lect1700.htm.

Vygotsky, L. S. (1987). *Thinking and speech*. Plenum.

Ward, S. J. (2016). *Understanding contradictions in times of change: A CHAT analysis in an art museum* [Dissertation]. University of Washington. Seattle, USA.

Wenger, E. (1998). *Communities of practice: Learning, meaning, and identity*. Cambridge University Press. https://doi.org/10.1017/CBO9780511803932

Wertsch, J. V. (1991). *Voices of the mind: Sociocultural approach to mediated action*. Harvard University Press.

Wertsch, J.V. (1998). *Mind as action*. Oxford University Press.

Wertsch, J.V., & Rupert, L.J. (1993). The authority of cultural tools in a sociocultural approach to mediated agency. *Cognition and Instruction, 11*(3–4), 227–239. https://doi.org/10.1080/07370008.1993.9649022

Yamagata-Lynch, L. C. (2010). *Activity systems analysis methods: Understanding complex learning environments*. Springer.

Yamagata-Lynch, L. C., Skutnik, A. L., Garty, E., & Do, J. (2016). Interactionist qualitative research as a semiotic mediation activity. *SAGE Open, 6*(3). doi:10.1177/2158244016666889

Yoon, S.A., Elinich, K., Wang, J., Schooneveld, J. B., & Anderson, E. (2013). Scaffolding informal learning in science museums: How much is too much?. *Science Education, 97*(6), 848–877. http://onlinelibrary.wiley.com/doi/10.1002/sce.21079/

8
WHAT DO WE MEAN BY EQUITABLE TEACHING IN MUSEUMS?

Overview

Museums offer a variety of approaches to professional development (PD), which refers to how museum educators are taught to teach. Currently, museums face the immediate challenge of providing to a wide range of visitors the services of a flexibly trained education staff, aware of deficit beliefs and who are critically reflective of their personal and professional views of learners and learning.

In this chapter, I pose the essential question: "*What do we mean by equitable teaching in museums?*" There are few research studies that have directly traced transformative teaching practices in museums, subsequently linking them with larger institutional rules, ideologies and hierarchies or within an expansive view of equity (Jennings & Jones-Rizzi, 2017). Research on PD is expanding, though, and becoming increasingly theoretically informed (Anderson et al., 2015; Martin, Tran & Ash, 2019; Patrick, 2017; Tran & Halversen, 2021; Ward, 2016).

I examine here the power relations that cut across all levels of museums and especially impact how we can best conduct PD that leads to equitable teaching. Equally challenging is being able to conceive of what fully equitable teaching in museums looks like. I focus on one PD case study, in which structural resistance arose and both collective and individual agency shifted notably (Ash, 2014a; Ash, Lombana, & Alcala, 2012a).

Using CHAT, we link individual educators, groups of educators and their entire institution in reciprocal relationships.[1] The structure agency dialectic (SAD) helps us map and reflect on the power struggles between museum educators' personal agency and the structural constraints within the specific science museum. My focus is on the contradictions between the status quo 'teaching as telling' and a newer 'teaching as flexible scaffolding' (Ash, 2014b; Mai & Ash, 2012). This case shows the potential for studying expansive learning and exploring educator deficit/othering

DOI: 10.4324/9781003261681-8

orientations while seeing the SAD in action. It helps reveal neoliberal principles of individualism and commoditization at work in subtle and not-so-subtle ways. It provids a specific example of structural constraints, in the form of mid-level managerial resistance to new teaching practices and shows how these constraints stifled collective and individual agency on the part of educators.

> **VIGNETTE**
>
> This National Science Foundation (NSF)–funded, five-year research intervention project in a large science museum traced how a newly hired cohort of museum educators came to be 'equity-/scaffolding-trained', reflective *blue-shirted* educators[2] while working in a self-contained, hands-on exhibition. The existing PD practices in different parts of the same museum explicitly required its *purple-shirted educators* to show visitors how to 'do the exhibits' in didactic format, often using scripts and explicitly explaining specialized content. The following segment illustrates the struggle over power and agency that ensued.
>
> About six months into the scaffolding teaching intervention research at the science museum, one of the scaffolding museum educators (*blues*) discussed negative experiences with and resistance from *purple* (didactic) mid-level managers. Ken, who had been hired during his *blue*-shirt training to temporarily join the *purples*, said,
>
>> One day I came in [to be a *purple*] and I was told that the [mid-level manager] said to ignore everything I've learned as a [*blue*] and go back to [*purple*] training because that's what they want to see…. They [*purple* manager] said we should be the "dragons" of the floor.
>
> He said he felt violated. His understandings were mocked and overridden with deficit-oriented arguments.
>
>> That was the way they were taught…to be loud and boisterous and obnoxious…. That's what they are used to. If they don't see it then they assume we aren't being effective. And they'd like us to be effective, so they'd like to see that.
>
> Ken argued that to be an effective *purple*, he was told to be pushy and controlling.
>
>> If they [*purple* shirt managers] were to walk around the floor and I'm talking with someone, they aren't going to hear "hey, I'm doing science and it's really loud over here," I think they expect that because that's the way it's been done in the past. They want to hear us yelling about science.
>
> This was a classic double-bind situation.

Introduction

Knowing the right way to teach[3] equitably in informal settings is a historically contested activity reflecting competing underlying ideologies.[4] Just as in our studies of the paired topics of demographics and dollars, and story and objects, learning and teaching reflect how museums are at the crossroads of 'figuring out' how to implement socially just teaching practice. All three aspects, learning, teaching and equity, highlight contradictions concerning whether museum educators, like visitors, are treated as commodities or as collaborators, or as passive or active. To explore this, I apply analytic tools, such as deficit views of learner and learning, normed expectations, diminished agency and constraining structure, as well as commodification and false individualism, where they are useful.

Reculturing is best studied by focusing closely on the 'on the floor' work of museum educators at an intermediate level of analysis (White, 1989). Existing frameworks for museum teaching practice have only tangentially addressed the power-laden issues of equity and social justice, focusing instead on vaguer notions of diversity and equality (Dawson et al., 2020).

Just as I asked in Chapter 7 how we position learning and learners, I ask here how we position teaching and educators, focusing particularly on how they are taught to teach equitably in their PD. Just as I linked learning and equity in Chapter 7, I link teaching and equity here. The central contradiction I discuss concerns the tension (secondary contradiction) between *teaching as telling* vs. *scaffolding in the ZPD*.

Museum educators occupy an important intermediate position between visitors and administration in the larger activity systems of museums; they are the 'message keepers and senders', the face of the museum. They are often asked to become change agents of museums (Martin et al., 2019; Tran & Halversen, 2021; Ward, 2016), yet there is a stark difference between these educators' power (low) and job expectations (high) (Gurian, 2020; Henry, 2006; Karim-Jaffer, 2013; Toohey & Wolins, 1993). They earn lower salaries than curators and their offices are often tucked away. They do important work for the museum, interface with the public, but have little power or status. "*Why is it that we have paid little attention to museum educators' work, professional development and equitable teaching?*"

I have chosen to focus my research on museum educators because they occupy a critical mid-level position in the hierarchy of museums. What they do affects visitors, and they also are affected by administration and management. Since equity is one of the most pressing changes we need to advance in museums, it is logical to start here, to place the burden and reward for change in their hands. This intermediate status makes the educator level of hierarchy a useful fulcrum for change.

I consciously integrate issues of equity in all my research. Here it is no different. I chose this *case study* project to explore what *is* possible for museum educator PD in order to develop equitable teaching practices in museums. There have been several theoretically informed museum educator PD studies over the past few decades (Anderson et al., 2015; Bevan & Michalchick, 2013; de Gregoria Kelly, 2009; Patrick, 2017; Piqueras & Achiam, 2019; Tran & Halversen, 2021), all of which inform this chapter. They provide the background for the change I wished to study. I will describe this case study later in this chapter. It is an 'on the floor' example of a theoretically based research intervention program (see also Martin et al., 2019).

Teaching for equity involves critically reflecting on how we position learners, as well as identifying what we believe to be essential in the teaching process. These are in turn linked to the socially, historically, culturally and politically bound understandings of learners, learning, power dynamics and hierarchy, roles and what motivates learning and learners. Using CHAT perspective language, learning must include the object of the activity, such as aesthetic appreciation, fun or learning new content.

Connecting learning and teaching and equity together in a PD equity curriculum with a critical theoretical grounding has great potential for showing us how we can better advance a museum's ability to meet its goals of working effectively for and with an increasingly diverse public (Chapter 3). I use CHAT's concept of expansive learning to situate this case study of the rupture and change in teaching practice in a large museum of science to analyze in detail how contradictions both disrupted educator PD and reflected the competing ideologies of a large museum. This struggle is a proxy for smaller and larger ideological battles in other institutions.

There have been increasing calls for museum educators to "interrogate the ways in which racism manifests in interactions with exhibitions, audiences, and colleagues" (Dewhurst & Hendrick, 2017, p. 103). The Center for the Future of Museums (CFM) (2010) has argued that "it's ironic that even though everyone is talking about innovation being the most desirable 21st-century skill, educators and students are still held captive in the least innovative teaching and learning environments" (p. 24).

Some equitable museum teaching practices have been explored in prior research, for example, 'belonging', being comfortable, not being treated as 'different', assimilationist expectations and 'barriers' (Archer, 2008; Dawson, 2014a, 2014b; Dewhurst & Hendrick, 2017; Garibay, 2009). This is reflected in the language of diversity, equity and inclusion, a current attempt to help those in charge learn what they do not yet know in order to be able to trace dynamic processes of power at work and know how to apply research results in ways that promote individual and institutional behavioral change.

A focus on teaching museum educators so that they can learn to interact and facilitate visitor learning more equitably forces us to adopt a stance of mutuality. Just as visitors are active participants in their own learning, so too are museum educators. Such research often uses teaching dilemmas of educators attempting to grapple with differences in museums (Achiam & Holmegaa, 2017; Agrawal, 2016). In this chapter, as in all the others, I agree with these aspirations but, again, rely on CHAT to ground our analysis.

My research has demonstrated how museum educators are expected to learn to be flexible and collaborative with minoritized visitors (Ash, 2019; Ash & Lombana, 2012). Unfortunately, the increasing emphasis on the bottom line and solvency has eroded educator agency. The commodification of educator work as an integral aspect of what museums are expected to do has created the same tensions we have found in prior chapters, leading to the same effects from increasingly persistent neoliberal policies (Dailey, 2006). In this case, we study the secondary contradictions that arose from the difference between a traditional didactic/showman teaching style and teaching as responsive listening and scaffolding in the ZPD.

Just to be clear, from a Vygotskian perspective, it is essential to know what learners already know in order to meet them with appropriate responses in the ZPD. A helpful response needs to be aimed somewhat higher than what learners already know, but not too high as to be out of reach. We can think of the ZPD as the area between a learner's current ability and the future growth the learner can achieve with the assistance of a number of things, such as a teacher, a more skilled peer, a book, a computer or an exhibit (Ash et al., 2009; Brown et al., 1993).

With the help of the Ken vignette, I discuss ideology, change and power and then return to the case study as an example of incomplete expansive learning. I tie together the theoretical strands at the end of the chapter.

Change Is Hard When All We Know Is 'Business as Usual'

Changing core teaching practices in well-established museums of science, art, history or culture is challenging (Martin et al., 2019; Patrick, 2017). As Gurian (2020) noted, it is as challenging for large institutions to change course as it is for ocean liners. DiMaggio and Powell (1991) noted,

> If institutions are, by definition, firmly rooted in taken-for-granted rules, norms, and routines, and if those institutions are so powerful that organizations and individuals are apt to automatically conform to them, then how are new institutions created or existing ones changed over time?
> (DiMaggio & Powell, 1991, in Seo & Creed, 2002, p. 222)

Promoting change when all we know is 'business as usual' is, of course, the essential question I raise in each chapter. As I have argued, only a dynamic theoretical framework will allow us to focus on the interlinked processes of museum work and uncover how power, structure and people affect or impede each other. *Reculturing* involves understanding the potential agency and power attached to administrators, managers, educators and visitors, as well as the particular institutional structural constraints (Varelas et al., 2015). The SAD and the power it reflects is one means to trace the dynamics of an organizational structure, while it acts either as a gateway or impediment for any organizational change.

Agency and Resistance

Changing any belief system/ideology/epistemology requires critically monitoring and transforming existing power structures (Dawson, 2019). Power inequalities (Gurian, 2009; Karim-Jaffer, 2013) generally show up in the details of division of labor, job categories, hours of work or designated salaries and also within rules, cultural norms, organizational guidelines and standards or political behavior (Oliveros et al., 2010).

The vignette provides a clear picture of the painful work-based contradiction that led to Ken's suffering. It is personally painful to be treated like a cog in the machinery. As a *blue* scaffolding educator, Ken had just learned how to listen first and respond later, to scaffold in the ZPD with minoritized families. He had watched videos of himself on the floor and gradually learned to step back and respond, rather than tell. He was fully engaged and had learned to trust the visitor to let him know what they needed. Sometimes, he noticed, he didn't need to talk at all. Then he was ordered to forget what he knew was good teaching practice by a mid-level, *purple* didactic manager. He was ordered to be 'a dragon on the floor', to take charge and to be loud, all of which he had come to experience as poor and ineffective educator teaching. His distress and his sense of diminishment were palpable signals of dynamic tensions at work. He was put in a double bind. There was no easy solution. Shortly after this, he quit his *purple* job, rather than compromise his ability to teach well.

Feinstein and Meshoulam (2014) asked whether museums treat visitors as collaborators or as clients; the same question holds for museum educators. The client view positions visitors as customers.[5] Ken was being forced by a manager to take on the client stance as an educator and to treat his visitors as customers rather than collaborators. The client view superimposes a 'one-size-fits-all', assembly-line approach, both for visitors and educators. These qualities are ill-suited for meeting equity goals, but they do align well with neoliberal-oriented efficiency practices.

We recognize Ken's experience of diminishment when he said, "They [*purple* manager] said we should be the 'dragons' on the floor". The *purple* management acted 'as if' neither visitors nor educators could think for themselves, and *both* needed scripts to achieve the 'right' content.

Ken's *purple* supervisor's reprimand was not an idle comment. Another *blue* educator in a similar situation was told she would be 'written up' if she did not comply with the demand to 'yell and tell'. The result for the *blues* working as *purples* could be fewer hours and a bad mark on their record and, of course, less pay. Such comments were meant to keep the educators in line. Here are obvious hierarchical, division of labor power dynamics acting overtly to squelch educator agency in the name of efficiency.

Ken resisted; all *blue* educators were by then aware they were challenging the status quo. They felt they were learning a better way; they had research findings to support their work! Structural constraints pushed back, though only after *blue* educators expressed an increased ability to teach (identity), an enhanced sense of agency (self-efficacy[6]) and increased capacity to reflect on their own practice (Ash et al., 2012b). The scaffolding intervention in this research study helped educators like Ken to critically challenge existing deficit[7] and neoliberal orientations and to recognize powerful and visible structural constraints. Ken's vignette allows us to identify the punishment and reward system for 'correct' work that middle managers used to control what happened on the museum floor. Looking at Ken's diminishment with a less personal lens but more sociopolitically highlights usurping and/or resisting power, a view consistent with R. Gutiérrez's (2013) argument that "researchers who have a long history of addressing anti-racism and social justice issues in mathematics have moved beyond this sociocultural view to espouse sociopolitical concepts and theories, highlighting identity and power at play" (p. 37). Here we are in the discipline of science, yet core features of power and identity cut across disciplines and contexts.

We can specifically recognize how 'work' with minoritized visitors was minimized at the museum through this example; these actions are fundamentally sociopolitical as educators pushed for equitable rather than equal treatment of visitors, and by default, for themselves (Ash et al., 2012b; Dawson, 2019). Ken, the other educators, the researchers and at least one museum administrator were all trapped in the museum's attempts at efficiency and control of identity (Apple, 2017; Golden, 2017; Harrison, 1997) and deficit ideologies.

If museum educators are expected to work effectively with minoritized visitors in a museum that reifies deficit, colonialist, genderist, racist views, then several nodes of the museum's activity system will experience tensions, which will, in turn, generate several secondary contradictions. The primary contradiction between use value (work/service) and exchange value (salary) when applied to work-based conflicts such as hours, salary or status will be exacerbated when educators engage in critical reflection (Marstine, 2017) on deficit beliefs. Because secondary contradictions emerge as tensions between the specific nodes, we can imagine that subjects (Ken and the *blues*) and rules (yell and tell) create one such contradiction. As museum educators learn to actually 'see' the dynamics of their work, they come to recognize differentials between agency and power at other institutional levels, as well (Varelas et al., 2015). To understand systems and structures in a holistic way at any level in an institution is to see them throughout the institution. Understanding a museum's settled expectations concerning visitors, teaching, learning and 'difference' leads educators to be able to resist these deficit beliefs (Ash, 2019; Ash, Lombana & Alcala, 2012a).

Generally, educators have lower positions in any museum hierarchy and lower salaries when compared with curators. This pattern holds across different types of museums, as well as geographical areas.[8] Educators are often hourly, part-time or temporary staff. Such ranking tells only part of the story. We also take into account what Nolan (2011) noted of some of her colleagues in museum education:

> Their education department offices were tucked away in museum basements or other far reaches of the institution, and they felt marginalized by their

leadership. Competition for power and resources between departments was high, and the educational mission of the institution was not lived out in practice.

(p. 1)

Beyond the details of salary, hidden offices and rank, there is the principal issue of *what to teach and how*.

Gurian (2009) commented on the tension between teaching the *canon* vs. moving to a more flexible stance. She argues that "curators have increasingly come under pressure to defend or change their traditional position by those…agitating for change…[yet, they] have been successful in their resistance" (p. 98).

The conflict over what content to teach is also ideologically informed; this question has undergone an epistemological shift in the 1980s (Prottas, 2019), which has changed the museum from "being about something to being for somebody…[in short] the public was foregrounded as…discussions of how educators should define their role in the museum began in earnest in the last years of the 1980s" (Weil, 1999, p. 3). This shifted the burden for educators to being responsive to visitors, rather than responsible for objects.

As we have seen in other chapters, essential aspects of power are often hidden. Educators and museums can and do ignore the conflicting conditions under which museum educators are asked to work and visitors are expected to learn. Teaching educators to teach equitably requires learning a heightened critical reflective capacity, as well as theoretical grounding in curriculum and research. It also requires sociopolitical savvy. Providing educators with this type of PD can strengthen any museum's ability to work with an increasingly diverse public if they are brave enough to do so. Research suggests they will encounter strong neoliberal headwinds.

Deficit/Neoliberal Ideologies in Practice

Just as do formal educational settings, museums fall prey to deficit ideology; there has been research directly uncovering and analyzing how deficit ideology informs and permeates museum practices (Coffee, 2008; Dawson, 2014a, 2014b; Harrison, 1997; Marzec, 2017; Ng et al., 2017).[9] Museums are coming to recognize that those 'new to museums' might need something different than 'one-size-fits-all' (CFM, 2009).

Obviously, "differing belief systems about how people learn inform our views about how people teach" (Barab et al., 2004). In some places, this translates to treating visitors as passive recipients, when educators engage in 'telling' at exhibits. If we think people need to be led to the content, we may tell them what we think they need to know instead of helping them to understand it in their own frame of reference. We have known this since constructivism arrived on the scene in the last century, but museums have not entirely caught up. More difficult, though, is

TABLE 8.1 Sample deficit discursive traces

—*It's too expensive to have free days; those people break the exhibits*
(McFelter, 2007, p. 61).

—*Why can't we find qualified people of color for this job?*
(Dewhurst & Hendrick, 2017, p. 102).

—*Why don't they (people of color) come here (to our museum)?*
(Feinstein & Meshoulam, 2014, p. 369).

—*Those students from (insert predominantly Black and/or Latino neighborhood) probably won't be able to focus on three artworks, so I'm just going to show two easy ones*
(Dewhurst & Hendrick, 2017, p. 102).

—*They don't know how to use the exhibits*
(Ash, in preparation).

treating educators as passive recipients in their own PD, by asking them to recite scripts.

As we examine ideologies underneath the work museum educators do, we recall Lucy Suchman's important point: "How people work is one of the best kept secrets in America" (Suchman, 1995, p. 56).[10] This certainly has in the past been true regarding museum educators' PD and work. Researchers in this growing field have broadened and deepened their analyses, yet it remains critical to understand that differences within museums concerning educator work necessarily reflect fundamental ideological contradictions.

By and large deficit views remain as pervasive at the museum educator level of museums, as they do throughout the museum. The discursive traces that follow from museum educators and administrators from Dewhurst and Hendrick (2017) and others give us a taste of how *deficit* is spoken in Table 8.1.

These discursive traces, a reflection of implicit or explicit deficit orientation, are surface markers revealing places where nodes of the activity system are in tension (Engeström & Sannino, 2010, p. 85).

Change at the Intermediate Level

McCall and Gray (2014) argued that in Great Britain, "The ambiguity surrounding policy, roles and practice also highlighted that museum workers were key agents in interpreting, using and understanding wide-ranging policy expectations" (p. 19). I have already suggested that museum educators occupy a crucial intermediate place of leverage in the museum hierarchy. Increasing attention from research projects and targeted practice recognizes the potential promise in this positioning.

Barbara Y. White discussed using an intermediate level of analysis or *middling out* for learning research design (White, 1989). In the past decade, studies have focused on educators' roles as change agents in museums (see Martin et al., 2019; Tran & Ash, 2019; Tran et al., 2019). The *blue/purple* case study working with educators, specifically focused on this intermediate level of analysis. We have argued that movement between levels within a hierarchy can be brokered at the intermediate level (museum educator practices), influencing both the administrative levels and visitor experience positively and negatively (Ash, 2014a; Ash et al., 2012a). The *blue/purple* case, an example of using the intermediate level of analysis, follows.

Blue/Purple *Case*

This *blue/purple* research intervention project was the impetus for me to reevaluate my relationship to systems analysis, reorient my theoretical framework fully to a CHAT framework, and fully integrate CHAT with critiques of deficit/othering. I reexamined fundamental questions such as "*Are educators clients or collaborators?*" (Feinstein & Meshoulam, 2014). I wanted to fully collaborate on an equal footing with educators conducting action research on their practice, and my team and I received an NSF-funded research grant to do so. The intervention project included observations of educators' existing and new ways of teaching, related work practices, supervision, evaluation and compensation (Ash, 2019; Ash & Lombana, 2012; Mai & Ash, 2012). The tensions that arose over the years-long study exemplify exactly what agents of change often experience within institutions well positioned to resist change (Ng et al., 2017). I have had to use critical reflection on the experience of the project and improve my theoretical framework to capture and make sense of what occurred.

In the case study, 12 newly hired *blue*-shirted educators met weekly. They were paid hourly; the group was composed of individuals of mixed age, ethnicity and educational backgrounds, and the group was assigned to work at a specific new hands-on, child-centered exhibition that had previously had no educators and very little signage. These *blues* worked at the same large museum as a group of a dozen existing *purple shirt* interactors, the 'regularly scheduled' floor educators for other exhibits. The *purples* wore the institutional color carried on all logos and promotional material of the museum. The *blues* wore the NSF logo and the research color. Over time, the two teams shared several members, depending on the time of year. The two groups were overseen by different vice presidents and mid-level managers. Both groups were paid an hourly wage, except for the *purple* and *blue* mid-level managers, who were salaried.

The theoretical cornerstone of the *blues* educational training and work was scaffolding in the ZPD (Vygotsky, 1978). They began their training by learning and practicing ethnographic watching and notetaking, emphasizing *noticing* visitor's existing resources, as well as how visitors were taught on the floor, both with and without educators. They met at weekly day-long meetings, practiced reflection, ethnographic note taking on the floor, watched and assessed selected video-taped examples of a spectrum of practices, as well as readings on the theory behind scaffolding theory. The goal was to understand how to best *respond* with an appropriate action pitched within the learner's ZPD. This activity required waiting and learning to listen and noting salient words and behaviors before responding. Palincsar and Brown (1984) said about working in the ZPD:

> [It] requires continuous adjustment on the part of the teacher to [the student's] current competence...on-line diagnosis that will guide her own level of participation.
>
> (p. 120)

It became apparent to the university researchers, myself included, that, as the *blue* museum educators became more involved with and responsible for their own learning, they became more agentive both for themselves and for their visitors. We were able to track how critical reflective practice changed the educators (Ash et al., 2012a). They became empowered to design new tools and strategies, and to give more power to the visitors.

Conflictual tensions mirroring Ken's began surfacing in the *blue* group's collective discourse during a regular Saturday meeting in the second half of the first year. Several *blues*, who had been subsequently hired as *purples*, were now experiencing negative interactions with *purple* management. They began sharing their unease with the group. Up to that point in meetings, the *blues* had been engaged as usual, in ethnographic note taking, viewing videos of practice (their own and others), discussing their ideas and making and revising the noticing and responding protocols and tools they used to concretize working in the ZPD. The institutional tension (secondary contradiction) between rules and subject, as well as between division of labor (hierarchy) and mediational means cracked open for everyone to see.

What Was Going Wrong?

Normally, when a case like this occurs this low in the hierarchy of an institution, the temptation is to try to sweep differences under the rug and make the best of it. The individual educators, disgruntled with the system, might think they had done something wrong. A CHAT perspective, which tracks how and where the systemic is personal, and the personal is systemic, allowed us, the university and museum researchers and *blue* educators, to address the real, larger underlying sociopolitical issues of power and identity.

Using the analytic tools of CHAT, we recognized that the subject, object, mediational means, rules and hierarchy nodes had come into tension at various times during the study. In terms of object/outcome, *purples* expected known outcomes, while *blues* expected many possible, often unknown outcomes. In terms of mediational means, *purples* relied on scripts,[11] while *blues* were expected to flexibly scaffold visitor's activities. In terms of power and hierarchy, *blues* were asked to critically reflect on their and the museum's practices (Ash, 2019; Ash & Lombana, 2012, 2019), while *purples* were punished for doing so. Through their own action research, *blues* became empowered to share power with families, embrace visitors' resources and challenge their own deficit views, and were finding a new freedom in teaching. They began to excitedly 'spread the word' to the rest of the museum.

As this transformation began to be understood at the museum management and administration levels, both subtle and overt institutional resistance emerged. The first expressions of pushback came from mid-level *purple* managers and their vice president, who all used both passive and active strategies to maintain the didactic teaching status quo (Ash, 2019). *Blues* were publicly shamed for scaffolding rather than yelling on the floor. The museum's Director remained silent, which functioned as tacit agreement.

The 'business as usual' institutional ethos overroad the study's new approach. An insistence on reasserting 'deficit beliefs' regarding both educators and visitors could be discerned in subsequent interactions within the institution (Ash, 2019). Although some of the practices developed by the *blues* migrated to the larger mainstream *purple* community, the core commitment to critical reflection, scaffolding and non-deficit views of nondominant populations did not. This is not uncommon in intervention programs; often particular teaching strategies remain, but the theoretical commitments and core principles disappear (A. Brown et al., 1993).

Expansive Learning

CHAT is designed to analyze systems. An expansive transformation approach allows CHAT analytic tools to focus on "how contradictions are approached and resolved" (Murphy & Rodriguez-Manzanares, 2008, p. 446). The *blue/purple* case provided an opportunity to do this.

In the expansive learning cycle, Figure 8.1, we see the contradiction, here the tension between scaffolding or telling was accompanied for the *blues* by the

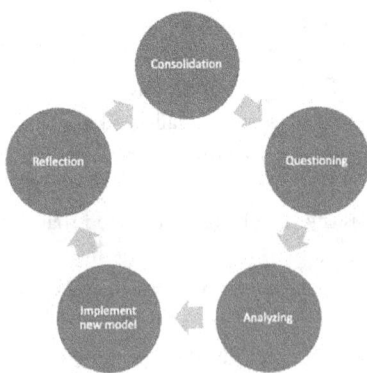

FIGURE 8.1 Expansive learning cycle

epistemic action of questioning the status quo of 'teaching as telling' (step 1); followed by analyzing existing practices, especially in serving the needs of an increasingly diverse public (step 2); followed by providing a new model (adapted and borrowed from classroom teaching) for 'teaching as scaffolding' (step 3); and, finally, applying these steps and attempting to generalize them throughout the museum (step 4).

As they became increasingly responsible for their own learning, the *blue* museum educators continued to ask questions, develop new scaffolding tools for understanding educator/visitor interactions, analyze the results and create new models and generalize their application across the museum; they followed the steps in Figure 8.1. For many systemic reasons, the museum system did not allow institutional consolidation (step 5, see Figure 8.1).

This lack of consolidation is unsurprising. Russell and Schneiderheinze (2005) noted that "contradictions may not always be resolved or lead to change" (in Murphy & Rodriguez-Manzanares, 2008, p. 447). Further, Engeström et al. (2013), in their detailed study of expansive learning cycles on three levels, revealed multiple spaces for uncertainty and creation:

> [A]nalysis shows that in a real-life formative intervention expansive learning actions emerged in the midst of a fairly large number and diversity of non-expansive learning actions…deviations from instructional intentions and plans demonstrates that expansive learning is indeed more than mere replication or imposition of the interventionists' plans. The very process is punctuated by deviations which open up space for learner agency and creation of truly new solutions and concepts.
>
> (p. 81)

It is comforting to know that deviations are normal and lead to creating new opportunities. One of those new opportunities for me has been to reframe how I view intervention research and to share these insights with others who might have perceived such outcomes as failures.

Educator Resistance

Hubbard et al. (2006) argued that even though "tensions and discontinuities are often considered harmful…they can be important opportunities for learning, both among the students and their teachers, as well as across whole school communities" (p. 98). In museums, we can see the same forces at work, as the *blue* researcher/educators increasingly came to collaborate with, rather than entertain, families from culturally and linguistically diverse, nondominant backgrounds while simultaneously enhancing their own and the families' agency and power.

The *blues* acted 'as if' the teaching in the museum, as Gutiérrez and Calabrese Barton (2015) suggested, "needed to redefine itself", and they introduced new forms to 'fix' the system. The *blues* 'resisted' the dominant teaching narrative in the museum. R. Gutiérrez (2016) noted that creative resistance to norms and strategies for interruptive insubordination are essentially political:

> [P]olitical knowledge for teaching, including understanding that all decisions are political acts, is as critical as other forms of knowledge that are normally touted as important for teachers to develop.
>
> (p. 58)

The *blues*' resistance to hegemony was quiet and professional. As part of their resistance, *blue* museum educators learned new ways to support minoritized learners while simultaneously advancing their own agency. They did not start out as a force for resistance. They began as an enthusiastic force for better teaching, explicitly using theory to inform practice. They were met with considerable institutional structural resistance. We heard from Ken. Another *blue* educator, Jamie, who also acted sometimes as a *purple*, reflected on why she thought things went wrong:

> [T]hat's where a lot of the resistance, from mostly permanent (salary/*purple*) staff really came from…
> we (*blues*) came up with this great new thing and we think you should change how you do it.

The SAD can help uncover the power dynamics these statements trace.[12] As Jamie said,

> [I]t wasn't for lack of trying…we tried a lot of different strategies, we did try and bring in people that we knew who had powerful personalities to try and get them on board.

Over time, the *blues* came to understand that they were being treated differently from the *purples* with regards to work expectations, power relationships, agency and identities.[13] Suchman (1995) discussed how workers can begin to understand underlying constraints in their work as they gain agency over some of the most important aspects of that work. The *blues* did just that, but their enhanced agency collided with institutional power.

Power Struggles

Scaffolding was not only efficacious for visitors; it was also good for the educators. As the *blues* transformed their practices, recognizing previously unrecognized visitor resources, they altered the way they assessed and facilitated visitor interactions. This was a profound behavior change for those originally expecting to be 'showmen' and tellers. Some of the *blue* museum educators had begun with the attitude that "*these families just don't know how to use the exhibits*", but they increasingly moved away from this deficit orientation and embraced the visitor resource stance (Ash et al., 2012a).

The *blues* learned and practiced increased agency and grew resistant to the institutional master narrative of deficit thinking. Most importantly, they came to understand institutional and personal power in new ways. How might we understand this? From a neoliberal business stance, the *purple's* standardized, 'one-size-fits-all' strategy was more efficient because it required less time and money than scaffolding training. Moreover, the *blues* oriented collectively rather than individually. And the public face the *blues* showed was not showman-like, so perhaps not sufficiently promotional.

This conflict showed how much the *purples* were stripped of their own agency. They were showy (but powerless) educators using standardized scripts. They were not allowed to 'spend time' with and listen to visitors. The rich reciprocal relationship the *blues* had come to experience as normal was completely missing for the *purples*.

This is eerily similar to the medical dilemma we discussed in Chapter 2, reflecting an assembly-line production system for both patients and doctors, and now visitors and educators (Apple, 2017). In medicine, the question was "*does the doctor take time to treat the patients or adhere to a time limit imposed by the system?*" One irony here is the fact that neoliberalism claims to champion individualism, while it strips away any real agency for doctors, educators, patients or visitors (Harvey, 2007).

In the museum system, the very people most in need of equitable personalized, respectful attention are those visitors new to museums. Of course, just as all learners do, when they receive more time for their questions, in slower-paced conversations, perhaps in their native language, they are engaged, knowledgeable participants. It is possible to deconstruct a 'one-size-fits-all' *efficient* system that discourages those unfamiliar with 'normed' museum culture from participating. The *blues* learned to scaffold 'listening and responding', signaled to visitors a welcoming and respect for visitor resources. This then enhanced visitor agency. It appears the existing museum ethos wanted neither visitor nor educator agency to emerge.[14] These familiar inequities, examples of so-called collateral damage, are insidious and difficult to change when administrators and board members argue that the money saved by staying with the standardized approach may help keep the museum afloat.

Many important lessons were learned through this case study, especially regarding the potential role of educators as agents of resistance and change in museums (Ash, 2019; Bevan & Xanthoudaki, 2008; Gilbert, 2016; Ng et al., 2017). These include

1. Educators actively and reflectively do reculture existing *deficit orientations* (Ash, 2019; see Chapter 7);
2. Educators can become empowered change agents (de Gregoria Kelly, 2009; Martin et al., 2019) but also must share that power with those they teach (Mai & Ash, 2012; Ash et al., 2012b);
3. Educators can recognize and counteract institutional resistance in the workplace (Varelas et al., 2015); and
4. Structural constraints need to be explicitly addressed rather than covered over by cosmetic changes (P. Moore, 2014).

These *blue* educators helped establish new hybrid spaces where marginalized visitors could share power, gain agency and jointly create ideas as collaborators (Ash, 2014b); these same qualities applied to the educators' own experience at work (Mai & Ash, 2012). Visitors responded (as measured by deeper and longer discourse) as museum educators increasingly acknowledged visitor cultural, linguistic and other resources (Ash & Lombana, 2019). In short, the *blues* successfully recultured their own teaching.

Blue/Purple Secondary Contradictions

Secondary contradictions can be resolved by "incorporating new elements into the activity to reconfigure it" (Bonneau, 2013, p. 12). *Blue* educators, in fact, were able to "question and change their practices…analyze their activities to try to solve the resulting problems…[and] lead subjects to question and change their practices" (Bonneau, 2013, p. 13).[15] As Foot (2014) suggested, "The motive for introducing a new object to an activity system is typically to find relief from one or more secondary contradictions and the tensions stemming from them" (p. 23).

The *blues* were trying to find relief from the tensions (Foot, 2014) arising in the teaching as telling activity system. The vignette with Ken reveals that the two nodes of tools and rules were in conflict. Ken was told (rules) that he could not use the new scaffolding tools (mediational means) to work with visitors and was threatened that he might not be paid as a *purple* (rules). In addition, Ken wanted to pay attention to what the visitors were saying by using a resource view, rather than a deficit view. In this, he challenged museum's covert efficiency policy by taking time with visitors and paying attention in new ways. This tension, especially as it was described by Ken, can also be situated between tools and rules. Finally, Ken's increased individual agency and the *blues'* increased collective agency ran up against strong resistance to undo any changes to the existing 'teaching as telling' system. This reflects tension between rules and the division of labor.

In Table 8.2, we note some secondary contradictions, including new elements (tertiary contradictions) introduced into the system as a result of secondary contradictions.[16]

TABLE 8.2 Secondary contractions in museum teaching from the *blue/purple* case study

Secondary contradiction	Specific conflict	Nodes involved	New element/tertiary
scaffolding vs. telling	time with visitors/ one-size-fits-all	rules/tools	reading/theory borrowing strategies from classrooms
visitor's deficit vs. resource	deficit/*other* orientation vs. resource orientation	rules/tools	fostering *belonging* with families with nondominant histories, listening/responding
agency vs. structure	individual vs. structural agency and power	division of labor/ rules	flexibility vs. specific script, 'working in the ZPD'

Figure 5.1 showed how and where some secondary contradictions may have arisen as tensions between nodes. Note the wavy lines between rules and tools, and tools and division of labor. Such representations are one way to make visible the tensions that often may seem inchoate as we work on the museum floor.

The *blue/purple* case illustrates how these seemingly innocent changes to the system affected the rules which the mid-level managers could use effectively to scuttle systemic change, as well as to maintain the existing hierarchical status quo.

Neoliberal Tendencies in Museums

The *blue/purple* case demonstrates that challenging the resistant neoliberal principles of consumerization and othering may lie beyond the purview of educators (Dailey, 2006). If not educators, though, who can exert the leverage to embrace the contradictions and expansion that lead to change? Museums are plagued by power structures that reinforce themselves, bolstered by neoliberal and deficit ideology that reinforces and is reinforced by the status quo (Coffee, 2008; Harrison, 1997).

Change can occur throughout a system but only if the arbiters of power agree to the change. In the case study, the museum's existing educational systems appeared to be threatened and became resistant when some educators appropriated a resource mindset, questioned the authority of deficit ideology and pursued critical reflection of the status quo.

If we assume a neoliberal ethos in the museum (Harrison, 1997), then we can expect that 'new ways of doing things' will usually be resisted. Further, when new ways threaten to change the status quo, managers may be loath to follow, as their own limited powers may seem to be being diminished. Neoliberalism is, first and foremost, about power and money, with a focus on the individual, which therefore resists any collective agency aimed at changing existing power structures. Underneath all of this was the real collateral damage done, notably through disregard for the quality of teaching and welcoming for minoritized populations (Apple, 2017; Harrison, 1997). If neoliberalism subverts the "goals, motivations, methods, standards of excellence and standards of freedom in education" (Ross & Gibson, 2007, p. 8), how can change happen?

As I already noted, White (1989) argued that by 'middling out' one can move between levels, for example, toward the museum administration or toward the visiting public. Other research projects in museums have found mid-level PD research in the museum workplace[17] a valid entry point for tracing how power and transformation do and do not occur (Seig & Bubp, 2010; Tran & Halversen, 2021; see also Martin et al., 2019 for a review in aquariums, science centers, museums, zoos and other settings). For this reason, this particular intervention and analysis started at the intermediate level of the system, the level of PD for educators. Museum educators are the lifeblood of many museums. Whether they can also function successfully as agents of change remains to be seen.

Summary

Any activity system such as a museum or museum education department uses mediational means, has 'objects of activity', tools, rules and divisions of labor, which are transformed across time in important and dynamic ways. To function well in their role, educators in informal settings need to understand the learning theory or mediational means they espouse and learn to reflect on how that understanding of theory impacts how they teach and learn to teach (see Chapter 7). Fundamentally different ideological views of learners, in particular, whether they are considered to be passive recipients or active participants, and deficit views of learner potential, both inform teaching practice. The *blue/purple* case study never reached the stage of stable consolidation in the expansive learning cycle (Figure 8.1); rather, it devolved into a relatively unstable hybrid state. We found individual and collective uptake of new forms of teaching activity but the expansive cycle did not eventuate in large-scale institutional change. The project program was only partially successful, as it was never fully consolidated throughout the home institution. The study highlighted several critical aspects of museum educators' work, such as the reciprocity that develops between visitors and educators when each is given the power to decide whether or how to participate collaboratively. The case study also provided a powerful opportunity for CHAT analysis of museum educator PD.

My team and I used both SAD and deficit orientations to 'see' power inequalities more clearly, using critical reflection[18] (Ash, 2019) to examine the intertwining of agency and structural constraints (Ash et al., 2012b; Varelas et al., 2015).[19] One insight emerging from these and other findings of the reflective practice movement, for both classroom teachers and museum educators, emphasizes 'not only reflecting' but following such reflection with 'concrete action' (Ash, 2019).

We cannot ensure that educators will teach well if those in power (managers, department heads, vice presidents or executive directors) do not share power with them. We have seen this repeatedly in the course of societal change. "The structure–agency dialectic exposes forces that may stifle access, participation, learning, and achievement" (Varelas et al., 2015, p. 443).[20]

Appendix 8.1: Levels of Interaction

It is difficult to affect change at any one level of activity in a museum without also activating change at other levels. At least three levels of analysis were involved in the *blue/purple* study; each level was part of and informed the larger system: top-level administration, mid-level managers, and floor staff who work directly with visitors.

Educator/Family Interactions

Educators first *noticed* learner behaviors as family groups interacted at one of four selected exhibits, observing the learner's level of activity and engagement, as well as how comfortable they appeared in the exhibit space, the topic of conversation, how they approached the content, as well as who led the interaction in the family group. *Blue* educators were asked to observe visitor activity as ethnographers as a necessary precursor to recognizing or "noticing" the subtle cues provided by families. This was followed by designing and selecting scaffolding strategies to respond to the diagnosed needs of the family. Overall, it appears that an ethos of careful listening and scaffolding encouraged educators and families to acculturate to and empower each other, without expectations of assimilation.

Educator/Administration Interactions

The two education teams had separate mid-level managers who led their teams differently, using specific markers of power. The purples had rules and scripts for 'how to teach' at exhibits (client stance). The *blues* management agenda had a more flexible collaborative team structure; the *blues* were co-researchers of museum practice, and most importantly, joined in the work as critical researchers of their own practices (collaborative stance).

Appendix 8.2: Museum Educator History

Prottas (2019) argued that museum education started with the French Revolution:

> The opening of the Louvre in Paris in 1793 marked a dramatic democratization of access to art, when the possessions of the former royal family were transferred to the public and made accessible. Sternfeld suggests that the Louvre's place in the history of modern museums highlights a tension within the institutions that continues to this day.

On the one hand, the museum emerged as part of a nationalistic, colonialist display of power.… But on the other hand, the act of making once-private art objects the property of and accessible to all citizens marked a radical critique of power and claim to access for all. (p. 3)

Notes

1. And, as in any sociocultural activity system, I incorporated people, mediational means, object/outcome, rules, division of labor and community (Ash, 2019).
2. The 12 new *blue*-shirted educators (paid staff of mixed age, ethnicity and educational backgrounds) worked at a specific hands-on, child-centered exhibit that had in the past had no active educators and minimal signage. A second group, the *purple* shirts, had been previously taught to teach didactically. Over time, the two groups, each about 12–15 people, shared several educators, at least for a short time.
3. Interpret, lecture, explain, demonstrate, facilitate guide, scaffold, etc.
4. These are several current active areas of scholarship—for example, Gutiérrez & Vossoughi (2010); Morales-Doyle et al. (2020).
5. Just like schools use standardized tests, using standardized scripts. As Golden argues, "[L]earning is increasingly governed by discourses of human capital and efficiency…[and] loss regarding teacher agency and relationships" (Golden, 2017, p. 1).
6. These were reflected by diagnostic discursive manifestations in Ken's and other educators' speech (Engeström & Sannino, 2011).

7 Anti-deficits have been examined within a variety of theoretical frameworks, including but not limited to issues of: cultural competence, deconstructing racism, inclusion, critical reflection (Ash, 2019; Coffee, 2008) and enhancing diversity more generally by engaging with racism (Dawson, 2014 a & b; Kendi, 2019; P. Moore, 2014).
8 Salaries average $38,619 for educators and $65,241 for curators in the United States (Glassdoor, 2020). In France, educators earn 32,597 €. The average museum curator salary in Japan is ¥7,019,930 ($67,124; Salary Expert, 2020).
9 Some scholars are beginning to use critical race theory in research in informal settings (P. Moore, 2014) to unpack some underlying belief systems at play.
10 While the focus here is professional development, we sometimes touch on how closely intertwined museum educators' PD is with other factors affecting how museum educators actually teach on the museum floor. Tran (2008) suggests that earlier museum researchers were focused on the students' and classroom teachers' experiences, developing curriculum and assessment for field trip experiences rather than focusing on museum educators (docents, explainers, interactors, etc.; p. 135).
11 We know this from considerable pre-intervention interviews, video and ethnographic observation.
12 Note that while the museum advertised as a hands-on science center, implying equal opportunity to learn at exhibits, this did not appear to be the case in actual practice.
13 Importantly, the executive director also did not advocate for the new pedagogies based on equity. He deferred to the *purple* leaders, even though the intervention brought in a good deal of (temporary) money to the institution.
14 Gutierrez and Barton suggest "[a] shift from 'fixing' the individual to re-mediating and transforming the functional system [which] is key to reimagining new forms".
15 Engeström (2005) further suggested that secondary contradictions "seek new ways to visualize and organize work in order to solve the tensions people experience" (p. 78).
16 Foot (2014) argued, "It is important to note that secondary contradictions exist *a priori* to and independently of tertiary contradictions. Tertiary contradictions…arise when the object of a more 'culturally advanced' activity (Engeström, 1987) is introduced into that system. The motive for introducing a new object to an activity system is typically to find relief from one or more secondary contradictions and the tensions stemming from them" (p. 23).
17 *The Reflective Museum Practitioner* (Martin et al., 2019) analyzed combined efforts to effect long-lasting change in museum educators and institutional culture. The institutions studied cut across a wide swath of scientific interests.
18 There are now numerous reflective practice PD programs (see Martin et al., 2019), some of which can work at least indirectly to recalculate power inequalities through enhancing museum educators' agency (see also Ward, 2016).
19 As before, much of the theory and practice undergirding such research has come from formal education, which teacher PD had focused on for several decades.
20 The structure agency dialectic as a theoretical frame has been prominent in formal schooling (JRST special issue, 2015) and only recently migrated to informal settings.

References

Achiam, M., & Holmegaa, H. T. (2017). Informal science education and gender inclusion. In L. S. Heuling (Eds.), *Embracing the other. How the inclusive classroom brings fresh ideas to science and education* (pp. 32–40). Flensburg University Press.

Agrawal, N. (2016). *Curator Kimberly drew on black art, social media and taking selfies in museums*. Broadly. https://broadly.vice.com/en_us/article/evgd9e/kimberly-drew-museum-mammy-interview.

Anderson, D., Cosson, A., & McIntosh, L. (2015). *Informing the practice of museum educators: Diverse audiences, challenging topics, and reflective praxis*. Sense Publishers. https://doi.org/10.1007

Apple, M. W. (Eds.). (2017). *Cultural and economic reproduction in education: Essays on class, ideology and the state* (Vol. 53). Routledge.

Archer, L. (2008). The impossibility of minority ethnic educational 'success'? An examination of the discourses of teachers and pupils in British secondary schools. *European Educational Research Journal*, 7(1), 89–107. https://doi.org/10.2304/eerj.2008.7.1.89

Ash, D. (2014a). Positioning informal learning research in museums within activity theory: From theory to practice and back again. *Curator: The Museum Journal*, 57, 107–118. http://dx.doi.org/10.1111/cura.12054

Ash, D. (2014b). Creating hybrid spaces for talk: Humor as a resource learners bring to informal learning context. *National Society for the Study of Education*, 113(2), 535–555.

Ash, D. (2019). Reflective Practice in Action research: Moving beyond the "standard model". In L. Martin, L. Tran, & D. Ash (Eds.), *The reflective museum practitioner: Expanding practice in science museums* (pp. 23–38). Routledge. https://doi.org/10.4324/9780429025242-3

Ash, D. (in preparation). Expansive learning in a large urban museum: Contradictions in teaching and learning, power, resistance, and transformation. To be submitted to *Cultural Studies in Science Education*.

Ash, D., Brown, C., Hunter. L., & Kluger-Bell, B. (2009). Becoming hybrid experts: Inquiry as professional development for college science faculty. *Journal of College Science Teaching*, 38(6), 68–76.

Ash D., & Lombana J. (2012) Methodologies for reflective practice and museum educator research. In D. Ash, J. Rahm, L. M. Melber (Eds.), *Putting theory into practice. New directions in mathematics and science education* (pp. 29–52, Vol. 25). SensePublishers. https://doi.org/10.1007/978-94-6091-964-0_4

Ash, D., & Lombana, J. (2019) The reflects model of action: Reflective practice for collaborating with non-dominant populations. In L. Martin, L. U. Tran, & D. Ash (Eds.), *The reflective museum practitioner* (pp. 165–181). Routledge.

Ash, D., Lombana, J., & Alcala, L. (2012a). Changing practices, changing identities as museum educators: From didactic telling to scaffolding in the ZPD. In E. Davidsson & A. Jakobsson (Eds.), *Sociocultural theory and museum practices* (pp. 23–44). Sense Publishers.

Ash, D., Rahm, J., & Melber, L. (Eds.). (2012b). *Putting theory into practice: Methodologies for informal learning research*. Sense Publishers.

Barab, S. A., Evans, M. A., & Baek, E.-O. (2004). Activity theory as a lens for characterizing the participatory unit. In D. H. Jonassen (Ed.), *Handbook of research on educational communications and technology* (Vol. 2, pp. 199–214). Lawrence Erlbaum Associates Publishers.

Bevan, B., & Michalchick, V. (2013). *Where it gets interesting: Competing models of STEM learning after school*. Afterschool Matters. http://www.niost.org/pdf/afterschoolmatters/asm_2013_17_spring/ASM_2013_spring_1.pdf

Bevan, B., & Xanthoudaki, M. (2008). Professional development for museum educators. *Journal of Museum Education*, 33(2), 107–119. https://doi.org/10.1080/10598650.2008.11510592

Bonneau, C. (2013, September 1–28). *Contradictions and their concrete manifestations: An activity theoretical analysis of the intra-organizational co-configuration of open-source software*. Proceedings of the 29th EGOS Colloquium, Montreal, Canada.

Brown, A. L., Ash, D., Rutherford, M., Nakagawa, K., Gordon, A., & Campione, J. C. (1993). Distributed expertise in the classroom. In G. Salomon (Ed.), *Distributed cognitions: Psychological and educational considerations* (pp. 188–288). Cambridge University Press.

Center for the Future of Museums. (2009). *Demographic transformation and the future of museums.* American Alliance of Museums. http://www.aam-us.org/resources/center-for-the-future-of-museums/demographic-

Center for the Future of Museums. (2010). *Demographic transformation and the future of museums.* American Alliance of Museums. https://www.aam-us.org/wp-content/uploads/2017/12/Demographic-Change-and-the-Future-of-Museums.pdf

Coffee, K. (2008). Cultural inclusion, exclusion and the formative roles of museums. *Museum Management and Curatorship, 23*(3), 261–279. https://doi.org/10.1080/09647770802234078

Dailey, T. L. (2006). *Museums in the age of Neoliberalism: A multi-sited analysis of science and health museums.* [Master's thesis, Georgia State University]. ScholarWorks. https://scholarworks.gsu.edu/anthro_theses/20

Dawson, E. (2014a). "Not designed for us": How science museums and science centers socially exclude low-income, minority ethnic groups. *Science Education, 98*(6), 981–1008.

Dawson, E. (2014b). Equity in formal science education: Developing an access and equity framework for science museums and science centres. *Studies in Science Education, 50*(2), 209–247.

Dawson, E. (2019). *Equity, exclusion and everyday science learning: The experiences of minoritised groups.* Routledge.

Dawson, E., Archer, L., Seakins, A., Godec, S., DeWitt, J., King, H., Mau, A., & Nomikou, E. (2020). Selfies at the science museum: exploring girls' identity performances in a science learning space. *Gender and Education, 32*(5), 664–681. https://doi.org/10.1080/09540253.2018.1557322

de Gregoria Kelly, L. A. (2009). Action research as professional development for zoo educators. *Visitor Studies, 12*(1), 30–46.

Dewhurst, M., & Hendrick, K. (2017). Identifying and transforming racism in museum education. *Journal of Museum Education, 42*(2), 102–107. https://doi.org/10.1080/10598650.2017.1311745

DiMaggio, P. J., & Powell, W. W. (Eds.). (1991). *The new institutionalism in organizational analysis.* University of Chicago Press.

Engeström, Y. (1987). *Learning by expanding: An activity-theoretical approach to developmental research.* Helsinki: Orienta-Konsultit. http://lchc.ucsd.edu/mca/Paper/Engestrom/Learning-by-Expanding.pdf

Engeström, Y. (2005). *The future of activity theory: A rough draft.* http://lchc.ucsd.edu/mca/Paper/ISCARkeyEngestrom.pdf

Engeström, Y., Rantavuori, J., & Kerosuo, H. (2013). Expansive learning in a library: Actions, cycles and deviations from instructional intentions. *Vocations and Learning, 6*(1), 81–106. https://doi.org/10.1007/s12186-012-9089-6

Engeström, Y., & Sannino, A. (2010). Studies of expansive learning: Foundations, findings and future challenges. *Educational Research Review, 5*, 1–24. http://dx.doi.org/10.1016/j.edurev.2009.12.002

Engeström, Y., & Sannino, A. (2011). Discursive manifestations of contradictions in organizational change efforts. *Journal of Organizational Change Management, 24*(3), 368–387. https://doi.org/10.1108/09534811111132758

Feinstein, N. W., & Meshoulam, D. (2014). Science for what public? Addressing equity in American science museums and science centers. *Journal of Research in Science Teaching, 51*(3), 368–394. https://doi.org/10.1002/tea.21130

Foot, K. A. (2014). Cultural-historical activity theory: Exploring a theory to inform practice and research. *Journal of Human Behavior in the Social Environment, 24*(3), 329–347. doi:10.1 080/10911359.2013.831011

Garibay, C. (2009). Latinos, leisure values, and decisions: Implications for informal science learning and engagement. *The Informal Learning Review, 94*, 10 –13.

Gilbert, L. (2016). "Loving, knowing ignorance": A problem for the educational mission of museums. *Curator: The Museum Journal, 59*(2), 125–140. https://doi.org/10.1111/cura.12153

Glassdoor. (2020). *Museum educators salaries*. https://www.glassdoor.com/Salaries/museum-educator-salary-SRCH_KO0,15.htm

Golden, N. A. (2017). Narrating neoliberalism: Alternative education teachers' conceptions of their changing roles. *Teaching Education*. http://doi.org/10.1080/10476210.2017.1331213

Golding, V. (2016). *Learning at the museum frontiers: Identity, race & power*. London: Routledge.

Gurian, E. H. (2009). Curator: From soloist to impresario. In C. Fiona & L. Kelly (Eds.), *Hot topics, public culture, museums* (pp. 95–111). Cambridge Scholars Publishing.

Gutiérrez, K., & Vossoughi, S. (2010). Lifting off the ground to return anew: Mediated praxis, transformative learning and social design experiments. *Journal of Teacher Education, 61*(1–2), 100–117.

Gutiérrez, K. D., & Calabrese Barton, A. (2015). The possibilities and limits of the structure–agency dialectic in advancing science for all. *Journal of Research in Science Teaching, 52*(4), 574–583.

Gutiérrez, R. (2013). The sociopolitical turn in mathematics education. *Journal for Research in Mathematics Education, 44*(1), 37–68. https://doi.org/10.5951/jresematheduc.44.1.0037

Gutiérrez, R. (2016). Strategies for creative insubordination in mathematics teaching. *Teaching for Excellence and Equity in Mathematics, 7*(1), 52–60.

Harris, C. I. (1995). Whiteness as property. In K. Crenshaw, N. Gotanda, G. Peller, & K. Thomas (Eds.), *Critical race theory* (pp. 276–291). The New Press.

Harrison, J. (1997). Museums as agencies of neocolonialism in a postmodern world. *Studies in Cultures, Organizations and Societies, 3*(1), 41–65. https://doi.org/10.1080/10245289708523487

Harvey, D. (2005). *A brief history of neoliberalism*. Oxford University Press.

Harvey, D. (2007). Neoliberalism as creative destruction. *The ANNALS of the American Academy of Political and Social Science, 610*(1), 21–44. https://doi.org/10.1177/0002716206296780

Hein, G. (1991, October 15–22). *The museum and the needs of people* [Conference presentation]. CECA (International Committee of Museum Educators) Conference, Jerusalem, Israel. https://www.exploratorium.edu/education/ifi/constructivist-learning

Hein, G. (1998, 2015). *Learning in the museum* (museum meanings). Routledge.

Henry, B. (2006). The educator at the crossroads of institutional change. *Journal of Museum Education, 31*(3), 223–232. https://doi.org/10.1080/10598650.2006.11510549

Hohenstein, J., & Moussouri, T. (2018). *Museum learning theory and research as tools for enhancing practice*. Routledge.

Hubbard, L., Mehan, H., & Stein, M. K. (2006). *Reform as learning: School reform, organizational culture and community politics in San Diego*. Routledge.

Jennings, G., & Jones-Rizzi, J. (2017). Museums, white privilege, and diversity: A systemic perspective. *Dimensions, 18*(5), 66–67. ASTC. https://nemanet.org/files/9615/0228/7672/Dimensions-DiversitySpecial-Edition_JenningsJonesRizzi.pdf.

Karim-Jaffer, S. (2013). *Making power visible for museum educators: A theoretical framework for multicultural museum education*. Bank Street College of Education. http://educate.bankstreet.edu/independent-studies/129

Kendi, I. X. (2019). *How to be an antiracist*. One World.
Mai, T., & Ash, D. (2012) Tracing our methodological steps: Making meaning of families' hybrid "figuring out" practices at science museum exhibits. In D. Ash, L. Martin, L. U. Tran, & D. Ash, (2019). *The reflective museum practitioner*. Routledge.
Marstine, J. (2017). *Critical practice: Artists, museums, ethics*. Routledge.
Martin, L., Tran, L. U., & Ash, D. (2019). *The reflective museum practitioner*. Routledge.
Marzec, C. (2017). *Literature review: From deficit to dialogue and action: Natural history public engagement for a rapidly changing planet*. https://doi.org/10.13140/RG.2.2.26292.35205
McCall, V., & Gray, C. (2014). Museums and the 'new museology': Theory, practice and organisational change. *Museum Management and Curatorship, 29*(1), 19–35. https://doi.org/10.1080/09647775.2013.869852
McFelter, G. (2007). The cost of free. *Museum News, 86*(1), 60–67.
Moore, B. (2013). *Understanding the ideology of normal: Making visible the ways in which educators think about students who seem different*. [Unpublished doctoral dissertation]. University of Colorado.
Moore, P. (2014, January 20). *The danger of the "D" Word: Museums and diversity*. The Incluseum. https://incluseum.com/2014/01/20/the-danger-of-the-d-word-museums-and-diversity/
Morales-Doyle, D., Varelas, M., Segura, D., & Bernal-Munera, M. (2020). Access, dissent, ethics, and politics: Pre-service teachers negotiating conceptions of the work of teaching science for equity. *Cognition and Instruction, 39*(1), 35–64. https://doi.org/10.1080/07370008.2020.1828421
Murphy, E., & Rodriguez-Manzanares, M. A. (2008). Using activity theory and its principle of contradictions to guide research in educational technology. *Australasian Journal of Educational Technology, 24*(4). https://doi.org/10.14742/ajet.1203
Ng, W., Ware, S. M., & Greenberg, A. (2017). Activating diversity and inclusion: A blueprint for museum educators as allies and change makers. *Journal of Museum Education, 42*(2), 142–154. https://doi.org/10.1080/10598650.2017.1306664
Nolan, T. R. (2011). The leadership practice of museum educators. *Dissertations, 99*. https://digitalcommons.nl.edu/diss/99
Oliveros, M. E., Halliday, S. V., Posada, M. M., & Bachmann, R. (2010). Contradictions and power play in service encounters: an activity theory approach. *Cadernos EBAPE.BR, 8*(2), 353–369. https://doi.org/10.1590/s1679-39512010000200011
Palincsar, A. S., & Brown, A. L. (1984). The reciprocal teaching of comprehension fostering and comprehension monitoring activities. *Cognition and Instruction, 1*, 117–175.
Patrick, P. (2017). *Preparing informal science educators: Perspectives from science communication and education*. Springer Nature.
Piqueras, J., & Achiam, M. (2019). Science museum educators' professional growth: Dynamics of changes in research–practitioner collaboration. *Science Education, 103*(2), 389–417. https://doi.org/10.1002/sce.21495
Prottas, N. (2019). Where does the history of museum education begin? *Journal of Museum Education, 44*(4), 337–341. doi:10.1080/10598650.2019.1677020
Ross, E. W., & Gibson, R. (Eds.) (2007). *Neoliberalism and education reform*. Hampton Press.
Russell, D. L., & Schneiderheinze, A. (2005). Understanding innovation in education using activity theory. *Educational Technology & Society, 8*(1), 38–53.
Salary Expert. (2020). *Museum curator salary Japan*. Salary Expert. https://www.salaryexpert.com/salary/job/museum-curator/japan.
Seig, M. T., & Bubp, K. (2010). The culture of empowerment: Driving and sustaining change at Conner Prairie. *Curator: The Museum Journal, 51*(2), 203–220. https://doi.org/10.1111/j.2151-6952.2008.tb00306.x

Seo, M. G., & Creed, W. E. D. (2002).Institutional contradictions, praxis, and institutional change: A dialectical perspective. *The Academy of Management Review, 27*(2), 222–247. doi:10.2307/4134353

Sternfeld, N. (2018). *Das radikaldemokratische Museum*. De Gruyter.

Suchman, L. (1995). Making work visible. *Communications of the ACM, 38*(9), 56–64. doi:10.1145/223248.223263

Tolbert, S., Spurgin, C., & Ash, D. (in preparation). 'Staying with the trouble': Praxis crisis in science teacher education for emergent bilingual learners.

Toohey, J., & Wolins, I. (1993). Beyond the turf battles: Creating effective curator-educator partnerships. *The Journal of Museum Education, 18*(1), 4–6. http://www.jstor.org/stable/40478946

Tran, L. U., & Halversen, C. (2021). *Reflecting on practice for STEM educators: A guide for museums, out-of-school, and other informal settings*. Routledge.

Tran, L. U., Halversen, C., Werner-Avidon, M., & Trahan, L. (2019). Reflecting on practice. In L. Martin, L. U. Tran & D. Ash (Eds.), *The reflective museum practitioner* (pp. 7–12). Routledge.

Tran, L. U., & King, H. (2007).The professionalization of museum educators:The case in science museums. *Museum Management and Curatorship, 22*(2), 131–149.

Tran, L. U. (2008). The professionalization of educators in science museums and centers. *JCOM: Journal of Science Communication, 7*. https://doi.org/10.22323/2.07040302

Varelas, M., Settlage, J., & Mensah, F. M. (2015). Explorations of the structure–agency dialectic as a tool for framing equity in science education. *Journal of Research in Science Teaching, 52*(4), 439–447.

Vygotsky, L. S. (1978). *Mind in society*. Harvard University Press.

Ward, S. J. (2016). *Understanding contradictions in times of change: A CHAT analysis in an art museum*. [Doctoral dissertation, University of Washington]. ResearchWorks Archive. http://hdl.handle.net/1773/37091

Weick, K. (1979). *The social psychology of organizing* (2nd ed.) Addison-Wesley.

Weil, S. E. (1999). From being about something to being for somebody:The ongoing transformation of the American Museum. *Daedalus, 128*, 229–258.

White, B. Y. (1989). *The role of intermediate abstraction in understanding science and mathematics. 11th Annual conference of the Cognitive Science Society*, University of Michigan.

9

HOW DO WE RECULTURE AN INSTITUTION WHILE OLD SYSTEMS ARE STILL IN PLACE?

Overview

Throughout this book, I have recommended *reculturing* at multiple levels of analysis within museum activity systems. I have emphasized using dialectical logic, founded on sociocultural principles, for reculturing at each level because this allows us to capture the many competing views that underlie issues regarding museum finances, story, teaching, learning, objects, and demographics.

In Chapter 1, I introduced the major themes of reculturing such as equity and social justice, comparing them to common views of diversity and equality and positioning them relative to competing ideologies. They serve as lenses through which to view the challenges in modern museums. Reculturing focuses on change from the '*inside out*', what I call *inreach* instead of expecting those outside the museum to change, what is called *outreach*.

In Chapter 2, I delineated the four theoretical underpinnings. CHAT, the main theory I offer for the analysis of successful reculturing, provides an analytic tool for complex museum systems and for tackling deeply embedded contradictions. CHAT is the only current theoretical framework that carries this particular holistic vision of change, or what Engeström has called 'expansive learning' (Engeström, 1987, 2016). I introduced the SAD as a theoretical lens for studying agency and resistance in relation to power and structure, as mutually constitutive activity. I critiqued deficit ideologies as they apply to museum systems and described the roles deficit and neoliberal ideologies play in stifling challenge through individualism, efficiency commodification and competition.

In Chapter 3, I described the ways some of the deep ideological differences that create competing interpretations of shifting demographics. I clarified how we can protect ourselves from lies told with statistics as scare tactics and as invisibility cloaks over power dynamics. Chapter 4 positioned finances as a way to expose ideological conflicts in museums, using entrance fees as a focus. I reviewed several alternative pricing models currently under consideration.

In Chapters 5 and 6, I explored how highly contextualized and historically bound our understandings of both narratives and objects are. I exposed how strong, ideological biases provide a rationale for 'normal' as they influence the meaning of narratives, as well as the treatment of objects.

In Chapters 7 and 8, I reviewed museum views of learning, and its fundamental connection to teaching, as well as the connection between certain teaching modalities and *othering* and *neoliberalism*. I have throughout attempted to call into question what once seemed *settled*.

I have traced the dynamics of power in each chapter, and I wish to discuss this further here. I have come to understand that in order to study change in a systemic and systematic way, we must draw upon larger theories of transformation. Because CHAT encourages expansion toward aspects we may not have known before, this more generative theoretical stance allows us to anticipate and thus make space for as-yet unknown outcomes. I have argued that a sociopolitical stance underpins reculturing as defined here, exposing the roots of neoliberalism and deficit orientations.

THE IDEOLOGY OF NORMAL

Heaton (2014) stated in "Museums and Racism: Are Museums Accidental Racists?",

> I have had more than a few conversations with senior persons in public institutions who have said to me, in effect,
> Our programs, our collections, everything that we do is intended for all comers.
> We are certainly not programming for white audiences. All are welcome and welcomed at our doors. Is that not enough? What else must we do?"
> They seem to be asking,
> Isn't the status quo, in terms of our product and my color blindness, sufficient?"
>
> (paras 2, 8–9)

Similarly, Dewhurst and Hendrick (2017) asked the museum educators engaged in an anti-racist workshop to raise their hands if they had ever heard one of the following statements:

> "She's just not the right, um, fit here."
> "Here's a work by the Black artist Jacob Lawrence. And here is another work by the famous artist Henri Matisse."

> "Why can't we find any qualified people of color for this job?"
>
> "You know how it is; she was just so aggressive in our educator meetings."
>
> "Those students from (insert predominantly Black and/or Latino neighborhood) probably won't be able to focus on three artworks, so I'm just going to show two easy ones."
>
> Looking around, the authors said that the auditorium was filled with raised hands.
>
> (p. 102)
>
> Heaton was asking, "So are museums [just] exclusionary or racist?" Perhaps we can wonder if it matters which is true. The experience of unintentional racism (we didn't mean it…) hits just as hard as if it were intentional. It is part of the myriad culturally-normed microaggressions all persons of color experience daily (Sue et al., 2007).

Introduction

After reviewing the myriad aspects of what constitutes a museum, I hope we can now more fully appreciate how challenging it is to actually *reculture* museums in substantive ways. I suggest reculturing works best from the '*inside out*' (*inreach*) with a focus on changing museum structure, policies and practices, instead of expecting those outside the museum to change (*outreach*).

I have engaged in a sociocultural, historical analysis of many critical areas of museology, exposing how ideologies define museum norms. I have touched on a number of contradictions that help *resist* and/or support 'business as usual', discussed power at multiple levels of analysis, and I have explored contradictions concerning money, demographics, narrative, objects, learning and teaching. All of these are the topics of interest that need to be explored in large and small experiments in the field in order to help move museums more gracefully into the 21st century. There is a need for a theory of change that can meaningfully emphasize equity, institutional norms, historicity, ideological commitments, power dynamics and critical reflection.

I have argued that deep ideological differences cannot be rectified by temporary solutions.

We cannot be surprised that there are inequities in museums when we see that inequities are ubiquitous in all the institutions and structures of our world. We may not be surprised that attempts to deal with inequity have been piecemeal, and not yet aligned with institutional *reculturing*. We can no longer be surprised that demographics are rapidly shifting. It may be surprising, or at least disheartening, however, to observe how these demographic shifts have served *deficit/othering/racist* views. *Deficit/othering* keeps the emphasis on the *other* who are expected to assimilate and serves forces that resist the construction of hybrid spaces of communication and experiences of belonging (Gutiérrez et al., 2009; Powell & Menendian, 2017). This hybridity (Ash & Race, 2021), as it becomes more common, will more accurately reflect the multivoicedness we expect in activity systems.

With the help of CHAT as my main theory, adding the structure/agency dialectic, and critiques of neoliberal and *deficit/othering* orientations, I intend in this last chapter to connect and synthesize the interconnected and emergent themes of the chapters of this book. I aim 'to hold up the mirror' to museums, to show the relationships between issues not often treated relationally in museology. CHAT has proven itself a versatile tool, helping us untangle how, and under what circumstances, contradictions intertwine and operate reciprocally. We can use the results of these analyses to promote the kind of transformation that leads to expansive museum systems. Ken's (from Chapter 8) experience showed that CHAT can analyze the personal as well as institutional experiences of power dynamics.

Specific contradictions, defined as "historically accumulating structural tensions within and between activity systems" (Engeström, 2009, p. 57), were the focal point of every chapter. Contradictions are not positioned as insurmountable problems, nor are they signals of failure. They don't respond to 'quick fixes' (Foot, 2014). Rather, identifying and studying tensions provides opportunities to formulate and understand secondary contradictions as they emerge. Secondary contradictions provide the visible instantiation of the primary contradiction at work and set in motion tertiary and quaternary contradictions. They are starting points for imagining change, especially with regard to equity, inclusion, and socially just, culturally accurate and historically bound policies and practices. I hope museums can learn to welcome them as opportunities for facilitating change.

CHAT has opened the door to a cyclical theory of expansive learning involving a multi-dimensional, systemic approach that includes both psychological motives and tools, as well as the ever-present dynamics of power, money, culture and history. With CHAT we can analyze complex and evolving institutions (Foot, 2014, p. 2).

I have deliberately posed real-world questions with no easy answers. In these past chapters, we have brought attention to tensions generated between nodes and across time that bring the contradiction (and the dialectical relationship) to light. The primary contradiction between use and exchange is old and ever present. Many of the secondary contradictions we also have studied are currently being generated, expanded and/or transformed but some have also been studied for decades using other frameworks (Bennett, 1995, 2013; Dubin, 1999; Gurian, 1995; James, 2013). Bennett (1995), for example, used a Foucauldian analysis to examine power in museums. I hope this book is a worthy companion to Bennett's powerful analysis.

I have applied *othering* and *deficit* orientation, and neoliberalism at several levels: at the institutional levels, examining Board rooms and hiring practices; at the intermediate level, looking at exhibit design and professional development for museum educators: and, at the personal, day-to-day level exploring how family visitors learn and have fun. All these levels have been explored relative to the broader system of the museum as a whole.

Finally, I have argued throughout that all systemic museum issues cannot be separated from the tenets of neoliberal principles of individualism, commodification and competition that currently undergird our society; thus, the sociopolitical is organically interlinked with the sociocultural.

Replacing Old With New While the Old Is Still in Place

> *"How will museums change if all they know is 'business as usual', 'norms' and 'settled expectations?'"*

This conundrum has been addressed by museologists for decades with many suggestions, but little comprehensive theory. Exactly 25 years ago, Elaine H. Gurian (1995) edited a chapter called "Moving the Museum" in *Institutional Trauma: Major Changes in Museums and Its Effect on Staff*.[1] She addressed many of the same contradictions discussed in this book, arguing for "collective institutional coping mechanisms" for the traumas or crises of the time" (p. 19).

Those who have written about institutional change in museums suggest that institutions are remarkably resistant to change. Engeström (1999) anticipated systemic contradictions and proposed expansive learning cycles in part to analyze change. He summarized common organizational upheaval, saying, "When whole collective activity systems, such as work processes and organizations, need to redefine themselves, traditional modes of learning are not enough" (p. 21). Elieli and Gould (1995), argued that any crisis

> generally brings in its wake a period marked by disorganization and confusion, general sense of ineffectiveness, in particular in relation to the specific solution of the crisis.... People in the system long to return to the previous familiar routine. The knowledge that there is no going back to the point of departure, other than by paying the price of ignoring reality is very painful.
> (p. 29)

According to CHAT, such trauma and disruption are both normal and predictable. Using tools that allow systematic analysis, we may be able to accept and facilitate transformation of museums as whole systems. This may soften the expected disruptions, especially when participants experience transformative agency by being involved in the change (Stetsenko, 2019).

When we can consider disruptions to be expected aspects of expansive learning, we can stay open to "learning what is not there yet" (Engeström, 2016), rather than expecting a settled or fixed answer. What is not there yet may be answers to questions concerning *deficit* ideologies, *othering*, and possibly new teaching or curating strategies. There might be multiple possible stories about the artifacts in museums that represent culture, history and social structures. Taken together, *learning what is not there yet* and *following the dialectic* offer a pathway toward transformed museum policy and practice.

In the following sections, I explore four overarching themes museums may wish to consider as they seek to reculture.

Staying With Complexity/Resistance

We have witnessed resistance to change in museums in each chapter, typically encountering neoliberal or *deficit* rationalizations for maintaining the status quo. I argue that complexity that does not rely "on simple and static categorizations" (Vossoughi & Gutiérrez, 2014, p. 603) is an essential ingredient in trying to transform systems. Complexity's opposite, simplicity, is the essence of the 'quick fix', and simplicity does not work within the inherently sociopolitical, historically bound,[2] socioculturally rich world of museums. Gurian (2019) argued for complexity in museums:

> [W]e have…an obligation, to aid in reestablishing a more complex and nuanced dialogue, by revamping our conventions of language and content presentation so that audiences, while still trusting in our veracity, will learn to expect density in public dialogue.[3]
>
> (para. 12)

Vossoughi and Gutiérrez (2014) similarly suggested we

> move away from assertive simplicity…problems are complicated, their solutions intertwined, estimated, and cumulative…beyond reductive dichotomies…[and move] toward methods that focus on the multiple activity systems.
>
> (p. 604)

Gurian (2019) also argued, "Exploring complexity theory in museums is a form of subtle political resistance. Resistance here means going against the dominant narrative of our times, especially when it is simplistic. Resistance is complex" (para. 18). An example from Jones-Rizzi and Mann (2020), who discussed racism and museums, illustrates why change is so hard:

> [Within] a group of community advisors who represented a number of groups we wanted to attract…one of the advisors who was of African descent commented that an exhibition in the museum was "hung white".
>
> (para. 2)

The pervasiveness of a European American white ethos points out how deep our reflections and analyses need to go. Most curators are white, and they develop, interpret and curate 'whitely'. This museum asked for feedback and received it distilled from complex and harsh lived experience. Jones-Rizzi & Mann (2020) have reminded us that

> change is hard—anything worth doing usually is…[so resist taking] the path of least resistance.… We need to stop making excuses: [such as] "That's not

how we do things." "That's not their role." "This is too disruptive."... None of this is new. These conversations have been happening for decades.... [These times may be different, because] emboldened disruptors are taking this work to a new level.... We are going to experience growing pains as we continue to move through these issues and define solutions.... We will make mistakes.

(para. 5)

Such 'emboldened disruptors' or resistors are essential in these turbulent times, especially when the instinct may be to hold steady to what we already know. Gurian (2019) noted that "research shows that going from simple to complex is not automatic, and requires training and experience" (para 17). This is true for all levels of the museum: administrators, managers, educators and visitors. Regarding visitors, she echoed Poole (2014), asking for educators to expect that "our audience will grow to expect cogency, complexity, creativity, non-conformity and overt dialogue" rather than simple, easy answers (Gurian, 2019, para. 12). Other scholars have echoed the need for more complex analysis and the awareness that ideologies inform all narratives and interpretations (Ash, 2019; Coffee, 2008; Dawson, 2014). Taken together, these researchers advise deliberately keeping the conversation complex as an important strategy to counteract any normative stalling.

Good Intentions Are Not Enough

B. Moore (2013) suggested, "Inequities…continue to exist when educators unconsciously ascribe to an unexamined ideology of 'norm'" (p. 4). Unexamined is one thing, unintentional is another. The claim of unintentionality is common and asks us to presume that the person or institution may be forgiven for having expressed racist, sexist, ageist, ableist or other normative attitudes.

If an overt intention cannot be proven, is the actor then absolved of the consequences of the impact of actions? Museums and their staff often say they have good intentions as they struggle to find relevance and to balance visitor demographics, narratives, objects, finances, learning and teaching in the 21st century.

I have presented multiple conflicts with so-called good intentions throughout these chapters. We can ask ourselves, as Heaton (2014) did, how much intention actually matters when larger issues are at stake? In Chapter 5, we saw Native American families embarrassed that their people's artifacts and memories resided next to animals in natural history museums. In Chapter 6, I described the dishonoring of Indigenous bones that has been sacrilegious and contentious for decades. I quoted an administrator in Chapter 4 who claimed visitors *need to pay* for what they saw in order to fully appreciate it. In Chapter 8, the museum educator described a family of color at a hands-on exhibit as "doing it all wrong". Very important assumptions were buried in such discursive statements, including expectations of speaking and behaving in the 'right' way and the need to act more like *us*. Yet, in all of these examples, the individuals or institutions could possibly claim that their *intentions were good*.

Intention works at all levels. A person might say for example, "I didn't mean", to imply that a particular statement does not constitute racism because racism was not *intended*. At the collective/institutional level, we find statements like, "His dean is making him hire a person of color when there are so many great writers out there" (Rankine, 2014, p. 15), and "she's just not the right, um, fit here". Such statements are relatively common and often accepted. If challenged, they are often followed by "I didn't mean", as well.[4]

The more obvious structural constraints in museums are hiring practices, budget constraints tied to deficit ethos, claiming that good intentions will be enough, refusing to learn and understand the role of white privilege and the dynamics of belonging and othering, as well as how systems perpetuate, recreate and reify these over time.

The most obvious answer to claims of unintentionality and the undergirding of structural constraints is the simple statement, "It's not about intent; it's about impact." Gorski (2010)[5] said it plainly: "Intentions may be honorable, but good intentions are not enough" (p. 515). Van Sluytman (2015, in Yosso et al., 2009) has suggested, "While ignorance of how something will be received is not an excuse for what can be less-than-conscious acts, more damning is the dismissal of the recipient's perception" (p. 670). He argued that not paying attention to what people of color may have to say impacts all levels of the organization—that is, individual, group and institution—and such deficit instantiations at any level impact the entire institution.

The National Museum of African American History and Culture (2020) website *Talking about Race* provides an overview of the issues and challenges museums at individual, interpersonal and institutional levels. Jones-Rizzi and Mann (2020) have argued that museums are beginning to monitor themselves from within, to reflect and change such behaviors. They suggested that

> the Museums & Race movement has expanded with an intentional mission of shining a light on the role that race and racism play in the museum industry—in both the obvious, visible ways and the smaller but sometimes more insidious, invisible ways. It also provides a space within a predominantly white field for those of us in the industry who don't identify as white.
>
> (para. 11)

There is much work to be done and we have just started. As with all expansive learning, we don't yet know the outcomes.

Mind the Dialectic

Most activity theorists understand that traditional dualistic frameworks do not help us understand today's deep social transformations (Engeström et al., 1999). Remember that Seo and Creed (2002) suggested that *following the dialectic* allows us to delineate concrete mechanisms embedded in social systems and in their contradictions, thus giving another pathway for tracing how contradictions can change systems. Dialectical logic is fundamental to studying the change process. Next, we follow the dialectic at three levels of analysis.

Sociocultural Dialectic Between Individual and Social: The ZPD

The dialectical relationship and mediation between the individual and the social are key concepts in understanding how they interact with and inform each other. Vygotsky addressed the individual and the social directly through using the zone of proximal development, the ZPD. For research, the ZPD allows us to trace how our academic and everyday concepts meet and interact, and help qualify especially the role of mediational means (called artefacts in the following quote):

> The understanding of artefacts...circulating between inner and outer worlds in which meaning is developing, presents a complex, layered, dialectical view of human engagement with the world.
>
> (Daniels, 2012, p. 73)

In Chapter 8, I described using the ZPD[6] to 'see' the dialectic in action—for example, to train museum educators to scaffold visitor interactions. The notion that artifacts mediate between inner and outer worlds in the ZPD is fundamental and functional as the ZPD *links* the individual and social, and their reciprocal interactions.[7]

ZPD, Dialectic and *Deficit/Othering*

How can ZPD dialectics enhance our analysis of social justice and inequities such as *othering* and *deficit* ideologies? To answer this, I begin with the language we use and the ideologies that inform them. Wertsch (2007) claimed that "our contact with the world is indirect or mediated by signs" (p. 178). These signs include the language of all the 'isms'. Leonardo and Manning (2017) have concluded that these signs "support a hierarchical racial structure" (p. 7). It has been argued that "the mediating tools of whiteness have become the common sense embedded in everyday practice" (Leonardo & Manning, 2017, p. 7). We can examine any dialectical relationship in the ZPD by its language and thus find this 'common sense' of whiteness, for example, in what Leonardo and Manning (2017) conceived of as 'white zones of proximal development' in order to investigate the relationship between whiteness and the ZPD:

> When [the] ZPD is used to explain racial disparities in the service of inclusion, it is usually connected with the lives of people of color. This leaves out a critical understanding of racially dominant experiences, or whiteness.
>
> (p. 32)

I want to connect this discussion of the ZPD, the dialectic and *othering* in order to deepen the analysis. This is a crucial aspect of museum reculturing. Based on the assumption that the relationship between individual and social context is dialectical. Leonardo and Manning (2017) noted that

> mapping Vygotsky's ZPD with whiteness studies provides a larger window into individual and social reciprocity of beliefs and behaviors that are part of common ideologies like whiteness.
>
> (p. 32)

This expansion of the dialectic and the ZPD is exciting because it allows us to reconsider how to frame *othering* and *deficit* views in more current interpretations of whiteness. In addition, given that

> [G]lobal white supremacy has structurally shaped history, politics, and economics...using Vygotsky's insights, we also analyze how whiteness functions as a sign system (Vygotsky, 1987; Wertsch, 2007) that organizes our experiences of the world.
>
> (Leonardo & Manning, 2017, p. 33)

We are never trapped by implacable ideology when we find a way to confront it. Understanding the dialectical relationship of the ZPD at multiple levels, we recognize "the influence of nature on man...[as] man, in turn, affects nature and creates through his changes in nature new natural conditions for his existence" (Vygotsky, 1978, p. 60). As Leonardo and Manning have expressed it, "Using the ZPD as a focus is one way to counteract 'the ossifying role of whiteness' in US society [which] is resistant to change and is precisely a perspective on the world that would prefer to forget race history" (p. 35). Vygotsky reminds us of the ubiquitous roles of resistance and constant revolution in history, captured in the dialectical method:

> [P]ersonal evolution is part of an ongoing social revolution....A new society requires a continually evolving (i.e., revolutionary) pedagogy, Vygotsky insisted on a keen appreciation for the dynamic nature of social relations.
>
> (Leonardo & Manning, 2017, p. 18)

We need these new studies synthesizing whiteness studies and sociocultural theory, what Fisher and Larkin (2008) have called the critical 'struggle' in the ZPD', in order to effectively recognize and counter *othering*.

Structure Agency Dialectic

Examining power, identity, agency and structure dynamics is important for all levels of museum staff.

Giddens[8] referred to the inseparable intersection of structure (rules and resources) and agency without giving primacy to either. What then can we say about the dialectical relationship between structure and agency in relation to equity and *othering in museums*?

SAD, a tool for exploring structures and individuals across multiple levels of activity, moves freely across the micro- to macrolevels and back (Bronfenbrenner, 1976 in Varelas et al., 2015). SAD has already been applied to studies of the student/teacher, principal/administration interactions in schools in science teaching (Gutiérrez & Calabrese Barton, 2015; Varelas et al., 2015). It has not been much used to analyze museum organizational functioning. Gutiérrez and Calabrese Barton (2015) have explicitly linked SAD to equity concerns:

> A more expansive approach to making sense of the structure–agency dialectic and how it frames opportunities to learn and become in science is important in moving forward an equity agenda in science education.
>
> (p. 546)

Let us consider again the structural constraints the *blue* museum educators faced in Chapter 8, both individually and then collectively. Any individual or collective action on the part of educators to reduce the deficit orientation in the museum was actively resisted. Agency remained diminished.

Engeström et al. (1999) took note that structural forces were held separate, at least in the behavioral and social sciences, where

> the individual may be seen as an acting subject who learns and develops, but somehow the actions of the individual do not seem to have any impact on the surrounding structures.
>
> (Engeström et al., 1999. p. 25)[9]

As one way to balance this inequality, Engeström (2001) and colleagues have advanced the notion of *transformative agency* at an individual or collective level. I introduced this briefly in Chapter 2, referencing Stetsenko's (2019) counter-approaches to static agency. Stetsenko characterized current models of agency as having a "residue of passivity", suggesting Gidden's doctrine "unsuccessfully attempted to invent a palatable version of capitalism". Conversely, Stetsenko considered

> each individual's agentive contributions to *communal practices*, [so that] these practices are changed as a whole every time a person acts as an active member of community…[the whole is] constantly transformed and realized (literally made real) by people themselves—and, importantly, by people not as isolated, autonomous entities but as agentive actors or active agents of social practices.
>
> (p. 4)

Stetsenko reframed agency as collective and transformative within an institution so that workers are not isolated and powerless. Stetsenko further argued,

> This position puts emphasis on a complex relational and dynamic network of continuous processes of material sociohistorical practices as *the nexus of*

people purposefully changing their world while simultaneously being changed by and in this very process of their own transformational practices.

(p. 80)

Agency can be transformative. A collective dialectic transformative view of active agency allows us to analyze systems with a goal of participants becoming active agents of new social practices in the museum world. This view fits well with Haapasaari et al. (2014) who argued,

> As changes in work organizations are profound and often destructive, agency that acts proactively to initiate and steer changes is needed, and all the innovative potential in the organization should be mobilized.
>
> (p. 233)

Transformative change can proactively initiate and steer needed changes. It is also a vehicle for resistance. Stetsenko concluded,

> [E]ffecting dissidence (including in challenging canons of passivity and behaviorism in psychology and education) de facto also means going beyond our present conditions in creating radical possibilities for social transformation.
>
> (p. 19)

Shifting the Burden: Neoliberalism and Outreach

Finding out *where the burdens lie* is an eye-opening activity for museum staff. McDermott (2015) recognized how the "neoliberal-influenced claims of individualistic acquisition of knowledge metaphors promote competition and disproportionately affect non dominant populations" (p. 338). Hall and Pulsford (2019) suggested that "hostility, blame, distrust and disempowerment…are themselves an ongoing outcome of the internalisation of neoliberal demands for responsibility and productivity" (p. 243). These insights help us understand how *outreach* functions as a not-so-subtle form of *othering*. I suggest that the dialectic between outreach and *inreach* is pervasive. How does this dialectic map onto a neoliberal focus? The focus on individualism without actual enhanced agency for individuals is prominent in each of our neoliberal critiques; this is individualism in name only. At the same time, collective organizations such as unions are discouraged. This is the neoliberal power dynamic laid bare. Transformative agency, as Stetsenko suggested, pushes on that power as a force for change.

This dynamic also underlies museums' practice of trying to change the other (*outreach*) rather than themselves (*inreach*). Focusing on change outside the museum while evading internal change can masquerade as 'doing something', perhaps even with efficiency. This perception meets neoliberal expectations of action, without actually making any substantive internal change. This is a well-known phenomenon among public universities that collaborate with community organizations in the name of public good but actually reflect market economics (Brackmann, 2015). Public service thus is disguised as another form of neoliberal cultural capitalism.

Outreach also carries implications of deficit expectations. "If only minoritized populations could assimilate to the norms of the museum" (Dawson, 2014, p. 986). Dawson's argument specifically dismissed the simplistic *barrier* model, "which risks perpetuating a cycle of social exclusion and nonparticipation" (Dawson, 2014, p. 986).[10] Dawson challenged this posture that continues to focus on the ones behind the barrier rather than on the structures that create the *barriers*.[11] Feinstein and Meshoulam (2014) critiqued this question from museums: "Why don't they come here?" It reifies the barrier model without recognizing how contentious a barrier model actually is. At best, the barrier model promotes piecemeal actions without delving into the structural issue of how different barriers interlink and potentiate or exacerbate each other. As Dawson and others have noted, seemingly disparate aspects are intertwined in important ways; these ideological and practical differences exist at different levels of analysis, and they have deep cultural, political and historical roots.

Norms in a Dialectical World

What is called 'normal', or normalized practice, is socially, culturally, politically and historically produced, and pervades all levels of functioning in museums. The norm sits in an uneasy relationship with anything that may not conform to it, for example, counter-narratives, the 'disruptors' mentioned by Jones-Rizzi and Mann (2020), Leonardo and Manning's 'whiteness ZPD' (2017), Stetsenko's transformative agency (2019) or the giraffe and elephant parable. While it may not be entirely clear what we mean by *normal*, most museum regulars and staff will claim to know it when they see it. It is the status quo. This view is reflected when staff members complain that minoritized visitors 'break things on free days' or, 'don't ask the right questions'.[12]

Coffee (2008) argued that norms "enforce discrimination and domination and white privilege". P. Moore (2014) and others have suggested that it is crucial to examine the ideologies that inform the creation and maintenance of any norm. This extends to all the subjects we have discussed: demographics and finances, narrative and objects, and learning and teaching. These categories make norms seem overly theoretical but, simply, they are actually 'the way things are done around here'.

Normed symbols, rules, and narrative are conveyed in so many unspoken and spoken ways, and they function as deeply held 'common culture' in any museum. Assimilation to norms is an unspoken demand across most formal and informal educational settings (B. Moore, 2013; Sleeter, 1996). Yet, as we saw with the Braydon family in Chapter 7, *their* resources allowed or compelled them to *resist* the norm in interesting ways. For reculturing, then, it rests on museums, staff and boards to recognize and challenge the old norms that no longer fit.

As an activity, norms could become some of the first things museums examine collectively.

Working the Dialectic Across Multiple Activity Systems

We have now seen ways CHAT can be used as a practical tool for examining the seemingly disparate elements of what is otherwise an unwieldy and multifaceted museum system. One way to start 'examining and managing the many seemingly disparate elements' is to excavate and identify norms at all hierarchical levels.

First and foremost, CHAT requires us to minimize reductionist or simplistic solutions of policy and practice in museums.[13] This means museums must stop focusing only on isolated facts of complex situations. Museums cannot afford, for example, to continue minimizing the role of context, ignore motivation and possible alternative outcomes, pay attention only to numbers, expect objects to speak for themselves or expect those new to museums to know how 'to do' them. Reductionism and oversimplification have never served museums well.

Third- and fourth-generation activity theory offers tools to analyze the complexity we want to understand. Activity systems can be networked, nested or interlocked into multiple-interconnected activity systems; this reflects the dynamic realities of larger systems functioning. In this way, we can see how and where *one system impacts the others*. Vossoughi and Gutiérrez (2014) argued that "as third-generation activity theorists, our work is organized around the principles that people are part of multiple activity systems, and that learning should be studied accordingly" (p. 603). We have already seen third-generation CHAT used as two communities seek to negotiate an object. Recently, Engeström and Sannino (2021) suggested the evolution of four generations of activity systems:

> [O]f the unit of analysis through…our generations, from mediated action to a collective activity system, to multiple-interconnected activity systems, and most recently to heterogenous work coalitions aimed at resolving wicked societal problems.
>
> (p. 4)

Third-generation activity theory allows us to envision and represent how multiple activity systems interact and reciprocally transform each other, which in turn helps us to envision how organizations can change from within. Figure 9.1 is a possible representation of interconnected activity system relationships relevant to any museum, here represented by three levels of activity with macro, intermediate and micro. We presume here that the larger object of the museum system is to provide a 'belonging'-based equitable learning environment for visitors.

In Figure 9.1, we see four systems interacting. It is obvious, even visually, that as one system changes others do as well. This helps us conceptualize why so-called quick or piecemeal fixes in one part of the system may harm, rather than help, attempts to resolve a particular contradiction. With CHAT's expansive learning cycle as the foundation and interlinked activity system analysis, we can leave space for the unexpected and for the as-yet unknown to emerge. In other words, we have the tools for open-ended dialectical system analysis.

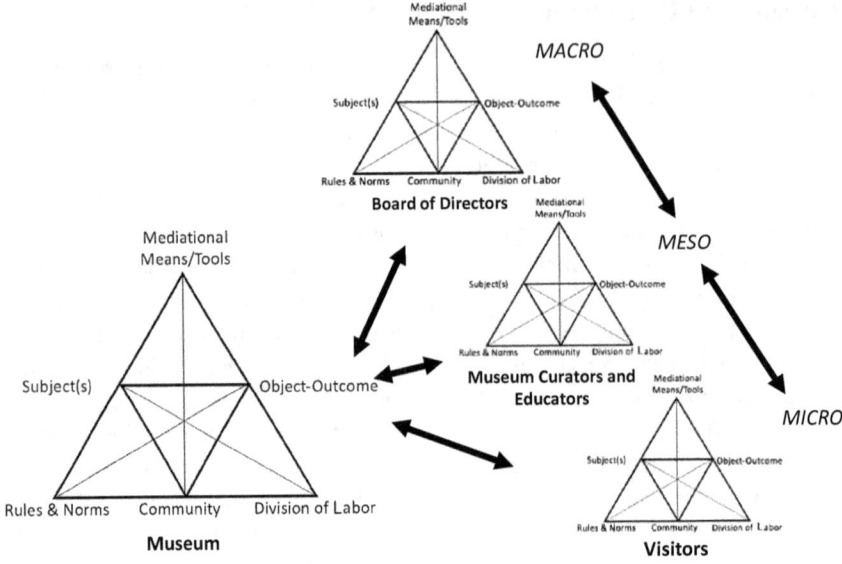

FIGURE 9.1 Multiple-interconnected activity systems

With more research, it will eventually be possible to make a more complete and systematically interlinked analytic network with which to visualize challenging issues such as equity as they impact each of the intertwined systems. It *is* **possible** to interlink these seemingly disparate aspects into a large, networked, interlinked system in order to understand how the interlinkages work. In this way, using CHAT, real museum conundrums can be analyzed more fully: the personal and systemic frustrations arising from museum educator teams viewing learning and teaching differently, the failure of entrance fees to create financial solvency for a not-for-profit institution, weighted ethical choices among contradictory narratives of history and the ethical and scientific dilemma of studying or honoring the bones of human ancestors. In all of these cases, an aspect of the museum system is negotiated or has been negotiated or will be negotiated. The effects of such negotiation carry over into other subsystems. More than one activity in the nested system may be activated in subsequent negotiations.

Follow the Power

This discussion is meaningless without touching on power and how power dynamics operate at every level and in every aspect of the museum system. Normative culture in museums rests on the locus of power, as does an assimilationist (become like us), individualistic (rather than collective) or hierarchical (rather than lateral) stance. Further, we have observed displays *of power* (Bennett, 1995; Dubin, 1999) at every level.

Power plays a role in other ways. "*Who gets to participate? What impacts do exhibits have on visitors?*" Think of a family of color abruptly challenged at the front door to provide proof they had been given a free ticket to the science exhibit. Imagine the cabinets full of poi pounders in a Hawaiian museum where Native Hawaiian descendants of those who created the pounders are not allowed to see or touch any of them. Think of the family new to museums who must sit and listen to a lecture about an exhibit or painting instead of participating in dialogue. Think of modern Indians listening to someone talk about how primitive their ancestors once were. Imagine the descendant of slaves looking at the artifacts of slavery displayed as if they were precious items.

In Chapter 8, threatened mid-level managerial forces resisted *blue* museum educator scaffolding teaching; in Chapter 7, the Braydon family used *their* resources to break the norm in quite interesting ways. In Chapter 6, sacred objects, ancestral bones, were appropriated to far-distant museum collections and only after years of negotiations returned for burial. In Chapter 5, we encountered the power of a master narrative and the resistance of the counter-narrative. Recall the fear of demographic shifts and white power losing the struggle against demographic shifts. The list of power inequities is extensive. The following are some examples from this book, followed by the nodes that may be in tension (Table 9.1).

These are only some instances of power in action. Those without power are quite conscious of how it plays out. Those with power take it for granted, and they may

TABLE 9.1 Some aspects of power in museums

Power in artifact selection/collection/interpretation; power to buy, sell, use money as necessary to override other concerns
(rules, division of labor, object negotiation)
Power in selecting the master narrative; recognizing/not recognizing alternative resources, stories, interpretations
(rules, division of labor, object negotiation)
Power of hierarchical organization
(rules, subjects, community, divisions of labor)
Power to choose dominant ideology
(rules, tools)
Power in interpreting, learning and teaching theory and practice
(didactic vs. scaffolding)
(rules, division of labor, object negotiation)
Power in the curriculum/exhibition/exhibit selection
(rules, division of labor, object negotiation; choice of exhibit, exhibition, signage, etc.)
Power of inreach vs. outreach—choosing one community's values or language practices over another's
(rules, division of labor, object negotiation)
Power in hiring and firing; rewarding, punishing for work; setting hours, clothing, salary, etc.
(rules, division of labor, object negotiation)
Power choosing representation, logos, public relations
(rules, division of labor, object negotiation)
Power in ALL budget decisions
(rules, division of labor, object negotiation)

work to remain unaware of the consequences. On a more global level, displays of power are often accompanied by the hegemony of political and cultural values and what has been labeled dehumanization of others.

Change Labs

But what is the actual mechanism for change and challenging power? What does CHAT tell us about dealing with intractable conflicts? The Change Lab can become a tool to engage participants in the possible creative production of new practices (Ward, 2015, p. 67). The Change Laboratory (CL) is

> a space that offers…practitioners…instruments for analyzing disturbances [and] bottlenecks in…prevailing work practices…[toward] constructing new models and tools, and…putting them on trial.[14]
>
> (Morselli, 2018, p. 37)

The Change Lab puts into practice all the tools we have already described but in specific instances focused on practical real-world problems. As Ward describes it,

> Developmental Work Research…by Engeström (2007)…is used to study complex learning environments, or activity systems…the Change Lab, a process that gives practitioners the opportunity to organize and plan for change by allowing them to reflect on data collected by researchers, as well as their own objects and motives.
>
> (p. 65)

But what do we actually do in Change labs? CL implements the steps we have already seen in expansive learning (Figure 8.1)—that is, questioning, analyzing, creating and testing new models, etc., typically with in person attendance in a dedicated physical space.

> The new joint activity becomes the object of CL work…typically focusing on producing a new model of activity that defines a Zone of Proximal Development for the group…the conceptual space where the group can expand the object of its activity, to produce…a new object…the new model is evaluated by the group by means of reflective tools (mirroring diagrams, video, diaries, etc.), so that it can be questioned, and improved.
>
> (Adapted from Senteni, 2020)

Reculturing as We Now See It

Based on the themes we just reviewed, I offer a beginning list of actions for critical reflection (Table 9.2).

TABLE 9.2 Some suggested actions to take

Locate the ideology:
—Examine mission statements, long term goals, and public documents.
—Examine internal symbols, signs, advertising and normed phrases—e.g., museum X always...

Follow the power:
—Conduct analyses of department structure and a master organization chart; be explicit.
—Find your job and your boss's job.
—When was the chart last updated? Who makes it?
—How vertically organized is it?
—Is there significant room for movement?
—Don't forget to compare salaries.

Communication:
Communication is key and one of the chief things that will ruin a project, if not done well.
—How is the community involved in exhibition design and evaluation?
—Are lines of communication within the museum clear?
—Are communication paths vertical, horizontal or both?
—Can you talk with your superiors any time you want?

Mind the dialectic:
Identify dialectical relationships in your department, other departments and the museum overall.
—Start with something well-known, SAD. Find the trade-offs. What are the rewards and punishments regarding individual/collective freedom and structural constraints?
—Figure out how to maximize collective agency. See what other museums are doing.
—Is there a union, a staff collective for bargaining?
—Are the rules well-known? Is there an ombudsperson?

Use theories:
Theories can be your friend.
—Theory can help you understand your degree of agency, which may help you negotiate conflicts.
—Notice how understanding contradictions makes transformation seem less daunting.
—Work the dialectic.

Examine the norm at your museum?
The norm is often so embedded that we do not recognize it as such.
—Are there unwritten rules; can you name them?
—Who speaks the most/least?
—Where do disagreements go?
—Are POC hired as tokens?

Be critically reflective:
Reflection is good, but it is not enough; you also need to do something.
—Consider all educational and entertainment institutions to be under the spell of neoliberal principle and policies.

(Continued)

TABLE 9.2 (Continued)

—Examine commodification locally in the subsystem and across the museum at large.
—Are external evaluators expected to agree with the institution?
—Find out boards composition and how they are selected.
—Research what other museums have done.

Learn about learning and teaching:
Do ethnographic learning and teaching studies on the floor, five to ten minutes every day.
—Examine for signs of 'knowledge economy', banking model of learning.
—Do educators/docents have the freedom to interpret?
—Are minoritized visitors welcomed? How/how not?
—Are sociocultural, equity-based theories put into practice?
—Examine museum educator professional development for degrees of freedom— remember the *blues*.

Find the deficit:
—Identify deficit orientation in all its guises; make a list.
—Look for/listen for *othering* of minoritized populations.
—How does your museum 'position the other'?
—Is it overly reliant on 'outreach' as a solution?
—Analyze discursive manifestations of *othering*.
—Look at hiring statistics, visitor statistics.
—Critically examine whiteness.
—Are there current decolonizing efforts?
—Examine pricing models.
—What are the master narratives; are counter-narratives allowed?

Engage in the Change Lab process:
—Work the dialectic.
—Use the expansive learning cycle to guide your work; conduct a Change Lab.

Last Words

I have promoted a systems approach throughout this book. It can be challenging to recognize the whole system when everyday details loom large, but it is extremely important to keep seeing the big picture. The Change Lab relies on this. CHAT allows us a 'best fit' theoretical perspective for systems thinking in educational research, specifically locating and dissecting contradictions in action in a dialectical fashion.

The particular contradictions I noted were generated and regenerated at multiple levels of the museum system. We need only to learn to recognize their existence and note when they enter the system in which we are embedded. Contradictions help museum staff to become the change agents they wish to be and to foster the subsequent change processes. Many more contradictions will emerge from the myriad field experiments now being conducted as local and global attempts to change policy and practice emerge. By experiments, I refer to the many small and large, often externally funded programs, interventions and other efforts aimed at changing museums from the inside out.

The one constant in all *systems* is power, who has it, who does not and how it is negotiated or not. I have placed *power* front and center in my analysis. Once again, I ask what change processes will facilitate transformation? I argue that we must look to CHAT for any effective answers, as successful change processes will be system-wide. Finally, to answer the question of why and how contradictions continue to define museums large and small across all levels of analysis, we must uncover the reigning underlying ideology, the deep-seated beliefs carried in the organizational charts, master narratives, and processes and procedures ubiquitous to each institution.

Appendix 9.1: Summary of Major Themes

I synthesize here the main themes of Chapters 1 through 9, using Table 9.3 for reference and review.

TABLE 9.3 A summary of questions/contradictions/themes used for this book

Chapter title	Contradictions	Questions	Themes
Introduction to the Main Theories and Themes of *Reculturing Museums*	Inreach/outreach us vs. them equality vs. equity	-What is reculturing? -Why is reculturing essential? How is this political?	-Demographics -Ideologies not numbers -Deficit ideology -Power
Why Do We Need Theories? CHAT/SAD Neoliberal/Deficit critiques	Primary contradiction— use vs. exchange value Theory vs. practice	-Why theory? -Why is a system approach important?	-Tipping point -Contradictions drive expansive learning cycles
Who Will Go to Museums? Ideologies not numbers	Us vs them Client/collaborator Power	-What is normative behavior in museums? -"Why don't *they* come here?"	-Demographics -Ideologies not numbers -Deficit ideology -Power
Who Will Pay for Museums?	Free for all/charge popular good vs. revenue Service/populist vs. budget/monetary Client vs. collaborator	-What is the purpose of museums? -What is the intended goal of charging admission fees?	-Entrance fees as proxies for ideologies -Neoliberalism Money and power -Three museum Pricing models

(*Continued*)

TABLE 9.3 (Continued)

Chapter title	Contradictions	Questions	Themes
Whose Story Is It?	Master vs. counter-narratives Frozen vs. dynamic Primitive vs. advanced Dehumanized vs. humanized Romanticized vs. real Commodification vs. conservation	–Who owns it, and what happens when it is challenged by counter-narratives? –How are master narrative constructed in museums? –What are some ideological contradictions in master narratives?	Story and museum exhibit design/critiques –Three controversies: Native American in museums Sutter Buttes Californios Smithsonian, and –One counter example Ziibiwing Center/core values –Power
Who Owns the Artifact?: Contingent Ownership in Context	Decolonizing/colonizing Secular vs sacred Monetary vs. cultural Contingent vs. solidified	–Is the purpose of objects to represent their culture or prove theories about science or history or both?"	–Retrenching/Deaccessioning Repatriation –Kennewick man –Iwi Kapuna –Containment, Objectification and Reduction
Where Is the Learning and Who Gets to Learn?	Individual or social Deficit or resource view ZPD as dialectical space for individual to social	–What are we supposed to do here? –How are deficit orientations and learning theory intertwined? –What is the role of mediation?	–Deficit ideology –Taxonomy of learning theories Whiteness in the ZPD –Mission statements
What Do We Mean by Equitable Teaching in Museums?	Didactic vs scaffolding teaching theory Resistance vs. status quo Structure vs. agency Deficit vs. resources *Blue* vs. *purple* case	–What does it mean 'to do' the exhibit right? –Whose norms? –Which level of analysis is best for reculturing?	–SAD –Scaffolding in the ZPD –Expansive cycle as a practical guide –Transformative agency
How Do We Reculture an Institution While Old Systems Are Still in Place?	Power revisited Complex vs. simple Individual vs. collective SAD	–Where is the power? –What can museums do right now? –Where is the norm in a dialectical world?	–Welcoming contradictions –Change Lab Review Resist Reflect –Follow the power

Appendix 9.2: Involving the Community

The question of reculturing has shifted from "Should the community be involved in exhibitions?" to "How should the community be involved with exhibitions?" Amy Lonetree (2009), Robert James (2013), Nina Simon (2013), John K. W. Tchen, (2005) and many others support face-to-face, talk-based collaboration or what Simon has called a participatory museum and Tchen and others have termed community-based dialogue.

There are tools that museums can use to listen effectively to outside voices and to change how they negotiate the ways they usually do things. This may sound simple; as many museums are finding out, however, critically reflective listening is a challenging process, requiring the expenditure of many person-hours at many levels of communication. There are past wrongs to be righted and sensitivities to consider on all sides, which may have yet to be acknowledged or understood. Many of these collaborations and dialogues have been inchoate at best. Community members are sensitive to tokenism and past experiences may or may not have been productive.

Simon (2013) suggested three main reasons that cultural institutions engage in co-creative projects:

- To give voice and be responsive to the needs and interests of local community members,
- To provide a place for community engagement and dialogue and
- To help participants develop skills that will support their own individual and community development.

She noted that "co-creation projects run into trouble when participants' goals are not aligned with institutional goals, or when staff members are not fully aware of participants' goals at the outset" and that "visitors and staff members often have very different ideas about how cultural institutions work and what they do" (p. 214). In CHAT talk, a negotiated common object between multiple activity systems has not yet been negotiated or even attempted. Therein lie many communication gaps. Misalignments, misattunements and actual interactive ruptures do provide the most useful information on how to improve dialogue about the object(ive), the mediational means, the rules and/or the divisions of labor to achieve better communication. And they require careful repair when they occur.

Once the community is involved, how does reculturing within the organization proceed? Which is the most appropriate professional level to leverage to create change in a museum? Research using the professional development of the museum educators is a good start. Over the last decade, such a mid-level approach has been used in attempts to transform large museum institutions. These attempts have been direct or indirect. Often these professional development efforts may not have begun with an explicit intent to change the larger organization, but larger change can and often does become part of the work. As would-be museum change agents have discovered the hard way, change in one level of professional activity in a museum affects other levels. This is exactly what activity theory predicts will happen.

Listening

One of the many communication strategies used has been 'listening to the audience' in museums (Vogel, 2008). By this we mean surveys (Vogel, 2008) to get feedback but also actually listening in person to real people in local museums, especially those who have experienced *othering*. This listening takes time and effort and a good deal of patience on all sides, as the very populations that have felt most unwelcome are now being asked to participate. Museums need to hear what they do not want to hear. Active, non-defensively received listening is critical to re-positioning 'outsiders' as collaborative partners.

Appendix 9.3: Critical Reflective Practice

Many researchers have found middle-level professional development work in the museum workplace to be a valid entry point for tracing how change does and does not occur (Bevan & Xanthodouki, 2008; Martin et al., 2019; Tran & Halverson, 2021). These researchers working in or collaborating across different institutions, including aquariums, science centers, museums, zoos and other settings, have found similar dynamics to apply throughout all these settings. All these contexts can and sometimes do incorporate critically reflective practice—that is, to ask educators and curators and administrators to examine their own and the museum's theories and practices, both as subjects for action research and to actively promote the goals of greater equity and inclusivity (de Gregoria Kelly, 2009; Ash & de Gregoria Kelly, 2013).

We are creating a larger group of museum scholars and practitioners to conduct theoretically informed research to effect long-lasting change in museum educator programs and to enhance institutional culture. The institutions we have studied cut across a wide swath of disciplinary interests. As a group, we are using critical reflective practice as a central organizing theme, although each of us has a different view of what it means for institutions to change, and each of our efforts has taken a slightly different approach.

Appendix 9.4: One Example of Museum Reculturing

Oakland Museum of California (OMCA): Reorganization and Going to the Community

Lori Fogarty, OMCA's director and CEO, says the museum isn't just a place people visit and passively receive information. It is increasingly becoming a community resource, an interactive place for public discourse and an activist organization dedicated to social justice. "I often get asked, 'Are you a museum or a cultural center?'" Fogarty says. "And I say, yes. Because we are both, and I don't think there's a conflict in being both".

One of the ways OMCA has achieved this is by welcoming people who aren't considered "traditional" museumgoers. California's demographics are much different than they were even a few years ago, with a growing Latino population, aging baby boomers, a huge number of millennials and reconceived definitions of what constitutes a family. OMCA has made it a top priority to connect with these changing populations, often by reaching them in their own communities beyond the museum's walls.

> The result of this process was a structure that is reflected in an organizational chart that is affectionately known internally as "the flower." The structure incorporates six cross-functional, cross-disciplinary "centers," all focused on an outstanding visitor experience and participatory community engagement.

"We are addressing these demographic shifts in many ways", Fogarty says. "We create inclusive social experiences, such as Friday Nights @ OMCA; we offer multilanguage materials in our galleries; and we have increased accessibility for all by reducing the cost barrier through our monthly First Sundays @ OMCA program and the Museums for All program". Additionally, OMCA partners with community organizations including the Oakland Asian Cultural Center and the YMCA of the East Bay to bring cultural experiences into different neighborhoods and increase civic engagement.

The OMCA's Barbara Henry (2006) suggests that "institutional strategies to achieve greater relevancy and public value can, and have been, initiated through the Education Department" (2006). She situates the educator at the crossroads of institutional change, suggesting among other things:

> The educator is in the crossroads of promoting collaborations—both internally across museum departments and externally with different communities—for advancing the museum as a publicly valued resource that contributes to building healthier communities.
>
> (p. 223)

Henry advocates for what we have called an intermediate level of professional development in the museum. She makes clear that the brokering activity she describes fits neatly into the perspective of two activity systems meeting to negotiate a joint objective, in this case a new exhibit. Henry argues that educators can serve as brokers between those outside and inside the museum—that is, *outreach and inreach*. If the museum education professionals can change their ways of thinking and their practices and language by interacting with a broader and more diverse public community (perhaps by directly addressing the controversies described in previous chapters), then part of their function becomes the translation of these ideas to those in the museum hierarchy. As such, they are in a position to potentially make change a less polarizing and more palatable experience for the administration.

Henry (2006) described such an example, in this case a controversial project that promoted community dialogues regarding *Whose history is recorded and validated for public memory?* It challenged the museum to experiment with how to collaborate and make connections between diverse groups:

> I learned that in serving as liaison, cultural broker, and experimenter, the educator[s]…contribute to deepening civic engagement…as an inclusive process in which the educator is actively facilitating the exchanges…across museum divisions and with the community. This expanded role of the educator is directly related to advancing institutional core values.
>
> (p. 228)

The educators in this instance acted as intermediaries, rather than merely house spokespersons. In short, they were given more autonomy and power. The outcome of this brokering process was described by Henry: "Putting the audience first has been a deep commitment for the OMCA". As noted earlier, OMCA (CFM, 2013) reorganized itself in 2011.

Lori Fogarty, the director, stated then,

> So, how are we doing now two years into our organizational transformation? When we embarked on this journey, I felt we were in a boat at sea, tossing around in turbulent waters, without a compass or life preservers. I can now say with confidence that we've landed, pitched our tent on the shore, and our new "flower" structure and culture is taking root.
>
> (OMCA website, 2013)

The language of community and the reorganization plan match in this case.

Excerpts from Future of Museums (http://futureofmuseums.blogspot.com/2013/08/flower-power-story-of-organizational-re.html).

Notes

1 Gurian's website lists this as *Reflections on Institutional Trauma*.
2 Gutiérrez and Calabrese Barton (2015) cite the work of Bang and Marin (2015) regarding "why it is important to make sense of how the historicity of structures shape the ways in which epistemologies and ontologies become settled in the design of learning environments" (p. 578).
3 As Gurian (2019) has said, change includes these beliefs: "[P]ushing for change and that everyone, no matter where they fit within the organizational hierarchy, has power to alter their collective situation. I favor action over inaction by using methods congruent with ideals; I remain committed to trial and error and think approximations, as the best we can hope for, should be celebrated; I think hand-crafted logical next steps beat ideological dogma; I remain persuaded of the importance of multiple answers over the victory of the single response" (para.18).
4 "Excuses for *unintentional actions* in terms of 'mere' ignorance include claims that they had never been taught the correct or appropriate information—"I didn't know"—and therefore cannot be prejudiced or racist. While such statements may be factually correct, most will argue that ignorance does not justify racism or mitigate the effects of their actions" (University of Calgary, 2018).

5 As Gorski (2010) argued, "attaining such an intercultural education requires not only subtle shifts in practice and personal relationships, but also important shifts of consciousness that prepare us to see and react to the socio-political contexts that so heavily influence education theory and practice" (p. 515).
6 To repeat, the ZPD represents an ideal spot in development where activity takes place in the space between what one can do individually and what one can achieve in collaboration with others, particularly with the help of what Vygotsky described as a more capable peer or teacher (Vygotsky, 1978; Leonardo & Manning, 2017, p. 16).
7 Again, Vygotsky's universal *law of development*, according to which human mental functions first emerge as distributed between the person and other people (i.e., "inter-psychological ") and only then as individually mastered by the person himself or herself (i.e., "intra-psychological"), and Rubinshtein's principle of "*unity and inseparability of consciousness and activity*", according to which human conscious experience and human acting in the world, the internal and the external, are closely interconnected and mutually determine one another (Kaptelinin, 2007, para.10).
8 Hunte et al. (2013) argued: "Giddens (1984) prioritize[d] neither the individual actor nor the structural-functional aspects of the social whole…[but]…their dialectic relationship…human action as a continuous flow of conduct…intertwined with the reproduction of the structural conditions that support social activities to become social practices… across space and time" (p. 3).
9 "The behavioral and social sciences have cherished a division of labor that separates the study of socioeconomic structures from the study of individual behavior and human agency. In this traditional framework, the socioeconomic structures look stable, all-powerful, and self-sufficient" (Engeström et al., 1999, p. 25).
10 As Rahm and Ash (2008, p. 60) suggested, "[M]any ethnically and linguistically diverse youth from low-income backgrounds are positioned as 'problems' by the [science education] system, which then results in the positioning of them as outsiders" (Dawson, 2014).
11 Dawson has argued, "On the one hand, the barriers model appears to make sense, of course people living in poverty struggle to afford a science center visit. On the other hand, the barriers model does little to explain how barriers might overlap (e.g., combinations of poverty and lack of interest) or the resilience of demographic patterns in ISE (informal science) participants despite attempts to change such patterns" (2014, p. 987).
12 Yet as we already noted, ideologies can and do change (Leonardo, 2009). And, as B. Moore argued, "While it seems evident that an ideology of normal changes over time.…I would argue that a shift [in] normal must involve a conscious effort on the parts of those who can see and envision a *new normal* where diversity is recognized, valued and privileged" (B. Moore, 2013, p. 68).
13 "More generally, [reductionism] can also refer to the 'omission of important co-determinants of a multi-causal situation' (Sayer, 2010 p. 34), or the choice of an inappropriate perspective or conceptual framework…Reductionism affects policy and administrative systems as well as related research paradigms, but goes right down to fundamental assumptions about learning and knowledge" (Wrigley, 2019, p. 1).
14 The typical form of Change Laboratory relies on the physical attendance of the community in a dedicated physical space.

References

Ash, D. (2019). Reflective practice in action research: Moving beyond the "standard model". In L. Martin, L. Tran, & D. Ash (Eds.), *The reflective museum practitioner: Expanding practice in science museums* (pp. 23–38). Routledge. https://doi.org/10.4324/9780429025242-3

Ash, D., & de Gregoria Kelly, L.Â. (2013). Thoughts on improvable objects, contradiction and object/tool reciprocity in a study of zoo educator professional development. *Cultural Studies in Science Education, 3*, 587–594.

Ash, D., & Race, A. (2021). Hybridizing equity-focused, field-based theory and practice for pre-service science teachers. *Journal of Informal Science and Environmental Learning, 1*(1), 1–16.

Bang, M., & Marin, A. (2015). Nature-culture constructs in science learning: Human/non-human agency and intentionality. *Journal of Research in Science Teaching, 52*(4), 530–544. https://doi.org/10.1002/tea.21204

Bennett, T. (1995). *The birth of the museum: History, theory, politics*. Routledge.

Bevan, B., & Xanthoudaki, M. (2008). Professional development for museum educators. *Journal of Museum Education, 33*(2), 107–119. https://doi.org/10.1080/10598650.2008.11510592

Brackmann, S. (2015). Community engagement in a neoliberal paradigm. *Journal of Higher Education Outreach and Engagement, 19*, 115–146.

Bronfenbrenner, U. (1976). The experimental ecology of education. *Teachers College Record, 78*, 157–158.

Coffee, K. (2008). Cultural inclusion, exclusion and the formative roles of museums. *Museum Management and Curatorship, 23*(3), 261–279. https://doi.org/10.1080/09647770802234078

Daniels, H. (2012). Dialectic and dialogic: The essence of a Vygotskian pedagogy. *Cultural-Historical Psychology, 8*(3), 70–79. https://psyjournals.ru/files/56309/kip_2012_3_Daniels.pdf

Dawson, E. (2014). "Not designed for us": How science museums and science centers socially exclude low-income, minority ethnic groups. *Science Education, 98*(6), 981–1008. https://doi.org/10.1002/sce.21133

de Gregoria Kelly, L. A. (2009). Action research as professional development for zoo educators. *Visitor Studies, 12*(1), 30–46.

Dewhurst, M., & Hendrick, K. (2017). Identifying and transforming racism in museum education. *Journal of Museum Education, 42*(2), 102–107. https://doi.org/10.1080/10598650.2017.1311745

Dubin, S. C. (1999). *Displays of power: Memory and amnesia in the American museum*. New York University Press.

Dubin, S. C. (2014). *Displays of power: Memory and amnesia in the American museum*. New York University Press.

Engeström, Y. (1987). *Learning by expanding. An activity-theoretical approach to developmental research*. Orienta-Konsultit. http://lchc.ucsd.edu/mca/Paper/Engestrom/Learning-by-Expanding.pdf

Engeström, Y. (1999). Activity theory and individual and social transformation. In Y. Engeström, R. Miettinen, & R. Punamäki (Eds.), *Perspectives on Activity Theory (Learning in Doing: Social, Cognitive and Computational Perspectives)* (pp. 19–38). Cambridge University Press. https://doi.org/10.1017/CBO9780511812774.003

Engeström, Y. (2001). Expansive learning at work: Toward an activity theoretical reconceptualization. *Journal of Education and Work, 14*(1), 133–156.

Engeström, Y. (2009). The future of activity theory: A rough draft. *Learning and Expanding with Activity Theory*, 303–328. https://doi.org/10.1017/cbo9780511809989.020

Engeström, Y. (2016). *Studies in expansive learning: Learning what is not yet there*. Cambridge University Press.

Engeström, Y., Miettinen, R., & Punamäki, R.-L. (Eds.). (1999). *Perspectives on activity theory*. Cambridge University Press.

Engeström, Y., & Sannino, A. (2021). From mediated actions to heterogenous coalitions: Four generations of activity-theoretical studies of work and learning. *Mind, Culture, and Activity, 28*(1), 4–23. https://doi.org/10.1080/10749039.2020.1806328

Fisher, R., & Larkin, S. (2008). Pedagogy or ideological struggle? An examination of pupils' and teachers' expectations for talk in the classroom. *Language and Education, 22*(1), 1–16. https://doi.org/10.2167/le706.0

Feinstein, N. W., & Meshoulam, D. (2014). Science for what public? Addressing equity in American science museums and science centers. *Journal of Research in Science Teaching, 51*(3), 368–394. https://doi.org/10.1002/tea.21130

Foot, K. A. (2014). Cultural-historical activity theory: Exploring a theory to inform practice and research. *Journal of Human Behavior in the Social Environment, 24*(3), 329–347. https://doi.org/10.1080/10911359.2013.831011

Giddens, A. (1984). *The theory of structuration*. University of California Press.

Gorski, P. (2010). *Unlearning deficit ideology and the scornful gaze: Thoughts on authenticating the class discourse in education*. EdChange. http://www.edchange.org/publications/deficit-ideology-scornful-gaze.pdf

Gurian, E. H. (1995). A blurring of the boundaries. *Curator: The Museum Journal, 38*(1), 31–37. https://doi.org/10.1111/j.2151-6952.1995.tb01033.

Gurian, E. H. (2019, December 22). *Elaine Heumann Gurian on the importance of and*. Museum Next. https://www.museumnext.com/article/the-importance-of-and/

Gurian, E. H. (2021). *Centering the museum: Writings for the post-Covid age*. Routledge.

Gutiérrez, K. D., Morales, P. Z., & Martinez, D. C. (2009). Remediating literacy: Culture, difference, and learning for students from nondominant communities. *Review of Research in Education, 33*, 212–245.

Gutiérrez, K. D., & Calabrese Barton, A. (2015). The possibilities and limits of the structure–agency dialectic in advancing science for all. *Journal of Research in Science Teaching, 52*(4), 574–583.

Haapasaari, A., Engeström, Y., & Kerosuo, H. (2014). The emergence of learners' transformative agency in a Change Laboratory intervention. *Journal of Education and Work, 29*(2), 232–262. https://doi.org/10.1080/13639080.2014.900168

Hall, R., & Pulsford, M. (2019). Neoliberalism and primary education: Impacts of neoliberal policy on the lived experiences of primary school communities. *Power and Education, 11*(3), 241–251. https://doi.org/10.1177/1757743819877734

Hunte, G., Wears, R., & Schubert, C. (2013, June 24–27). *Structure, agency, and resilience*. Proceedings of the 5th Symposium on Resilience Engineering, Managing trade-offs, Soesterberg, Netherlands. https://www.resilience-engineeringassociation.org/download/resources/symposium/symposium-2013/Hunte%20et%20al.%20(REA%202013).%20Structure,%20agency,%20and%20resilience.pdf

Heaton, J. (2014, January 20). *Museums and race*. Tronvig. https://www.tronviggroup.com/museums-and-race/.

Henry, B. (2006). The educator at the crossroads of institutional change. *Journal of Museum Education, 31*(3), 223–232.

James, R. (2013). *Museums and the paradox of change*. Routledge.

Jones-Rizzi, J., & Mann, S. (2020, July 1). *Is that hung white?* American Alliance of Museums. https://www.aam-us.org/2020/07/01/is-that-hung-white-a-conversation-on-the-state-of-museum-exhibitions-and-race/.

Kaptelinin, V. (2007). Activity theory. In M. Soegaard & R. F. Dam (Eds.), *The encyclopedia of human-computer interaction* (2nd ed.). The Interactive Design Foundation. https://www.interaction-design.org/literature/book/the-encyclopedia-of-human-computer-interaction-2nd-ed/activity-theory

Lakoff, G., & Ferguson, S. (2006). The framing of immigration. *Huffington Post*. http://www.huffingtonpost.com/george-lakoff-and-sam-ferguson/the-framing-ofimmigration

Leonardo, Z. (2009). *Race, whiteness, and education*. Routledge.

Leonardo, Z., & Manning, L. (2017). White historical activity theory: Toward a critical understanding of white zones of proximal development. *Race Ethnicity and Education, 20*(1), 15–29. https://doi.org/10.1080/13613324.2015.1100988

Lonetree, A. (2009). Museums as sites of decolonization: Truth telling in national and tribal museums. In S. Sleeper-Smith (Eds.), *Contesting knowledge: Museums and Indigenous perspectives* (pp. 322–337). University of Nebraska Press.

Martin, L., Tran, L.U., & Ash, D. (2019). *The reflective museum practitioner*. Routledge.

McDermott, R. (2015). Does "learning" exist? *WORD, 61*(4), 335–349. https://doi.org/10.1080/00437956.2015.1112956

Merritt, E. (2013). *Flower power: A story of organizational re-blossoming*. American Alliance of Museums. https://www.aam-us.org/2013/08/13/flower-power-a-story-of-organizational-re-blossoming/

Moore, B. (2013). *Understanding the ideology of normal: Making visible the ways in which educators think about students who seem different* [Unpublished doctoral dissertation]. University of Colorado. https://www.semanticscholar.org/paper/Understanding-the-Ideology-of-Normal%3A-Making-the-in-Moore/7a7900fb8e44338c360921fd28d52ca00648f1e9

Moore, P. (2014, January 20). The danger of the "d" word: Museums and diversity. *The Incluseum*. https://incluseum.com/2014/01/20/the-danger-of-the-d-word-museums-and-diversity/

National Museum of African American History and Culture. (2020, June 2). *Talking about race*. https://nmaahc.si.edu/learn/talking-about-race

Oakland Museum of California: A Bay Area Art, History & Science Museum. (n.d.). https://museumca.org/

Poole, N. (2014, November 25). *Change*. Medium. https://medium.com/code-words-technology-and-theory-in-the-museum/change-cc3b714ba2a4

Powell, J., & Menendian, S. (2017, June 29). The problem of othering: Towards inclusiveness and belonging. *Othering and Belonging: Expanding the Circle of Human Concern*, (1), 14–39. https://otheringandbelonging.org/wp-content/uploads/2016/07/OtheringAndBelonging_Issue1.pdf

Rahm, J., & Ash, D. (2008). Learning environments at the margin: Case studies of disenfranchised youth doing science in an aquarium and an after-school program. *Learning Environments Research, 11*(1), 49–62. https://doi.org/10.1007/s10984-007-9037-9

Rankine, C. (2014). *Citizen: An American lyric*. Graywolf Press.

Sayer, A. (2010) Reductionism in social science. In R. Lee (Ed.), *Questioning nineteenth-century assumptions about knowledge, II: Reductionism* (pp. 5–39). State University of New York Press.

Seo, M. G., & Creed, W. E. D. (2002). Institutional contradictions, Praxis, and institutional change: A dialectical perspective. *The Academy of Management Review, 27*(2), 222–247. doi:10.2307/4134353

Senteni, A. (2020). *Change laboratory*. http://edutechwiki.unige.ch/en/Change_laboratory

Simon, N. (2013). *On white privilege and museums*. Museum 2.0. http://museumtwo.blogspot.com/2013/03/on-white-privilege-and-museums.html

Sleeter, C. E. (1996). *Multicultural education as social activism*. State University of New York Press.

Stetsenko, A. (2019). Radical-transformative agency: Continuities and contrasts with relational agency and implications for education. *Frontiers in Education, 4*. https://doi.org/10.3389/feduc.2019.00148

Sue, D. W., Capodilupo, C. M., Torino, G. C., Bucceri, J. M., Holder, A. M., Nadal, K. L., & Esquilin, M. (2007). Racial microaggressions in everyday life: Implications for clinical practice. *American Psychologist, 62*(4), 271–286. https://doi.org/10.1037/0003-066x.62.4.271

Tchen, J. K.W. (2005). Homeland insecurities: Teaching and the intercultural imagination. *Imagining America, 2*. https://surface.syr.edu/ia/2

Tran, L. U., & Halversen, C. (2021). *Reflecting on practice for stem educators: A guide for museums, out-of-school, and other informal settings*. Routledge.

University of Calgary (2018). *Courageous conversations speaker series*. https://www.ucalgary.ca/equity-diversity-inclusion/education-and-training/calling-me-racist-webinar

Varelas, M., Settlage, J., & Mensah, F. M. (2015). Explorations of the structure–agency dialectic as a tool for framing equity in science education. *Journal of Research in Science Teaching, 52*(4), 439–447.

Vossoughi, S., & Gutiérrez, K. D. (2014). Studying movement, hybridity, and change: Toward a multi-sited sensibility for research on learning across contexts and borders. *Teachers College Record, 116*(14), 603–632.

Vogel, C. (2008, March 12). Museums refine the art of listening. *The New York Times*. https://www.nytimes.com/2008/03/12/arts/artsspecial/12visitors.html

Vygotsky, L. S. (1978). *Mind in society: The psychology of higher mental functions*. Harvard University Press.

Vygotsky, L. S. (1987). *Thinking and speech*. Plenum.

Van Sluytman, L. (2015, November 17). Many small microaggressions add up to something big. *The Conversation*. https://theconversation.com/many-small-microaggressions-add-up-to-something-big-50694.

Wertsch, J.V. (2007). Mediation. In H. Daniels, M. Cole, & J.V. Wertsch (Eds.), *The Cambridge companion to Vygotsky* (pp. 178–192). Cambridge University Press.

Wrigley, T. (2019). The problem of reductionism in educational theory: Complexity, causality, values. *Power and Education, 11*(2), 145–162. https://doi.org/10.1177/1757743819845121

Yosso, T., Smith, W., Ceja, M., & Solórzano, D. (2009). Critical race theory, racial microaggressions, and campus racial climate for Latina/o undergraduates. *Harvard Educational Review, 79*(4), 659–691. https://doi.org/10.17763/haer.79.4.m6867014157m7071

INDEX

Page numbers in **bold** indicate tables, page numbers in *Italics* indicate figures and page numbers followed by n indicate notes.

activity theory 28n6, 40, 43, 45, 150; *see also* cultural-historical activity theory (CHAT) theory
Alex, B. 198
alienation 199, 207
American Alliance of Museums (AAM) 76, 78, 79
American Association of Museum Directors (AAMD) 78, 133, 136n2
American Indian narratives 158
American Museum of Natural History (AMNH) 152–153, 209n21
American museums 3–4, 114–115, 121, 128, 208n11
Ancient One 190, 195–196
Anderson, G. 76
Andrews, M. 145, 148, 149
Apple, M.W. 2, 14, 15, 59
appropriation 188
artifact 181; *see also* Indigenous artifacts; alienation 207; Australia 208; contingency and context 191–192; contingent *vs.* solidified 201–202; decolonizing/colonizing 192–193; DNA testing 205; mediational, positioning ideologies as means 190–191; ownership 186–187; repatriation in the United States 205; repatriation of a sacred item from Scotland to Canada 182–183; sale of Kwakwaka'wak masks in Chicago 182;

secondary contradictions of uses of **189**; secular *vs.* sacred 199–201; selling/deaccessioning *vs.* culture 202–204; who owns Nazi loot? 205–207
Ash, D. 210n26, 239, 299n10
Asian Art Museum 200
Asian National Museums Association 78
assimilation 1, 15–16, 21, 81, 95, 101n13, 286; and resistance 23, 230–231
Association of Science and Technology Centers (ASTC) 78, 99–100, 136n2
Association of Tribal Archives, Libraries, and Museums (ATALM) 152
attendance, museum 23, 55, 65, 77–80, 90–91
Au, W. 2, 24
Australian museum 208

backstory 192
balancing the budget 4, 121
Bamberg, M. G. 145
Bang, M. 8, 66n9, 152, 164, 298n2
Barker, A. J. 151
Barnes, B. 170
Battell Lowman, E. 151
beautiful trouble (social media) 97
Bell, P. 19, 76
belonging 16, 83–85, 87–88, 114, 252, 287
belongingness 24

Bennett, T. 28n2, 277
Bevan, B. 101
Bingham, G. 101n5
Black, G. 150
Blackler, F. 48
Blud, L. M. 238
blue educators 254, 259, 262, 264, 266
blue/purple research intervention project 258–260
blue/purple secondary contradictions 264–265
boards of directors and power 128; board power 129–130; deaccessioning art 132–133; quick fixes 131–132; retrenching efforts 130–131
Boast, R. 121
Bogost, I. 62, 63
Bonnici, S. 84, 85, 101n14
bottom line vs. social good 117–119
Braddock, K. 143
Brady, M. J. 193, 202
Bransford, J. 221
Braydon family 220, 223, 224, 232, 289
British Museum 39, 115, 192
British Petroleum (BP) 39
Brooklyn Public Library 120
Brown, A. L. 221, 259
Brown, K. 118, 137n6
Brown, M. 210n30
Bruner, J. 155, 156, 161, 165
Burke Museum 195, 196, 209n19
'business as usual' museum circles 7
Butsch, R. 171n4

Calabrese Barton, A. 13, 58, 261, 268n14, 284, 298n2
calculated indifference 49, 60, 150, 193
Californio Indians in California (controversy) 161; dehumanized vs. humanized 164; frozen in time vs. dynamic 162–163; primitive vs. advanced 163–164; romanticized vs. real 164–166
Callanan, M. A. 239
Callihan, E. 74, 94
Campfens, E. 187
Carpio, M. V. 145
Case, R. 226, 228
Center for the Future of Museums (CFM) 7, 76, 252
Chaiklin, S. & Lave, J. 221
change 3–5; expectations of 81–82; at intermediate level 257–258; numbers and 77–80
Change Laboratory (CL) 290, 299n14

changing core teaching practices 253; agency and resistance 254–256
cherry-picking data vs. impartial 92
Chinese Association of Museums (CAM) 78
Christen, K. 210n31
Chung, J. 100, 115
Clegg, M. 198
Cleveland Museum of Art (CMA) 89
Clifford, J. 101n8
Cobb, A. J. 156
Cobb, P. 226, 236
Coffee, K. 8, 16, 17, 60–61, 286
Cole, M. 228, 233–236
collateral damage 42, 49, 52, 60, 152, 193, 263
collectivism, individualism versus 18
colonist narrative, altering 152–155
commodification 87; vs. conservation **157**; and objectification 202–204
commoditization 42, 44, 182, 193
community of significant others 47, 49
conflicts 12
Conn, S. 183
conservation, commodification vs. **157**
consumerism 114
containment, objectification and 201–202
contingency and context 191–192
contingent collaborations 210n31
contingent ownership in context 202
contingent vs. solidified 201–202
continuing cultural link 187
contradictions 4, 5, 50–51, **52**, 64, 85, 91, **158**, 231–233; cherry-picking data vs. impartial 92; creative attendance counting (or sausage making) vs. impartial 92–93; diversity, museums and 88–89; from diversity to intersectionality 94–95; at individual/small group with an educator 64–65; at mid-level management 65; museum attendance 90–91; primary 51–53, **119**; quaternary 53–54; secondary 53–54, **117**, **119**, 150, 155, **156**, 158, **162**; tertiary 53–54, **119**; tokenism vs. transformation 93; at top-level management 65; visitor numbers 87–88
contradictions, ideological 116–118; bottom line vs. social good 117–119; financial/business model 121–122; us vs. them 119–121
Contreras, D. 201
cooperative vs. client distinction 123
corporate museums 116
corporate schooling 116

Cortell, S. 113, 117
counter-narratives 143, 145, 167–168; as resistance 147–148
COVID-19 pandemic 78, 112, 130, 133, 184
creative attendance counting (or sausage making) vs. impartial 92–93
creative counting 93
Creed, D. 4, 10, 154
Creed, W. E. D. 4, 10, 154, 281
Crenshaw, K. W. 94, 102n25
critical conflicts 12
critical reflection 16–18, 298
Crowley, K. 239
cultural appropriation 193; and misrepresentation 165
Cultural Competence Learning Institute (CCLI) 79
cultural-historical activity theory (CHAT) theory 1, 5–6, **6**, 9–10, 28n4, **40**, 41, 44, 45, 86–87, 110, 117, 185, 186, 222, 232, 241n2, 249, 275, 277; breaking down the Exxon/Valdez using 45–48; contradictions 50–51, **52**; exhibit design 56–57; expansive learning in 54–56; neoliberal educational system 59–61; primary contradictions 51–53; quaternary contradictions 53–54; secondary contradictions 53–54; tertiary contradictions 53–54; third-generation activity theory 48–50, 87; transformative agency at work 57–59
culture: normative 21; selling/deaccessioning vs. 202–204
'culture of power' (Delpit) 100
Curtis, N. G. W. 182, 192, 193

Dailey, T. L. 14, 51, 52, 67n33, 95, 122, 134
Daley, P. 211n37
Dallas Museum of Art (DMA) 128
Danielsen, A. 117, 135
Dartt-Newton, D. D. 161–163, 165, 167, 174n36, 174n38
Davis, N. 24
Davis, P. 15
Dawson, E. 20, 22, 23, 25, 76, 188, 220, 222, 286, 299n11
deaccessioning 132–133; vs. culture 202–204
decision-making 27, 89, 128
decolonizing 147, 151, 192–193; decolonizing actions 193–194; Hawaiian iwi kūpuna (case) 197–199; Kennewick Man (case) 195; repatriation 194–195;

settler colonialism/westward expansion vs. decolonization 151
deficit-laden discursive traces 62
deficit/neoliberal ideologies in practice 256–257
deficit orientation 11, 221, 257, 262, 266, 277, 284; vs. resource orientation 21–23
deficit thinking 8, 15–16
dehumanization 152
dehumanized vs. humanized 164
DEI (diversity, equity and inclusion) 79, 80, 88, 252
Delpit, L. 29n19
Delpit, L. D. 100
designed environment 240
Design Thinking for Museums 11
Detroit Institute for Arts (DIA) 133
Dewey, J. 228
Dewhurst, M. 257, 275
dialectical logic 56, 65n3
Diamond, J. 222, 239
Di Domenico, M. L. 203
Dierking, L. 222, 239
dilemmas 11
Dilenschneider, C. 81, 82, 95, 113, 118
DiMaggio, P. J. 253
discursive manifestations 10–13, 50, 61, 88, 116
diversity 19, 74, 80, 88–89
diversity, equity, accessibility and inclusion (DEAI) in museums 79
DNA testing 190, 195, 196, 205
Donaghue, N. 60
double binds 12–13
double deficit 29n15
Dubin, S. 16, 23, 148
'dumbing down' 62–63
dynamic pricing 126–127

Eakin, H. 200
educational system, neoliberal 59–61
educator/administration interactions 267
educator/family interactions 266–267
Ekström, K. M. 112, 29n14
elephant and giraffe parable 82–83
Ellenbogen, K. M. 239
emboldened disruptors 280
empathetic museum 97
Engeström, Y. 11, 37, 40–44, 48, 51, 52, 55, 64, 65, 66n5, 221, 228, 261, 268n15, 274, 278, 284, 287, 290
entrance fees 110, 112, 114–115
'entrance fee wars' 117
equality, equity/social justice vs. 18–19, *20*

equitable teaching in museums 249; blue/purple case 258–260; change at intermediate level 257–258; changing core teaching practices 253–256; deficit/neoliberal ideologies in practice 256–257; educator/administration interactions 267; educator/family interactions 266–267; expansive learning 252, 260–262, *260*; interaction, levels of 268–267; museum educator history 267; power struggles 262–265

equity/social justice 1, 7, 19; *vs.* equality 18–19, *20*; and learning theories, intertwining of 221–223

European museums 114–115

executive pay at New York City Museums 135–136

exhibit design 44, 56–57

expansive cycle, stages of 55, **56**

expansive learning 152–155, 252, 260, *260*; in CHAT 54–56, 67n24; educator resistance 261–262

expansive transformation, cycle of 55, *55*

Exploratorium 222, 228, 229, 239

externalizing 20

Exxon Valdez oil spill 38, 45–48, 64

Falk, J. H. 241

Feinstein, N. W. 21, 66n21, 123, 188, 254, 286

Feldman, K. 74, 94

Fernando, C. 87

Ferrare, J. A. 2, 24

financial/business model 121–122

financial crisis affecting museums 114, 116

first-generation activity theory 9, *9*, 44

Fisher, R. 283

Fonseca, F. 170, 171

Foot, K. A. 5, 6, 40, 42, 45, 51, 53, 67n37, 118, 190, 264, 268n16

fourth-generation activity theory 287

Fraser, A. 123, 128, 130

free-choice learning 241, 245

frozen in time *vs.* dynamic 162–163

furloughs 131–132

Garibay, C. 76, 188

Ghosh, J. 172n13

Giddens, A. 13, 29n13, 283, 299n8

Gill, R. 60

Gjorgjioska, M. A. 67n31

Glenn, J. 184–185

Global Diversity & Inclusion Benchmarks (2014) 82

Golden, N. A. 267n5

Gombault, A. 112, 114, 127

Gorski, P. 15, 19, 22, 281, 299n5

Grant, D. 119, 121

Gray, C. 257

Greeno, J. G. 226, 228

Grimes, R. L. 199

Groleau, C. 6, 40, 53, 190

Gurian, E. H. 3, 6, 25, 63, 76, 101n9, 119, 121, 253, 256, 278–280, 298n1, 298n3

Gurian website 98

Gutiérrez, K. 267n4

Gutiérrez, K. D. 13, 48, 58, 222, 223, 261, 268n14, 279, 284, 298n2

Gutiérrez, R. 255, 262

Haapasaari, A. 285

Hall, R. 67n29, 285

Halperin, J. 136n3

Hands-on learning 220, 224

Hannah-Jones, N. 77

Harris, C. I. 173n33

Harrison, J. 67n32, 184, 186, 199, 207, 208n5

Harvey, D. 14, 87

Hawaiian *iwi kūpuna* (case) 197–198

healing spaces 168

Heaton, J. 275, 276, 280

Hein, G. 229

Hendrick, K. 257, 275

Henry, B. 297–298

Heritage Center 38

Hess, H. 174n44

hierarchy 23–24

high-quality recreation 160–161

history of modern museums 267

Hobsbawm, E. 8

Hodkinson, P. 226

Hood, M. G. 236

Hooper-Greenhill, E. 76, 188

Hopi Katsinam 203

Hopi Tribe 203

Horgan, J. 143

Howard, J. 195

Hubbard, L. 261

Hunte, G. 299

Hutterer, K. 188

hybrid model 123–124

ideological contradictions and master narratives 150; conflicting ideologies 151; native American story power 151–152

308 Index

ideological mismatches 18; assimilate or resist 23; deficit *vs.* resource orientation 21–23; equity/social justice *vs.* equality 18–19, *20*; individualism *versus* collectivism 18; outreach *vs.* inreach 19–21; power, stratification, hierarchy 23–24
ideologies 16–18
idle curiosity 189
impartial: cherry-picking data *vs.* 92; creative attendance counting (or sausage making) *vs.* 92–93
Incluseum 98
Indianapolis Museum of Art 127
Indianapolis Zoo 127
Indian Removal Act of 1830, 152, 166, 167, 170–171
Indigenous artifacts 181; *see also* artifact; competing ideologies regarding ownership of 187–190
Indigenous Peoples and Museums Network 152
individualism 18, 28, 60; versus collectivism 18
individual/small group with an educator, contradictions at 64–65
individual/social turn 225; assimilation and resistance 230–231; contradiction 231–233; learning theories in mission statements of museums 229–230
inferior race/class 60
informal learning 240
inreach, outreach *vs.* 19–21
institutional racism 100
interaction, levels of 268; educator/administration interactions 267; educator/family interactions 266–267
International Council of Museums (ICOM) 3, 130
Interpersonal racism 100
intersectionality 94–95
Iwi 190
Iwi Kūpuna 195, 198

Jackson, H. H. 164
James, R. 295
Jenkins, T. 78
Jennings, G. 82, 84, 88, 93, 94, 99, 102n24
John-Steiner, V. 5, 221
Jones, J. 90–91
Jones-Rizzi, J. 82, 84, 88, 93, 94, 99, 102n24, 279, 281, 286
Jornet, A. 242n8

Kalin, N. M. 52, 122, 134
Kalshed, D. 77, 185, 201
Kanders, W. 93
Kaptelinin, V. 5, 6, 10, 37, 40
Karp, I. 14, 67n34, 95
Kelly, L. 174n44
Kendi, I. X. 82, 152
Kennewick Man (case) 195
Kidman, J. 151, 186, 193, 201
knowledge economy 60
Kundu, R. 52, 134
Kurin, R. 191–192
Kuutti, K. 40, 51

landowners, private 160
Langemeyer, I. 57, 67n26
Larkin, S. 283
late capitalism 14
Latinx 19, 29n18
Lave, J. 221, 224, 228
Leading with Intent 93
learning 218; equity and learning theories, intertwining of 221–223; expansive 152–155; free-choice 241; individual/social turn 225–233; individual *vs.* social views of **237**; learning research pragmatics 237–238; mediational means, role of 233–236; naming 239–241; repertoires of practice 223–225; social learning research in museums 238–239; taxonomy of **227**
learning research pragmatics 237–238
learning theories in mission statements of museums 229–230
Lee, C. 62, 63, 66n17
Lee, C. P. 62, 67n35
Lee, O. 23
Lefthand, P. 193
Leonardo, Z. 17, 18, 44, 282, 283, 286
Li, S. 77, 79
Lindqvist, K. 115
livelihood 48
Lonetree, A. 76, 146, 156, 166–168, 188, 194, 199, 295
Lowry, G. 129–130, 135
Lucariello, J. 155, 156, 161, 165

MacDonald, S. 188
MacLachlan, N. 188, 199, 209n15, 210n29
Mahn, H. 5, 65n4, 221
Mallett, W. 128
Mandelbaum, L. 171
manifest destiny 149, 150, 152, 154, 164, 170

Mann, S. 279, 281, 286
Manning, L. 282, 283, 286
Marin, A. 8, 66n9, 298n2
marketization 123
Martin, L. 265
Marxist dialectics 50
MASS action toolkit 98
master narrative 155–157; American Indian narratives 158; Californio Indians in California (controversy) 161–166; high-quality recreation 160–161; NMAI (controversy) 166–167; private landowners 160; sacredness 159–160; Sutter Buttes (controversy) 158–159, *159*, 160
McAfee, K. 157
McCall, V. 257
McConnell, M. 174n44
McDermott, R. 60, 220, 226, 231
McDonald, S. 48
McManus, P. 222, 238
McMullen, A. 188
mediational means 10, 13, 27, 28n5, 39, 45–47, 233; applying Cole and Wertsch to the Braydon visit 234–236; positioning ideologies as 190–191
Meighan, C. W. 188
Menendian, S. 15, 24, 81, 84
Merritt, E. 80, 89, 126, 127
Meshoulam, D. 21, 66n21, 123, 188, 254, 286
Metropolitan Museum of Art in New York 4, 131
Middle Mountain 159
mid-level management, contradictions at 65
Migration Museums, in Europe 8
mission statements of museums, learning theories in 229–230
Mjoberg, E. 209n17
Modest, W. 85
Moore, B. 23, 24, 280, 299
Moore, P. 76, 83, 89, 102n20, 188, 286
Morales-Doyle, D. 267n4
Morrissey, J. 189
Moss, I. D. 83
multiple activity systems, working the dialectic across 287–288
Multiple-interconnected activity systems 287, *288*
multivoicedness 42
Murray, D. 241
Museum 2.0, 98
Museum Audience Insight in 2012, 78, 92
museum curators and educators 39
museumization of migration 78

Museum of Modern Art (MOMA) 129
'museum outsiders' 1
Museums & Race report card 99
Museus, S. 15
Mwanza, D. 66

NAGPRA (Native American Graves Protection and Repatriation Act) 12
naming 18–19
National Museum of African American History and Culture 281
National Museum of Australia 201, 204
Native American Graves Protection and Repatriation Act (NAGPRA) 190, 203–205, 208n8, 208n11, 210n29
Native American Holocaust 167, 171
Native Americans 26, 46, 95, 145, 147, 159–160
native American story power 151–152
Native Hawaiians 197
Native narrative 165
Nazi loot 205–207
neocolonialism 151, 155, 172n12, 201
neoliberal educational system 59–61
neoliberalism 18, 60, 114, 172n12, 186, 265; and outreach 285–286; power and 134
neoliberal policies 14–15, 52, 75
neoliberal tendencies in museums 265
Network of European Museum Organizations (NEMO) 78, 130, 136n2
neutrality 98–99
Newcomb, S. 164
new mainstream 19, 74, 101n12, 128
Ng, W. 75, 82, 83, 87–89
NMAI 166–167, 192
Nolan, T. R. 255
norms 24, 152; challenging 7–8; in a dialectical world 286
numbers and change 77–80

Oakland Museum of California (OMCA) 158, 161, 296–298
Obama, M. 2, 3, 5, 85
objectification: commodification and 202–204; and containment 201–202; reduction and 199–201
O'Connor, A.-M. 211n41
O'Connor, J. 208n2
O'Donnell, N. 131, 133
O'Mara, J. 82
ookaan headdress 185, 187, 192, 193
Orsoss, J. 120
othering 2, 8, 15, 20, 83–85, 87–88, 114, 121, 152, 163, 283

outreach 1, 6, 7; *vs.* inreach 19–21
ownership 186–187, 189, 197, 207

Palincsar, A. S. 259
Parker, C. S. 19
payment for museums 110; boards of directors and power 128–133; bottom line *vs.* social good 118–122; cooperative *vs.* client distinction 123; executive pay at New York City Museums 135–136; financial crisis affecting museums 114–116; ideological contradictions, uncovering 116–118; power and neoliberalism 134; pricing details 135; pricing models, museum 123–128
Penney, D. W. 146
People of Color (POC) 77
Perkins, D. N. 225, 242n7
Pew Charitable Trust 3
Piaget, J. 228, 229, 233
pluralism 204
Pogrebin, R. 128, 131, 132
Poole, N. 280
Powell, J. 15, 24, 81, 84
Powell, W. W. 253
power 8, 23–24, 95–96, 191; analysis 61–63; hierarchies 24; and neoliberalism 134; of stories 148–150
power struggles 262; blue/purple secondary contradictions 264–265; neoliberal tendencies in museums 265
pricing details 135
pricing models, museum 123–126, *125*; going free for all 128; hybrid model 123–124; one price for all 127; variable and dynamic pricing 126–127
pricing war 113
primary contradictions 51–53
primitive *vs.* advanced (contradictions) 163–164
private landowners 160
professional development (PD) 249
project implicit 99
Prottas, N. 267
provenance 187, 206
public funding 114
public good 189
Pulsford, M. 67n29, 285
purple supervisor 254

quaternary contradictions 53–54

racism: institutional 100; interpersonal 100; levels of 100; structural 100

Rahm, J. 299n10
Raicovich, L. 120
Ramos, B. 101
Ranger, T. 8
Rasmussen, M. 205
Reach Advisors 100, 114, 130, 172n10
recreation, high-quality 160–161
reculturing an institution 274, 290–292; Change Laboratory (CL) 290; complexity/resistance, staying with 279–280; critical reflective practice 298; dialectic and deficit/othering 282–283; following the power 288–290; good intentions 280–281; involving the community 295–298; minding the dialectic 281–282; multiple activity systems, working the dialectic across 287–288; neoliberalism and outreach 285–286; norms in a dialectical world 286; Oakland Museum of California (OMCA) 296–298; replacing old with new while the old is still in place 278; sociocultural dialectic between individual and social 281–282; structure agency dialectic 283–285
reduction and objectification 199–201
Rentschler, R. 112, 114, 124, *125*, 127
repatriation 194–195; of a sacred item from Scotland to Canada 182–183; in the United States 205
repertoires of practice 222–225, 232
resist 23
resistance: assimilation and 230–231; counter-narrative as 147–148
resource orientation, deficit *vs.* 21–23
retrenching efforts 130–131
revenues of museum 115
Richeson, J. 77
Robert, N. 94, 95
Roberts, L. C. 50, 59, 150, 154, 171n3
Robertson, S. 59
Rodney, S. 91
Rodriguez, G. 19
Rogoff, B. 222, 240
romanticized *vs.* real 164–166
Rosenbaum, L. 120
Roth, W.-M. 6, 57, 67n26, 242n8
Rubin Museums 200
Russell, D. L. 261

Sacred, secular *vs.* 199–201
sacred items 199
Sacred Land Project 159
sacredness 159–160, 200

Saginaw Chippewa story 167–168
sale of Kwakwaka'wak masks in Chicago 182
Salomon, G. 225, 242n7
Sannino, A. 11, 40, 43, 50, 66n5, 66n15, 287
Schneider, K. 128
Schneider, T. 128
Schneiderheinze, A. 261
science museums 99–100
secondary contradictions 53–54, 150, *155*, **156**, 158, **162**
second-generation activity theory *45*, 47
secular *vs.* sacred 199–201
self-knowledge 24
self-reflection 24
selling/deaccessioning *vs.* culture 202–204
Seo, M. G. 4, 10, 154, 281
settled expectation 8, 147, 152, 162
settler colonialism 151–152, 154
settler colonialism/westward expansion *vs.* decolonization/native rights 151
Sewell, W. 13
Sfard, A. 225, 226, 231, 242n5, 242n6
shared authority 146
Sheets-Pyenson, S. 157
Shoenberger, E. 183, 209n14
Siegal, N. 115
Simon, N. 3, 92, 98, 115, 119, 122, 209n12, 240, 295
Skorten, D. 119
Smagorinsky, P. 9
social good, bottom line *vs.* 117–119
social justice *vs.* equality 18–19, *20*
social learning research in museums 238–239
social media, museum 97; beautiful trouble 97; empathetic museum 97; Gurian website—Elaine Hermann 98; Incluseum 98; MASS action toolkit 98; Museum 2.0, 98; museum neutrality 98–99; museums and race 99; project implicit 99
sociocultural dialectic between individual and social 282
solidified, contingent *vs.* 201–202
Starn, R. 173n24
State Park and Recreation Commission 160
Statistica 91
Stetsenko, A. 28n3, 59, 284–286
stewardship 160
story 143; counter-narrative as resistance 147–148; counter-narratives in new museums 167–168; expansive learning 152–155; ideological contradictions and master narratives 150–152; master narrative 155–167; power of stories 148–150; two recent exhibitions about controversy 169–171

stratification 23–24
Strauss, M. 189
structural racism 100
structure agency dialectic (SAD) 1–2, 9, 13, 249–250, 253, 283–285
Suchman, L. 24, 58, 257, 262
Sutter Buttes (controversy) 158–159, *159*, 160

Taneja, M. 151
Tang, G. 242n10
Taylor, A. 38
Tchen, J. K. W. 81, 88, 295
tensions and emerging contradictions 91; cherry-picking data *vs.* impartial 92; creative attendance counting (or sausage making) *vs.* impartial 92–93; from diversity to intersectionality 94–95; tokenism *vs.* transformation 93
tertiary contradictions 53–54
Theme Index and Museum Index Report 90, **90**
theories, need for 37; contradictions 40–42; contradictions at three levels of analysis 64–65; cultural-historical activity theory (CHAT) theory 44–61; Exxon Valdez oil spill 38; levels of analysis 43–44; multivoicedness 42; power analysis 61–63, time 43
theories of *Reculturing Museums* 1–29; assimilate or resist 23; change 3–5; cultural-historical activity theory (CHAT) **6**, 9–10; deficit/othering 15–16; deficit *vs.* resource orientation 21–23; discursive manifestations 10–13; equity/social justice *vs.* equality 18–19, *20*; ideological mismatches 18–24; ideologies and critical reflection 16–18; individualism *versus* collectivism 18; neoliberalism 14–15, 18; norms, challenging 7–8; outreach *vs.* inreach 19–21; power, stratification, hierarchy 23–24; structure agency dialectic (SAD) 13
third generation activity theory 48–50, *49*, 95, 287
third-generation CHAT analysis 87
time 43
Timmis, S. 57, 241n2
Tishman, S. 220
Tobin, K. 6
tokenism 148; *vs.* transformation 93
Tolbert, S. 18
Tomicic, A. 67n31
top-level management, contradictions at 65

Tran, L. U. 268n10
Trans-Alaska Pipeline System 38
transformation, tokenism *vs.* 93
transformative agency at work 57–59
Tripadvisor 38
Tsoukas, H. 10
Turner, V. 94

UNESCO 130
unintentional actions 298n4
Ünsal, D. 79
us *vs.* them 119–121

Vadeboncoeur, J. A. 241
Valdez Museum 38
Valdez Museum and Historical Archive 38
Valdez Native Tribe (VNT) 38, 66n7
Van Gogh Museum 90
Van Sluytman, L. 281
variable and dynamic pricing 126–127
visitors of museums 74; change, expectations of 81–82; contradictions 85–91; 'culture of power' (Delpit) 100; elephant and giraffe parable 82–83; numbers and change 77–80; othering and belonging 83–85; power 95–96; racism, levels of 100; sciences 99–100; social media, museum 97–100; tensions and emerging contradictions 91–95; visitor numbers 87–88
Vossoughi, S. 48, 222, 223, 267n4, 279
Vygotsky, L. S. 5, 9, 10, 37, 43–45, 65n4, 221, 222, 228, 233, 236, 240, 241n1, 282, 283, 299n6, 299n7

Walker, R. 209n16
Ward, S. J. 4, 52, 67n24
Wenger, E. 221, 228
Wertsch, J. V. 228, 233–236, 282
Western Australian museum 208
Westward expansion 152
White, B. Y. 257, 265
white fear 113
Whitney Museum of American Art 2
Whyte, J. 42
Wilcox, M. 185
Wilkening, S. 115
Woerner, D. 127
Woody, R. C. 130, 132

Ziibiwing Center 167, 169
zone of proximal development (ZPD) 5, 10, 45

For Product Safety Concerns and Information please contact our EU representative GPSR@taylorandfrancis.com
Taylor & Francis Verlag GmbH, Kaufingerstraße 24, 80331 München, Germany